THE SUBJECT
MEDIEVAL / MODERN

Figurae

READING MEDIEVAL CULTURE

THE SUBJECT
MEDIEVAL / MODERN

TEXT AND GOVERNANCE

IN THE MIDDLE AGES

Peter Haidu

Stanford University Press, Stanford, California 2004

Stanford University Press
Stanford, California

© 2004 by the Board of Trustees of the
Leland Stanford Junior University

Printed in the United States of America
On acid-free, archival-quality paper

Library of Congress Cataloging-in-Publication Data

Haidu, Peter, 1931–
    The subject medieval/modern : text and governance
in the Middle Ages / Peter Haidu.
        p. cm. — (Figurae)
    Includes bibliographical references and index.
    ISBN 0-8047-4743-1 (cloth : alk. paper) —
    ISBN 0-8047-4744-X (pbk. : alk. paper)
        1. French literature—To 1500—History and criticism.
2. Literature and society—France.   3. Politics and literature—
France.   4. Subjectivity in literature.   5. State, The, in literature.
6. France—History—Medieval period, 987–1515.
I. Title.   II. Figurae (Stanford, Calif.)
    PQ155.S7 H35 2004
    840.9'001—DC22

                                        2003020557

Original Printing 2004

Last figure below indicates year of this printing:
13   12   11   10   09   08   07   06   05   04

Typeset by Tim Roberts in 11/14 Garamond

I am a subject,
and I challenge law.

This book is for Mike Flug, Columbia CORE, and the Faculty Civil Rights Group at Columbia University ca. 1964–68. Their memory shone through years of labor as the sign of a debt:

> Knowledge doesn't grow
> in human hearts like a tree in an orchard.
> Something else is required:
> *to hear, contradict and discuss, to learn;*
> *retain, reinscribe, demonstrate by action.*
> Lacking that, no man of any age,
> is courageous, worthy or wise.
>> Benoît, *Chronique*
>> *des ducs de Normandie*

Debt encountered fidelity, and asked: How will I exceed my self? Continue *to think*, to maintain in a singular time of multiple being, the sole material of this being, the Immortal a truth brings into being through me, the composition of a subject?
> After Alain Badiou, *Ethics*

> Have I done so? If so,
>> evening bears witness to the day.
>> Adam de la Halle,
>> "Congés"

This book is for those who survived, and for our children:

> Imagine the darkness drawn away
> The new day falling equitably
> In the valleys of the living. Imagine.
>> Philip Levine, "Burned"

Acknowledgments

The first drafts of this book were written during my tenure as a fellow with the John S. Guggenheim Foundation in 1995–96—a grace of money, time, and freedom. The Foundation has also generously provided a publication subvention, to help reduce the book's retail cost. My debt to the Foundation is profound and incalculable, as is my gratitude. The Guggenheim fellowship was supplemented by an additional quarter's leave from the University of California. The Academic Senate at UCLA has provided regular research support.

Stanford University Press underwent major changes as this work wended its way toward appearance. It must have been one of the last books accepted for publication under the brilliant editorship of Helen Tartar: I am proud to have been one of "Helen's boys," to steal a phrase from Daniel Boyarin. After her, Kim Brown and Tim Roberts shepherded the manuscript as it grew into a proper "book," tussling with the stubborn, occasionally irascible author as necessary. Rob Ehle and Janet Wood saw to its elegant dress. Alex Giardino's copy editing was precious, especially when its agonistic moments forced the book's potential into being. By contrast, there were no agons with Norris Pope or Alan Harvey, only courtesy and understanding.

Two dear friends, Matilda Tomaryn Bruckner and Timothy J. Reiss, generously read early, desperately long drafts and provided invaluable encouragement, support, and suggestions. Sarah Kay gave attentive readings that were models of patience, probity, and wise counsel. All three have my deepest gratitude for their insights, their rigor, and an intellectual largesse proffered in rare friendship and professionalism. Although much credit goes to them for any grace herein, they bear no responsibility for surviving infelicities. What they cannot elude are my forcible, my warmest, my most heartfelt thanks!

Contents

THE SUBJECT
MEDIEVAL / MODERN

Introduction

> The years since 1968 are lapsarian. . . . The subjective is
> not continuous. It surges into being, and then ceases to exist:
> it lapses.
>
> *Sylvain Lazarus, Anthropologie du nom*

> The past can be seized as an image which flashes up at the instant
> when it can be recognized and is never seen again. . . . For every
> image of the past that is not recognized by the present as one of
> its own concerns threatens to disappear irretrievably.
>
> *Walter Benjamin, "Theses on the Philosophy of History"*

The modern subject was invented in the Middle Ages, such is the thesis of this book, destined to disturb medievalists and modernists (including postmodernists) alike. Both are deeply invested in the binarism "medieval versus modern," which constitutes their historiographical self-image by Othering its opposite. If the modern subject is medieval, it follows that the Middle Ages are modern, or that modernity is medieval—a troubling result either way. The self-assurance of academic specialists, their job security, and their epistemic authority are undermined by such transgressive revisions. A modernity that defines itself by unceasing change in perpetual self-reinvention projects a "Middle Ages" that is flatly self-identical under a pall of theological closure. Both images are delusional and ideologically determined.

Determined currents of critical scholarship have worked for generations to dispel that simple-minded binarism. More than a century ago, Paul Viollet proclaimed, "We issue from the Middle Ages. . . . The roots of our modern society lie deep in them. . . . The Middle Ages are alive in us."[1] More recently, Jacques Derrida recognized that "all the concepts of the modern theory of the State are secularized theological concepts. . . . One must start from theology if one is to understand them."[2] The disciplines as institutionalized, however, remain largely anchored to their constitutive assumptions: the exclusive alterity of the "modern" and the "medieval."

Modernity's ignorance of the Middle Ages licenses its self-image and hides the revolutionary character of the Middle Ages which constituted modernity. Far from flat, stable, and unprofitable, the millennial interregnum of the medieval period *is* the revolution which cast the die of futures we tremble in. That revolution was political, taking the term in its broadest sense, as the armature of collective life. Governance divides those in power and those subject to power. The "state" is one very particular, historical form of governance. The state's beginnings—not "origins," but a specific set of transformations that shift the course of history—are found in France and England in the eleventh and twelfth centuries: that is when the first foundations of what would become "modern" states begin to take a recognizable shape.[3] But state-formation is only a somewhat more visible aspect of the transformation in European civilization. The eleventh-century investiture controversy was, in effect, a "Papal Revolution"[4] which reformulated relations between religion and secular life in "a mighty iceberg of change,"[5] a disengagement whose release of lay energy and creativity has been compared to a "process of nuclear fission."[6] That energy was channeled into disciplinary rationalities of culture and politics, transforming the remains of the Roman Empire into the states, the cultures, the institutions of the so-called early modern period: from the Renaissance on, the West builds on the labors of the Middle Ages, equally monumental and monstrous.

"Literary" texts and historical practices from the Middle Ages participate in the cultural invention of the subject as part of the political invention of the state.[7] This concept of subjectivity is a far cry from one that flattens out Emile Benveniste's paradox: "Is 'ego' who says 'ego.'"[8] Against a long continental tradition of philosophical subjectivity, Benveniste asserted a speaker's capacity to posit himself as a linguistic subject by the simple act of saying "I." His paradox resolved nothing: it posed an enormous challenge to thought, largely ignored. Reducing subjectivity to the use of "I" denies subjectivity to any discourse—a figure of irony, Chaplin's silent muster of innocence, Buster Keaton's stone face, a portrait by Paul Klee— lacking the verbal subject "I," which is patently ridiculous. If

> A poem dreams of being written
> Without the pronoun "I"[9]

does it forswear subjectivity, or render it as paradox? The linguistic subject is equivalent neither to the subject of consciousness nor to the subject of action: it is frequently their simulacrum. The centrality of language remains uncontroverted: society does not exist without it. But if language is essential to collective life, it is as the condition of possibility for heterogeneous constructions that exceed language itself. Nor does subjectivity reduce to identity, as in current identity politics: on the contrary, contradictions between subjectivity and identity are frequent—as the ensuing pages will show. Contradictions produce the political subject, sometimes by challenging identity.

The subject, collective or individual, exists in passive and active phases. In the passive phase, it is the object of manipulations of parents, its own unconscious, and a world of representations that gather ideological value. This first, "objective" phase produces an aporetic image of self-mirroring,[10] which is both undermined and overdetermined by the later entry into a symbolic domain of language and culture. This passive phase has been extensively explored from the psychoanalytic quarter: Lacan himself, after him Žižek and others, tease out with disturbing mastery involutions of subjectivity which reduce textuality to symptomatic formations. The second phase of subjectivity extends the symbolic to the incorporation of social identities and ideologies. It recognizes the efficacy of the unconscious, but encounters the demand of social action as the world springs the necessity of making choices—often binary and framed by external conjunctures over which the subject has no immediate control—on the individual. This is the necessity of narrative, slighted by generations that, after May 1968, disengaged themselves from social action.[11] Faced with such choices, the individual, as agent, wagers his or her subjectivity, an ongoing dialectic between subject and history with ideology as mediating term.[12] An alternative mode of subject-creation, explored by Foucault, is that of discipline, whose early stages were "ethical," more recently transformed by the development of specialized professions.[13] In both cases—ideology and discipline—the repetition of choices and actions may construct the identity of a habitus.

In historical societies, ideologies and disciplines are multiple: the individual is a site of multiple traversals, constituted in the disruption, breaking, and reknitting of multiple semiotic strands,[14] his or her subject position(s) targeted by multiple interpellations.[15] In that manifold, interferences and contradictions necessarily occur.[16] Individual encodings are interrupted, requiring choices among the multiple interpellations: "A subject is that term which, submitted to the rule which determines a place, punctuates it with the interruption of its effect."[17] It is in that interruption, in that disjunctive moment, when interpellation fails,[18] and the subject is forced into excess over its cause,[19] that subjectivity is attained and that text is formed, in the burdensome, enforced freedom of making choices. The identity of post-Althusserian theory of the subject is the subject's nonidentity. Nonidentity in two senses: not the same as "identity," and not identical to itself. Furthermore, the contemporary discovery of subjectivity's fragile nature makes of it more a goal, a hope to be attained, than the stable ontological assumption of political life: subjectivity is always under construction. It is constructed by the choices the subject makes as narrative, historical agent.

It is this latter, active phase of the subject that medieval texts explore. The degree to which they respond to psychoanalytic readings has been established by critics from Roger Dragonetti to Alexandre Leupin.[20] The validity of the enterprise calls for a major theoretical discussion, not broached here, regarding the presumed permanence of psychic structures across historical and cultural divides, and the elision of textual structures that define textuality itself. From this quarter, serious examination of the ways the unconscious and political life impinge on each other is rare. In the *Ethics of Psychoanalysis*, Lacan more than once alludes to the threat of nuclear self-destruction, frighteningly present at the time of his seminar, neither as a political issue nor as a discourse to be psychoanalyzed, but as an obscenity dismissed in horror and disgust: a civilized, psychoanalytic "Othering." Nor, in a work that claims to be an "ethic," is there any guide to choices of action other than loyalty to one's own desire: both modern and medieval history demonstrate how that principle can lead to ultimate horrors.

The constitution of the subject is an integral part of medieval state-formation, with its increasing reliance on ideology and discipline. The beginnings of "modern" practices of governance are examined in the chapters titled "Representation": they spearhead a more encompassing change, the elaboration of a disciplined civilization, of which subjectivity is one precipitate. Aspects of the process are found in medieval history, linguistics, philosophy, political theory, even a protolegal anthropology. Above all, however, practices modernity categorizes as "literature"—a modern institution with no medieval equivalent—do the ideological work of their polity in exploring and constituting subjectivity by providing performative models of human comportment. They do so in a manner that retains "deniability": works of fantasy and fiction, they are easily appropriated by the category of ornamental entertainment, "the aesthetic" of modernity. As such, they have formed the traditional canon of French medieval "literature." Texts were selected out of the mass of documents in the course of the nineteenth century's philological explorations of European archives, and canonized because of their undefined pertinence to the researchers' subjective constitutions. The "literary" history of the Middle Ages told the story of how we came to be what we are, in strange disguises. It is a story we (do not) recognize: some sense of its import glances across our reading, but only peripherally, insofar as its meaning escapes us. The canon is an uncanny allegory of the state and its discontents, which grips us, often against our taste and will, because it tells the story of our coming to the untenable site of subjectivity we occupy. The canon is an allegory whose code has been misplaced, or, more precisely, repressed.

Some medieval texts participate in the canonic "national allegory" Fredric Jameson has noted.[21] As with the Third World, not all texts do so:[22] some develop narrative figures of self-reflexivity superficially exclusive of any political problematic;[23] others radiate complaisance in the pleasures of the Same.[24] Texts, however, are strange, unpredictable, polyvocal subjects, as constituted in contradiction as the human subjects who produce them. Contemporary speculations on theory and method approach the sophisticated semiotic sense of medieval thinkers and writers, allowing those medievalists who engage them to reveal, not only unsuspected productions of medieval meaning, but a "New Middle Ages."[25] A new subjectivity is generated by textual and political practices, starting in the eleventh and twelfth centuries, initially affecting only a few and slowly spreading as the center of a new mode of collective life—a culture and "civilization"—of which state structures are the central armature.[26] To recapture the flickering evanescence of the subject of freedom for a material and agonistic historiography is the goal of this book.

One lesson of textual awareness is the inherent polysemantics of textuality. All texts, by their nature, are compounded of multiple structures, which do not necessarily deliver unitary meaning neatly wrapped to passive readers. On the contrary, they require active intervention, a self-aware construal of meaning from a historically and theoretically informed reader. We do not garner preestablished meanings, we construct them. Insofar as the cultural autonomy and integrity of the text are respected, we construct its meanings in an overt act of structural interpretation. The pretensions of historicism—to recapture a single, "correct" meaning located "within" the text and verifiable in its own time—are beside the point. No reading totalizes the import of a book: at most, we approach a reasonable and a partial adequacy, well short of closure. Readings contemporary to the text—when available—enjoy no absolute privilege: they are almost as incomplete, as subject to criticism vis-à-vis the text, as modern readings. This book performs an initial survey, no more: far more texts are to be read in its optic, both as furthering political subjectivity and as eluding that proffered function. Furthermore, the subject is protean and takes a variety of textual forms. Rather than repetitions of a single formula, the following pages explore different medieval "takes" on the processes of subjectivation, in their relations to violence, voice, and textual structure.

Subject and text, state and civilization, are profoundly ambiguous icons of problematic interdependences. This book does not sing their praises: it views them with suspicion, convinced of the profound continuities between the medieval period and modernity, between violence and the state-form.[27] The discourse of this work, constantly nagged by theory, is both semiotic and historical: its focus is on praxis, both textual and historical. If society's history is "read" as text, it must always be with its *hors-texte* in memory. The weight and strain of muscle and bone, of blood and the single eyelash, may not be perceptible outside a *texte*: they are not adequately accounted for as text. Those suspicious icons—subject, ideology, text, state, and civilization—have effectivities: they exist. They require examination as objects of historico-theoretical research, an examination impelled by the multiple passions of beauty, justice, and knowledge, as part of an effort to deal with a world increasingly seductive and terrifying.

PART I

BEFORE THE STATE

CHAPTER I

The Peace Movement

A Crisis in Ideology

Two Models of Subjectivity

ABJECTION: BENEDICT OF NURSIA (SIXTH CENTURY)

Two models of subjectivity appear early in the Middle Ages. One indexes what is often designated as the "medieval" subject, committed to the subjection of complete abnegation. For the monk living under the rule of Benedict of Nursia, founder of the Benedictine order, submission to the Rule was absolute:

> No one in the monastery should follow the will of his own heart, and neither inside nor outside the walls should anyone presume to argue with the abbot.[1]

In this world, none under his rule (*regula*: a straight-edge, measuring stick, a staff to whip inattentive schoolboys, a pattern or model for behavior: the means and symbol of "discipline"). Under a *regula*, the *subjectus* is an inferior, thrown under the authority and command of another, reduced to "passive . . . reflex-type conduct."[2]

The medieval church and theology knew the modern subject, however. Ideological campaigns, the persecutorial machines of the Inquisition, were constructed against it. Correct belief and submission was seen as granting freedom: "To have liberty is to be led by the spirit of the Lord; not to have liberty is not to be led by the spirit of the Lord."[3] Wrong beliefs and practices, the absence of belief, arrogance toward established authority, the conviction or fear that the universe offered a void filled with independent desire, judgment, and self-assertion, rather than a plenitude of closure, were what had to be repressed, excluded, exorcised. In its effort to enclose and limit the damages of this potential of self-assertion as always already culpable desire, the medieval Christian imaginary constructed a theological diegesis which possessed a kind of objective reality but lacked an outside: the other side of nonbeing was God, its sustaining center, allowing only a flat, depthless surface of existence to thirsty humanity.[4] The church knew the subject: it was the antagonist, the Devil incarnate.

AGENCY: THE OATHS OF STRASBOURG (842)

Charlemagne's surviving son, Louis the Pious, leaves three sons, who engage in repeated, violent conflicts. Two—Louis the Germanic and Charles the Bald—unite against the third, Lothaire. His defeat allows a negotiated division of the empire in three parts. Charles will rule Western Francia, to become France itself; Louis gets Eastern France, to become Germany; Lothaire's intermediary zone runs from the Netherlands to northern Italy: "Lotharingia." The Oaths of Strasbourg divide the Carolingian empire in 842, establishing the ancestor-states of modern France and Germany. They mark the linguistic division between Latin and the vernaculars, and between French and German.[5]

The Oaths, on February 14, 842, are political performatives. Each brother concedes to the other his territory. Each swears not to ally himself with Lothaire against the third. Each swears aid and protection to the other. The reporter is one Nithard, warrior, court diplomat, historian. Along with the official Latin text, he includes the oath in early forms of French and German. The oaths actually pronounced were not the official Latin: the Germanic king swears in Romance, the French king in German. The oaths' effectivity depends on their being understood and trusted, not only by the kings, the enunciator's other, but by their men: their own, and their brothers.'[6] Their content is quite extraordinary. Each king has his men swear that if he, their prince, betrays his brother, they, his own men, will not follow him, their own lord, against the brother: if the king betrays his brother, his men are to break their loyalty to him. Vernaculars were essential for the success of the diplomacy. Adherence presumes the investment of speakers in their language, and their belief in its performative value. This social contract links, in its initiating historicity, issues that modern modes of thinking separate: polity, language, and textuality. Each implies the others.[7]

Nithard documents a calculated recognition of a new and complex reality: multiple cultures, multiple languages, work in the same political space, calling on subjects in different languages—a necessitated multiculturalism. A new order reigns: new power, political and military, resides in the vernacular. Latin long survives, among monks and clergy who "died to the world" and retired from overt competitions for power and wealth. It also remains an administrative and legal language, even in secular domains. Decisions, bureaucratically recorded in Latin, must have been argued and decided in the vernacular. Henceforth, power in the world belongs to men who speak, think, and live the vernaculars. Among speakers of Latin, popes, bishops, abbots, retain power. Governance operates across a linguistic discrepancy. Bilingualism was the order of centuries.

That the Oaths mark a crucial moment in the development of the vernacular as political discourse is incidental to their role in a calculus of political forces.[8] Not only the kings swear: their men swear and commit themselves to a course of future action that could pit them directly against the king who claims their loyalty. The kings' underlings are placed in the position of having to judge their lord and leader: if they judge him to have betrayed his word, they are mandated to rebel against him. Under prescribed circumstances, the subject is to judge the Subject, in spite of ordinary bonds of loyalty. The subject is bound between two ideologemes, loyalty and truth, a double bind whose name is "freedom": he is expelled from ordinary codes of submission into the unaccustomed autonomy of ideological choice. That is the model of the "modern" subject: a specifically political subject, negotiating the fundamental loyalty to the governor and his rule, is defined in the ninth century.

The Oaths of Strasbourg designated territories that grew into modern nations. It is an error, however, to consider the event constitutive of those modern nation-states: state-formation requires more than words, even vernacular. In fact, history flowed in the contrary direction. The Oaths, confirmed by the Treaty of Verdun in 843, signal the beginning of a long devolutionary process. The division of the empire into three parts reveals centralized governance disintegrating: effective power devolves to successively lower rungs of the hierarchical order, in three stages.[9] Men appointed as agents of central power increasingly act in their own name, assuming the prerogatives and profits of power. Great, independent principalities develop as hereditary states around the turn of the tenth century: Flanders, Burgundy, Aquitaine, Normandy, and Britanny.[10] Then, counts assigned as administrators of a single *pagus* (> *pays*) set themselves up as autonomous chieftains in regions like Anjou, the Mâconnais, Auxerrois, Nivernais, becoming "princes" (*principates*) in their own name. Finally, a yet lower level of authority intrudes: the castlemaster of one or a group of fortresses in turn assumes the chieftain's role in a small, autonomous cell of political and military power: individual castles become "power containers." Some degree of public order might survive, but the decried expression of "feudal anarchy" signals that a substantial number of contemporaries judged the fragmentation of power "exorbitant and calamitous."[11] Political devolution continues until what is now called France is covered by multitudinous cells of local force, vying with neighbors and superiors for power and profits: "feudal society."[12]

The Social Paradigm

Producers and masters occupy opposed subject positions. Society depends on peasants for the production of its food and surplus value. Consumers of the latter are divided into two subclasses: the nobility and the clergy. The latter, especially their leaders—abbots, bishops, popes—generally come from noble families, often destined as younger sons to religion by the inheritance system of primogeniture. While clergy and nobility both live by capturing the fruits of peasant labor, the value-systems of their ideologies are sufficiently antagonistic to make of them different social agencies. From the perspective of an exploited peasantry, would the difference have been that marked?

The answer is not easy to come by. Reconstructing the daily lives or opinions of ordinary peasants is difficult: archives do not resound with their voices. The microphysics of power leaves occasional, indirect, and scattered traces. Peasant history is also produced, like peasant labor itself, as the slow, patient accumulation of detail of an archaeological assemblage. The peasant village itself is a historical product. It begins with survivors' reverence for the dead: first the cemetery, as a town coalesced around its interred dead, who continue as an integral part of the town. Centuries later, servicing the dead still preoccupies a major institution in thriving Arras.[13] After the cemetery, right next to it in metonymic colonization, a church is built, the physical anchor for the developing fabric of parishes, covering the continent in religious cells. Robert Fossier calls this the "cellularization" of the peasantry, ironizing on the neologism's carceral associations.[14] The underground is possessed; then earthen surface is colonized; at a third stage, "gothic" integrates the light of sky. The social unit is elaborated around its dead: peasants as well as nobles venerate their dead. A spectral dimension persists through the Middle Ages.[15] "Ghosts" have effects in material life: they connect to money, violence, and domination. Death weighs on the living, even revolutionaries: its spectral density burdens the living with taxation, debt, accusation, and summons of all sorts.[16]

A curious unifying thread is a widely traveled peasant song, surfacing in Latin, French, and English. Adalberon of Laon, an opponent of the Peace Movement, ridicules the Peace Movement with it: "Naked bishops need only follow endlessly the plow, Goad in hand, singing our first parents' song."[17] In the vernaculars, it associates with insurrections. In France, it is heard during the fourteenth century:

> Lorsqu'Adam bêchait et lorsqu'Eve filait,
> Où alors était le chevalier?[18]

It is already commonplace in English by 1381, when John Ball used it as text of a sermon:

> Whan Adam dalf and Eve span,
> wo was thanne a gentilman?[19]

As against the functionalist ideology of the three orders—laboring peasants, praying religious, and fighting nobles—who needs a knight or a noble? sings a peasant in the fields or a woman at the spinning wheel. The text may have signaled equality in death;[20] others sought equality in life. Traces of peasant culture survive mainly in hostile citations of clerics or noble documents, suggesting that cultural systems of value, independent of clerical and aristocratic codes, capable of nurturing claims of equality, freedom, and human dignity, operated in villages and small towns.[21]

As power coalesced in local cells, warriors residing permanently or in rotation at their leader's fortification, they rode forth in regular cavalcades: the *chevauchée*, showing the flag of domination to the peasantry in the surrounding countryside, guaranteeing its continued exploitation.[22] This was governance reduced to its simplest terms: the overt use of force, or its threat, to guarantee the extraction of surplus value, in a binary division of society into the laboring plebe as against the specialists of mounted force, *milites, chevaliers*, or knights. Between the two, a central, constitutive, relationship: production, force, and terror as policy,[23] with the aristocracy as ultimate beneficiaries.

Class interdependence was perfectly well understood. Relations of the nobility with peasants form the seigneury in French: lordship, or in the more pastoral vocabulary of English medievalism, "manorialism." Both designate the relationship between dominance and submission, nobility and peasantry. Social dependency on peasant labor is universally recognized, even by a conservative theologian. Adalberon of Laon outlines society's functioning. Human law imposes two conditions, nobility and serfdom. The serf's innumerable labors provide food, wealth, and clothing for all:

> No free man can live without serfs.
> When work is needed and they choose to pay for it,
> Kings and bishops submit to their serfs.
> The lord who hopes to eat feeds off his servant.[24]

The anticipation of Hegel's discourse on the Master and the Slave is laced with ironic references to food and the nourishment that nobles ideologically claim as their social function, but that peasants actually provide to all society. Adalberon's formulation also anticipates modern experts in taxation: the income of all feudal magnates derived from labor services on their holdings of land, and payments in kind. Differences were simply a matter of scale, "under the political economy of feudalism a man's wealth and authority were directly related to the size of his holding."[25]

The term *feudalism* has been criticized.[26] Its broad use for the totality of the socius labels an agricultural society of peasants working the land under brutal oppression for the very small part of that society—less than 1 percent of the population according to one calculation[27]—which lived off their labor, a class that dubbed itself "noble." That is a disproportionate metonym. A more specific sense may be salvaged, centered on the fief: a revenue-producing grant by a lord, most frequently of land, in exchange for a vassal's mounted military service. Feudalism names the economic and political relationship among members of the ruling class, its internal relations of dominance organized around the structure of fief-holding. It is a recursive relation of superiors and inferiors, lords and vassals, ideologically melded around the turn of the eleventh century into a single class. Its internal organization unifies two sharply distinguished strata, or a continuum with two extreme points.[28] As a complex class, ideologically unified in spite of internal contradictions, the warrior-nobility faced the two other classes of society—the religious and the peasants—from the vantage point of the fief.

After cemetery and church comes the castle, not the imposing stone constructions of modern tourism, but the earlier, primitive "motte and bailey," an earthen mound typically fifteen meters high, topped by a platform 100 meters square, a construction of forty days' labor by fifty men.[29] On the platform, a tower surrounded by a palisade, both of wood. By persuasion or terror, the lord obtains not only the construction of fortifications but also the agglomeration of service trades at their foot. This was the castling of the countryside (*incastallamento*) in successive waves: defensive works against foreign attackers under central government followed by a proliferation of "private" fortifications in the "first shock of the castellans,"[30] a new regime of fragmented rule by local force. The strong were linked by "lineages," a molecular rhizomatic of noble linkages. This political dislocation produced a scattering of hundreds of power containers: called a "castlemasters' revolution" by some, a "mutation" by others, it is denied by yet others.[31] The seigneury was based on territory or the power of the *ban*: the power of command, taxation, and punishment.[32] Exactions were ideologized as counterparts of the lord's "protection." To what degree was this a "protection racket"? This "exchange" can seem to have gone tacitly unquestioned by the peasants themselves, as an early form of the social contract,[33] but docility was not universal. Nevertheless, the seigneury becomes the definitive framework of social life in the hundred years after 1075, according to the varied chronologies of different regions.

Extraction of surplus value in monetary form initially took the form of a bewildering variety of taxes, touching every aspect of ordinary life. Even at the local level, intermediaries harvest the profits: subalterns do the dirty work of collection, deflecting hate, fear, and resentment from the master, preserving the social contract by disguising its reality. Pressure to increase the profits of lordship was permanent, the means of extortion multiple and varied: direct and indirect taxation on land, the harvest, on necessary services like the communal oven, the flour mill, and the wine press, on social relations like marrying outside the village, etc. A euphemistic vocabulary develops: terms like *entreaty*, *custom*, and *quest* double the more precise and harsher register of *exaction*, *cut*, and *takings*.[34] Most taxes eventually are annualized, but the *taille* remains: a sudden demand for emergency payments, in amounts and at times determined by the lord at his will. The "cut" remained a mark of servitude. The size and rate of flow into coffers of dominance was related to the efficacy of the lord's henchmen, the knights, acting as enforcers of the collection process: the functional equivalent of the IRS.

Violence and Historiography

The literary scholar's normal role is as a comfortable guest at the historian's table, gratefully gleaning the latter's harvest. When current interpretation conflicts with established tradition and occasions major differences of opinion within the historical discipline, the *littérateur* is forced to look anew, and independently. The violence of medieval society has recently given rise to a historiographical dispute. Far from a tedious quarrel of specialists, the disagreement engages the character of historical change: whether rapid or slow; whether its violence affects only parts of the socius or its totality; whether specific groups can be identified as its agents.

The dispute bears a heritage. "Violence" is a standard component of the "barbarism" by which the Middle Ages is systematically Othered. *Vide* Vico: "Everywhere violence, rapine, and murder were rampant, because of the extreme ferocity and savagery of these most barbarous centuries."[35] Modern, empirical history retains the trait. Marc Bloch saw violence as characteristic of the epoch and its social system.[36] Today's leading military historian of France sees feudalism as the militarization of sociopolitical structures. Fragmentations of power multiply rivalries and diffuse violence, depradations, and destructions, fueled by high costs: construction and upkeep of fortresses, purchase and upkeep of knightly armaments, servants, and training.[37] Weakened central authority left men in a state of perpetual and painful insecurity before the permanence of menacing threats of unleashed violence, as external invasions ruptured ancient frameworks of power. Externally incited violence had internal repercussions.

This remains the view of most modern and contemporary historians, none of whom can be charged with "Othering" the Middle Ages: Georges Duby, Pierre Bonnassie, Eric Bournazel, Jean-Pierre Poly, Thomas Bisson.[38] The charge of a revisionary historiography is led by Dominique Barthélemy, whose rhetoric is not unrelated to the topic: initial aggressive ridicule of an opposing opinion modulates to a conclusive nuance in which the difference from the initial object of ridicule is nearly imperceptible. His work has occasioned scholarly debate and rejoinders.[39] At issue is the construal of feudal violence as violence among the nobles themselves. Much violence was attributed to the *faida*, the pattern of insult and revenge characteristic of noble culture and frequent in its narratives. The code was potent: "honor," the morality of heroism, fused with *honor* meaning "fief": material interest fused with social regard. The medieval nobility granted itself the right of "private" war against any other noble, so long as hostilities were preceded by a challenge, a formal declaration of hostilities. Barthélemy denies denying violence, but claims it was self-limiting and eventually generative of order,[40] buttressing his argument by a foray into legal anthropology. Given the cyclical potential of revenge to go on indefinitely, pressure for conciliation and settlements by negotiation was built in. The feudal feud-pattern was self-limiting, an early medieval form of conflict management.[41]

This argument has limited validity, on two conditions: participants must have access to comparable, credible sources of violence; and feudal families of the medieval nobility are considered tribal. Even among nobles, the utility of the feud in conflict resolution is limited by gender. The feud was an activity of males. Women did not enjoy its advantages: they most frequently figure in the texts as intraclass victims of male vengeances in lineage feuds. Nor did commoners have access to comparable means of violence. A major methodological issue arises. Self-limiting violence may operate to some degree within the specific social class that made of it a profession: the knights. Barthélemy goes beyond that to suggest a larger, transcendent social utility by portraying knightly violence as beneficial "*perhaps even* to peasant villages," with a further qualification: "*in a defensive mode.*" In other words, by forcing peasants to unite defensively against knightly depredations, noble violence sustained village cohesion.[42] Aggression has beneficial effects: it gives victims reason for defensive unification. What violence, oppression, systematic torture, and terror could not be legitimated in this manner? How far can ideology go to defend the violence of a particular social class?

Patrick Geary's account provides the scholarly basis of Barthélémy's revisionism: only nobles and clerics appear. No peasant, no serf, in an article on "living with conflicts in a stateless polity." The "peasant in general" is mentioned twice, once as a potential occasion of conflict and again at the very end, in a discussion of modes of justice. Conflict among secular nobles and men of the church (often of noble provenance themselves) was managed by various modes of arbitration through informal social networks. Voluntary courts of arbitration did not develop into permanent institutions issuing binding decisions and adjudication, with the "*coercive power*" to enforce peace. Such courts existed, but had authority only over those who were not "fully 'free'"—peasants and townspeople, the *vilain*. These courts did not settle disputes in order to build a better, more peaceful society. Rather than implement an abstract ideal of justice, their function was "to improve income, control dependents through *coercive judicial force*, and thus demonstrate the power of lordship." When new judicial systems developed later, they did not signal a new social contract among free men, or issue "from a joyful acceptance of a better quality of justice"—the historian's irony is palpable. Such judicial innovations were imposed from above, "as counts, kings, bishops and popes managed to expand their *coercive judicial authority* from their serfs and slaves to the free warriors, nobles, and clerics of Europe."[43]

This shivering conclusion confirms what one suspected. "Conflict management" sometimes reduced the social violence of "private war" in the dominant classes. Men who made their own law informally settled conflicts among themselves in negotiations that accounted for relative potential force, without being called to account at any bar of justice. A formal system of law was enforced only on the lower orders by "coercive power," "coercive judicial force," "coercive judicial authority." This classic article ends by yielding what it argues against: the fact of a class society. One dictionary definition of "coercion" is "government by force." "Conflict management" governs the internal relations of the ruling class, which applies coercion, force, violence, or "brutality"[44] to the peasantry, from which it *coercitively* extracts surplus value in the form of "judicial punishments," which "improve income" and "control dependents," through a judicial structure that is a mode of oppressive governance of the weak by the armed, mounted machines of war, and a means of financial extortion. Q.E.D.

The appeal to legal anthropology elides the central fact of medieval society. Far from a tribal society, medieval society was a historical society, with a division of labor reflected in its class structure—a concept that, like violence, arouses Barthélémy's ambivalence: using it repeatedly, he denies its existence. Lineage was indeed important to the medieval nobility: feudalism's layered tribalism was a self-serving ideology. For a tenth-century cleric—Rather of Liège—it is not lineage that renders lords powerful, but property and possessions.[45] Some modern scholars cast doubt on the concept of class, notoriously problematic. The fact is that in the Middle Ages, class structure was enforced by the dominant class to its own advantage. One of its characteristics was the differentiated distribution of freedom: some were "free," others not. Take the trial of one "Vital": the name could not have been more appropriate! His father was accused of burning a monastic grange. Unable to pay the fine, the father became a serf of Saint Martin at Marmoutier, along with his wife, Plectrude. That was not enough. The monks also claimed the son Vital as their serf. Plectrude fought them off as long as possible, up to but excluding trial by hot metal. Vital escaped their *dominium* as long as possible. When it became unavoidable, he went through the ritual of submission, but later reneged. Finally, in the year Pope Urban II dedicated Saint Martin's basilica, Vital acknowledged his sin, underwent the ritual of submission again, and capitulated to the extent of declaring his own son to be Saint Martin's serf as well.[46]

Barthélémy cites this case in a discussion of voluntary servitude, but never addresses the question: Why the effort to avoid becoming Saint Martin's serf? Why the avoidance of clerical *dominium*? Could it be that, lacking noble networks of negotiation or arbitration, escape from domination—even from monks—was the best Vital and Plectrude could hope for? That they felt a desirability of "freedom" and appreciated its material and spiritual advantages, even in eleventh-century terms that differ from the modern? Modes of justice varied by class, as today, defined by the subject's relations to economic production and distribution, as well as to the settlement of disputes. "Free" and "unfree" were class characteristics: peasants knew the difference and resented it. Commoners were subject to a more compelling system of justice than the nobility.[47] Differential distributions of "freedom" and "justice" are aspects of class identity.

The legal anthropology invoked represents the recrudescence of a functionalism long dismissed in anthropology. "Peace in the feud," the notion of "conflict management" through the *faida*, is old news, ridiculed and dismissed more than forty years ago.[48] Renato Rosaldo, concerned with the interplay of anthropological frames and historical evolution, ironically cites the "extraordinary optimism" of a simple functionalism that attempts to portray the violence of feuding as a stabilizing force.[49] A different anthropology makes aggressive warfare the ultimate, foundational level of determination, responding precisely to the topographical characteristic of feudalism, its fragmentation. For Pierre Clastres, the serial juxtaposition of autonomous primitive societies, analogous to the independent fiefdoms of feudalism intent on preserving their autonomy against other groups identified as potentially inimical Others, leads to violence at a level more primary than economic exchange.[50] If the feudal cell is to be examined anthropologically, the anthropology of violence is at least as pertinent as the anthropology of juridical reconciliation.

The Middle Ages were a society returning from a major historical disorganization, a dynamically evolving historical society whose strong class structure was integrally related to its evolution.

Why would the relationship between warriors and peasants be violent? In a medieval cliché: *seniores omnia tollunt*, "lords grab everything." Exactions, taxes, were so excessive in the late eleventh century, they threatened "reasonable surplus value" and imperiled farming itself. The total fiscal arsenal around 1100 constituted "*supertaxation*," "*overtaxation*."[51] In fact, the value of fixed taxes was reduced by inflation. As revenue by taxation lagged, another modality of the *ban* came increasingly important: "justice." Processing legal claims and punishments was profitable: its assignment to different levels of lordship was negotiated between lords and vassals. Traditional punishments—cutting off ears, noses, fingers, or other extremities—were not productive: justice in the form of fines was preferred. Cash replaced payment in kind as the financial mainstay of the seigneury. Profits were substantial. Innumerable small penalties added up, in one English manor, to 4,000 pounds: the value of 70,000 days of labor.[52]

The seigneurial framework is ambiguous: a lord is both protector and extortionist; the principle of his governance is questioned directly infrequently.[53] But alternative vocabularies in the body politic testify to ideological conflicts. An oxymoron such as "new customs" for new taxation does not erase the alternative *mals usos* (abuses). Both have ideological weight. One wonders about the readiness of French or English peasants of any epoch to gracefully yield the substance earned by their muscle-twisting labor. The castle and its effect on the surrounding countryside formed the central link in feudalism. Fortresses are power containers, military bases, a major instrument in the subjection of peasants to the lord's power. Castles, supposedly protective of peace, were also the bases of "private" wars among lineages capable of devastating the countryside: "sources of violence."[54] They extend power into the surrounding countryside: farmers, formerly free, are forced to submit to arbitrary *seigneurial* judicial powers; free peasant holdings disappear; new fiscal burdens are levied.

The powers claimed by the lord of the manor were so strong that villagers could seem in helpless bondage. In spite of huge discrepancies in available force, even in the early period relations between tillers of the soil and landlords were not one-sided. The village, as an organized community, commanded forms of economic pressure: passive resistance, the slowdown, the strike, even sabotage, could disrupt the economy of the manor, and force on the lord "a tacit agreement to co-operate" as commoners took on the running of the landlord's estate with the latter's implicit agreement, allowing them "a measure of self-government."[55] When pressure failed, rage and revolt beckoned.

The model of seigneurial lordship, based on agricultural labor, applies to town life as well.[56] A communal movement took form between the River Somme and the Rhine, affecting cities in northern France—Saint Quentin, Valenciennes, Arras, Amiens, Gand, and so on—between 1090 and 1125. Townsmen swore a common oath, a *conjuratio*. When successful, they purchased specific, limited freedoms from their lord, such as replacement of the *taille* by annualized taxation. Towns were ruled by property owners, excluding many from power. Possessing a seal, central offices, a bell tower, even a castle, the commune was a collective lordship, exercising the same legal, financial, and military powers as a noble *seigneur*. Among clerics, it incited horror and repugnance.

The combination of feudalism with the seigneury adapted governance to radically altered circumstances, incorporating for a time what retrospectively stands out as its opposite, the protocapitalist commercialism of the towns. It was no idyllic, frictionless communalism. Although pressure tactics could produce accommodations, violent conflict was not unknown. A monk, recording a charter in 1138, attributes the following phraseology to a minor lord, who grants a given property "free of all financial obligation, of all exaction of the *taille*, of all obligation of labor . . . and of *all these things by which the violence of knights ordinarily extorts from the poor.*"[57] Medieval texts often attribute to evil characters a condemnation they would not pronounce on themselves. The narrative "slip," if such it is, inscribes a fact obvious to the social consciousness of the time, namely that violence played a functional role in the nobility's extortion of surplus value from peasant production. It was answered by assassinations frequently enough to become ritualized.[58]

Three arguments are key to the revisionary dismissal of medieval violence: its documentation masks clerical interests and is unreliable;[59] it was not as bad as imagined, and amounted to no more than conflict resolution;[60] finally, it was no worse than the violence of any other period.[61] A fourth issue remains subtextual, that of opposed models of social change: sharp, rapid change, termed "revolution" or "mutation," as against slower, incremental evolution. This revisionist quarrel implies major issues in historiography, political philosophy, and the shape of human nature.

The key documents issue from a major social movement, the Peace and Truce of God. Local bishops called councils:[62] mass demonstrations held in fields and meadows outside towns, attended by large masses of the *populus*—women were noteworthy in attendance—by clerics, some local nobles, and knights. Crowds were drawn by relics, brought forward and venerated. Speeches were made, position papers read; the meeting demanded oaths of reform; sanctions of excommunication were threatened for those who refused or relapsed. The individuals addressed were the bearers of violence, the *pugnatores* or *bellatores*: the mounted warriors called knights. These councils did not merely *call for* peace. They instantiated what the Middle Ages meant by *pax*: not the absence of war and conflict, but the active process of negotiation, the social construction of peace as order.[63]

The Latin documents unquestionably represent clerical perspectives. In the competition between clerics and the lay aristocracy for control of labor, land, and profits, developing cultural differences led to tensions. Earlier lay donations to abbeys and monasteries, made as part of "a fluid, imprecise, and custom-governed pool of reciprocal gifts and favors"[64] were caught in an epistemic shift, as a new sense of property undermined those donations and as ennobled knights reclaimed "their" properties. Cultural changes had produced differentiated value schemes, recodings that resulted in concrete conflicts of interests, as ecclesiastical claims on lands previously donated by nobles were now questioned. Violence was a possible result of shifting cultural patterns and inadequate legal processes.

The documentation of judicial disputes between ecclesiastics and knights is one-sided. The distribution of military force and ideological power takes the form of a chiasmus.[65] Military force was the domain of the lay nobility, but the dominant discourse was that of the church: the voices of feudal knights and nobles were an "occulted dominant discourse."[66] That institutional documents represent institutional interests is hardly news. The question is the extent to which such investments vitiate their documentary value. The putative referents in social reality are unavailable. The events have passed, no reliable statistical representation of knightly criminality is available. The knights themselves were both "police" and the accused perpetrators; they rarely possessed the technology of writing. The documentation is clerical, because writing was a clerical skill. All our documentation is slanted: What else is new in History? Discard all slanted documentation, and the discipline of history vanishes.

The documents were polemical and self-interested. They were also overdetermined, representing other social interests for which the church assumed a pastoral responsibility and a moral duty: such is hegemonic practice. Prelates labeled themselves *pauperes* and identified their interests with those of the poor, in part as a tactic to recover rights over properties seized by laity.[67] Their claims were *both* expressions of *caritas* and self-interested. Economic interests impelled some clerics to strategies that parlayed their interests into social alliances with others who had grievances against knights: peasants, merchants, undefended women and children, and so on. Self-interest alone does not invalidate clerical claims. There are concrete stakes in peace: limbs, lives, treasure. Does that vitiate demands for peace?

The question is not whether clerical documentation bears clerical interests, but whether such self-interested documentation is the sole evidence of violence. The major revisionist work, Barthélemy's huge study of the Vendôme—it runs more than 1,000 pages—repeatedly voids the question of feudal violence without actually denying it.[68] He denies denying violence, but derides it as a topic. A participant in the debate, the historian Stephen D. White provides evidence that counters the latter's thesis. Drawing on an archive central to Barthélemy's research, at an abbey in the Vendôme, White shows that clerical evidence is *not* the only documentation of medieval violence. On the contrary it provides "an inventory of eleventh-century violence":

> the plundering and burning of an entire village; burning barns and houses, seizure of horses, cows or pigs; killing horses; damaging a mill; destroying fishing-nets; cutting down trees; uprooting vines; homicide; attempted homicide; abusing hospitality; improperly pasturing animals; beating peasants and seizing their goods or money; issuing threats; digging up corpses and taking them away for burial elsewhere; evicting a tenant; ejecting a plough; seizing a beehive; collecting tithes or customs; usurping a mill; taking over a church; and invading land.[69]

The list is unsurprising: it is entirely consonant with Peace documents. It demonstrates that "*identical images of lay plunderers and lay violence appear in charters and [clerical] records.*"[70] That this list is based on an archive central to Barthélemy's magnum opus, whose contents the latter disregards, raises questions of historical method. White's evidence shows that, in spite of self-interest, clerical documents were not pure fantasy. They indexed events in the world of social relations. Indeed, Barthélemy himself acknowledges: "The entire order of lordship rests on relations of force."[71]

Finally, it is argued that the Middle Ages were no more violent than any other period: "As violent as it may have been, [the period] comported *certainly* no more nor less disorder than any other epoch."[72] The defense already comports an implicit admission of violence. *That* argument, made at the end of the twentieth century, is puzzling. It has a limited, literal validity, which deconstructs any claim of a nonviolent feudalism. Comparative judgments of violence are admittedly difficult. But the assertion that "the Middle Ages were not more violent than any other period" makes a limited kind of sense, particularly in comparison to the twentieth century, "the most bellicose in human history,"[73] "the most murderous era so far recorded in human history,"[74] whose megadeaths from the modern religious wars among capitalism, communism, and fascism from 1914 to 1990 are estimated by Zbigniew Brzezinski to reach as many as 187 million. What *weight* should such a comparison be accorded in view of two world wars, the first of which left "a black deposit of ruthlessness and violence," while the second was "the greatest school of barbarism of them all," marked by a resurgence of torture as a systematic governmental resource? Eric Hobsbawm notes the double collapse of the political and social orders in a "descent into Hobbesian anarchy," in which "unspeakable things" are done by people lacking all social guides to action: "We have learned to tolerate the intolerable."[75] Compared to the twentieth century, the eleventh was not worse, not more violent. The absolute number of dead and tortured was smaller, given discrepancies in population and the technological means available. Proportional statistical comparisons are absent. To grant that one might favor the Middle Ages, is perhaps somewhat ridiculous, even odious. What *is* comparable in modernity and the Middle Ages is that in neither case is the violence simply illegal, anomalous, or "opposed to legitimate rule."[76] In both, violence is deployed, not outside the rule of law, but as a policy of those in power, those who claim legitimacy in the practices of governance. In the eleventh century as in the twentieth, law itself is violent: it is the violence of "legitimacy" that is barbarous. To ignore the possibility that a legitimately established government would turn violence against its own population is to disregard both modern and medieval history.

As a simple, exclusive binarism, the opposition of continuity and rupture in medieval history obviously oversimplifies: "revolutions," "mutations," and slower evolutions all occur. History consists of their interplay, not their opposition.[77] That interplay is most likely to be perceived through attention to the dialectical relations among social classes. This, finally, is the crippling fault in the revisionist historiography eager to dispel "the violent Middle Ages." It proceeds by a radical synecdochic exclusion, of the largest part of society—the peasantry—for the sake of an exclusive focus on the smallest part, what has been called "an infinitesimal and discontinuous film" of the social surface—the self-designated nobility.[78] This "dust of history" defines revisionist history's epistemological bias and informs the blindness of its insights.

Othering performs a function for the enunciator. Condemning violence, medieval or tribal, modernity implicitly claims a reasonable peaceability. Once modernity (even a medieval historian's) recognizes its own anchoring in a temporality of violence, the recognition of medieval violence no longer constitutes Othering. What counts is taking the measure of an other—the past, another culture—without making it the mirror image, positive or negative, of the viewer. A view as jaundiced of modernity as of the Middle Ages can help. Medieval violence was not gratuitous, not a marginal exception to an otherwise serene society. It functioned as a technique of governance for the extraction of profits. Violence—Marc Bloch and Walter Benjamin got it right—inhered in law itself. Customary law legitimated usurpations of power. The tradition of the *faida*, which led from private vengeance to private war, was a "noble" practice: but "war" and "legitimate policing" had direct effects on commoners, their violence ricocheted throughout the socius. Violence lodged in mores that allowed for a brutal expressions of passions in the direct deployment of physical force. Burchard, bishop of Worms, notes around 1024 that murders are a daily occurrence among parishioners,

> thanks to drunkenness, pride, or for no reason at all. In the course of a year, thirty-five serfs of Saint-Peter's have been murdered, in all innocence, by other serfs in the same church; and the murderers, far from repenting, glory in their crime.[79]

In the state of general insecurity, peasants as well as knights acted violently. An English chronicler praises the harsh peace of William the Conqueror: henceforth, no man can put another to death, no matter the damage endured, anyone could ride through England, his purse full of gold, without incurring danger. Ordinary crime had double roots: vengeance and naked robbery.[80] Human potentials of violence are doubled by the grossest of economic motives:

> Knighthood is profitable. It brings in money, lots of it. As with everything else, it is, in part, perversely vicious: it has a dark side, where lurks that sharp spur, secret and intense, the lure of booty. But just like the silken coats thrown over metal hauberks, ideology serves to ornament all things with pleasing colors, and to reassure people. Lust for wealth is disguised as courage, masking itself under this ardent spirit, cool and uncalculating, which pleases women and which, so they say nowadays, no longer is so displeasing to God.[81]

The ideology of chivalry developed in epic and romances masked the forced extortion of wealth in unequal violences visited on the peasantry. Greed was woven into the gorgeous fabrics of chivalry.

The Peace Movement

The disintegration of centralized power, early feudalism's extremely localized mode of governance, scatters molecular cells of power across the face of France in rhizomatic dispersal. The written, legal basis of justice is shredded, along with centralized power and its bureaucratic literacy: in a new dispensation of "custom," exactions become "customary" and orally determined as fear and potential violence bend interpretations of law and its applications.

The regime of violence and terror causes widespread social revulsion. Texts from various regions suddenly begin to talk of new, evil, vicious, and unjust customs, imposed by willful violence.[82] Their coolest phrasing is *injustae consuetudines*. The noun signals what modern historiography idealizes as "the customary mode of law."[83] Absent written codes, customary practices acquire force of law. Law was oral, and *hence* customary: orality was characteristic of literature and law as well. In both, plasticity allowed for change, under local pressure, according to new conditions, while retaining the claim of ancient self-identity: thus is tradition invented.[84] Law became the relatively stabilized Interpretant of local practice. The documents' language implies the disjunction between two codes: that of justice, that of custom. The historical Real is fissured; its fissure points to something in the real, referred to as *violentia*. The perpetrators of violence are *raptores, pervasores, usurpatores, oppressores ecclesiarum et pauperum*: oppressors of churches and the poor. The vocabulary reveals both the sharpness of polemical rhetoric and the acuteness of conflicting social practices. "Customary" exactions are now called "forced"; "new customs" are called "evil," "vicious," "unjust" (*malae, pravae, injustae consuetudines*); they are also termed *pradae* ("depradations"), *rapina* ("rapine"), and closest to our own vocabulary, *violentia*—terms whose technical usage does not obscure their larger, more resounding meanings. They address new impositions by the masters of the social order and claims on ecclesiastical properties, as well as criminal assault, theft, rape, kidnapping, or arson.

The documents are integral to the dialectic of a protest movement against knightly violence. It may have combined self-protection for the church and the reestablishment of the principalities and larger seigneuries.[85] It promulgated demands that knightly violence be limited in the categories of its victims or in the time frames of its perpetration: the two stages are known as the Peace of God and the Truce of God. The Peace concerned relations between warrior-knights and the unarmed rest of society, by excluding categories of the population as the knights' permissible victims.[86] The Truce concerned relations among the members of this warrior aristocracy itself, attempting to limit the pleasures of fighting by excluding combat from certain times of the week: Saturday to Monday morning, later on Wednesday to Monday.[87] The two together are the Peace Movement.

Its documents are not neutral, objective records; they are written in Latin by prelates who were its spokesmen and organized its demonstrations. Representation normally bears values and interests: "objectivity" is a modernist normative ideology. The peace papers were rhetorical tokens in the polemic of political struggles.[88] Rhetoric and symbolic capital are themselves realities, integral parts of historic struggles. Their investment does not preclude historical reality: they are part of it. Representation signals reality; it also *is* a reality.

The documents' list of targeted behaviors resembles Stephen White's list from the charters of Marmoutiers in pungent specificity.[89] An act of

989 cites property thefts from peasants and personal attacks on or thefts from clerics.[90] Later documents add as victims noblewomen traveling alone, widows and nuns, peasants of either sex, as well as sergeants or merchants. Bulls, cows, pigs, sheep, lamb goats, asses and their burdens, mules and horses, mares and their untamed colts, mills and their grain, all are regularly stolen. One idealist demands:

> Let no man burn or destroy the dwellings of peasants or clergy. . . .
> Let no person dare seize or distrain a male or female villager or extort
> money from them. Let no one burn or cut standing crops, cut down
> an olive tree, or remove their fruits. Indeed let no one pour out
> another's wine.[91]

The "peace oath" formulated by Warin, bishop of Beauvais, and proposed to King Robert the Pious in 1023, prohibited the following acts to those who swore the oath: invading a church or its storehouse, assaulting an unarmed cleric or monk or their or their companions' horses, seizing bulls, cows, pigs, sheep, lambs, goats, asses or the burden they bear, mares or their untamed colts; seizure of villeins of either sex, sergeants, merchants or their coins, or holding these persons for ransom, or ruining them with exactions, or whipping them for their possessions; extortion of mules or horses, male or female, and colts at pasture; burning or destroying houses; uprooting others' vineyards or harvesting them; destroying a mill, or seizing the grain in it; knowingly harboring or assisting an admitted and notorious public robber; protecting a man who breaks this peace; attacking merchants or pilgrims; killing the animals of villeins; plundering villeins and taking their property; assaulting noblewomen traveling alone or their companions, as well as widows and nuns; taking wine from those transporting it, or their oxen; capturing hunters or their horses or their dogs; assaulting unarmed horsemen or taking their possessions, between the beginning of Lent and the end of Easter; or punishing a villein for attacking another without first making a complaint and waiting fifteen days.[92] Prohibition of crime marks its existence.

The Movement's goal is perspicuous. What was its success? Did it stop knightly violence? Continuing concern with knightly violence suggests its successes were mixed at best. Robert Fossier considers it a "failed revolution."[93] Nevertheless, it had pragmatic effect. Close reading of the documents reveals that it succeeded sufficiently to itself become a repository of symbolic power: it attracted political powers who wished to influence or even capture it. The documents bear traces of the negotiations that attended their promulgation. "Exceptions" to prohibitions of bellicose behavior were extensive enough to weaken the documents' intent. The oath of Beauvais (1023) forbids invasion of churches or their storehouses . . . *unless* to catch a criminal. Attacks on unarmed clerics are forbidden . . . *unless* they are committing a crime, or in vengeance for a crime for which they refused to make amends, and that only after a warning of fifteen days. Mills and grain are protected . . . *unless* the knight is on a cavalcade, or with the army . . . or it happens to have wandered onto his land![94] These loopholes to violence represent pressures of the bellicose class, brought to bear in negotiations, to allow for the presentation of a document acceptable to the secular sponsors of a council as well as to the clerics.

A political judgment had been made, that conciliar discourse bore sufficient symbolic capital, of enough potential effect in the social body, of enough potential hegemony, to justify efforts at damage control and cooptation. The process began early. Duke William V of Aquitaine sought to cooperate with the Movement and obtain control of its operations on his territory, shortly after its beginnings. Around the year 1000, he himself called a peace council in his capital of Poitiers, which designated "the prince of that region"—himself or his substitute—as judge in case of infractions:[95] thus were seculars placed as judges in a process initiated by the church. It is an ambiguous move: enthusiastic adhesion of the count to the principles of the Movement, or a wily effort to defang it? Both alternatives confirm the importance accorded the Movement by a prime mover in political power. Either makes sense only if William thought the legislation possessed potential social, pragmatic effectivity.

Could such ideological effectivity be thought possible, unless the documents, however oriented and interested, indexed some connection to a lived reality? Ideology is not pure fantasy; ideological posturing and maneuvering are not without attachment to a felt or potential social reality. The historical record, no less ambiguous than a literary text, leaves room for speculation. Indeed, it takes shape as historical record only on condition of becoming a text, even if the modern notion of ideology shadows its "literary" status. The historical record, neither uselessly fictional nor empirically objective, requires the skills of readers of poetry and narrative, grounded in medieval and modern theories of text and politics.

From the end of the tenth and into the eleventh century, the territory of France saw something radically new. A military historian considers the Peace Movement an original response to feudal fragmentation.[96] The participation of the *populus* led Carl Erdmann to call it "the first mass religious movement" of the Middle Ages.[97] It was perhaps the first nonviolent mass intervention in history since Aristophanes' *Lysistrata*: popular assemblies demonstrated peacefully against established military powers for peace. Existing social circumstances make the event remarkable. How does a society based in the exercise of force open itself to mass, popular political action?

Mass interventions are rarely made of pure spontaneity, particularly when engaging in as subtle and complex a course as nonviolence: Ghandi demonstrated how much canny strategizing nonviolence requires. Rage can do without ideology, nonviolence cannot. Nonviolence is the ultimate gamble on ideology. Georges Duby assumed the aggression of the knightly class, arguing that when the Peace of God suppressed its aggressivity, it needed another outlet: the crusade.[98] He understood the Movement as a political entity, producing ideology that targeted differentiated social classes: aimed at knighthood and chivalry, it was not directed against the seigneurs.[99] Rather, it allied prelates and princes against turbulent knighthood. Its effectivity was long-lasting. Future kings followed its prescriptions.[100]

Violence did not disappear with its legislations: Urban II, at what was in fact yet another peace council at Clermont in 1095, chastised the French knights who murdered and waged war with each other, in preaching the crusade. His prescription is essentially: since you're going to continue to fight anyway, let's export the product offshore and expend your violence more usefully, against populations we disdain: "a race from the kingdom of the Persians, an accursed race, a race utterly alienated from God."[101] Knights reproduced as a social class. Their subculture reproduced violence: that was what knights were for. The praxis, the *habitus*, the pleasure, the profit, the status, the self-image of knighthood—its "honor"—were based on it. They were a key element of social structure, a force of violence on which depended the hierarchical dominance of the seigneurial system. No one proposed their abolition. The idealized crusades were a form of export "dumping" of surplus violence produced on the European terrain.

The Peace Movement was a risky and courageous gamble by clerics directed at the specialists of mounted violence. The economic basis of the church was the same as that of the secular feudals: the manor, the seigneury. It depended on the continued production of surplus value, harvested in the form of tithes and other dues, or by co-opting peasant labor into the structure of the church itself as lay brothers (*convers*). Both required continued domination by warrior-knights.[102] The Peace Movement broke the potential hegemony between the two segments of the dominant class, condemning the violences of the *milites*, not only toward the clerics themselves but also toward all the poor, all the *inermes*.[103] It tried to circumscribe the social damages of violence without delegitimizing the violent class itself, by limiting the classes of its victims and the times it could be practiced. Given its dependence on knightly force, the church risked its own socioeconomic fundament in delegitimizing violence. Such a risk was not undertaken without grave occasion. Dependent on the force it condemned, the church must have thought the damages endured severe. This historical aporia undoubtedly limited its efforts.

The Peace Movement was "one of the seminal institutions of the age" and left its imprint on the social and political agendas of the Middle Ages.[104] Its futurity included momentous if ambiguous effects: the crusades, clerical reforms to separate church and secular power, the rise of the communes, the monarchy's return to power, and initiations of state governance and pastoralism. Incapable of enforcing it, the Movement succeeded in placing peace on the political agenda as a central concern of public policy. Its ultimate beneficiary was the French crown, as it reestablished political dominance to lay the bases for the state at the turn of the thirteenth century.

Ideological Crisis and the Scene of Ideology

In spite of efforts to differentiate the medieval mass movement from modern analogues,[105] the morphological resemblances are striking:

—organization by organic intellectuals who planned events, formulated demands, and negotiated in the name of the mass;
—sequencing marching formations with stationary discussions;

—the massive acts of presence by individuals providing popular support at the risk of life and welfare;

—co-optation by existing power structures.

Even what seems completely different, the veneration of relics that drew the *populus*, has its modern equivalent: the presence on the dais of veterans of the Movement, those who earlier "put their bodies on the line." Relics and veterans are different encodings in which concrete reality fuses high ideals of futurity with a shared and mediating past.

Methodologically, a calculated presentism, deploying modern notions of ideology, may be instructive historically. Three reasons for the immediate failure of the Peace Movement come to mind.

(1) State ideology works, not alone, but in combination with the potential violence of a repressive state apparatus.[106] The church did not command its own repressive forces: it relied on those it sought to control, the knights. It shared interests with secular powers and was itself implicated in the economic and political structures that were dependent on the exercise of knightly violence.

(2) Ideology must encounter the subject addressed on its own terrain. It works in the self-recognition of a potential subject, accurate or not: it inaugurates new subjectivities only by starting with the codes of the old subject. That hardly occurs in a foreign language that condemns the subject's values and behavior. Legislation in Latin that aimed at suppressing the lifeblood of mounted warriors did not readily enter the knightly culture. Ideology must speak the subject's own language—in every sense—addressing the subject's own culture and value-systems.

(3) Ideology consists not of abstract elucubrations or disembodied disquisitions on "values," familial or institutional. An imaginary relation to real conditions of existence, it addresses real practices, institutions, and interests. Its (re)constitution of subjects can succeed only if it enables them to operate in the real parameters of their social formation. Ideology helps constitute those parameters, but its elasticity is not total. It can be profoundly misleading; it also can be an instrument for pragmatic or revolutionary programs of social action. It negotiates the potential subject's conditions of existence, his or her real-life interests.

Above all, the fusion of economic considerations with the subjectivity of existing political structures may have been determinative. The needs and greed of the lower nobility, the castlemasters and their knights, just acquiring direct control of the instruments of violence for the profitable extraction of surplus value, vivified by the desire to emulate the great aristocrats at whose expense that relative autonomy was wrested, may well have preferred to continue on the violence of their acquisitive process, even at the cost of incurring condemnation from the hegemonic ideological institution of its society—the church. Still operating within the model of "*ravir, offrir*,"[107] warrior-knights saw neither countervailing violence to make them fearful of loss, nor alternative means to perform their values and achieve their goals—profits, the pleasures of dominance, status, and collective identity—within the parameters of the Peace Movement.

The "ideological crisis" of the Peace Movement is characterized by a striking imbalance in the historical record. While the clerical perspective is amply represented—the prologues of the peace councils set forth its values—there is remarkable mutism of the other side. There are no counterarguments to the presentations of the churchmen, there are no discursive representations of the values and norms of knighthood, justifying and legitimating their practices, which can be juxtaposed and compared to the clerical documentation. Two documents are frequently named as historical specifications of "feudalism." One is the vague idealization of a letter by Fulbert of Chartres, responding to William of Aquitaine in 1020.[108] Cited as a classic definition of feudalism, it is remarkably lacunary of "feudo-vassalic ideals,"[109] especially in the reduction of the superior's duty to the single notion of reciprocity: Is that all the lord owes the vassal, given the latter's risk of limb and life? Fulbert's letter, written for a great prince, one-sidedly insists on the vassal's obligations and remains distant from concrete issues arising when vassals felt unjustly treated. It hardly reflects a value-system sufficiently developed for ideological encounters. Exemplifying vassals' problems with feudalism, another document is even more puzzling. The prose narrative of Hugh of Lusignan, roughly contemporary to Fulbert's letter, displays the endless conflicts that beset feudalism, as in Hugh's own relations with William of Aquitaine. Its status as a historical document exemplifying "the realities of feudal relationships,"[110] previously assumed, has recently been challenged: it may be fictive, the source of a later epic, or the summary of a lost chanson de geste.[111]

Little is known of the Imaginary of mounted warriors in the tenth and eleventh centuries: our earliest texts date from the late twelfth. Marx, whose grasp of medieval fundamentals was often acute, noted that social conflict in the Middle Ages was less hidden, less covert, than in modernity. "Feudalism itself had entirely empirical relations as its basis."[112] There was no need for the labor process to assume a "fantastic form" different from reality: the social relations of labor appear as people's "own mutual personal relations, and are not disguised under the shape of social relation between the products of labor."[113] The ideological self-representation integral to all culture may have been limited to establishing small-group identity for the knights. At the bottom of the devolutionary curve, it is not the individual's relation to a distant king or emperor, to a count or duke far from the individual psyche that counts, but the face-to-face relation of men-at-arms to each other, including their chieftain, in close quarters, in tours of castle-duty and on mounted cavalcades into the surrounding countryside. Ideology worked through peers of violence, in illusory equality with glorified chieftains, and in Othering dominated peasants. Group identity formed by individual identifications with specular alter egos and warlords. Equality with the latter and superiority over peasants were wrapped in the mystique of immediate, corporeal presence, hence the emphasis on loyalty and *compagnonnage*. The devolutionary shift, from empire and kingdom to the single "power container" of the medieval fortress, erased the topographical absence that was—and is—an essential axis of state ideology. Or so one may speculate, in the face of the absence of documentation.

Knightly ideology, at this early stage, may have been minimal and insufficiently articulated to allow effective negotiation with opposite numbers, for example, the Peace Movement. Indeed, the fundamental requirement for negotiations was missing, at its beginning: the existence of *a scene of ideology*, a praxis of ideological exchange to stage the encounters of articulated ideologies. Such encounters, borne by multiple narratives or discourses, requires a new form of arbitration: not the hierarchized logocentrism of doctrinal theology or clerical ideologies of stabilization, but discourse as active critique and intervention, whose very existence acknowledges multiple value-systems. Such an encounter does not occur by itself. Prior conditions are required. A confrontation must be stage managed, creating a public scene for polemics leading to resolution, failure or revolution. The Peace of God Movement was a dramatic step toward a postclassical (re)creation of that scene, by clerical intervention in a field constituted by the opposition of "warriors and peasants" to allow a play of contradictory interests. A partial success can be inferred from the multiple exceptions in the final documents of its legislations. At the beginning, however, before that intervention, the *différends* were not merely unresolved issues within a given political framework. They occurred at the level of a more fundamental discrepancy. The *différend* was one of incommensurables: not different discursive genres,[114] but discourse and its defining contrary: physical violence.

The warrior-knights were perhaps little susceptible to ideological manipulation at all. Freud's second primary drive (*Thanatos*) is given multiple representations, as a tendency toward death, destruction, and aggression.[115] If that drive, a speculation shocking many, has any substance to it, then tenth- and eleventh-century knights had fallen on a remarkably satisfying solution to the problem of living. Their nights might be spent in the discomforts of cold, dank fortresses, but their days were spent in healthy exercise, riding horseback through magnificent French countryside, exercising muscles, psychic thirsts for domination and the blood of others, earning status, the respect and admiration of peers and superiors, as well as status and a livelihood above that of most of the population. Their lives fused these gratifications, melding sedentary and nomadic cultures, the "nomadic" trajectories of the *chevauchée* leading back to stable points of issue and return. So long as ideological questions do not interfere, the warrior-knight of devolution had found a personally satisfactory solution to the question: "How to live?"

The "ideological crisis" of the tenth and eleventh centuries was the encounter of ideology with its alterity: violence itself. The early oral epic—for which no actual text exists—would have sung the joyful glories of riding, fighting, and killing. Its texts exist, for us, only as woven into the palimpsests written down as of the end of the twelfth century, well after the crest of the Peace Movement. The written versions of the early chansons de geste represent, not a direct evidence of these warriors' embodied value-system, but a nostalgically idealized ideology of imposing stature, skilled physical force, heroism, courage, and, above all, the honor that devolves from loyalty to the point of death: one's own, or the other's. Read in context, these texts reveal that such ideological values cohabited, not only with brutality but also with the crassest material interests. In addition to their nostalgia for a world that may never have existed, the written texts we inherit also incorporate, in counterpoint to their nostalgia, an unexpectedly earnest yearning for peace.

The ideological negotiations that characterize twelfth-century epic, the increasingly complex perspectivalism, and subjectivism of late-twelfth- and early-thirteenth-century narratives would have been undertaken as deferred dialectical reactions to the shocked encounter of ideology and violence in the Peace Movement: in recognizing and responding to ideological alterities implicit in material action and structures, the ideological scene was created. That encounter later produced not only the ideological responses that characterize the surviving texts but the field of ideology itself, in its relative autonomy: a vernacular field of cultural representation, constituted by a problematic different from officially recognized clerical ideology, within which the value-codes of different social subgroups encounter to negotiate with each other, even within individual texts constituted in and drifting out of the codes of particular classes.

Dialectics of the Multitude

The historical question: Were the eleventh century and the feudal dispensation particularly violent? is unanswerable in the absolute. The social evenementiality in question, "reality," is unavailable. It never existed as a singular entity: different participants, constituted as different social groups, experienced that evenementiality differently. The ideological self-consciousness of the period was convinced of its own violence, seeing it from multiple perspectives. The multiple Reals of the period resound with the violence that runs through them. This is equally true of the clerical documents of the Peace Movement and of the vernacular epics.

The real historiographical question is: What explains the sudden appearance of a mass movement, asserting the irreconcilability of an "imagined community" not yet a "nation," and the practices of violence? How to explain the invention, in the eleventh century, of a "politics of violence"?[116] What explains the transformation of the multitude into a mass movement, even with clerical leadership? That is the stupendous Moment of the tenth and eleventh centuries. An increase in actual violence? An internal political contradiction, as the ethic of *ravir, offrir,* based on Carolingian military expansion, was interrupted by the very success of that expansion, placing targets of pillage, booty and slaves, at ever greater distances? Violent, aggressive impulses earlier played out in foreign domains now turned inward. The attitudes and traits of an earlier economy based on rapine, pillage, and theft, on a taste for violent acquisition by depradation (*praeda*), were now turned against internal populations.[117] Internal competition, factionalism, and particularism in turn created the sharp fissures that produced new, "noble barbarians," whose rapacity fed on increasing agricultural production in overdetermined behaviors we call "violent," as did medieval clerics. Economic benefits appeared first in the higher circles of aristocracy, whose conspicuous consumption made knights and castellans yet more eager for acquisitive expropriations that would permit imitation of high social models.

A shift in mental attitudes toward greater acquisitiveness, the appearance of new notions of property, combined with changing economic and political circumstances, led to conflicts between the clergy and the laity. The clergy, more disciplined, its ideology condemning wealth and direct expenditures of moneys for personal pleasure, excelled at accumulating treasure. It sought stability for practical reasons and peace for ideological reasons. At the monarchy's political nadir,[118] against the violences of the seigneurial system of exploitation, the Peace of God Movement entered the political scene as a strikingly original contribution to Western history. Ideology, never completely absent, now emerged as a relatively autonomous field for the negotiation of social conflicts, first in Latin, later in the vernacular, sometimes projecting hypothetical models of social behavior more desirable than "real" comportments or normative encodings. Its effects, then as now, are unpredictable. Both its form and its first effect was the transformation, the crystallization, of a "pure," dispersed multitude into an ideologically constituted mass movement. This is the Event of the tenth and eleventh centuries: kings, states, and philosophers will slowly learn to negotiate with this mass—normally inchoate, occasionally assuming its role as collective subject—until Spinoza's "multitude" in the seventeenth century lays the ground for the revolutions of the eighteenth.

CHAPTER 2

War, Peasant Revolt, and the *Saint Alexis*

O f the subjective structures in texts from the twelfth or early thirteenth centuries, the major narrative types are saints' lives (hagiography), epic (the chanson de geste), and what is ordinarily called *romance* in English, a confusing term for which I prefer *novel*.[1] Even the earliest epics are late, deferred inscriptions of a susbtantial but lost oral tradition that precedes the novels. As of the mid-twelfth century, however, epic and romance overlap and continue to do so for centuries.

That said, *epic* and *romance* also retain a broader sense, designating overlapping cultural moments in a long-term dialectic of political history and representation. Each deploys different modes of representation to address historical forms of violence. Early epic explores the ideological problematics of violence in a class of warriors and aristocrats beset by feudal fragmentation. That violence explains, at least in part, monasticism's insistent rejection of the *saeculum* in hagiography.

Romance includes most surviving lyric, relatively short narratives called *lais*, and the longer verse narratives usually called *romances*—a prejudicial term that, by excluding serious content, misled the readings of great scholars like Erich Auerbach, Northrop Frye, and Fredric Jameson.[2] These texts are associated with the courts that, becoming stabilized, are integral to a process of recentralization and state-formation that eventually subsumes "feudalism." This process occurs initially at the level of the principalities that dominate European politics in the eleventh and twelfth centuries, including the royal demesne of the Ile-de-France.[3] These courts are characterized by several traits: preoccupation with power, its imposition and organization; processes of representation, written and personal; the growth of bureaucracy, incremental at first but reaching an explosive level as church schools meet a demand for administrators by shifting curricula from the literary to the "practical"; and the development of "discipline" as a social practice whose diffusion in texts and practices constitutes new subjectivities. The texts modernity considers "literary" are integral to this social revolution. The textual archipelago attached to the court, intensely attentive to formal and structural coherence, bears inscriptions of multiple ideological concerns. Their coherences are not those of simple messages, but rather of complex signifying systems within evolving class contradictions of political power and economics.

Although the earliest epics antedate the earliest novels by a generation or two, we paradoxically owe the inscription of oral epic to the cultural revolution of "romance." An extraordinary *prise de conscience* caught oral epic on the edge of disappearance to record its last oral vestiges. Our knowledge of the earlier epic form is grounded in the historical literacy which suppressed orality and reduced it to a subordinate cultural feature. The later form of consciousness preserved the earlier, englobed it, and reinvigorated it. The inscription of early oral texts was part of the dissolution of oral dominance: this cultural embrace left its traces. All medieval texts represent various mixtures of orality and writing. Late epics especially incorporate novelistic influences even as they convey more ancient narratives, often with early historical reference. In the sliding temporality of oral storytelling, such texts do not possess a recoverable moment of originary composition: they are not "of" one historical moment alone. A historical palimpsest, text packs layered memories from *all* the periods it traverses.

A sliding temporality minimally allows for two chronologies. The simplest might base itself on dating the primary manuscript. This would radically reorganize literary history. *Raoul de Cambrai* could be contemporary to the *Song of Roland* (both at end of the twelfth century). It would precede Chrétien de Troyes, best recorded in the Guiot manuscript at the end of the second decade of the thirteenth century. This would rip the works from the historical and cultural web within which they initially appeared. It would replace them as elements of the coming to consciousness of a later generation that wrote them down: not unimportant, but a radical recontextualization.

I prefer the hazardous, sometimes speculative philological enterprise which attempts to locate specific texts according to both internal and external indices in a context of composition. Such localizations are rarely certain, always subject to revision, and—taking into account the complexities of cultural transmission—do not simplify the critic's work. On the contrary, they jeopardize certainty and clarity. This leaves open the possible enterprise of radically rewriting literary history on the basis of manuscript inscription rather than compositional invention—as another, possibly complementary, enterprise.

Vernacular Representations of Violence

Violence remains a recurrent theme throughout medieval textuality. It has too readily been assumed that the texts glorify the violence they represent. True, many reveal admiration for their subjects' heroic virtues, the beauty of accoutrements, and their collective ideology. Some view the accompanying violence as reprehensible; others problematize it; the values of a saint's life exclude it.

The historical referent of medieval textual violence is nowhere to be seen today. It cannot function as a criterion for historical accounts. It is the real on the other side of the chroniclers' and historians' Reals.[4] The closest we approach that real is to interpret the archives' documentary traces: the period's own "Reals," never "objective." Such traces are never a mirror reflection of reality being promenaded alongside a country road, as Stendhal described the nineteenth-century novel. They are always already part of the social and political processes, traversed by self-interests and ideologies, potentially performatives. What is unquestionable about these traces is their continuous concern with and reflection on violence. All forms of what modernity considers medieval literary self-reflection are haunted by violence, to the point of obsession.

THE SUBJECTIVITY OF VIOLENCE

Peace did not represent a universal social consensus. Radically opposed positions developed in the vernacular. For knights, war could be an occasion for joy, intensely desired, eagerly anticipated. In the *Thebes Novel*, a knight rushing toward battle gallops down the hillside, making the valley resound with hoof-clatter: "His whole heart laughed with joy."[5] Peace could arouse countercritique and ridicule. Bertran de Born, a minor baron who revolted against the English occupation of Aquitaine under Henry II, derided peace. Appropriating the love song's conventional spring opening, he sings it as the season of battle, in the delight of watching mounted and armed knights chasing off

> the rabble with their goods in flight
> pressed by the skirmishers, and behind
> outriders,
> the army crowding in . . .

and gives voice to the joy of violence:

> . . . I love beyond all pleasure that
> lord who horsed, armed and beyond fear is
> forehead and spearhead in the attack . . .
> Maces smashing painted helms,
> glaive-strokes descending, bucklers riven,
> . . . brast-out blood on the broken harness,
> horses of dead men and wounded.[6]

This brilliant lyric poses unresolvable questions. Nostalgia for a warrior purity already lost? An ideological tactic to invigorate allies and followers? Does the discipline of its poetic formalization itself undermine its violent content? It clearly textualizes violence as a positive. It enunciates a class subjectivity: to wager one's body in courage and hardiness for physical battle on horseback requires an emotive investment of aggression that takes form as either rage or joy.

WAR

The most frequent form of textual violence is that of war, which brings pleasure, glory, and profit to ennobled practitioners, but wreaks havoc and devastation on peasants. I am unaware of war recounted from the peasant perspective—medieval media were not hospitable to subalterns—but even accounts that supposedly glorify the warrior class frequently reveal the damages its wars wrought on local populations. War's destructiveness itself becomes a topos, a narrative convention, that shrinks neither from the de-

tails of violence nor from its pleasures. A male character describes war with
a note of sexual sadism:

> "I saw the entire land filled with enemies,
> burning towns, violating churches,
> chapel roofs melted down, bell-towers tumbled,
> *twisting the breasts of noble women*:
> so great a pity overwhelmed my heart
> I wept tenderly from the eyes of my head."[7]

The sadistic pleasure is immediately recouped by tears that signal the observer's empathy with the victims.

Siege warfare is a topos. Towns contain booty and are weakly defended.
Outside their walls, populations are defenseless. One late-twelfth-century
account will have to stand for dozens of others:

> That day they rode hard, in force.
> You should have seen those bright, shining helmets;
> They covered prairies, fields, open lands.
> First went the incendiaries;
> Grayhead Isoré led the scouts,
> Foragers ran out through the countryside.
> Tumult arose, clamor redoubled.
> People fled across fields,
> Cowherds assembled their cattle;
> They regrouped in the town for safety;
> They failed, the attack was too strong.
> The scouts set fire everywhere
> In the towns, smoke poured out.
> They chase the herds, lead off peasants as prisoners.
> People lament, clamors redouble.
> The attackers didn't slow down before Cambrai,
> Set flames to all small farms within a league.
> The call to arms resounded, the city gives the alarm . . .
> The seneschal went to the window,
> Across the plain he saw knights drawing near,
> Bright helmets shining, burnished in the sun.
> He saw the whole countryside covered with knights;
> Across the fields, he saw men seizing the herds,

> Seize and keep the donkeys and cattle;
> He saw the fire lit, the flame jump,
> Peasants and herdsmen of cattle flee.[8]

Devastations that might be thought regrettable side effects of chivalric war are nothing of the sort. Fire, pillage, theft are norms of medieval warfare, integral and essential tools: devastation was intentional strategy.[9] It deprived the enemy of food, supplied the attacker with same: starvation was a chief weapon. Fire was recommended by Jordan Fantosme, who assigns this speech to Philip of Flanders:

> "Destroy your foes, *lay waste their country,*
> *Set fire and flame to everything*
> So that no wood or meadow is left the enemy,
> With which to break fast in the morning.
> *Then* with *united* force besiege their castles . . .
> That's how to begin war: such is my advice.
> *First lay waste the land,* then attack the enemy."[10]

A scorched earth strategy was one choice. In the *Roman de Rou,* Harold's brother Gyrth specifically recommends and explains it:

> "go through this country with fire,
> destroying houses and towns,
> take all booty and food,
> pigs and sheep and cattle.
> Let Normans find no food
> nor any thing on which to live."[11]

To capture the opponent's strong points, the countryside is first ravaged to deprive him of supplies; *then* castles are besieged.[12] Strategy aims at non-combatants. The primary means is logistical and political devastation: destruction of enemy territory was the fundamental technique of medieval warfare; terror was a complementary method.[13] For Vegetius, the military authority revered during the Middle Ages, "the main and principal point in war is to secure plenty of provisions for oneself and to destroy the enemy by famine. Famine is more terrible than the sword."[14]

War without fire?—sausage without mustard! Setting a torch to the thatched roof of one wooden house set a whole town afire. Driving off cattle, slaughtering them, destroying vineyards, robbing the population, "the effects of a visitation by an army bent on doing its worst with fire and sword were appalling."[15] Besides economic damage and weakening the opponents' military, it showed the ruler unable to protect his subjects and undermined his political authority.[16] Total warfare was not the invention of World War II. It was the business of kings and "noble" warriors; peasants on any side were victims. It was merely another form of damage endured from social superiors. The story of Gurmund, king of the Africans, demonstrates that an entire society can be destroyed, with a savagery that exceeds any strategic rationale:

> They began to destroy the land . . .
> Burn the houses, destroy cities;
> Beat and hunt and kill
> Knights and villeins,
> Clerics and monks and nuns.
> They contravene the law of God.
> Fields were rendered useless,
> Women shamed, men transpierced,
> Infants disembowelled in the crib,
> Property seized, animals stolen,
> Towers shattered, cities burnt.[17]

Some poets accepted such warfare and considered its ravages "the normal business of war."[18] The grossest depradations commingle with claims of chivalry. William Marshall, an "ideal" knight, returned from crusade in 1188 to enter the service of Henry II. When Philip Augustus's attack on Gisors failed, he withdrew into Capetian territory. William counseled Henry to disperse his men, but with secret orders to reassemble and launch an expedition into French territory. The king complimented his marshal as "*molt corteis*" and followed his advice. William was credited with the maneuver and the ensuing plunder.

Next, Henry launched a midwinter attack from Chinon, ordering his men to ride day and night until they reach Montmirail, where they are ordered to "burn and destroy everything in sight, sparing nobody, seize the town, sack it and burn it. Led by the Marshall, that is exactly what they did."[19] Heroism was not necessary. Warfare was devious, sudden, and destructive. Deceit was not dishonorable, nor tricks like throwing chalk dust into the eyes of enemies. Knights directed tactics against the poor, against laborers, against their goods and chattels. In the war between Henry II and his son Henry, which set the English against the Scots in 1173–74, warrior booty included "any number of animals, oxen, horses, fine cows, ewes lambs, clothes, money brooches and rings."[20] The trend was not to limit the horrors of war, but to make them endemic.[21]

These practices are not only shocking to delicate modern sensibilities, they also contradicted Augustine's theory of the just war.[22] Three criteria determined whether a war was "just": (1) Was it declared by proper authority? (2) Was its cause legitimate?; and (3) Were the fighters' motives proper? Chronicle accounts differ markedly from theological doctrine. Few speeches in the chronicles stress the justice of the cause. Leaders label opponents evil and rationalize war as vengeance punishing the wicked for alleged injuries. The greatest differences occur in relation to the third criterion. Intentions, motives, and practices diverge widely. For Augustine, just war was fought out of Christian love for the enemy: hatred, revenge, and plunder were specifically ruled out. "The real evils in war are love of violence, revengeful cruelty, fierce and implacable enmity, wild resistance, and the lust for power, and the like."[23] Gratian, Aquinas, and Alexander of Hales continued the Augustinian tradition, excluding cupidity and the desire for booty. But the chroniclers' battle rhetoric contains not a single reference to charity or love for the enemy. The stress was on the enemy as evil, to arouse rage and hatred. The chroniclers' God legitimated vengeance. Leaders repeatedly promise plunder as inducement. Clerical theory of right intention had little pertinence to the chroniclers' representation: the warriors' motives were "hatred, desire for revenge, and lust for booty."

A critical attitude toward such practices was not unknown. Wace's descriptions emphasized their horror.[24] The stench of swollen, rotting corpses that cannot be burned hangs over an episode of the *Roman de Troie*.[25] More articulated critiques also occur. The troubadour Girart de Bornelh complains that he used to see

> barons in beautiful armor, following tournaments, and I heard those who had given the best blow spoken of many a day. But now honor lies in stealing cattle, sheep and oxen, or pillaging churches and travelers. Oh, shame upon the knight who drives off sheep, robs churches and travelers, and then appears before a lady.[26]

A century and a half later, in the fourteenth century, a canonist, Honoré Bonet, specifies the actual victims of war as the working poor:

> In these days all wars are directed against the poor laboring people and against their goods and chattels. I do not call that war, but it seems to me to be pillage and robbery. Further that way of warfare does not follow the ordinances of worthy chivalry or of the ancient custom of noble warriors who upheld justice, the widow, the orphan and the poor. . . . For these reasons the knights of today have not the glory and the praise of the old champions of former times.[27]

Medieval culture not only encoded an awareness of the horrors of the devastations of war, it also grasped its essential class character. Whoever fights, whoever wins, the peasant loses. William of Orange has wormed from King Louis a grant of territory: Spain. On the way south, William encounters a commoner who suggests the old Trojan horse trick of sneaking troops into Saracen Nîmes in a thousand covered carts. William implements the strategy. He requisitions carts and oxen from the locals:

> They take the carts, the oxen, the barrels . . .
> If the peasants murmur, Bertrand[28] doesn't give a damn.
> Whoever complained later was shamed:
> He lost his eyes and was hung by the jaw.[29]

No permission is sought from any local noble for this requisition, still less from the peasants themselves. The legitimacy of noble theft from peasants is unquestioned by the cultural codes of a noble text. Noble economic violence against an unprotected peasantry is untrammeled. Complaints are met by murderous punishment.

PEASANT REBELLION

The devastations of war, increasingly stringent nobiliary extortions, seen as violent and unjust, were not always ingested passively. Aggrieved villagers sometimes lodged protests in "memorials" of complaint against local nobles or their representatives.[30] The modern historian explicitly warns against imagining a mass of peasants against elite "exploitation."[31] And yet, that is the representation of medieval historians, recounting armed revolt by a collectively organized peasantry. The ordinary form of peasant resistance is hidden pilferage of a lord's lands, poaching in his forests, burning his crops, sabotage of labor required on his lands, nondelivery of payments in kind or in money, and even flight from his lands.[32]

Peasants also rebel, however. The English uprising of 1381 is famous.[33] Earlier revolts—open, large-scale peasant resistance in armed conflict against their lords—occurred.[34] Merovingian royal taxation occasioned popular revolts in sixth-century Francia; that of 548 was termed "a savage insurrection of the people" [*populi saeventis seditio*]. In the Saxon uprising of 841–42, one annalist reports that slaves "rose up violently against their lords [and] perpetrated much madness . . . the nobles . . . were violently persecuted and humiliated." The *Annals of St Bertin* report a peasant *coniuratio* in 859: commoners organized against the Danish invasions only to be wiped out by Carolingian lords uninterested in the distinction between defensive *coniuratio* and rebellious *conspiratio*. The *Annals of Fulda* mention *seditio* and *conspirantes* around Mainz for 848 and 866. The Liutizi, a grouping of pagan Slavs, rose up in great force against Saxon domination in 983: aristocratic weakness delayed a quick counterattack for two months. Again in 1073–75, the Saxon people and peasants "rose up and caused great destruction" during the civil wars between Henry IV and the Saxon princes.[35]

A peasant revolt occurs at the beginning of the Peace of God Movement in Normandy. It is recorded in a number of texts. William of Jumiège, a chronicler thought sober and reliable, writing a century after the event, notes a "sudden and widespread movement of discontent throughout the duchy among the peasants [*rustici*]."[36] Violently hostile to the rebellion, he stressed the will of the conspirators to live free [*iuxta suos libitus vivere decernebant*], noted the massive and unanimous character of their movement [*rustici unanimes*], and described a structure of political representation: local meetings took place in the fields, choosing delegates charged with presenting local decisions to a general and sovereign assembly held in the center of Normandy.[37] The story is retold in the vernacular, with variance in details, by Wace in the *Roman de Rou*, and by his replacement as Henry II's historiographer, the Benoît of the *Chronique des ducs de Normandie*: unless otherwise indicated, I follow the latter. Norman peasants swore to get rid of all lordship, to live henceforth as they wished, without representative or lord. They would no longer follow imposed laws, customs or judgments, nor any other establishment of law, but follow their own pleasure and will. All agree that lordship is killing them. It impoverishes them all, in their work in the fields, in their labor, in their food. Not work, labor or upbringing, not fatigue nor good years, prevent them from being victimized and stripped of all they earn. *They* have everything, *they* take everything, *they* devour everything, never do *they* lack anything; *they* make the commoners live in poverty and grief. Those established over them have no pity: seneschals, provosts, sheriffs, all do them harm and pain and shame, seeking aids and *tailles*, pretexts and cavalcades, excuses to take away their cattle and rob their houses.[38]

As the complaint continues, the text gives the peasants the collective voice of direct discourse:

> Who could endure so many provosts,
> Serve so many bailiffs willingly,
> So many foresters and beadles,
> Or perform their mandates? . . .
> We've been wrong, crazy
> To take so many blows,
> We're strong and tough,
> Hardened and confident,
> More muscled and bigger
> Than they or their like.
> We're a hundred for each one of them . . .
> No longer will they have rights over us.
> If heart and manliness don't fail us now,
> We'll have great plenty,
> Everything now taken from us,
> Everything we now can't eat:
> The stags, the boar, the deer
> No peasant eats now.
> We'll take all the good fish
> They now refuse and forbid us.[39]

And so they swore the *conjuratio* among themselves. But the duke is forewarned, repression is turned over to Count Raoul. Spies are sent out; harsh and hideous justice [*aspre justise*] is visited on the plotters. The leaders had their eyes put out, their noses, feet, or hands cut off, the teeth pulled out.

> It was in the time of Duke Richard the Second
> It happened as I tell you the story.

It was in 996–97. Benoît and Wace come a century and a half later. That an event occurred at the end of the tenth century was recounted in Latin in the eleventh, retold in vernacular histories of the midtwelfth, suggests continuing topicality. Conflicts between peasantry and nobility, even rebellions, were judged a recognizable potential reality, in the twelfth century as in the tenth.[40] Wace even suggests identification of the earlier peasant revolt with a phenomenon of his own time. The duke hears the peasants are creating a commune (*vilein cumune fasaient*: l. 911). After its defeat, "the commune was abandoned, the peasants since have made no gesture towards it."[41] Collective revolt was recognized as the unitary phenomenon of *cumune*, whether by peasants or burghers.

The peasant discourse of rebellion rejects all domination, asserts the injustice of lordship which blocks the peasants' material progress, the unacceptability of oppressive representatives of power, the greater strength and number of the oppressed, and the material rewards of claiming nourishments now reserved by the noble class for itself. These peasants were not without a political culture, an ideology of equality and materialism, and a rudimentary democratic praxis.[42] Undecidable is the degree to which the ideology enunciated in the text was widespread on the ground, as opposed to merely figuring noble fears. But the basic narrative structure—class struggle taking the form of a peasant rebellion—encoded a sufficient sense of likelihood for it not to seem absurd in a work of history. Enough *vraisemblance* was encoded in the story for its author not to be laughed out of court, in rhetoric reminiscent of the *Merchant of Venice*:

> We are men as they are [*Nus somes homes cum il sunt!*]
> We have limbs as they have,
> Our bodies are as great as theirs,
> And we can suffer as much as they:
> All we're lacking is heart.[43]

The word *equality* does not appear, but the concept is asserted. The principle of human equality, in fact, is widespread and generally understood in the Middle Ages, even as ideology insistently naturalized and sacralized social hierarchy. Concepts of free communities, free status and tenure, and the equality of man are readily encountered, as is peasant desire for freedom.[44] Existing inequalities are explained by making victims responsible for their fate: peasants are faulted for their own degradation, or more general social processes are held responsible, disculpabilizing those who profit from inequality. In spite of this, ideologemes of universal freedom and equality surface in the texts of medieval culture, clerical and noble, Latin and vernacular.

Class warfare is not a modern invention, nor a Marxist one. The texts demonstrate that the subjectivity of the rebellious peasants had been constituted by ideological interpellation, apparently spurred by excessive exactions and extortionate stratagems experienced as confiscatory and unbearable. Foucault's theory of the *plebs*, brought into being by oppressive governance, is apt. Closer in time and social structure is Spinoza's radical understanding that governance in all forms (including the feudal) necessarily addresses the relationship between sovereignty and the multitude— the *plebs* as organized for action. That potential, of organization for action as if with a single mind, recurs as a leitmotif in *The Political Treatise*.[45] It is what makes the greatest danger to the commonwealth its citizens rather than its enemies (6:6). If the ruler rules by violence, it is by violence alone that he may be resisted by the multitude (7:30). If absolute sovereignty exists, it is that of the multitude as a whole (8:3). Spinoza is unlikely to have known about the revolt of 996-97: few events could ground his reflections as well as those which tell of Norman peasants constituting themselves as the multitude of violent revolt, and its savage repression.

Foucault's *plebs* is pertinent. Apt as well is the historical observation, grounded in a different society, that "any conceptualization of exploitative class relations, e.g. slavery or serfdom, requires as a theoretical presupposition . . . a concept of 'communal property,'" as in Marx.[46] Whether peasant ideologies of equality and rebellion were recorded by court chroniclers with horror at past revolts, or as warnings of potential dangers, they inscribed the sociopolitical problematic of their time—the feudal period which, mutatis mutandi, extends in Marxist historiography to the Revolution.

Hagiography: La vie de saint Alexis

The church was split in its reactions to a world of violence. Some clerics assumed activist roles within lay society, especially as it impinged on church interests. Others surrounded a religious world with enclosures of language, culture, and monastic walls. Early vernacular texts translate and adapt saints' lives from the clerical Latin. In monastic representation, as in lay society, a dualistic system of dominance operates. The central relationship in hagiography is between the saint as subject and God, the absent presence that does not appear but whose absence makes itself felt, even at the level of names. Hagiography toys with the (im)possibility of language, of naming either God or the hero himself, descended from the negativity of the paternal euphemism: the father of Alexis (wordless) is named Euphemien (word-avoidance).[47]

But that play is overridden by narrativity. Hagiography employs narrative tripartition. The saint escapes from the world to rejoin God; he or she succeeds, in spite of obstacles, insofar as sublunary life allows; he or she dies, surviving in the memory of witnesses and the faithful.[48] The law at work in the subject's fidelity toward a destinator-God does not derive from a negotiated contract like those of feudalism or commerce. Unformulated, that law offers a binary alternative determining a choice that overrides, in the text's ontology, the play with language. The indirect reference of periphrasis nonetheless produces narrative action. Alexis, anonymous beggar in front of a church, is repeatedly identified as "the man of God" [*l'ume Deu*] by a voice that speaks to the sacristan.[49] He is the man of God. But if he remains after being identified, even by God, he will be unable to continue his total dedication to prayer as an anonymous, de-identified subject. Identity draws the attention of crowds: all honored him, great and small. But he does not desire honor: it "encumbers" him.[50] Identity, in the monastic ideology of the eleventh century, is inimical to complete submission to God.[51] Alexis eludes the identity offered by God, so as to remain utterly faithful, as subject, to a self-denial that is itself a form of prayer to the absent God.

That dynamic leads him also to reject his truth, his identity in the eyes of his family, even on his return to Rome, when he finds shelter again in his parents' home, by posing as an anonymous beggar. He thereby also rejects, as *l'ume Deu* earlier rejected wife and noble status, all possible thirds that might disturb the total abnegation and dedication to God. In this early, archaically elegant text, the narrative subject is an antihero whose antinarrative rejects all possible objects of value—*this* world's values. Its structure hinges on the repeated principle of the excluded third. All potential thirds—father, mother, wife, the status of an identity that social recognition might give—are invoked and rejected, categorically and absolutely.

More than the Latin text, the vernacular *Alexis*, which dates from around 1040, emphasizes the sorrow of the excluded thirds: a principle of perspectivism, hinging on divergent and contradictory ideologies, is already at work in the sophistication of this archaic text. The grief of the antagonists—parents and wife—is given enormously affective rhetoric, in order to set up its rapid deconstruction by the disdainful pope, for whom the death of the subject is not occasion for sorrow, but joy:

> "Lords, what are you doing?" said the pope.
> "What's the point of these cries, this grief, this tumult?
> Whoever may grieve, to us he is joy,
> By him we gain a good intercessor;
> Let us pray him to take us from all evil."[52]

The dead subject-saint will function as intercessor for the people of Rome. He will be Rome's third, vis-à-vis the absent God.

In the eleventh-century *Saint Alexis*, space for the absent third is textualized, emphatically negated by the narrative and words of the text and then reconfigured. Death posits a space of the included third, which allows Alexis to act henceforth for the sake of the collectivity, the role he refused while alive. That is where he will be reunited with his family, in the presence of God. Heaven contains that space of thirdness, unavailable on earth, though projected from earth. On earth, only the dualistic relation of superior and inferior, of Subject and subject as God and saint, is recognized by the saint's morality. No ethics is possible: none exists. The man of God is set against father, mother, wife, recycling the lesson of that earlier Master:

> I have come to set a man against his father, a daughter against her mother, a young wife against her mother-in-law; and a man will find his enemies under his own roof. (Matthew 10:35–36)

Those closest to him are metonyms of the *saeculum*, the world as the site of violence and distraction from God, the world to be rejected for the sake of God's salvation. Monasticism's lesson is harsh.

Alexis, as narrative subject, turns his back in total alienation on family, society, and the personal destiny of Roman aristocratic identity.[53] The textual subject is the monastery, whose ideology turns its back on mankind for the sake of prayer and salvation. The monk's *imitatio christi* requires not only renunciation of the world, but mortification of the flesh:[54] the saint "tormented his flesh in the service of God."[55] Monastic ideology requires public praise of God, celebration of the divine office, excluding work of the hands.[56] Action in the world is not required, not even pastoralism: some monasteries refused lay participation in their services.[57] The monk pays the price: a radical renunciation of the world.[58] His life is exile from country, family, society, material goods, earthly pleasures, anything that endows this life with value.[59] The prologue of Peter Damian's "Life of Saint Romuald" states the theme of *contemptus mundi*: "It is against you, O world of filth, that we raise ourselves in the most absolute manner."[60]

The subjective lesson of Latin hagiography is *askesis*, self-denudation to the point of denial of identity itself. But the monastery's population of monks is not self-sufficient. Its *askesis* is supported by peasant labor, in the form of tithes or the labor of lay brothers, the *convers*, laboring peasants wearing the cloth. It also depends on the protection of warrior knights and the good will of their lords. Hence the need to provide an ideological justification of the monastery in the language of the contributory untaught: the vernacular. Hence the translations of hagiography from the Latin, the medium in which the monks already know the saints' lives, into the people's vernacular.

Paradoxically, the resulting vernacularization reproduces the dualistic structure it shares with aggressively combative epic and knighthood . . . but inverted. Paradoxically also, the monastic program of ideological self-legitimation by vernacularization performs the first conjunction of the vernacular with writing, the basis for the twelfth-century explosion of a written lay culture increasingly autonomous from clerical control. In propagandizing the laity, the church endowed it with the weapon of cultural independence: its own cultural and ideological ground, its *suppositio*. Hagiography still condemned the values of the audience addressed, but aporetically: now that audience heard its own language as the material of textuality. The ground-bass of its daily existence, the linguistic skein that enveloped and structured its experience, acquired an existence that took its language beyond quotidian utility. Writing was one of the powers and mysteries of the church; it would envelop the awesome power of the state as well. In both, transcendence was harnessed to an institution, but undercut by the vehicle, the vernacular of the fields, the hut, the peasant's table and bed, the shop window of the artisan and merchant. Contaminated by religious values, these were not locations of purity. But they were also not entirely harnessed: their language and their experience had never been entirely subsumed by the official dogmas of institutionalized church. Now, their language entered onto an ambiguous "beyond": the adventure of a culture that, as praxis, could be neither completely subsumed nor completely independent of the official culture of the church.

Alexis's mother and daughter had awaited son and husband with intense desire; now they grieve and gaze at him lying dead. The wife's *plainte* contains the earliest stanza of passionate, carnal love in French. Implicitly condemned by the poem's structure and ideology, it rings vibrant even today:

> O lovely mouth, lovely face, lovely presence,
> How it has changed, your lovely face!
> I loved you more than any creature.
> Now so great a grief appears!
> Better for me, my love, had I died![61]

The Latin version contains no equivalent. The restatement of monastic ideology in the vernacular required recognition of the lay culture addressed and its values. It produced the first formulation of passionate, carnal attachment in the vernacular, antedating even troubadour lyrics of *fin'amors*. Religion, propagating itself, produced its own contrary. Linguistically and ideologically, religious propaganda constituted a secular, vernacular, cultural revolution. The effects of both textuality and ideology—overlapping concepts—are largely indeterminate.

Ideology emerged as a relatively autonomous field for the negotiation of social conflicts during the Peace Movement, to which the *Saint Alexis* is contemporary. Its effects, then as now, were unpredictable. Listening to a *jongleur* recite the *Life of Saint Alexis* more than a century later, Peter

Waldo, a wealthy merchant of Lyon, gave up riches, family, social position, in order to live, poor and homeless, as had the saint and the apostles.[62] His story demonstrates both the performative power of narrative and its indeterminacy. Imitating the saint's example, Peter committed himself to voluntary poverty. Disseminating the message, he undertook itinerant preaching and commissioned translations of the Bible. His *imitatio* of the saint's life and apostolic dissemination had unintended pragmatic consequences. It ran afoul of established, institutional control over the ideological field and incurred the wrathful discipline of the church, which forbade vernacular translations: it declared Peter Waldo a heretic.

CHAPTER 3

Epic and the King's Peace

The Song of Roland and *Louis' Coronation*

War itself requires no special motive but appears to be engrafted
on human nature; it passes even for something noble.
Immanuel Kant

Violence is inscribed at the deepest, most constitutive structural
levels of the epic chansons de geste's warrior heroism. An over-
simple identification of matter, meaning, and structure has led to a generalized impression that the epic universally glorifies the violence it portrays.
That is confusing meaning with problematics. Epic explores violence: Is
this automatically a glorification? Does Sophocles' *Oedipus Rex* endorse incest? Epic explores violence and its structures; in some cases, it projects
symbolic solutions to the political problem of violence. Violence is epic's
central concern, not the object of its praise. It is a matter toward which
epic takes a stance, not an identitarian embrace. That stance is often complex, a mix of admiration and critique.

How paradoxical this can be appears in one of the earliest Old French
poems extant. Itself not an epic, the *Voyage of Saint Brendan* was written
early the twelfth century. Its hagiographic background winds through an
exotic fantasy quest, en route to paradise—far from the motifs of contemporary epics. Nevertheless, their topic is inscribed in the poem's dedication
to Lady Alice the queen. Through her will divine law prevail, growing an
earthly law to make

> multitudinous wars disappear,
> Thanks to the weapons of Henry the King
> And the counsels you will deliver.[1]

The law of God and human counsel will pass through the queen to the king, human and divine laws will be respected, peace will arrive, war will disappear—thanks to the king's intervention with the weapons of war. The king brings an end to war by making war: war ushers in peace. The paradoxes of twelfth-century governance, and of governance ever since, are inscribed in this brief dedication. Hagiography rejected a warring world for the sake of salvation. The *Voyage of Saint Brendan* offers a glimpse of paradise within the framework of this life, one terminus of an escapist fantasy. The other terminus is that nexus of peace, power, and war as the means to achieve the peace.

After the Oaths of Strasbourg, the thin series of Old French texts are all of religious inspiration for nearly three hundred years, translated from Latin: the *Vie de saint Alexis* is merely the most imposing. Then, in the north, secular narrative predominated, in epics focused on transactions of violence and power. As is normal in oral culture, the content and even structures of individual poems evolved and changed continuously. Their actual manuscript inscription did not begin until the late twelfth and thirteenth centuries. Different manuscripts of the same text can bear substantive variations. *Manuscripts* can sometimes be dated; *works* are best "dated" by a temporal bracket.

The epic, in Greece, Rome and medieval Europe, thematizes war and its effects. Issuing from societies modernity deems "primitive," it can be extraordinarily sophisticated, complex, and highly articulated. The poems prize the heroic, lauding physical prepossession, technical fighting skills, courage, and loyalty above all, in recognizable conventions that can give rise to ideas of "genre." But conventions are often used in profoundly discordant ways. Seemingly conventional "war poems" may harbor structures pointing to peace and its disciplines, such concerns for peace being hidden by textual circumspection toward traditional conventions. Some of the most archaic stories are embedded in texts revised much later. The same *story* could be told in purely constative or admirative veins; its act of *narration* could reveal a sense of tragic loss deriving from a mingling of identification with distance—as in the case of *Raoul de Cambrai*, which aspectualizes its narrative through perspectivalism.[2] Different, even contradictory subjects of enunciation are implied by different tellings.

The Old French epic was class-specific, but the noble class was a complex one, and the jongleurs who were its entertainers were marginals. The oral epic, as it appears through later written recensions, was the cultural field within which segmental differences of the dominant political class were deployed and negotiated in ideological semiosis. Women, peasants, merchants, clerics, even the pope, make only occasional appearances, especially in the early poems. The essential, paradigmatic axis of the texts is that which defines feudalism: that between vassal and lord, often promoted to king or prince. Although feudalism has come under skeptical scrutiny as a principle of historical explanation, there is no doubt of its ideological reality in vernacular narrative. Not only does it structure most narratives: a subcategorization organizes the epic in three cycles according to a structural analysis of the fundamental feudal relationship. The texts are distributed according to legendary genealogical ancestors of heroes: Charlemagne, Garin de Montglane, Doon de Mayence.[3] The specific roles of heroes and kings, subjects and destinators, reveal an axiological surface distribution of positive and negative value to the two paradigmatic actors of feudalism: lord and vassal.

In "the matter of France," the king's cycle (for example, *Song of Roland*), both vassal and lord are given positive markers on the surface: both Roland and Charlemagne appear as "good guys." In the Garin de Montglane or William of Orange cycle, the king is weak, young, incompetent: he is negativized; his vassal, Count William or another, is the hero. In the last cycle, that of the rebellious barons, both lord and vassal are negatively valorized: both are "bad guys." The distribution is as follows:

	lord	vassal
King's cycle:	(+)	(+)
William of Orange cycle:	(-)	(+)
Rebellious baron's cycle:	(-)	(-)

The texts envisage three narrative possibilities: both king and vassal are admirable, and only a traitor explains tragic defeat; the king lacks the requisite qualities, but is supported by a great vassal; or the king's weakness or ill will leads to the dreadful cycle of revenge, both antagonists assuming negative markings. One further subtype is logically possible: the king would be given positive value, and the vassal negativized. That possibility does not actually materialize, marking the class enunciatory position.

The validity of this distribution is limited. As texts bespeaking a complex class, they are not only accounted for by a simple, binary ethic. Surface values "cover" the text's more serious exploration of fundamental political issues. The surface binary is an enabling condition for the textualization of the culture's "political unconscious." That unconscious operates, not at the level of surface verbalizations, but in developing complex political content for deeper narrative structures. Epic discourse is one of competing values and loyalties, where plural and contradictory value schemes take advantage of the enlarged framework of fiction to explore the constitutive aporias of feudalism—conflicts that can extend over generations without finding a resolution. Sometimes only the participants' exhaustion allows a cessation of devastating warfare.

The Song of Roland

Narrative logic undergoes specific modulations in the Middle Ages, sometimes ignored in favor of the new twelfth-century interest in dialectics.[4] It is characterized by episodic construction, in ill repute since Aristotle. Purely episodic narrative, which consists merely of "one thing after another" without differentiation of initial and terminal states, can only leave things as they are: it is inherently conservative. Only as a culture grasps the principle of narrative transformation does it obtain ideological purchase on its own historicity: its dependence on prior states of social forms, its potential for change that may flicker as glimpses of desire or, indeed, as tremulous threats or warning signs of degradation. "Narrative," as it grasps its own potential to move from a *state (a)* at the beginning, through a process of change at *state (b)*, so as to arrive in conclusion at a *new state (c)*, bears a potential of imagining historicity. Insofar as it embraces its own force, it attains a threshold of narrative performativity, the possibility of impinging on social praxis, so as to change the socius. The transformational narrative potential of the text also defines its potential of performative historical intervention.

Such narrative offers a "principle of hope" that can nourish people, texts, and political developments. A secular, vernacular culture inscribed its potential for historical transformation in complicated ways that coordinated contradictory imperatives. Epic deployed the ideological force of a distant Carolingian mythology to address more recent issues with a view to a cruelly "utopian" future. No text fuses the antinomies of warrior heroism with the transformative hope for peace more intently than the Oxford manuscript of the *Song of Roland*. The fundamental structural integrity of the text is precisely the reason it appears to moderns to transcend its own historicity, *and* the reason its transformations apparently had the historically performative power they did.

The *Song of Roland* is readily mined for ideology in the classic sense. Thus,

> A vassal must suffer great hardship for his lord,
> Endure sharp cold and great heat,
> Lose his blood and his flesh.[5]

Not only hortatory discourse, but the poem's narrative content furnish *exempla* of feudal ideology. All the Franks of the rearguard die for their lord, courageously performing vassalic duty at the mountain pass of Roncevaux. Oliver and Roland, for all their momentary differences, as well as the Archbishop Turpin, are merely the most individualized of the poem's vassalic heroes. What better examples to illustrate feudal ideology? And yet, the poem is equally cited as monarchical propaganda and testimony of religious hegemony—both inimical to feudalism.[6] None of these perspectives is entirely misplaced, but none takes account of the problem posed if all are somehow relevant to the interpretation of the text: the key terms—feudalism, monarchy, religion—imply different social systems and contradictory value schemes.

The poem's crucial ideological negotiation occurs at the structural level, when the entire narrative trajectory is examined as the relationships of constitutive parts.[7] That is where the poem organizes the multiple value-systems it incorporates and makes a deeper critique of its own surface representations of feudal, monarchical and religious values. Its beginning offers an idealized version of feudal nobility, heroically submitted to a wise and powerful leader marked off from ordinary men by communications with the divine. A surface reading lays the responsibility for the disaster awaiting in a mountain pass, where the returning army's rearguard is entrapped and decimated, on the shoulders of the traitor Ganelon. In fact, the violence of the feudal order is amply demonstrated as a self-generating mechanism, destroying individual lives as well as the service owed a higher authority. Hero and traitor both are courageous and loyal to feudal ideals. That is the paradox: feudalism self-destructs. When he returns to the battlefield to find his nephew Roland stretched out in death among the flowers of the field, Charlemagne bemoans the military and political disaster that has befallen him: it will weaken him in future politics. Neither the sincerity of his grief nor the severity of the disaster is open to doubt, in the affective rhetoric of his sorrow.

Nevertheless, Charlemagne mounts a new army, replacing Roland and Oliver, great heroes trailing the refulgence of past exploits, as if by verbal magic, with unknowns, Rabel and Guineman, reorganizing the army in effective divisions that will follow his orders precisely. Short the great heroes of the past, it begins to resemble the regimented, anonymous armies of the future, its soldiers not only serving a royal chieftain, but subjected to him. With this new army and God's help, Charles wins against a reinforced enemy: the emir Baligant's arrival from the east with huge, fresh contingents turns the conflict from a local skirmish to cosmological totalization. After Charles' victory, the text returns to unfinished business: the formal trial of the traitor Ganelon, which redefines the relations of feudalism and monarchy. Found guilty by a jury of his peers under pressure from the emperor, he is drawn and quartered at the latter's order. Ganelon's torture is both the unmaking of the feudal world, in Elaine Scarry's phrase, and the assertion of the approaching dominance of royalty spearheading the disciplinary society.[8] Extreme judicial punishment is governmental terror as policy, from the *Roland* to Damiens in 1757.

The argument that convicts Ganelon defines an important principle in politics and law. It is voiced by an unknown, an everyman. Heroes are blond and prepossessing; Thierry is slight, dark, and swarthy. He proclaims the hierarchical superiority of the king's service over any noble right or prerogative:

> Whatever wrong Roland did Ganelon,
> being in your service, that was his protection.
> Ganelon is criminal in that he betrayed him.
> Toward you, he's perjured in bad faith.[9]

Thierry, asserting the priority of royal claims over and against feudal values, defines the legal meaning of the trial. The *Roland* establishes a principle that does not obtain in the reality of the day. While the king's special aura was generally acknowledged, in cold hard fact, local vassals rebelled: the princes of adjoining principalities readily warred against their king as a merely equal antagonist. The poem argues a position of hierarchical superiority that is not evident in contemporary historical reality. It transforms the initial feudal context, in which the emperor-king performs as little more than parliamentary chair of the meeting, into a position of political preeminence. That will become a historically crucial transitional type, the "feudal monarchy," a stepping-stone toward the absolute monarchy and, ultimately, the modern nation-state.

The logic of the poem's narrative structure thus follows a sequence of four stages:

1. feudalism's self-destruction;
2. universalize the conflict [the Baligant episode];
3. resolve issues of culpability [Aude's death, Ganelon's trial];
4. suggest the new order.

A monstrous political economy structures the first stage. Although the traitor is nominally responsible for the disaster at the mountain pass, his performance as the king's messenger to the enemy reveal him to be a courageous, headstrong knight similar to the hero, his stepson Roland. Alone in the enemy camp, he is entirely prepared to fight and die for his king's honor. He and Roland share warrior traits and values; only in loyalty is there a difference, and even that remains problematic. Ganelon follows established feudal rules: a noble, he has the right to personal vengeance and issues the proper public challenge, before Charlemagne as witness, no less! He achieves vengeance in what seems to him a correct observance of judicial norms. The hecatomb of feudalism at Roncesvals is produced by the logical, systemic self-destruction of feudal ideology.

An issue remains as a narrative excess. The king, as feudal lord of his troops, owes them protection, a duty spelled out in frontline arguments with the enemy. The narrative repeatedly signals the emperor's burden of culpability and the legal principle that condemns him. Charlemagne remains the feudal lord who did not succor his vassals, hence an unresolved culpability. The enemy's entrapment, the traitor's obvious guilt, the self-destruction assigned Roland, do not relieve the emperor. Culpability pursues him to the last laisse of the poem, where he undertakes yet further missions, in a punishment he himself ascribes to God: "*si penuse est ma vie!*" (l. 4,000).

The text thus tracks a transformation from its initial feudal stage, to a historically later stage of monarchical predominance—a stage that would not be achieved for about one hundred years after the traditional dating of the poem (ca. 1100). The poem, along with other epics, (re)marks the problematic character of feudalism, producing feudal violence as an effect of the warrior class' character and ideology. It also designates the structure by which the present will be transformed into its futurity: monarchy will surpass the feudal order by taking every possible advantage of existing feudal norms. It will respond to feudal calls for help in solving feudal problems, thus overcoming the aporias of "the feudal system" over a period of centuries.

That the *Roland*'s narrative transformation had a performative effect on the historical social text is not demonstrable in evidentiary terms: as a hypothesis, it is not falsifiable. That is true for most fundamental notions of social life. It must retain the status in which it is proposed, a hypothesis that can be supported with various kinds of argument and subscribed to with greater or lesser certainty and conviction, but that cannot be established as positivistic fact: only vectors of likelihood are available. What is more certain is that this shift represents an ideological transformation. This was not unprepared in Latin discourses on the responsibilities of kingship. The effectivity of such discourse on peasants or knights was indirect and limited: the *Roland*'s language and narrative force was available to the entire population. It is in the vernacular that ideological transformations affecting the general populace, or a largely illiterate segment like the knights, had to be worked.[10] Most knights, even when agents of a prince's administration, remained ignorant of Latin.[11] And it was the knights who were the target of the ideological effort to instill the value of peace in nascent subjectivity.

The *Song of Roland* posed the effective subjection of the nobility to the monarchy as a desideratum: in historical context, it expressed a utopian hope. Elements of ideological fantasy are present: the transformation of violence against clerics, women, and peasants into military heroism against foreign invaders; creating a new army out of nothing; the assertion of continuing feudal loyalty as a military norm as against the historical introduction of mercenaries, accompanied by the princes' and kings' obsession with garnering money to pay these troops-for-hire; stopping the course of the sun, at the convenience of the Christian king and deity. Such narremes are ideologically oriented. Behind the fiction lay far less heroic social performances, structures of force, authority, and taxation—incipiences of the state disregarded by the narrative. The poem's response to the sociopolitical problem of violence mingled admiration for an aesthetic ethics of heroism, recognition of the feudal nobility's self-destructive mechanism (a sociological reformulation of the principle of tragedy), and an optative narration in which the hierarchical priority of the sovereign figures as a supersession of feudal fragmentation: it proposed a retotalization of the political field that subsumed feudalism rather than discarding it, under the domination of an ideologized mythology of kingship.

The *Roland*'s narrative structure states a starting point and an end point. It demonstrates the ideological starting point; it limns the new man required *after* the revolution (Rabel, Guineman) and the fundamental ideology that will generate him (Thierry). What it omits is the practical question: *How?* Just *how* is the switch in ideology and the resultant change in subjectivity and behavior to be achieved? What the poem does not envisage, what was perhaps unimaginable in its own historical context, was the process by which this subjection of violent warriors to a rule of state could come about. What would lead these creatures of violence, trained to violence, to find profit and gratifications in horsebacked violence, constructing violent identities in the close-knit fortress troop—what would lead these rough-hewn warriors to subject their taste for violence, the social status and financial advantages it won them, to the rule of a distant king? Psychic investments had been made in the practices and value-systems that made the warriors what they were. What was required was a fundamental shift of psychic adhesions—the kind of subjective shift at a level fundamental to society, where its ideological cement provides communal adhesion.

Louis' Coronation

The question would not be addressed until the arrival of "romance" on the cultural scene. In the meanwhile, a cultural problem of a different order blocked the conceptualization of a solution to the antinomy of power and legitimacy—its imagination, taking that word as a gerund. It is a lack in the world of cultural forms that impeded an imagined political solution. Characteristic of early epics (outside the *Roland*) is their entrapment in the irresolution of purely episodic form. In later narratives such as the novel, episodic differentiations do exist and yield a coherent structural paradigm.[12] Episodic structures may be overlaid with shifts of perspective, under the influence of the new romance discourse, with appeals to feelings over physical actions, attention to romantic emotions tangled in feudal conflict, and the priority of individual moral value over social status defined by legal criteria, as well as the insertion of pilgrimage and adventure into the traditional epic framework.

But these syncretisms prove insufficient to respond to the problematics of violence. So too, the installation of new aspectualities does not in itself allow for the operation of a crucial narrative potential. That is the fusion of anthropomorphic representation and sequential logic that offers a transformative potential. The early-twelfth-century poem, *Louis' Coronation*, belongs to the second epic subtype, the William of Orange cycle, traced genealogically to Garin de Montglane. Louis, a weak, frightened boy, is crowned king during his father's lifetime according to custom, in spite of evident inadequacies, by William, Duke of Aquitaine, who performs as guarantor of the throne and Louis's personal safety. In repeated episodes, William fights off attacks from external and internal enemies:[13] only thanks to his courage and loyalty does Louis survive multiple besetting dangers. A weak, inept superior survives to triumph over his enemies thanks to the personal heroism and military support of a vassal, a great prince of his realm.

Principalities such as Anjou, Champagne, Flanders, and Normandy were better organized, more powerful, less plagued by the insubordination of theoretical vassals, than the putative "kingdom." The king's domain, the Ile-de-France, was itself one of half a dozen major principalities in northern France. It was marked by relative weakness, and the survival of a vague, inchoate sense of the king's preeminent legitimacy. No cohesive theory of kingship had general currency in the eleventh and twelfth centuries to sustain royal preeminence: only hints of such a theory glimmer in Suger's writings. *Louis' Coronation* resolves the split between the two levels of rulership by the willing, loyal subordination of a principality's prince, the locus of real political power at the time of the text's composition, to legitimate kingship.[14] It is in the structures of the text, which organize its oppositions and narrative sequences, that its political (un)conscious, and that of the period, are inscribed. No distinction, in any polity, is more fundamental than that between violence and legitimacy. Their conjunction is all that distinguishes the king of France from his equals or superiors in power before 1180. Insofar as *Louis' Coronation* textualizes the political unconscious of the period, it is structured as a subject split between power and legitimacy.

The division of the textual subject is doubled by the indeterminacy of the narrative subject. The narrative subject is known as "William of Orange" in scholarship, but in this poem he is variously named. He is Shortnosed Bill (Guillelme al Cort Nés); William son of Amory of Narbonne the Proud and brother of Bernard of Brabant the Warrior; Strongarm Bill (Guillelmes Fierebrace); or just plain Strongarm. Each name is imbricated in narrative. Shortnosed William is explained in the narrative, as his first major antagonist, the pagan Corsolt, cuts off the tip of his nose along with his nosepiece, his shining hauberk and the hair on his forehead (ll. 1037–41). This may be an etiological narrative for the odd name of "Shortnosed," which looks like a misreading, striking in a supposedly oral text: "Guillelmes al Cort Nés" would be a misreading of an original "Guillelmes al Corb Nés," marking the Roman nose frequent in the South. The nose is turned to fun as it is subjected to Saracen sarcasm and William's own irony, who "avenges" his nose by killing a Saracen who insults him.

"Strongarm William" is also etiologized by narrative. In the poem's initial episode, William comes to court and finds already seated at the king's side one Arneïs of Orleans, the internal enemy who offers himself as regent during the weak prince's youth. Arneïs, in fact, is on the point of successfully tricking his lord and becoming the regent. Wild William stalked through the crowd to stand in front of the traitor. Rather than decapitate him with his sword—he suddenly remembered that killing is a mortal sin—William rolled up his sleeves:

He grabbed him by the hair with his left,
Raised the right, and slammed it back on his neck:
He broke his jaw in half,
And knocked him to the ground, dead at his feet.[15]

Names, like subjects, are produced by stories. Unlike the modern, medieval man is not onomastically trapped: identity and names are social constructs, sometimes individual choices or socially attributed "nicknames." William's onomastic dispersal parallels the split of power and legitimacy in the poem, and royalty's aporetic reliance on a rival for political support. Such an aporia marks a site of weakness and potential conflict in the political domain.

The Problematics of Peace

The desire to overcome violence made itself felt, not only among men of the church, among peasants distraught at having their labors come to naught as fields were burned, cattle stolen, themselves and their families beaten, harassed, even killed. Peace was integrated into the slow recapture of centralized power by princes and kings. The church had launched the Peace of God in the absence of a king capable of controlling excessive violence. Its failure left hanging the task of peace it had begun. The king's inability to rule (*rex inutilis, imbecilitas regis*), the church helpless in spite of alliances with secular power, peace turned into an instrument, a sign of achieved rule: an ideologeme.

Peace was not the absence of war. Peace had a structure, a political structure that incorporated political calculations and economic class. It was an ongoing project, engaged in negotiation and conflict, including *werra*. No polls exist, of course, but it is a reasonable supposition that at least a rough peace was heartily desired by the silent majority of the population. Its peasantry, fearful or angry at being ravaged by unpredictable irruptions of violence, whether in war, local terror, or the pure pleasure or aggression expressed by Bertran de Born, probably preferred the labor of the fields and the pleasures of its homes.

Differences of ethos dug a wide gulf between the warriors and the others of their society. Along with violence, overspending—largesse—was the knightly ethic. Going into debt was chic, in conspicuous consumption mimetic of the great aristocrats. Peasants resembled the monastic clergy in one respect: both accumulated value and valued peace. Abbeys and monasteries laid up treasure: foodstuffs in granges and larders, gold and silver in treasuries. Such accumulations of value made excellent targets of opportunity, inviting the devastatory proclivities that knights could also gratify in burning peasant fields and destroying their huts. These too turned a profit. Stolen metal implements could be resold, to be melted down and recast as knightly armor: ploughshares could be beaten into swords. How does one repress violence when its pleasure is doubled by profit? What the rest of society hated was both appetizing and lucrative to the knights.

The limited, punctual alliance between clerics and peasantry was based both on common economic interest and the religious ideology that cast the church as shepherd of the poor and the weak, the commonality disarmed in the knights' attempt to monopolize the means of violence. That alliance consolidated in the Peace Movement to face a dominant class that was fundamentally divided, economically, socially, and politically. The economic interests and culture of mounted warriors differed from those of great aristocrats, proud of ancient genealogies that legitimated status and fortresses.[16] By contrast, castellans and their bands of warriors were rank *parvenus*, pretentious, arrogant but dangerous Johnny-come-latelies. Local powers, they had to be negotiated with, both necessary instruments of the princes' power and their competition.[17] Legitimacy and power were split. The aristocracy saw its power base sapped as castellans acceded to local power. The lesser nobility had only weak and recent claims to legitimacy: all the more reason to assert these claims violently.

That split was a constitutive fissure in the political dominance of the nobility. The effort to impose unity on inherently contradictory class segments by ideological consolidation took several forms. The dubbing of knights became a sociosemiotic act so generalized among both segments that it can be studied as historical anthropology.[18] The upper nobility adopted the designation of its lower servants: all members of the new, compound class were now "knights," a mounted *chevalerie*. The horse gave mobility, increased height that leveraged the weapons of violence, and became the living symbol of sociopolitical superiority, both instrument and sign of the new order and ideology of "chivalry."[19] Most important, the knights, functionally armed retainers and enforcers, were inducted into the nobility as new members of an ancient class, endowing them with a new legitimacy and making them "free" men: free of onerous taxes levied on plebeians. The upper nobility exchanged the lower-level knights' customs for sociolegal promotion, conjoining what had formerly been two separate class segments competing for surplus value into a new class, "universal" insofar as it excluded peasants as quasi animals, monks as quasi women, and women as women. These semiotic and ideological exchanges, around the turn of the eleventh century, asserting the unity of the newly complex nobility, guaranteed the continuity of surplus value extraction for all of the newly constituted class. The abyss between the "two levels of feudalism"[20] was papered over by class unity, however factitious. The constitution of a new class also inched toward another phenomenon, only dimly perceived initially: the creation of a "disciplined" society, even as the social formation was producing new social types.[21] Society was becoming increasingly complex. Its constituent classes were forming a new kind of civilization, of governance, discipline, and ideology.

This ideological rapprochement resolved the problem of class unity at one level. The tension in the texts, however, was not only between the two levels of feudalism: it was also between the feudal class, especially the great feudatories, and the king. The status and effective power of the king decreased considerably during the devolutionary period. Earlier, attendance at the royal court had been a privilege, a sign of high status and authority, an occasion to participate in the interplays of influence and decision making, in the acquisition, creation, and strengthening of power. Great princes and bishops attended, and signed the king's charters and diplomas. But the rank of those in attendance dropped, first to chatelains and knights, and by the end of the eleventh century, to burghers, clerics, or monks, even farmers and village mayors: "very obscure characters."[22] Dialectically, the degradation of the court had advantages: the king's multiple links with people of little importance gave him deeper roots in the country—a royal populism. For administrative purposes, absent bishops and counts are replaced by the king's officers: seneschal, *connetable*, *chambrier*, and *bouteiller* take leading roles under Philip I (r. 1060–1108). Permanent members of the royal entourage, they came from the midlevel aristocracy of the Ile-de-France. They formed the kernel of governance in a turbulent political world as governance passed from bishops to laymen, from independent powers to more manageable subordinates.

A renewed conception of royal authority was affirmed under Suger and Louis VI (r. 1108–37): sacrality played a diminished role, political superiority in the kingdom a greater one. Nevertheless, in spite of these quiet developments in royal administration, the king's effective powers remained limited. Suger's *Life of Louis VI* shows the king spending an inordinate amount of time and energy on horseback, battling the rebellious barons of his own principality, establishing feudal control over his own territory only by dint of unceasing effort. Conflicts with great neighboring princes who were technically the king's vassals were normal and structured the initial phase of verbal ideology.

Required: Subjects and Kings

Max Weber's sociological theory of the state named as its essential elements territory, monopolistic control of violence, and the bureaucratic apparatus that incorporates not only policy but the very identity principle of statehood.[23] It elides an essential component. "A state exists chiefly in the hearts and minds of its people."[24] It requires the willing submission of its population. Such submission is taken for granted in the First World, constituted by populations who experience their "voluntary servitude"—produced by centuries of discipline and ideology—as freedom.[25] Such a population does not occur by nature or by accident: it is created. The *Song of Roland* did not benefit from centuries' worth of hindsight. That text addressed its futurity, stretching toward an imagined polity with tragic recognition of its ineluctable cost, but without specifying the process by which the requisite subjection would be achieved. It was not deluded into a purely idealized, optimistic utopianism. A new world was to be elaborated, requiring new kinds of subjects, to be constituted as integral to political (re)construction. Out of the fragmented seigneurial regime would be erected structures of state: the state's first form was *as* a seigneury![26] The process was neither linear nor uninterrupted. Violently cruel, often sudden and erratic, subject to losses, erasures, reversals, and rediscoveries, not at all an elegantly incremental progressive self-fashioning, what can seem merely accidental beginnings of state formation are discernible ex post facto; particular innovations lead to the political formation we inhabit. The inventors themselves were too busy dealing with concrete, ad hoc empirical issues on the ground to theorize.

These (re)beginnings take the form of a (re)centralization of power, but with a difference. The past was appealed to as ideology in the political mythology of Charlemagne, as well as in cultural commonplaces: *translatio studii, translatio imperii*. At the Carolingian court, clerics had been agents of royal publicity and ideology. Theocracy had served both kingship and church. But starting in the twelfth century, and reaching its apogee under Philip the Fair (r. 1285–1314), another ideology developed, that of a royalty that refused submission to ecclesiastical power. Medieval clerics in royal service created the first discursive ideologies of state.[27] In spite of Daniel Bell, history "consists of a long series of ideological conflicts": we are nowhere close to "the end of ideology."[28] Recurrent appeals to the past must not blind us to medieval pragmatism, oriented to the legitimation of the present.[29] Reference to the past in the Middle Ages is neither merely conventional or commemorative: it is addressed to the present inflected by an imagined future, desired or feared. Invocation of the past is a present force.

"Peace" was an ideologeme associated with rulership, from Charlemagne to Robert the Pious, who was told in 1023 that justice and peace were the roots of his office.[30] As with the Peace Movement, ideological discourse has to be apprehensible to the population addressed. That population, in the twelfth century, was a lay population, mostly "Christian" in the sense of overt adhesion and minimal beliefs, but which necessarily negotiated ideological issues in its own vernacular. Latin ideology was inadequate to the task of constituting subjects of the state—a task requiring endless repetition, variation, and adaptation. Some in the clergy realized this. During the century between 1150 and 1250, the ideology of the three orders was adapted in a variety of vernacular texts, including history, fiction, didacticism, and Etienne de Fougères' *Livre des manières*.[31] No discursive counterideology developed during the twelfth century: no authentic, self-generated discursive representations of the knights' or the peasants' political beliefs against the claims of clerics surfaced—hence the impression that the latter represented all of society. No vernacular prose discourse appeared in the twelfth century until its very end: just lyric poems, poetic epics, verse narratives, verse histories.

Ideological modes for the *illiterati* developed. While reserving ideational discourse in exclusionary Latin, the church developed nonverbal practices, rituals that marked public life with sacred sanction. The royal coronation became a major ritual, establishing the king's legitimacy.[32] Although ritual does not create the king, it is the symbolic instrument of his legitimacy. Before his death in 1226, Louis VIII urged rapid coronation of his oldest son. Joan of Arc's mission in the fifteenth century was to have the king crowned at Reims to assure his legitimacy. The coronation's judicial principle was retained even though the dynastic principle replaced royal election as of the birth of Philip Augustus in 1165. A descendant of Charlemagne through his mother Adèle of Champagne, he was saluted as "Karolid" by contemporaries, his reign hailed as a return to Carolingian roots (*redditio ad stirpem Karoli*). Ritual and genealogy responded to ideology.

Prepared and staged by the clergy, this royal propaganda stressed neither principles of monarchy nor the abstract idea of the state, but the concrete effect of the real person of the king in majesty presented as audio-visual ceremonial. The royal insignia, differentiated from feudal symbols by their religious aspect, represented the functions of power: military attributes, symbols of command, judicial power. Like the crown, they were concrete objects. The holy character of the sacred unction evoked the king's ecclesiastical nature, in analogy to a bishop's consecration. The coronation was presented as nearly miraculous. The legend of Saint Remy, the holy unction of Clovis, played decisive roles in making the king of France the successor, not only of Clovis and Charlemagne but also of David. Even absent directly political or social vernacular discourse, the king's clerics produced a panoplied symbolism of power. Ceremonial ritual and the production of insignia endowed secular power with the requisite touch of the sacred. King and state were identified: the concrete specificity of the former, enhanced by ecclesiastical symbolism, predominated. Suger records the coronation of Louis VI in an ABA form: words, ritual, words.[33] From the very first sentence, Suger uses the vocabulary of the Peace Movement, and has Louis enact its key ideologemes: protect the church; succor "the poor," peasantry and clericality melded together; repress violences of upstart tyrants, knights, and castlemasters who wield power illegitimately.[34] The ritual followed, in three major phases: the royal dubbing; application of the unction; grant of the royal insignia (tunic, ring, scepter, the hand of justice); at the end, the coronation itself and installation on the raised throne, symbol of the primordial mountain as the cosmic seat of power.[35]

The same topics recur at the beginning of the chapter that follows the coronation, with one difference. For the suppression of tyrants, Suger substitutes the young king's devotion to peace and the defense of the kingdom (*paci et regni defensioni insistere*). The substitution identifies two sides of the same coin: to subdue "tyrants," the nobles who pillage, rob, and murder, *is* to establish and defend the peace of the kingdom. Thus, restatements of the ideology of the Peace Movement frame the coronation. The Movement's triumph was to have produced a program that, though it failed in its own terms, became the ideology of the monarchy's return to a recentralized exercise of power. While this recentralization was only part of the momentous civilizational change under way, it was an integral and a necessary part: perhaps its kernel and backbone. Ideological packaging linked the exercise of the king's business of war with pastoral protection of the poor and the defenseless in the name of peace.

The drama of ritual, with music and imagery, with royal insignia, holidays, royal entrances, and the king's coronation, had a powerful effect. Ritual symbolism suggested a royalty of awesome nature, seemingly dependent on ecclesiastical structures for political and economic strength as well as legitimation. Strict limitations blocked the theocratic potential. The Capetian was not, and did not seek to become, a *rex sacerdos*. He remained a layman, to whom were granted "a few crumbs of ecclesiastical dignity."[36] The coronation ritual created a fiction, the image of an all-powerful sovereign.[37] In fact, none of the twelfth-century kings—Louis VI, his son Louis VII, or Philip II "Augustus"—was all-powerful, in spite of the implicit claim of unlimited powers lodged in the person who symbolized the *res publica*.

This is the limitation of ritual. Awesome and imposing, its effects are gross, not subject to subtlety or qualification. From the perspective of ideology, ritual falls short in formulating and articulating specificities. Verbal discourse is the only means of defining a program or imposing a policy.[38] Suger's own account frames the description of the ritual with two statements of the specific values Louis VII incarnated: he explicates the ritual's meaning verbally. Language allows for more specificity than other means of semiosis and remains the best medium for the development of ideology that provides performative models of behavior and the constitution of subjects.

There was also a practical problem with rituals, even when successfully staged. Their effectivity was limited by the requirement of physical presence. Ideological subjectivation is fragile and requires repeated reinforcement. Coronations were rare, particularly among the long-lived Capetians, who did not die and succeed each other frequently enough: only three during the twelfth century. Coronations fell into ineffectual forgetfulness. This limitation was parried. "Crowned courts" (*curiae coronata*) developed, held on great festival days where the king's coronation was renewed by the public wearing of the royal diadem.[39] Such ritual repetitions were not necessarily devoid of substance. At the *curiae coronata* of Bourges in 1145, the second crusade was initiated.[40] A decade later, in 1155, at Soissons, the historical process came full circle: the pale, semiclerkly figure of Louis VII who had lost glamorous Eleanor and Aquitaine to Henry II, reclaimed the historic function of centralized power by proclaiming, for ten years, "the King's Peace."

This was neither a completely unforeseen development, nor an anomalous one. Already in Louis VI's reign, great nobles had recognized the king's right to judge infractions of the kingdom's peace.[41] The specific contribution of Louis VII's reign was the "decisive strengthening of the king's prerogative as protector of churches and pacifier of his kingdom."[42] Although educated as a cleric who became heir apparent on the death of his older brother, Louis was capable of horrendous violence. In 1142, he invaded Champagne and set siege to Vitry, the main town of the Perthois, dependent on Thibaud de Champagne. His army despatched the burghers' militia, spread through the streets, pillaging and setting houses on fire. Soon, both city and castle were an inferno. Fifteen hundred villagers who sought refuge in the church died in the flames: the resemblance to Raoul de Cambrai's massacre at Origny is striking. The king wept over the event, which did not prevent him from carrying devastation into the very heart of Champagne with extreme violence: "Almost all that belonged to count Thibaud was pillaged, burnt and depopulated," wrote one cleric. Violence perdured as part of the king's effort to establish "peace."

Nevertheless, Louis VII's reign is remarkable for the dual development of ideology and efforts for internal peace. As in the coronation, he himself was sign of his own kingship and its main ideological vehicle. In spite of the debacle of the Second Crusade and the loss of Aquitaine, he came to figure in the popular imagination as a lay saint. This iconization masks the finesse that allowed him to conciliate three policies: a continuing alliance with the church; the independence of secular royalty as the church's equal; and increasing emphasis on peace.

In 1141, Innocent II affirmed the papacy's superiority over temporal power, at least in spiritual matters, subordinating the secular prince to the church and lowering kingship to a limited, purely lay power. Louis refused this conception and asserted the equality of sacerdotal and royal powers. The principle of dual powers was supported by Suger, regent during the Second Crusade. Addressing the pillage and ransoming of the Brabançons—unemployed mercenaries turned bandits, in a transformation to become familiar during the Hundred Years' War—Suger invoked the ideological symbol of two swords, "material and royal," on the one hand, "spiritual and ecclesiastical," on the other. The abbot of Saint Denis wrote the archbishop of Reims in 1149:

> The glory of the Church consists in the indissoluble unity of the regnum and the *sacerdoce*; what is of benefit to one benefits the other, and it is obvious that the temporal kingdom lives by the Church of God, just as the Church of God prospers and grows by the temporal kingdom.[43]

After Suger's death in 1151, from 1154–55, Louis lay down the bases of a complex policy, incorporating the interdependence of war and peace. He attempted to unite his own vassals in new alliances to contain Plantagenet ambitions. Blois-Champagne was turned into an ally: Count Thibaud became the seneschal of France. Securing justice and peace in the kingdom is the duty and prerogative of the king:

> The honor of the king, attentive to dispensing justice, should procure peace and tranquility to all, extending his long hands for the protection and care of all.[44]

The king's mission of justice, peace, and tranquility extends to the protection and care of his population: it (re)establishes the pastoral function of the state.

The *rex pacificus* was associated with new political alliances, eliciting the sympathy and adhesion of the churches and enlarging the royal purview. In the King's Peace, secular power took over a policy that had failed in the hands of the clergy: it became the lynchpin in a complex ideological image of a kingdom (re)united in sociopolitical peaceability. On June 10, 1155, an assembly of prelates and barons met at Soissons. Its final act resembles the legislations of the Peace Movement. At the request of the clergy, with agreement of the barons, Louis establishes "peace for the entire kingdom":

> We order that, as of next Easter [March 1156], and for a period of ten years, all the churches of the kingdom, with all their possessions, all the peasants with their livestock and herds, and all merchants, in all places, and the men dependent upon whomsoever, insofar as they are ready to seek justice from their ordinary judges, shall always have peace and full security. In full council and before all, by the royal word, we have said that we would hold inviolable this peace, and that, if there were infractions of this peace thus decreed, would make justice in their respect, according to our ability.

Those present swore support, "so that justice be done to the violences."[45] Two years later, a council of bishops (Reims) gave judicial definition to the policy of 1155. A lord refusing to enact justice will be considered "infractor" of the peace. Recourse to the king would be available to victims: "the king has the power to constrain evil people to amend themselves, from his office by virtue of which he must defend churches."[46]

A new order is being sketched out. The responsibility for a peace that had been God's through ecclesiastical intermediaries is turned into "a mission of public order" shared by bishops and princes, the king of France as its supreme arbiter. The mission was difficult. Its enforcement had to respect the kingdom's feudal structure.[47] Patient negotiations and compromise were required, between the ideology of the King's Peace and the realities of mid-twelfth-century power. But the essential step had been taken. Soissons substituted the King's Peace for the Peace of God.[48] A function that had been imperial before feudalism now returned to the monarch. Royalty assumes effective responsibility for peace and the welfare of its population. Foucault's "pastoralism of power" begins to take form with the nascent state.

The weakness of the marginal can be a strength. Latin continued as the language of official policy: vernacular texts did not encroach on its protected precincts. Lay, vernacular culture developed practices of fictional representation that possessed a great tactical benefit: the virtue of deniability. Vernacular writing was the cultural medium in which the essential ideological work of the nascent state was done, taking forms seen as mere amusements and distractions: poetry, epic, romance, vernacular history, and chronicle. Although men of the church disliked these texts, the danger they posed to the church's monopoly on ideological discourse did not appear until the beginning of the thirteenth century. Lay, vernacular culture developed for nearly a century, eluding dominant opponents before being subjected to concerted pressures that warranted changes in the way it transacted its ideological business.

What modernity misreads as the incomprehensible monstrosities of medieval epic violence, or the light-heartedly fantastic amusements of narrative romance, were a major ideological workspace of medieval society. These texts addressed violence as a social and a textual problem, from the perspective of a state in the process of creation and the recasting of subjectivity. Postmodernity lives the unwinding of the nexus whose complex construction began in the Middle Ages. That it will discover the solution to the question human violence poses to reflexive consciousness is not evident.

CHAPTER 4

The Love-Lyric as Political Technology

The imperatives of governance did not impose any simple functionalism on the semiotic process of culture, but the latter hardly occurred in the reserved and cloistered space of modernism's post-Kantian aesthetic. The cultural phenomena that rode the new wave of governance were produced and consumed at noble courts whose "civilizing" role has been celebrated in a manner that oversimplifies the virtues and debits of civilization as well as the complexities of the Middle Ages.[1] A syncretism like "the Christian-courtly agenda of civilizing," supposedly represented by romance as against the "militant nobles" of supposedly monosemantic epics, serenely overlooks more issues than it resolves.[2] The evolving princely court provided a vibrant and dangerously nourishing medium for the development of new ideological strains. The semiosis of courtly lyric, novel, and *lai* was continuous but not identical with another crucial cultural phenomenon, the development of social literacies. As cultural phenomena, lyric and "romance" are simultaneously formal and ideological. Relatively autonomous, their examination must take into account their specific and distinguishing complexities, in relation to each other and to a cotextual social evolution. Their relative autonomy produces relations that are complex, not reducible to the comforts of simple formulae.

The spread of literacy has received much attention.[3] An earlier view mechanized the politics of patronage: poetry ornamented a patron's politics. In fact, the process was far more complex. It integrated ecclesiastical literacies within secular politico-administrative structures, at the cost of individual psychic splits.[4] New textual subjects, trained as clerics, found employment at secular courts and viewed noble problematics through grids derived from the nobility's sociocultural alterity, the church, producing complex semiotic effects. Some of these subjects represented voices otherwise condemned to silences; others reached for the perspective of a putative "society-as-a-whole" in the course of development. Courts were not manufactures of monosemantic ideologies. They—and the texts written for them—staged encounters between differentiated and conflicting codes and interests. The results were often hybrid or contradictory, and ineluctably ideological.

The ultimate, formally overt criterion was always the interest of the prince, but ideological codes abroad in the total culture allowed for varied definitions of that interest. Even at court, power was viewed from perspectives colored by moral and political values that inherently conflicted with those of the nobility. And yet, for these perspectives and the values they bore to be effective, twelfth-century writers tended to lay aside their clerical background. Twelfth-century textual perspectivalism developed secularism by deferral of the religious, not by its negation. Lodged in the abeyance between an official and institutionalized, though varied, ecclesiastical culture and a nascent but still inchoate secular culture, the practices of cultural secularism began: vernacular, accessible in principle to all, addressing this-worldly problematics, these practices constituted a cultural revolution.

In England, one court counted for the development of vernacular culture, the king's. In France, each principality had his own court. The development of vernacular textuality occurred in these princely courts, the king's excepted: Capetian cultural policy remained in the hands of a clergy, its back turned on vernacular letters. Since England was a Norman colony, English vernacular culture developed in Anglo-Norman. Paradoxically, the cultural revolution which conjoined French literacy and vernacular narrative was first effectuated by the Anglo-Norman king's cultural policy. His interest was the creation of a vernacular ideology countervailing the Capetians' capture of the Carolingian legend. A rich blend of history and fiction resulted in the mid-twelfth century by writers who recast Roman, English, and Scandinavian materials in French octosyllabic couplets: Master Wace's *Brut* and *Rou*, that Benedict who replaced Wace as court historiographer to write a *Chronicle of the Dukes of Normandy*, as well as the adaptations known as the "romances of antiquity"—*Thebes, Eneas,* and

Troie—whose Latin origins allowed them to share the authority of history. Anglo-Norman texts reworked visions of history, producing multiple versions of "a usable past." In continental courts, legendary narrative materials from Celtic culture were adapted as exotic vehicles for fictional reflections on subjectivity and the political organization of society. The Anglo-Norman Real was more overtly political, that of the French more distantiated through fictional refraction: both aimed at an evolving real.

Hagiography and the chanson de geste share a fundamental characteristic. Both refer to a subject that defines the insufficiency of the present: a Latinate God or Charlemagne. The new cultural centrality of the principality's court implies the sociopolitical integration of the subject. The subject is now institutionalized, with the court as a reference point, even as the individual engages in multiple adventures. This required, as its hypothec, the scissions of subjectivity: they could lead to madness. The creation of subjectivity for the nascent state required not only labor but also the pain and grief of successive cuts; the integration of subjectivity requires its disintegration.

Lyric Submission and the Representation of Women

The first written vernacular texts to achieve cultural autonomy are lyrics at the courts of southern France. The first troubadour invalidates the poet-patron opposition: William IX, Duke of Aquitaine (1071–1127) was himself a prince of power and wealth. His poems construct a highly complex subject, announcing postmodern explorations of which, according to one optimistic estimate, "it is impossible for even a medievalist to remain innocent."[5] It is always "*je*," an "I" often morphologically implicit, who centers the text's contradictions and diffractions. "*Je*" is a shifter, a shifty pronoun of uncertain reference.[6] It can be taken for the author of the words; the composer of the music; or the performer who bodies forth text and music in the momentary illusion of presence for an audience: the lyric's primary mode of existence was in public performance. Through the normal processes of identification, the master shifter also captures individual members of the listening public.

The subject, in its potential universalization, is multiple and split in the earliest European vernacular lyric. The collection of William IX's poems is slim but varied, bearing multiple directions blurred by the later tradition. A preferred opening is the idea of opening itself, fusing self-reflexivity and self-ridicule with the very idea of poetry:

> I shall make a *vers* about
>   nothing,
> downright nothing, not
> about myself or youth or love
>   or anyone.
>   I wrote it, on horseback, dead asleep,
>   while riding in the sun.[7]

In the inverted reflexivity of systematic self-negation, this text initiates European lyric as a deconstruction of the transports of poetry. Another poem repeats the theme—

> I'll make a *vers* while sleeping here
> walking and loafing in the sun . . .[8]

but segues to brilliant and gross vulgarity. Two women, other men's wives, take "*Je*" for a fool, lead him to their room, feed him, bathe him, and "use" him sexually for eight days and more:

> So listen, how often I fucked them:
> a hundred-and-eighty, and eight times more,
> until I nearly broke my strap
>   and the saddle-bags with it.[9]

The duke also wrote a kind of poetry more familiar from the clichés of modern literary history: poems of *fin'amors*, the unrequited love for a lady distant from "*Je's*" desire, he kneeling in submission:

> I'll make a new song now
> before wind blows or it rains or snows,
> for my lady tests me out: how
> and how far goes my love.
> And no legal plea against me
> will get me
> loose of her bond.

Even here, some ironic undercutting operates.[10]

William's slim collection stands in for the absence of a lost, earlier tradition: it signals multiple directions in which poetry might have developed. A drastic selection folded self-reflexivity into all ensuing textualities, as it repressed vulgar fucksongs and allowed women's worksongs to survive only in aristocratic adaptations. *Fin'amors*, the subtle and intense exploration of a narrowly restricted poetic potential, became the dominant lyric tradition. Joined to this selection was the inversion of a secondary motif. "Love-sickness," widely recognized as a secondary metaphor by traditional scholarship, is a supplement which marks its origin. That origin is not divine or noble aspiration. The ennobling potential of *fin'amors* inverts a doubly negative view of love as medical pathology and Neoplatonic demonology.[11] Poetic inversion transforms both in a poetic revolution which discovers the fantasmatic character of the amorous process, a transformation that will be captured by the political domain for ideological purposes. The topos of "love at court," turned into *fin'amors*, is immediately captured for "ulterior" purposes of political ideology. Within a generation, between 1150 and 1180, the figure of woman migrates from the southern lyric to the north of France, where it is adapted, transformed, and integrated into narrative representations. Paul Zumthor's lyric "register" marked the aesthetic's remarkable repetitiveness, capable of endless recombinations thanks to its fusion of the semantic fields of love and poetry, founding the production of poetic meaning in a permanent, necessary ambiguity.[12] This potential, elaborated in Occitan and Old French, migrated to Italy as the *dolce stil'nuovo*, to Germany as *Minnesang*, persisting in "Renaissance" love sonnets to be renamed "courtly love" by nineteenth-century scholars; it perdures in modern poetry until André Breton and Paul Eluard, in film until *Breathless* and *Leaving Las Vegas*. Thousands of texts reinvent the medieval "register" of love as institution.

Courtly lyrics assume and replay the same negated narrative: the lover, on his knees, sings his desire for a haughty, distant lady, deploying suasions supposedly geared to produce her recognition and the lover's "reward." The same arguments, images, and vocabularies, in poem after poem, produce varying levels of complexity and comprehensibility, from the easy accessibility of *trobar planh* to the obscurity of *trobar clus*. The poems' repetitiveness insists on their inverted relation to reality. In social reality, the subjection of women to men was categorical. Individual exceptions existed, of course, when the new courtly ideology legitimated women's value and the church obtained their right of refusal, but women's usual role in aristocratic exchanges was as a token in forming alliances and expanding territories. Women attained positions of autonomy outside their own domestic circles after accidents in the lives of their men: the death of a father or husband, the youth of a princely heir requiring a regency. A "normal" female life was untouched by formal personal independence: she was submitted to the tutelage of a father, negotiated as a commodity in the biopolitics of lineage, and transferred to the tutelage of a husband ideologically conceived in the image of lord and God.[13] The ideology of female submission to male legitimated a conception of marriage in which women reflected their men's hierarchical superiority. Women acceded to juridical existence only in marriage.[14] What parameters of historical culture, in its social and political context, respond to this sudden efflorescence of intense love poetry, promoting the lady as superior, demoting the male as submissive victim, radically inverting the social realities of the time? How do we account for the cultural inversion of fundamental social codes in textuality?

This representation of women is no longer seen as the unmitigated cultural triumph of a liberatory cultural renaissance.[15] It is rather seen in the context of a patriarchal medieval society. This view is unimpeachable. Medievals themselves would not have impeached it. They would have asserted it proudly, invoking a biblical model. Medieval representations of women were elements in male systems of signification.[16] Figures of women in textuality are signifying integers within complex sign systems that embody male strategies and problematics. Q.E.D.

The historical experience of oppressed groups is that political advances are mixed. New representation of women is inherently progressive, but the first representative of women on the U.S. Supreme Court is a conservative; similarly, the current occupant of Thurgood Marshall's chair on the same court is a sexist reactionary; a leading black politico in California is a conservative businessman who opposes affirmative action. Et cetera. Politics is messy; so is history. Oxymoronic ideological cohabitations make strange bedfellows and surprising alliances. Paradoxical "bedfellows" cohabit the mental skin of persons and individual texts. No individual is adequately accounted for by a physical sexual identity—penis or vagina define no one's gender, an indeterminacy which complexifies the subject of gender immeasurably. If sexual subjects are conceived of as complex textures of various strands of sexualizing tendencies, no single voice of unified gender issues from any given speaker, or writer, or interpreter, or text. Even misogynists must be seen as complex genderings. Male writers are not more unified as subjects than others: they may still give voice to women's experiences and perceptions.

A widespread cultural strategy submitted the violences of male Thanatos to an Eros represented by women. Such strategies too were male. The romance paradigm transforms the violent, epic warrior into the individual knight who subordinates his violence to new behavioral codes, installing a female figure who replaces the dominance of a male seigneur or king. She becomes the sign anchoring the knight's subordination to a newly valorized secular love. Female characters in romance are metaphors men use to construct their own subjectivity: they are not "real" women. Guenièvre and Laudine are not "real women": who thinks Lancelot and Gauvain are "real men"? That criticism, that representations of characters are not "real people," repeats Erich Auerbach's error of imposing on medieval textuality a nineteenth-century aesthetic criterion, "the representation of reality."[17] Intervening scholarship and theory have shown the aesthetic correlation of text and reality in "realism" to be a historically limited phenomenon. Medieval "realism" was a version of Neoplatonic idealism funneled through Augustine; its alternative was a nominalism that separated sign and its referent. Except for the occasional and inevitable *realia*, social realities enter medieval textuality in ways that, from the mimetic perspective, cannot but be accounted oblique and indirect. Reference is secondary to the production of meaning, of signification. Guillaume de Lorris's *Rose*, early in the thirteenth century, oscillates between "realism" and nominalism.[18]

The sophisticated understandings of contemporary feminism remain essential: the voices of texts are not simply male or female. Neither in textuality nor in real life does one find "a clear resolution to the question 'who is speaking,'"[19] whether in the texts of female or of male authors. The female subject is voiced as a shuttle, in an unstable and shifting zone, defying absolute reduction to a male/female binarism.[20] So too, for all the real privileges and powers that attach to its gender, does the "male" voice. Along the way, the "erotic" strategies of courtly poems and novels, deployed to titillate and seduce men into tempering their violence, might benefit women, as an admittedly mixed blessing.

"Romance" marks a historical Event, a Moment at the deepest levels of the human psyche, which Lacan called a "stupefying paradox." Over a large geographical area, where mores of bandits were the norm, there suddenly appear courtly rules of behavior governing relations between men and women.[21] Lacan wrongly dresses this paradox as embarrassed compensation for "not getting any," part of his theme "there is no sexual relation."[22] More seriously, he reflects on the relation between the courtly lady and *Das Ding*, the subject's absolute Other, its first principle—the Object always sought, never found. The lady represents the Thing, the enigmatic, unspoken center of the text, even if in anamorphic form.[23] The lady of *fin'amors* and the Thing, while not nothing, do not exist in the ordinary sense: absent and foreign to the organism, they orient its position and its pleasure principle as an absent presence.[24] All aesthetic production is historical, however: Picasso doesn't paint like Velasquez, a novel of 1930 doesn't use Stendhal's style.[25] The paradox then is historical. A recognizably artificial, conventional language presents the lady as inaccessible and depersonalized, emptied of all passional substance; yet the Middle Ages was a period "when people fucked hard and fast."[26]

Not only aesthetics, ethics too is historical. Ethics, Lacan informs us, is inseparable from ideology, which leads him to discard "intellectuals" of the left as fools, those of the right as knaves. With astounding, oversimplifying naïveté, Lacan limns Freud instead as a "humanitarian," concerned with human nature rather than irrelevant ideas or ideologies. But *Civilization and Its Discontents* argues for man's native tendency toward evil (*méchanceté*), aggression, destruction, and cruelty: the death instinct.[27] Against the fundament of Christian ethics, "Thou shalt love thy neighbor as thyself," Freud argues that men are not gentle, friendly creatures who desire love and only defend themselves if attacked. A "powerful measure of desire for aggression has to be reckoned as part of their instinctual endowment." They happily aggress their neighbor, exploit his labor capacity without salary, use him sexually without consent, seize his possessions, humiliate him, cause him pain, torture and kill him. *Homo homini lupus*: the evidence lies in life and history. This aggressive cruelty "merely lies in wait for occasions. Men are savage beasts to whom sparing their own kind is alien."[28] Instinctual aggressiveness, the hostility of each against all and all against each one, oppose any program of civilization and culture that seeks to elaborate libidinal bonds among men. The paradox is ahistorical.

The twelfth century, its socius and polity, negotiated a traumatic passage through a fundamental conflict that still impinges on the future of Western history. It developed state structures that bore Lacan's "Law of the Father," initially in Christian monarchical form. The struggle of new disciplines to control historic violences that justify Freud's pessimism continued for centuries: it is not over yet. It required recasting the human psyche, the male in particular, to reduce indulgence of the taste for violence under the control of an outside agency. The superego's psychic role and its demands were immeasurably strengthened . . . and therefore its punitive aggressiveness against the ego as well.

Lacan's view is coordinate with Nietzsche's account of the origins of the guilty conscience in the creation of the state, "the most radical change" that man has experienced. It results in his becoming "imprisoned within the pale of society and of peace"[29]: what Norbert Elias called "civilization." In the process of "internalization," man's inner world, originally as thin-stretched as if between two layers of skin, burst apart; at the obstruction of external outlets, it expanded in all dimensions. Social organization now protected itself against old drives to freedom: "all those instincts of wild, free, prowling man" were turned backward *against man himself.* Enmity, cruelty, delight in persecution, in surprises, in change and destruction—all these instincts were turned against their subjects, hence "bad conscience," "the suffering of man from the disease called man." The "spasmodic plunge into a new environment and new conditions of existence," constituted "a declaration of war against the old instincts," which up to then had been the staple of Man's power and joy. It occurred as "a break, a jump, a necessity, an inevitable fate, against which there was no resistance and never a spark of resentment." Fitting "a hitherto unchecked and amorphous population into a fixed form . . . [started] in an act of violence": the establishment of the state. The "state" thus appeared

> as a ghastly tyranny, a grinding ruthless piece of machinery, which went on working, till this raw material of a semi-animal populace was not only thoroughly kneaded and elastic, but also *molded.* . . . Such is the origin of the "State."

The superego as society's representative in the individual psyche, conscience as the metonym of state culture, these are staples of psychoanalytic understanding. Oddly, Freud repeatedly appeals to the state code for a military metaphor to describe the impositions of constraints on aggression, just as did the twelfth century. Restriction of aggressiveness is the severest sacrifice required of the individual by society:

> The institution of the superego which takes over the dangerous aggressive impulses, introduces a *garrison*, as it were, into *regions that are inclined to rebellion*.[30]

In the Middle Ages as in psychoanalysis, the individual psyche is an allegoreme for the violent repression of historical violences. And in psychoanalysis as in medieval theology, man's evil transcends his efforts at self-control: "if we are to be judged by the wishes in our unconscious, we are, like primitive man, simply a gang of murderers."[31]

Medieval tangles with "the question of woman" are folded into this epochal crisis. The pollutions of complexity, of simultaneous promotion and domination, of conjoined adoration and subjection, underlay the evolutions of "romance" and its cultural after effects. The texts discussed here, except those of Marie de France, are oriented toward the construction of male subjectivity: their representations of women figure first as structural utilities. But such orientations are not exclusively functionalizations. The ambiguous promotion of women had varying and contradictory effects, resulting from the inherently complex nature of its readings. Such "readings" are also performative.

One response is the insight of contemporary psychology: the idealization of woman is nothing else than misogyny turned inside out,[32] a perfect example of Marx's formulation of ideology as inversion, where "men and their relations appear upside-down as in a camera obscura." Even inversion, however, is a social reality: it "arises just as much from historical life-process as the inversion of objects on the retina does from their physical life-process."[33] Courtly idealization becomes another ideological representation, instrumental in imprisoning women in a phallocentric society. Misogynous idealization negates woman's concrete personal reality, ultimately as damaging as deprecatory misogyny. While psychologically founded, this argument does not resolve the problem posed by the appearance of an image so radically contradictory to social codes. Medieval textuality in general does not offer a screen on which to deploy "personal concrete realities." Its conventionalisms *can* be inflected toward a problematized recognition of identity and the individual, but these tend to be addressed as collective issues. Secondly, while medieval textuality is hardly "realistic," and its texts produce *effets de réel* at their surface only occasionally, it is structurally coherent with contemporary social problematics at a deeper level. What is negated here is a structure not at the surface level of a story, but at the deeper levels of social life, where gender identities are constituted.

The poems do retain some thematic contact with ordinary sensuality (more in the troubadour lyric than in the northern version) and social realities. William IX imagines his hands under the lady's coat, he offers "ground-rent" in exchange for being "inscribed in her charter." He worries about the effects of his departure for the crusade on the politics of the region.[34] The later poetics of the northern lyric appropriates southern conventions in a purified, abstracted, and ascetic form; nevertheless, the texts retain similar marks of insertion in the material structures of society.[35] In the remarkable stasis of its central image—the lover frozen in passive supplication to the cold and distant lady—this lyric seems the contrary of narrative. And yet, it is exactly this situation a Chrétien de Troyes will textualize in *Yvain*, as the hero first meets the lady he has fallen in love with: he falls to his knees and her feet in submission.[36] Close examination of the lyrics' language reveals a complicated rhetorical strategy, not so much the absence of narrative, as the continual negation of a narrativity insistently invoked. Surprisingly, these narrative potentials are repeatedly drawn from a materialist historicity the poems seemed designed to elude, including economic change and legal traditions. Thus the lover, cheated by having the fundamental law of exchange disregarded, may lodge a legal complaint against the lady who, as feudal overlord, refuses to reward his services as a vassal.[37] Courtly rhetoric frequently touches on legal, political, and economic codes.

Another possibility is the paradoxical inversion of values. A poem recommends that the textualized subject remain in the lady's power . . . since he's already there, and that he flout common sense, preferring scarcity and deflation to wealth and inflation:

Remain in her dominion,
Since you're already there.
Never love plenty,
Nor fear the rising costs of scarcity;
A good thing's sweeter in deferral,
The longer the desire,
The sweeter the testing.[38]

In spite of an imagined transcendence of economics by an art of living, neither exchange nor transcendence affects the lover's frozen posture of submission. The central convention of negated narrativity allows only a static relationship. Various third terms are appealed to; all fail to change the two-term relation. The structure is the same as in hagiography: its secularization radically changes its content, but the structure of domination remains the same. The subject subjects itself to a superior instance, an Other: God, or the lady as cold, distant, and forbidding. He remains loyally suppliant in that Other's service, awaiting a hoped-for selection that never occurs. The lyric of *fin'amors* institutionalizes the regime of secularized absence.

The only hope of breaking out of the lyric register's frozen narrativity lies neither in continuation of feudal service, nor in judicial processes of appeal. The lover's only hope lies in an autotelic increase in value, as in the appreciation of a sum of money thanks to the interest earned. The process, forbidden by the church as "usury" (the prohibition of all forms of interest), was nevertheless well-known to merchants and knights, nobles and kings, who lent, borrowed, and paid interest in various disguises to evade clerical condemnations. Only by aping the forbidden commerce in money is the subject given hope of exiting the lyric's stasis. Only the process that announces capital formation promises hope of satisfaction to a knight imprisoned in inherited thematic conventions.

As a formula for ideology, pure "inversion" oversimplifies . . . but sometimes reductive simplicity pays. Extensive manipulation of the ideology of gender relations occurs in the twelfth century. The fundamental terms of marriage are being shifted in complex ways. The church undermines the commodification of women in biopolitical strategies. Henceforth, women will have at least a formal right of refusal in marriage. The church demands a formal approval be elicited, preventing—at least in theory—brutal disregard of personal preferences. In the best of circumstances, it could allow for strategies of negotiation. Less than full freedom of choice, this does represent an incremental advance.

This limited liberation, however, was paired with an extension of the prohibition of incest to the seventh degree of cousinage. This cast wide the net of the forbidden: given the endogamic tendencies of European nobility, and the tentacular reach of the lineage structure, any imaginable marriage was likely to transgress. This left the church to find excuses for particular exceptions, if it so chose. The church of males, eager to increase its control over politically dominant lay*men* in spite of the Gregorian reforms' separation of church and society, incidentally ameliorated the lives of women. The incest prohibition, coupled with women's new ability to refuse marriage, was part of the continuing struggle between the two subsections of the dominant patriarchy, the noble laity and the noble clergy. The real subjection of women, as opposed to the representations of male Reals, may well have been exacerbated by this rivalry. Progressive elements were enmeshed with the reactionary: that mix is not only modern. Not only do men use women to think with, men use women for reproductive purposes in the *ideological* reproduction of society as much as in its biological reproduction. The beginnings of women's amelioration were entangled with the politics of male ideologies.

The iconic figure of women's representation as dominant is anomalous, in the codes of the twelfth-century social cotext. This figure's unlikeliness shadows any representational value. The icon is aniconic. It decodes the normally subjected position of woman, and recodes it into an anomalous, nonreferential sign of domination. The discrepancy between text and social structure unhesitatingly and repetitively declares the poem's fictiveness. Precisely that fictiveness is the first function of the de-/recoding. It allows for a male auditor's identification with the figure of male submissiveness before a dominance figured as female. Literary identification here works, not by an equation of same with same, but an adherence of self to Other. Had the figure been less improbable, identification might have been painfully frightening, hence an object of disidentification. *Vraisemblance* is not the only basis of identification: sometimes its opposite functions more effectively. In ideology and aesthetics both, represented content is misleading. It may cover something else, standing for something not represented, which cultural censorship decrees cannot be represented overtly. Representation is a covert operation. Irony and allegory index the covert, hence their defining role as the acme of subjectivity and self-reflexivity. Ideology is goal oriented, but is borne in a medium inherently unreliable and unstable.

The very improbability of the situation in historical terms led nineteenth-century philologists to invent their own fictive narrative to account for the texts: that of adulterous love affairs between vassals and the wives of their feudal superiors. The narrative itself was fictitious—in only a minimal number of poems does the relation between lover and beloved take adulterous form[39]—and perhaps based more on contemporary realities among the philologists than on medieval perspectives. A male at a medieval court is invited to project himself into the text by identification with a submissive male subject, subordinating himself to a woman. What this image bore, in endless registral variations as dozens of poets composed hundreds of texts all setting into play the male subject's same submissive role, was precisely the repetition of male submission. Easily accepted because so fantastic, the radical submission of self to another was the invariant. Marked as unrealistic fantasy by its reversal of the historical roles of men and women, the poems of the *registre courtois* normalized a representation in which the male subject was not only cast in the role of subordination, but elected it regularly. Courtly lyric accustomed combative male subjectivity to its own subjectification.

Even better, the figure of dominance to which the male subject was invited to project himself was profoundly ambiguous. Authoritarian and domineering, the female figure was a presence defined as an absence. Decorporealized, the lady reigned over her subject by enforcing the regime of her absence in denying herself, from a position of distant superiority. Insofar as she retained any bodily reality, it was not a sexual, a sensual, or an intimate body, but only the abstract body of sovereignty, the king's "public" body feminized.[40]

The extraordinary flowering of lyric poetry in the twelfth and thirteenth centuries did not result from a conscious intentionality of the purpose just described. The poems' overt raison d'être was an intensely formal research, a modal quest for endlessly varied forms of the same register. The focus was on form, the content a mere excuse.[41] With *amor* and *canso* each other's metaphors, an erotic poetics occasionally selected the political iso-topy as metaphor. At a different level of analysis, however, that very meta-phor was the poems' raison d'être: it produced their social and historical meaning, their political ideology, their pragmatic effectivity. It depended on the poem's ambiguity, its nature as *bifrons*: two-faced. The "lady," an ideologeme male society used to think with, was a free-floating signifier, whose absence masks another, that of an effective sovereign, a sovereignty for which society was reaching, to be revealed, in the monarchical state, as the sovereignty of absence. The warrior's obeisance before this figure of multiple, layered absences, prepares his subjectification. It rehearses and performs that subjectification.

The "lady," an ideological counter in men's efforts to think political problems symbolically, acquired representational potential oriented less to-ward the past than toward present and future. Nor did its function as male ideologeme exclude women from the audience, or even as writers. All ide-alization frames the subject in a double bind that makes rejection of the representation as difficult as acceptance. A woman poet entering the world conventionalized by troubadours found only difficult identifications within masculine codes. The *trobairitz* Castelloza's inscription of passion required both intense identification with the voice of the self-humbling troubadour lover and multiple reversals as she turns the tables on the convention by envisioning death if her lover does not grant her "joy."[42] That complex ef-fect would have been compounded in being overlaid with the semiosis of real-life relations, in which the position of political and social dominance was man's: covert identification offered women by the figure of the "lady" was functionally with a man, not a woman.

For the male audience, did identification with the self-subordinating subject repeat something already present as desire? Had the ideological cri-tique of their violence by the Peace Movement had an effect on warrior-knights? Does the lyric's success indicate a dialectical relation to the her-itage of the Peace Movement, a congruence of textuality and desire? There grew, perhaps, in the knights whose violence posed such a problem for clerics and their feudal superiors, a desire for submission, seductively fed and encouraged by the courtly love lyric. The poems were heard and their poets patronized for the beauty of their formal invention, but they bore other, covert meanings. Poetry fused aesthetic formalism with the ideological function of disciplining the subject, a subject reconstituted by submission to the discipline of an *ars* of love. Was discipline itself an object of desire, submission to it a desired voluntary servitude? Should the translation of Andrew the Chaplain's scholastic *De arte honeste amandi* be, not "The Art of Courtly Love," or "How to Make Love as a Gentleman at Court,"[43] but "The Discipline of Love at Court"? For the female audience, was turning the tables on male dominance through identification with a functional dominance in female disguise, not a temptation? As necessarily discrepant parody?[44] For women as much as for men, the possibilities of identification tendered by the courtly lyric posed an ethical problematic. Accepting that identification played into the patriarchal role distribution, leaving the psychic structure in place even while reversing the players' sexual categories. It is not clear that modern feminism has found the answer to that conundrum yet.

CHAPTER 5

Chrétien de Troyes: The Perspectival Novel

T he subjectification proposed by the lyric is constituted in lack, twice over: its regime of absence is doubled by immobility. Not only is the destinator absent behind the lady's veil: What narrative trajectory is possible, in the apparent parentheses of that absence? Along with a "real" destinator, the lyric text repeatedly suppresses a narrativity whose fundamental axis is the (dis)satisfaction of desire. Desire returns insistently as each line invokes a potential for action only to negate it and its satisfaction. The suppression of narrativity insists on the knight's submission, without addressing the question of how to get the wild, erratic, brutal, destructive warrior to that place of submission, or what social use it may serve. The lyric is not transformative: its performativity is a weakened one, operating only by the high seduction of its elegant formal repetition. Like the chanson de geste, lyric repetition presents the end goal of a process, without exploring the process itself. But that repetition is also the experimentation required by a culture seeking out all possible forms of the Imaginary to forge ideological tools and constitute new subjectivities. The love lyric performs as an inverted mirror image of the *Roland*'s proleptic subject. Epic proposes a distant desideratum. Lyric presents it as achieved. The in-between is elided.

That is the advantage of overtly fictional narrative. Recently in bad odor in some critical quarters,[1] narrative remains an essential mode by which men and women apprehend and constitute their being, their desires, the meanings with which they surround their lives and constitute their subjectivity. A praxis of narrative was not lacking, of course, in the epic chanson de geste, whose problematic presented itself as collective. The epic subject is the subject of a lineage and a vassalic contingent. But the epic achieves transformative linearity only exceptionally. The novel is something else. The state would capture, subsume, undermine, and circumvent feudalism's double articulation of lineage and vassalism. Without directly attacking either, indeed while constructing itself on top of and out of them, the state addresses those whom it organizes not only as links in complex associations of familial and localized polities but as individuals. The long-term dynamic of the state severs social relations and group linkages, atomizing its subjects in the alienating absence of an ever-absent sovereign Other. At its beginning, however, it addresses the individual as the sign of a collective hope. The problematics of individual subjectivation, not the celebratory "discovery of the individual," defines the moment of romance.[2]

Romance here denotes a moment of cultural evolution.[3] It has also been used to denote a narrative genre by philologists and theoreticians, from Erich Auerbach and Northrop Frye to Fredric Jameson, designating texts of colorful marvels, supernatural heroes and events, appealing to fantasy and the public's taste for utter displacement from serious concerns.[4] Its medieval examples are written in verse form—itself a sign of "nonseriousness" for many. Such attitudes long precluded the study of these texts as meaningful symbolic considerations of the cultural and political issues that faced their societies.

Such neutralizing presuppositions were dislodged by close reading, which demonstrated that the systematic use of irony and comedy distanced the meaning of the text from the amorous and heroic ideologies it unquestionably bore.[5] These techniques enter a parodic function,[6] a suggestion in line with recent theorizations that dress textual self-reflexivity in the cloathes of parody.[7] This identification poses a problem for literary history, which ordinarily starts the history of the modern novel with Cervantes's parody of medieval romance in *Don Quixote*. If parody exists already in the twelfth-century text(s) whose imitations Cervantes parodied, then the element of parody, inherent in this writing from the beginning, was lost from sight as the tradition evolved. Cervantes reinvented the wheel of parodic self-consciousness: his great work—as is the case for many "renaissance" *chefs d'oeuvre*—was a continuation of medieval practices. But if this parodic element marked the initiation of the novel, then in fact, the twelfth-century texts are the first European novels since Petronius. The classicizing adaptations in the *romans* of Thebes, Eneas, and Troie at midcentury, focused on an analysis of the contemporary political situation. Those of Chrétien de Troyes and his school a generation later tie the political subjectivity addressed in the *romans antiques* and the nascent idea of the individual, to a subjectivity outside the framework of the mirror of princes.

The semantics of *roman* suggests as much. The transitional moment that fused the novels of antiquity with the beginnings of vernacular history at midcentury, introduced a new kind of narrative material with radical cultural implications. Its central concern is the constitution of individual subjectivity. The novels of antiquity address a single subjectivity, that of the ruler, adapting the "mirror of princes" tradition in narrative vernacular form. Their essential subject—in the multiple senses of topic, protagonist, narratee, and patron—is the Anglo-Norman king. Rewriting classical legend, chronicle, and epic, recording what can be gleaned of the history of Scandinavian invaders and their progeny, they propose the kingly figure as central. The generic distinction between "history" and "the novel" is modern.[8] Both are termed *romans* in the twelfth century. *Roman* was not a generic designation, but a linguistic one: in the romance language, in the vernacular, as opposed to Latin. It is used of fictions like the *Yvain* or the *Roman de la rose*, as well as of works modernity thinks historical. Wace's *Brut* concludes, "[In] the year one thousand and five hundred and five Master Wace made this *roman*.[9] Whether a text was "imaginary" or "historical" was secondary to the fact that it was in the vernacular.

The twelfth century was sophisticated enough to know the difference between veracity and the lie, between a recital of events that had taken place and simulacral representations that had not. That distinction is essential to the structure of their narratives.[10] They were sophisticated enough to grasp that the simple binarism "truth-or-lie" hid the more subtle category of "fiction." That "*roman*" refers both to "true" histories and to texts whose fictionality was patent does not signal mental incompetence. Rather, the conjunction of writing and the vernacular, the fact of vernacular texts being written at all, counted for more than questions of veracity, mendacity, and fictionality. Existence was more important than veridictory status: ontology trumped morality. Vernacular culture claimed radically new territory, making the written word its own, scripture next to Scripture. That counted for more than generic distinctions of history and fiction. "*Roman*" asserted the revolutionary junction of the vernacular with the literacy of power and the power of literacy. It was an assertion of cultural power that predominated, not genres. *Roman* signaled a cultural revolution.

More useful than the notion of genre are the formal and thematic conventions that furnish models for the analysis of individual texts that in using, transform them.[11] Particular texts make varying uses of the same traditional inheritance. Thomas and Beroul's versions of *Tristan et Iseut* deploy the same conventions as Chrétien de Troyes's novels, but with opposite meanings: the Tristan authors mostly omit warrior violence as a concern, they oppose passion and society, postulate no integration of love and social service, and allow for almost as much ruse, manipulation, and dissembling as the fabliaux. Insofar as one credits the literal truth of the love potion as a determinant of action, subjectivity is elided. As has long been recognized, Chrétien's *Cligés* turned the Tristan-material on its head. Meaning devolves from what the individual text does with its intertextuality, not from sharing conventions in a putative "genre."

In addition to associating vernacular culture with power, the *roman*'s elision of a perfectly well-known problematic of veridicity and mendacity also deferred differentiation between the texts of truth and those of fiction. It defined texts in their linguistic form, not in their referential status, as productive of meanings through which they attain performative effectivity. They are French, not Latin, and they are written, no longer relegated to the wild margins of orality in a cultural hierarchy that assigned official dominance to written Latin. They exist, in spite of the topos of truth-saying with which even obviously fictional texts begin their narration, not as functions of truth, but of power subsuming truth. They exist by virtue of their multiple pleasures, transgressive assertions of self, power, and relative autonomy within a previously decried vernacular culture. They are novels, in full realization of the powers of their fictions. Power is their focus, vernacular their vehicle, secular their problematic.

The *romans antiques* and the histories composed between 1150 and 1165 around Henry II's court, are part of the Anglo-Norman/Angevin growth of power. Their blend of classicizing narrative and vernacularization of the mirror of princes tradition problematizes the question of kingship: they perspectivize it. Their classicism legitimizes the entry into the narrative diegesis of large numbers of female characters and the thematics of sex and love as essential to the scene of a royal court. The courtly lyric casts the female as the male's superior in the idealization of *fin'amors*, accustoming the male knight to a subject position of inferiority vis-à-vis the female. The fantasy of the representation defangs the subject's necessary self-subjection.[12]

The *roman*'s fictionality becomes most obvious with the second generation, twenty years or so after the inception of classicizing adaptations. The introduction of Arthurian characters and themes, conjoined with *fin'amors'* inversion of gender relations, at a court of Champagne known for its commercial calculations and hard-headed, cohesive political governance, introduced the reflexivity of a self-conscious fictionality, and the distanciation effect of *ostranenie*. In a world of political realism, manipulating with equal effectivity old feudal bonds and new productivities of commerce in the count's active organization of his principality into a permanent, year-round center of international trade, the Arthurian stories ran no risk of being mistaken for reportorial "truth." Fictionality was their most obvious characteristic. Their claims to veracity and faithfulness to sources are themselves fictive, rhetorical conventions, part of a well-established code, common to writer and auditor, sharing in perceptions that allowed for multiple ironies. The ethico-political pertinences of their narratives are second-stage realizations, borne by absorbing, nonallegorical fictions of exotic diegeses, adventures defined by deictic difference, which addressed problematics of the "here-and-now" by representations of alterity.

Precisely this surface appearance of exotic fictionality allows for the development of fiction as a primary instrument of theoretical and ideological exploration, capitalizing on the deniability of the fantastic, the marvelous, the fictional, and on structural aspectualities. Its exploration was self-reflexive in its very historicity. It was fictional in the orientation of representations toward the production of meanings, rather than recounting ancient narratives for immediate political purposes. It was political in that, under the cover of fiction, it addressed the fundamental issues of its own civilization, not in confusion between truth and lying, but in the realization that the seriousness of fiction could best be pursued by bracketing and deferring such issues as that of fiction's "truth." It was ideological in its subjectifying productivity.

Early Arthurian romance sidelines kingship. The hero's effective superior is taken over from lyric and narrativized as the idealized lady. Heterosexual eroticism is substituted for homosocial *compagnonnage* and linked to the reproductive function in the marriage bond. Homosocial friendship is retained but ironized by the cardboard figure of Gauvain as the sometimes ridiculous other of all knightly adventure. Chrétien's first novel, *Erec et Enide*, largely remains within the mirror of princes problematic of the *romans antiques*, though its focus in the second part on Enide's subjectivity pushes the issue of woman to the forefront. But with *Cligés*, *Lancelot*, and *Yvain*, the courtly makes its grand entrance: the domination of the feminine principle, the subordination of the death drive of Thanatos in its form of knightly aggressivity to an Eros both eroticized and socialized in its very idealization.

Lacan finds courtly love a *"paradoxe stupéfiant."*[13] In fact, its instrumental idealization of woman is the price paid for her erotic domination of Thanatos: only to a superior being can that domination be ascribed. In these middle texts, Chrétien gives an ideal solution to the social problem of violence: males learn to subordinate their violence to the love incarnated by the women who dominate the narrative diegesis. A papier-mâché figure like Gauvain knows this subordination from the very beginning, but even passionate heroes like Lancelot and Yvain learn to control and dominate their passion so as to serve superiors and society, their ladies and others, faithfully.

Exchange and Subjectivity

The subject is the topic of all Chrétien de Troyes's work.[14] His first novel, *Erec et Enide*, continues the narrativization of the "mirror of princes" tradition.[15] Its first part conjoins hero and heroine as couple in the inherited ideology of love, adventure, and closure. The second part threatens the couple with social devalorization ensuing from uxoriousness: Erec is accused of abandoning knighthood for his wife. Ordering horses for himself and Enide, he commands her to ride ahead in complete silence. She repeatedly attracts hostile knights and is forced to face the ideological conflict of multiple semiotic roles: Will she follow her husband's order as a properly submissive wife, or will she act as subject, voicing independent judgment of the danger incurred by the couple and especially the husband? Repeatedly caught in the contradictory ideologemes of loyalty and obedience, she disobeys her husband repeatedly out of love and loyalty. Although this is Chrétien's first novel, its central decisionary focus is on the woman, caught in the contradictions of a patriarchal value-system.

The central characters of Chrétien's last three narratives share an identity problem: each is detached from his "real" name, at least temporarily. The knightly lover's shame resounds throughout the *Lancelot's* periphrasis, the "knight of the [shameful] cart." Yvain uses a pseudonym, "the knight of the lion." Perceval ignores his own name until it is suddenly revealed by a young woman who turns out to be his cousin. In all three, the disjunction between the person and the proper noun, between identity and subjectivity, is problematic. Lancelot's case is the most puzzling. He is labeled by an early, minor episode with a periphrastic appellation that then recurs as leitmotif. Pursuing his rescue of the queen, kidnapped by an unnamed antagonist, the hero loses his horse, encounters a peasant with a cart, a tumbrel that takes condemned prisoners to their punishment, hence a sign of dishonor and shame. Lancelot hesitates the time of two steps: Does a knight of honor mount the cart of dishonor? Anything must be endured to save the queen: he climbs on, to be tagged henceforth as "the knight of the cart," an oxymoron conjoining chivalry and shame.

The tag's *literal*, "historic" level of meaning refers to the narrative episode that earns him the sobriquet. Its *tropological* meaning is the accruing shame that haunts his quest for the Lady Guenièvre: she specifically holds it against him when they are finally united. Its *anagogical* meaning is a parodic reduction of the saintly injunction—the divestment of all subjective autonomy—so as to become the perfect instrument of the Other's will. Its *allegorical* meaning depends on the anagogical. In religion, the allegorical level is ecclesiastical: it pertains to the church as institution. Here, the allegorical meaning is directly contrary to clerical values. The deity in question is not the Christian God, all-powerful and ineffable. It is a woman, another man's wife. Lancelot, like Tristan, is vassal to the king whose wife he sleeps with. Lancelot's tropological shame is profoundly shocking to a religious hermeneutic grid. His divestment of self, of subjectivity and the freedom of choice it names, submits him, not to St. Alexis's God, but to the profane, adulterous love of the king's wife. As parody, it is gross, radical, and extreme. It is to be juxtaposed to the same author's ironic invocations of religious symbolism.[16] It does not directly attack religion: it eludes the question in deferral.

The obvious reluctance to incur the shame and dishonor of associating with criminality is later turned on its head by Guenièvre. It is not the association with criminality that she holds against Lancelot. On the contrary, it is his two-step hesitation. That was the moment which allowed him to reflect, to take distance from the choice he faced, the moment of freedom in which he evaluated the alternative of two ideologemes—knightly honor versus succoring the queen—the moment of subjectivity, in which he chose among the mandates of alternative codes. Lancelot hesitated in the exercise of freedom, judgment, and subjectivity: that is the crime against the religion of secular love with which he is reproached. The author who more acutely than any other writer of his time grasped the wrenching requirements of the new polity in the development of appropriate subjects, examined in the thought-experiment of *The Knight of the Cart* a counterexample, that of a willful, intentional self-desubjectification. The story's continuing popular success, the idealization of Lancelot, mark the eagerness with which abandonment of the burdens of subjectivity, the responsibility of freedom, are sought.

Chrétien's last, unfinished text, the *Perceval,* is a profound if inconclusive meditation on violence, nature, and nurture deferred. Previous texts take an amused but sympathetic stance toward knighthood. At the beginning of this text, however, a perception and judgment of "chivalry" is formulated that is remarkably harsh. Knighthood is mocked with bitter irony when Perceval's mother hears her son call the knights just encountered in the forest the most beautiful things in the world, more beautiful than God or all his angels. For her, knights are

> "the angels people complain about,
> who kill everything they see."[17]

The boy's brothers and father were killed or crippled in a narrative of knightly violence and devastations that led the mother to deny her son the noble heritage to which he was entitled by identity of birth. Her narrative, its critique of a knighthood earnestly sought by her son, perfectly exemplified by Gauvain and generally entertained as an idealized image of human potential, offers the perspective of a victimized subject-position from which the narratee may view the ensuing narrative.[18] It offers a judgment of knighthood, but does not enforce it. It frames the narrative subject's efforts to acquire the subjectivity to which he is entitled by identity and subject position. His constitutive desubjectification occasions the ensuing efforts to install subjectifying ideologies: the Mother's discipline of ordinary social life, Gornemant de Goort's chivalric discipline. The attempts are performatives that misfire, producing mechanical, Bergsonian comedy. The boy's youthful eagerness leads to an automaton's adoption of new rules without reflective mediation, hence his continued inability to find subjective freedom. Only in the blood drops in the snow episode is there even the suggestion of reflection: its content remains unverbalized, a question to the narratee. Perceval slides from one attempted subjectivation to another, without attaining subjectivity . . . even in the Hermit Episode.

Identity is a crucial concern of the author's narrative rhetoric, in his teasing deferral of protagonists' names. Such toying presupposes the normative functioning of a system of discursive identities, to which the deferrals allude in their divergence. Along with names, it assumes systematic, normalized identification as an encoding structure and allows the narrator's manipulation of an audience that has heard these stories as oral tales before and is now challenged to recognize the particular hero. Questions of identity are often problematized in intratextual relations: *Yvain* is full of these, not all manipulated by Lunete, the heroine's lady-in-waiting. When Yvain discovers her imprisoned in a stone keep, the narrator leads the reader to participate in his recognition of the identity of the woman in the stone keep, while she first remains ignorant of his identity.[19] These deferrals constitute a communal relationship between author and auditor, on the basis of shared codes: elements of a fictional contract.

Multiple systems of identification function simultaneously in twelfth-century society. The practice of the signature, an indexical, physical trace of bodily presence inscribed in documentary textuality, is one practice of individuation which has survived to modern times from a complex identificatory process.[20] Other practices of individuation included the development of heraldic signs of identity, whose expansion necessitated the development of a social specialization: the herald, who identified specific individuals in the sudden plethora of identitarian signs.[21] Another was the use of the seal, which quickly came into nearly universal use, not only by kings, princes, and great nobles, but by knights, merchants, and peasants as well.[22] It was the semiotic means of the individual's capacity to act as a legal person.[23] Individualizing identitarian signs spread to corporate bodies as well. Along with their bell towers, retainers, and centralized bureaucratic offices, towns had their own seals: the modern ideologeme of the corporation as a fictive person has medieval beginnings. None of these signs of individual identity was forced on the population and its classes: the wave of individual identifications appears to have responded to a strong, widespread social desire.

Deferred identification of subjects as a textual game was one form of taking them lightly. A fabliau laughingly demonstrates that one might wish to flee identity. Outside London, a jongleur crosses paths with the king. The king asks courteously:

> Whose man are you, lord jongleur?
> Milady's lord, by God.
> —Who is your lady, in all good faith?
> —Milord, my lord's lady.
> —How are you called?
> —Milord, like my father.
> —What name had your father?
> —My very own, milord.
> —Where are you going?—Over there.
> —Where are you coming from?—From here.[24]

Such circular games rely on the existence of more straightforward, systematic identities and a normative cultural practice of self-identification: occasional refusals to identify oneself are evidence *a contrario*. But the novels reveal concerns beyond formal identity. They develop structures to establish qualitative differentiations among individual actors. In novel after novel, Gauvain and Keu the seneschal are comparative terms that define social norms of positive and negative values.[25] Heroes and others engage in knightly combat against these two mounted benchmarks, to establish individual relative value within a sociotextual system. Once such values are established, communications networks register those values in a kind of social value bank. The hero sends a succession of vanquished antagonists as signs of their own defeat and of his glory to Arthur's court, functioning as an "Arthurian Bank of Social Value" (ABSV).[26] Entire novels are given over to constructing and testing such values.

Identity, as the site of values that define the specific individual, is fundamental to narrative. It is the interface of the body and the social encodings of subjectivity. At one point, Yvain's identity is established by a cicatrix, the trace of a wound that inscribes personal identity as a knight on his face. Identity inheres in the body, but the mark devolves from a social practice: combat. Identity is not primary. Being unmarked is primary. The metaphysics of being are social and therefore historical. Identity, though necessary, is far from accounting for the problematic of subjectivity. Individual identity is only one term of a paradigm, whose other key term is the subject. Identity and subjectivity entertain complex relations, to the point of contradiction. In the play between the two lies the crux of the novels. Perceval's identity is hidden from him in childhood, which results in the lack of training as a knight and his inability to achieve proper knightly subjectivity in spite of a burning desire to do so. The text's incompletion leaves Perceval as the great example of deferred and unsuccessful subjectification—an anticipatory desubjectification.

Desubjectification followed by successful resubjectification in social integration is the structure of Chrétien's *Yvain, the Knight of the Lion*. The acme of novel writing in the twelfth century, it brilliantly balances a remarkable number of contraries. It fuses the unforeseeability of "adventure" with structure. And yet, its cohesive structuration of the unforeseeable produces an extraordinary proliferation of significations. It fuses irony and comedy with the seriousness of social thought, so that "style," once thought the essence of the medieval text,[27] becomes one with the process of subjectification. But "the duplicity of language makes of the word (*parole*) itself one of the major energies of the plot."[28] The paradoxical interdependence of moral, narrative, and political duplicities is essential to its structure. Yvain conquers feudal love, wealth, and power through a betrayal of feudal rules of engagement tantamount to murder, abandons personal identity in madness, and reestablishes a proper identity and subject position through pseudonymy. Only after multiple adventures, performed under specific constraints, does he attain a newly reconstructed subjectivity, appropriate to a functional subject-position, defined by the social and political parameters of the role of the *châtelain*—the castlemaster.

What is this identity Yvain must relinquish for half his narrative in order to obtain an appropriate subjectivity and place in society? Earlier, public denunciation by his wife's messenger led to the first European scene of love-madness and its loss of identity. Yvain is not one of those heroes whose name the narrator defers. Instead, he loses that name, as part of the identity by which the cultural system defines the individual. The identity of a socially constituted self is abandoned in "madness." Madness from the perspective of human sociality is animality from the perspective of cultural anthropology: he behaves like a wild animal in the forest, an unsocialized and abhorrent mode of being.

Narrative Exchange

Yvain inscribes a reflection on the fundamental terms of sociability in the very structures of the text: identity, subject position, and subjectivity; charity, contract, gift, exchange, and debt; the subject, his self-constitution, and service to the society of the needy. These terms structure the narrative and its diegesis. It deploys existing sociotextual norms, then tells the destruction of a social identity, and its reconstruction in the form of pseudonymous subjectivity that transforms a knight of honor into a mobile functionary of social services.

Yvain's story is bipartite, with a gaping hole of desubjectification in the middle. Although presented individually, Yvain enacts the same values as epic heroes: family honor and revenge lead from the Arthurian court to the violence of a forest killing. At court, Yvain hears his cousin Calogrenant narrate his own story: wandering in the forest seven years ago, he encountered the hospitable daughter of a lowly knight, a terrifying peasant who was more animal than human, and finally, the magic fountain, shaded by the world's most beautiful pine, to which is attached a golden basin. When emptied of water, the basin caused a wild tempest, savage lightning and thunder cracking open the sky. The storm's end brings a dual aftermath: birds cover the entire tree to sing a symphony of joy; a knight, wild as a lion, rides out and challenges him for the damage the storm wreaked on his castle . . . without warning.

That last phrase is crucial. Just as in the *Song of Roland*, a challenge previously issued is crucial to a case both legal and moral. Yvain, at court, reacts as any feudal hero constituted by the ideology of honor, shouldering the burden of his cousin's "tale of shame, not of honor." Revenge is as much a motive as in the *Roland* or *Raoul de Cambrai*: it is essential to social identity and status. Taking French leave from the court to avenge that shame, he repeats his cousin's adventures. That identity defines both the narratee's ironic distance and the subject's deontological fault. Unlike Calogrenant, Yvain already knows the plot: he knows that the storm at the fountain damages a nearby castle. He knows that indulgence in the magic fountain's marvels entails damage that the other knight considers an attack on his fief and his honor. That knight had complained to Calogrenant of the harm and shame done him without challenge or warning (*sanz desfiance*. l. 492). When that knight rides out again after the storm, Yvain kills him. Enveloped by magic invisibility in the dead knight's castle, Yvain will hear the beautiful, grieving widow call him "a murderer, a traitor" (l. 1207), and repeatedly—five times in six lines—hurl "coward" at him in the varied forms of paranomasia (ll. 1222–27). She returns to the essential point of the feudal warrior's honor—betrayal of the rules of knightly engagement, which distinguishes justified homicide from cowardly murder.

The issue is handled lightly by the narration, with dexterous distractions of verbal and structural games, but a perspectival undercurrent, both narrational and moral, haunts the hero. Doubt is cast on Yvain's integrity in the terms of his constitutive code as a feudal knight. Was his act murder? Are not his quick marriage to the widow, his rapid accession to the role of reigning castlemaster, grounded in moral quicksand? The text delivers no heavy-handed condemnation: it signals a possible questioning, leaving it to the reader to pursue. The text offers evidence that undermines an otherwise admirable knight, tainted by the inescapable violence at the heart of warrior desire.

Protected by an invisibility the text suggests may be cowardly, Yvain voyeuristically observes his victim's widow in her intense grief, and immediately falls in love with her. In comically rapid succession, he is fearfully led to her, performs a catechism of love, and elicits a marriage: he achieves the fantasy daydream of his class, Duby's "*jeunes*": "young," not in age, but socially liminal so long as their father lives and prevents them from assuming the political functions and social status of the chatelain.[29] It can be a protracted liminality lived among troops of peers in the identical subject-position, wandering from one tourney to another. Homosocial bonds and heterosexual daydreams are its fodder of psychic survival: marrying a noblewoman with a castle in fief, without abandoning buddies, is every *jeune*'s fantasy. Its satisfaction has realistic aspects. Marrying Laudine, Yvain assumes the joys, responsibilities, powers, and profits of matrimony and a fief. In exchange for the seminomadic, liminal life of the unattached knight, he achieves the adult status of husbanding a lady with a major *châtellenie*. "Protecting her fountain"—his wife's delicate phrasing of Yvain's new responsibility—is erotically teasing, but he has lucked into an appropriate subject-position: the realized daydream of his class.

Gauvain's ability, old homosocial buddy, to persuade his newly married friend to abandon wife and fief for a return to the *jeunes*' adventurous life is all the more paradoxical. He recognizes his proposition's absurdity: he himself would not follow his own advice! But Yvain bites: having just solved the problem of living by realizing the male fantasy of marrying a beautiful woman with fief and fortune, the hero reverses field, negates his own success, and—according to the norms of cultural development—regresses to an earlier stage of life: he leaves for another year's nomadic errancy, as if still a *jeune*. The change of direction is not undertaken lightly. It requires negotiation with his wife, leading to a contract . . . which lays the basis for its betrayal. Contracts are crucial to Chrétien's text, his culture, and its civilization. That between Yvain and Laudine is merely the most detailed interpersonal contract. Its carefully negotiated clauses, modifications, and specifications try to cover all foreseeable eventualities: each party specifies clauses he or she requires. She insists he return within a year, or her love will turn to hate. He pleads that is a long time: were he a dove, each time he desired her, he would rejoin her. But the future cannot be known:

> expecting an early return,
> you don't know what's coming . . .

qu'est a avenir, that is to say, what *avanture* might occur, what unforeseeability erupts in human life: precisely what is sought in leaving wife-and-fief. Yvain asks for an exception, in case of obstacle, bad luck, or prison.[30] Laudine agrees, but no obstacle awaits you, *so long as you remember me.*[31] The magic ring she gives him precludes any jail, so long as a true lover remembers his lady. Negotiations close, husband and wife part.[32] The contract is drawn, its legalism transposes the tension of an odd and complex lovers' parting. Both parties enter into it freely, both know its terms, hence Laudine's right to reject the contractant who does not observe the terms of a contract so precisely and openly arrived at.

Contracts, negotiated and implicit, subtend the entire narrative. Yvain will repeatedly despatch an antagonist hurriedly so as to get to the next episode, having promised to defend another defenseless lady—a personal contract! Such contracts are the structural form of thirdness, invoking a law of exchange that poses the negotiators as synallagmatically free subjects. That freedom in establishing contractual bonds is presupposed by social contracts, feudal and marital as well as the commercial contracts of merchants at the fairs of Champagne.[33] In a civilization constructing itself at the edge of abyssal violence, contractuality seems sweet security: law is the fundament of social life. Medieval narrative insistently addresses questions of law and contract. The very concept of law is changing. Chrétien anticipates the return from oral, customary law to the Roman model of written law.[34] When narratives structure themselves in legal terms, the very basis of sociability is textualized. Outside law, there is only conflict, antagonism, the chaos of violence all too familiar.

Absent explicit negotiation, mutual reciprocity may occur *as if* by contract. When Yvain is first trapped by Laudine's sliding portcullis, neither he nor the reader knows the identity of the young woman who comes to his aid. It looks like pure gift, until she reveals her identity: years before, when Lunete visited Arthur's court, Yvain was kind when all others were mean. Lunete already bears a debt, contracted before the story's beginning: her help to Yvain repays that debt, even if it leads to (seeming) betrayal of her own mistress, as her stratagems deceive Laudine and favor Yvain.[35] They lead to the odd marital contract between Yvain and Laudine's "fountain" and place Yvain in Lunete's debt. That will be repaid in turn, when he saves her life, which in turn imposes on Lunete a new debt, to be repaid at the end of the romance by their last exchange, when Lunete manipulates her lady once again, to reconcile and reunite the couple.

Panurge's praise of debts in Rabelais's *Tiers Livre* was anticipated in the twelfth century as social praxis and narrative structure. Indebtedness initiates the exchanges of vital narratives, subsumed by contractualism. Exchange of needs and satisfactions constitute society, formalized by contracts, a formalization not taken for granted in an emergent complex society. Contracts, specified or implicit, are the basis of sociality, and not only of a commercial, capitalist society: feudal reciprocity also was contractual. Well before Rousseau, a theory of the social contract was at work in the structure of vernacular narrative. When Yvain disregards the contract so carefully negotiated with Laudine and overstays his year's leave, he imperils not only a particular social relationship, but sociality itself.

That betrayal—ironically referred to as "forgetting"—leads to the first recorded example of love-madness: its progeny is legion. Publicly denounced by Laudine's messenger, Yvain goes mad. He loses mind and language (*sans et parole li faut*: l. 2777), then he turns hate against himself: he has killed himself, stolen joy from himself, no vengeance is possible (ll. 2792–99). He runs off into solitude, far from tents and pavilions, a vortex whirling in his head: he strips naked and flees into the forest.[36] A man insane and wild (*hom forsenez et salvage*: l. 2830), lacking name, language, identity, or clothing, he is reduced to a level of presocial animality. Language, memory, and social positionality are necessary to the identitarian paradigm: Yvain discards human identity.

The Hermit's charity enables the human animal's return to human status. Charitable pottage leads to habitual returns and entry into a system of exchange: the wild man brings the carcasses of animals he has killed, in exchange for the Hermit's meager soup.[37] The Hermit skins the animals and exchanges them in some nearby, unspecified location for the kind of flour appropriate to the nobleman he recognizes in the quasi animal. Identity is divisible: it returns in small increments. Inversely to modern economistic assumptions, the free gift of charity initiates the exchange systems at the basis of society.[38] Yvain's madness is a desubjectification. The narrative's fundamental transformation begins in this brief episode. In the ensuing episodes of the second half of the novel, he pulls himself up by his psychic bootstraps with the aid of a sequence of individuals whom he serves in implicit structures of exchange, reconstituting himself as a subject. These exchanges define the modular, episodic structure of the novel's second half.

Helpless, sleeping naked in the forest, Yvain's identity is signaled to a passing troupe of young women by a scar on his face. He establishes reciprocity before accepting even desperately needed help. Awakening under the eyes of a watchful lady-in-waiting—Lunete's functional equivalent—he finds himself unable to walk.

He needs to find help
to help and lead him off.[39]

The theme is repeated, identifying the knight periphrastically as "he who had great need of help."[40] When the lady-in-waiting rides into view, addressing him with kindness and courtesy, inviting him to the castle nearby, he first asks:

"Young lady, tell me then,
have you need of me?"[41]

Only if she has such a need (*besoing*) can he accept her help for his needy state (*besoing*). The exchange of the word signals the reciprocal exchange of needs being established as the basis for social relationships. Yvain is looked after for two weeks: in exchange, he defends the lady's castle. By contrast, the ironic eroticism as the lady-in-waiting overuses a precious and magic unguent registers as a purely wasteful version of the gift: it ridicules both waste and economy.

In the episodes of the longer, second half of the novel, Yvain's prowess transforms knightly combat from the destructiveness cited by Perceval's mother into social services for those who, unarmed and lacking all alternative recourse—the *inermes* of the Peace of God Movement—find themselves in desperate need. Yvain selflessly succors a series of defenseless women by knightly force of arms, fighting against increasingly terrifying opponents. Reciprocally, his efforts will be rewarded. Women themselves will be offered as the hero's reward. But he, already fixated elsewhere, will comically turn them aside repeatedly. More important, his social value in the form of reputation will be increased at the Arthurian Bank of Social Value, the king's moveable court functioning as a savings bank of personal value: each vanquished opponent, his life spared, trumpets the hero's achievement when reporting to the king's "prison."

Thirdnesses

The tendency to equate the category of exchange—in spite of Lévi-Strauss—with commerce and capitalism, obscures its function as an essential mode of social relations outside economics. Contracts define the terms of a deferred exchange and operate at the bases of intersubjective relations in both private and public domains. The feudal contract records the results of negotiations between a lord and his vassal: their relation, unequal by definition, is assumed to be synallagmatic, that is, to occur between equals. Exchange is an essential category of narrative: it is the structural basis of the *Yvain*. Its exchanges regularly function contractually, by informal contracts generally assumed as well as by contracts formally negotiated. As narrativized, contractual negotiations imply the equality of the contractants—whether the negotiation bears on marital or on feudal relations. It would be absurd to pretend that external relations of force have no bearing on such negotiations, but the equality of the negotiators who will be bound by the eventual contract is an implication integral to the process of negotiations.

The principle of equality is both an assumption of the process and its product as a rule: it is the law of the process. Negotiation ordinarily occurs between two parties: that is a matter of "secondness." Negotiating a contract implicitly generates a "thirdness": the rule of equality, and the separateness of the contract itself from the being of the two parties even as it governs their relations. The process generates its own transcendence: secondness produces a third.

The Lacanian Symbolic is a thirdness, as the Imaginary is a secondness: culture lodges in the individual Imaginary, and transcends it. The *Yvain's* reconstituted subject is indissolubly linked to the sociosymbolic. Individual value is constructed by intense effort and risk of self in the service of others. In each episode, a two-term Imaginary relationship produces an exchange of services whose advantage for the subject is deferred. The episodes are organized by the subject's individual others as a string of the social symbolic. The episodic sequence indexes a totality composed of small sociological groups (the *maisniees*: households) and large-scale socioconcepts (economics as production, distribution, or consumption, the dispensation of justice).[42] The totality indexed is neither religion nor the state, but a political society: human life as collectively interdependent, though short a totalizing institution of governance. Both instances which accumulate deferred value—the "ABSV" and its enfolded alterity, "society" as the totality indexed by the individual episodes are symbolic constructions which represent forms of C. S. Peirce's thirdness: the formulation of general values, principles, or rules, often in the form of ideologemes and laws, empirical or deontological, that raise dyadic relations to a new relationality.[43]

Another thirdness is the aspectuality of the text, the text's structured apperception of the narrative. Each episode deploys the three fundamental functions of narrative: *displacement* from one scene to another, and a *conflict*, in the specifically feudal form of mounted combat. But in the *Yvain*, combat, constitutive of each episode, is subsumed by a three-term figure of *communication*: combat produces a value that redounds to the benefit both of immediate beneficiaries and indirectly to that of the heroic subject. Combat here is not so much oriented toward selecting a winner by incapacitating the loser, as it is to the creation of value. Combat is transformed into labor; it produces value, in three forms: Yvain's victory; the beneficiaries' liberation from oppression; and in a further loop of surplus value, the communication of the errant knight's achievement to the ABSV, operating on the principle of anonymity, as in a Swiss numbered bank account. Known only as "the knight of the lion," his value accumulates as an account of deferred reputation, ultimately cashed in as Yvain's subjective value—perhaps with compounded interest!

The "number" of his account is a false identity: a pseudonym, the heraldic sign of "The Knight of the Lion." This pseudonymous identity allows for the reconstruction of a subjectivity defined by earned social value. Paradoxically, his simulacral personal identity is a class identity. A transformation of identity systems began at the end of the Carolingian period, surfaced in the eleventh century with coats of arms, and explosively multiplied in the twelfth with the system of heraldry.[44] The subject's sign, the lion, is the heraldic sign most frequently chosen by knights, the favorite sign of chivalry. The lion's disappearance toward the end of the narrative signifies the hero's integration of the quality it represented: the signifier absorbs the signified. Yvain's pseudonymy asserts his heroic election of class identity: his adventures demonstrate his ability, not only to fight threatening antagonists at increasingly hostile odds but also to observe "loyally" the terms of multiple, potentially contradictory contracts. Pseudonymy removes identity as an impediment to the free exercise of a subjectivity intent on reclaiming identity, hence the necessity for pseudonymy: it is integral to subjective authenticity. To become oneself requires being another: *je est un autre.*

As the narrative constructs (dis)identifications of its subject, so its narration engineers implicit (dis)identifications of the reader-auditor. A distantiated narratee results. The reader-auditor, that variable fragment of history, is invited to triangulate a complex relationship with the text's narrative representations, both identificatory (hence Imaginary) and distantiated (hence Symbolic). Both in-the-text and out-of-it, both narratee and reader, the complex construction of an uneasy lectorial subjectivity proceeds out of the text's negotiations. Unease is the condition of an autonomous potential of judgment.

The narratee is also held at a distance by the nonverbalization of subjectivity—a major difference between modernity and medieval practices. Modern subjectivity is an individual matter of personal interiority, most readily signaled by the pronoun "I" taken as a radical.[45] But in this narrative, all about the destruction and reconstruction of subjectivity, what is not represented are the psychic workings of an individual ego. Our perception of Yvain is almost entirely external. The text rarely enters into his putative interiority. The major exceptions are two lyrical love monologues at the beginning. But love, in these monologues, is textualized in the ordinary register of the *grand chant courtois*, a conventionalism that negates individual interiority. There are also, toward the end, two brief notations as Yvain decides to return to Laudine.[46] Again, their courtly conventionality blocks any particularized interiority-effect. At precisely the points where a modern rhetoric of fiction would anticipate entry into the internal world of subjectivity, a wall of conventionalism faces the reader.[47] For the latter, the narration seems to betray the narrative. It aims at subjectification, but recounts only action.

That is both the interpretive crux of the text, and a lesson it might teach modernity. Subjectivity is not only an ocean of inchoate feelings, from terror to orgasmic pleasures of the sublime, awash in an individual interior. Nor is it only symptomatic enunciations of an unconscious substituted for subjectivity. Subjectivity is a potentiality for action inscribed by ideologies, the multiple systems of values abroad in the culture. Emotions and the unconscious are not irrelevant to such potentials for action, but they do not exhaust the field of subjectivity. Psychoanalysis and deconstruction recognize with difficulty the ultimate necessity that besets the individual, of eventually taking action within a social and political sphere, action that has further constitutive effects of subjectification: the relations of subject and society are marked by loops, dialectic as well as repetitions, each constitutive of the other. But the subjectivity that is a potential for action is not given by descriptions of interiority or structures of the unconscious: it is only reconstructed on the basis of the subject's actions. Subjectivity issues in action; action and the ideology it packs construct the individual. In a textuality focused on the narration of action, the hero does not figure a radical individualism.[48] The individual is a necessity of narrative, not necessarily an ontological existent.

Is there no center to this totalizing diegesis? Besides the hero's interiority, the most obvious figuration of absence is Arthur, absent even to himself in the *Perceval*, who stumbles in the *Yvain* from postcoital dormitude at the beginning into his vassal's wedding as an uninvited guest (a wedding that he, as his vassal's lord, ought to have arranged), and thence to the Solomonic wisdom of a royal justiciar in the penultimate episode—a free-floating signifier if ever there was one. Earlier chronicles show Arthur as a capable war chieftain; after *Cligés*, the king undergoes a "fading," a distinct degradation, turning much less heroic. He nearly becomes a background figure, no longer knighting vassals or encouraging chivalry, to the point of a paradoxical passivity.[49]

Textually, however, Chrétien's Arthur is not a *rex inutilis*.[50] Not only has he specific narrative utilities, such as punningly pulling justice out of a Solomonic hat: absence is an essential aspect of kingship. In addition to actual powers and functions, the king represents two unrepresentables: God and the polity. Under the dispersals of feudalism, kings spent much of their lives traveling from one vassalic hospitality to another, in repeated acts of presence that countered the ground bass of absence. Beyond that, the character's somnolence marks the absence of the real ruler from the textual diegesis. The really existing prince, the one operating on the ground— Thibault, or Henry surnamed the Generous, successive counts of Champagne—was anything but absent. The count was a real presence, shrewdly calculating, strategically planning in all-controlling secrecy the ways governance could impose discipline, extracting value and force from the burgeoning economy, and increasing political centralization.[51] The real count operated as a prince in his principality, an effective ruler lacking only the aura of kingship. The textual Arthur marks a necessary space whose "real" occupant was not represented in the text: he had no Real. Did this absence result from the encounter of panegyric expectations and the realistic cast of Champagne? Or in the anticipation of another figure, the text being written within the time bracket of Louis VII's death in 1180, the designation of his son Philip II as his successor the preceding year, and the latter's accession to the throne, only later to be designated as "Augustus"? Was there a sense abroad in the kingdom, of a desired accession of the king, not only to the throne, but to a new level of effective power, beyond the princes of the principalities? Chrétien's Arthur occupies the space of a form of governance undecidable at the time of writing. The textual Arthur is a lieutenant: he holds the space of a highly determinate and effective prince competing with the figure of an indeterminate and future monarch: an irreconcilable hesitation is historically exact. Chrétien's Arthur is an absence holding place for a real of uncertain identity: Arthur is a self-acknowledged Real of an unknown king, a *lieutenant* for the real of state rule.

The subject is coordinate with the state. Yvain serves instances of society, the ruler's identity left unspecified. When a ruler arrives, "Yvain" will be ready: the knight will become the king's representative. Subjects are those who bear the necessity of representing an absent instance outside themselves. Representing an absent power requires them, as its representatives, to operate with some degree of autonomy. Subjectivity, at its beginnings, is not a universally recognized characteristic of the body politic. It is a specialized trait of functionaries. Their subjectivity is the representation of the state within the psyche of the individual subject. An alternative subjectivity exists in negations: rebellions against rule, or its evasions.

"Gender Trouble"

The violence in epic was that of warrior combatants. That of lyric was doubled and sublimated: its idealization of the lady is a violence performed on woman's concrete specificity. The linearization of the lyric's narrative kernel, in the shift from the *grand chant courtois* to narrative, split the representation of woman on the axis of power. Its idealization absorbs the representation of women into a cold distance of power and domination. Guenièvre and Laudine have little depth or substance. They are the narrative utilities of a patriarchal structure of domination overlaid by a rhetoric of female beauty and, in Laudine's case, the weakness of susceptibility to comedic manipulation. To neither are attributed discernible signs of affection for their lovers, nothing like Laudine's passionate grief for her dead husband, or Yvain's passion for her. There is nothing comparable to Héloïse's passion for Abelard or Iseut's for Tristan. At most, a socialized eroticism is stirred by Lunete's vaunting of Yvain's prowess.

At the other extreme of the female axis are the numberless victims of violent rape who, to a degree unacknowledged by earlier criticism, dot the narrative landscape of the "courtly" diegesis.[52] Idealization once led to an interpretation of woman's historical promotion in the course of the twelfth century; should her repeated subjugation in rape scenes now lead to the opposite interpretation, that of uninterrupted patriarchal degradation?[53] Are idealization and rape nothing but two faces of the same misogynistic tradition, fusing clerical, theological prejudice with generalized male fears and brutality in defining the medieval attitude toward women? Or is the assumption that all female representations index a singular referent—"woman-as-body"—itself a form of misogyny, even if presented as "feminist"?

Gender exemplifies the tendency in Western historiography to reduce the Middle Ages to modernity's Other by a single, totalizing trait. The medieval period was not monolithic about women, its views entirely shaped by a single, hegemonic misogyny. Varying views of women occur, even in ecclesiastical documents. Pastoral manuals reflect encounters with actual human experience in the confessional: "a practical understanding of the interaction of women and men that belies the idea of a unitary medieval discourse of misogyny."[54] Marriage was theorized as a hierarchical relationship, but realities of social and economic interdependence required cooperation even in hierarchical relations. Today, scholars reach beyond "the superficial appearance of a monovocal, clerical discourse of misogyny," open to the variabilities of real-life subjects, and reject as simplistic the monovocalic ideology. Instead, they revel in the "complex, competing, and frequently discordant chorus of medieval women and men."[55]

The discordances of individual texts negotiate gender issues with complex, varied means and results. Content could have different meanings and be seen from different perspectives. Rape, along with prostitution, seduction, and forced marriage are alternative narremes in the gendered plot of female hagiography.[56] Hrotsvitha, the tenth-century writer of Latin hagiography, plays, and epic histories, thematizes rape, not as a report on women's victimization, but as an ideologeme to contradict the patristic equation of woman with sexuality and sinfulness. Women are the center of theatrical action: "their *response* to male aggression" is what determines the plot.[57] Here, rape tropes something admirable in the representation of women's power, virtue, courage, and superiority. A comic parody of the rape scene can transform its voyeuristic eroticism into laughter. A physical rape is always horrifying; as a narrative syntagm, it can produce different meanings.

Chrétien de Troyes stands accused of aestheticizing rape in voyeuristic fascination with the language of sexual violence, subordinating the "*literal* experience" of rape to its narrative instrumentalization, its horror to the flattery of male honor. His staged rapes are said to shift attention away from the body of the victimized female character with a moral ambivalence that condemns but aestheticizes rape in a titillating manner that "ignore[s] the *literal* consequences of violent behavior."[58] This criticism insists on the *literal* effects of rape. Its insistent focus on what it calls the "*literal* level" of the text—as if the text were a news report—disregards the twinned inter- dependences of narrative structure and its ideology. Chrétien's amusing brilliance has led to charges of "mystification." To what degree do our "de- mystifying" readings go "against his grain," and to what degree do we merely follow the clues left for us, when we grasp their sophistication? Once the fundamental principle of self-reflexivity is formulated, the text is seen to foreground the process of female appropriation precisely so that the reader may criticize the mystifications of the process. The dead-end issue of authorial intentionality is bypassed, and the reader, male or female, is left to struggle with the text's multiple perspectives. Textual self-reflexivity is demonstrable; authorial intentionality, never. And textual self-reflexivity, when successful, encompasses the reader's own self-awareness within an open text.

The perspectival structuration of narrative texts incites the production of meanings. They reach beyond themselves and their own reflexivity, de- ploying potentials of signification to construct figures never concretized in the texts themselves: their narratees. In Roberta Krueger's potent ambigu- ity, narrative "*engenders* its readers." The difficulty is that the "real" readers, the historical individuals who pick up the story in manuscript or in print, each read differently, with greater or lesser attention to the indicators strewn about the text. As there is no innately female mode of reading, nor any single category of woman reader, there is no single type of male reader either. Reading only with a view to gender relations, one might conclude that a knight's identification with Yvain's increasing honor would find his "dreams of sovereignty" fulfilled and "his desire to be the active subject" confirmed.[59] A knight, however, might also see that the satisfaction of "dreams of sovereignty" depends on disciplined submission to a contract and to the lady whose vassal-husband he has become. It all depends how the story is being read. Yvain, at the end of his story, might read it differently than earlier on.

That may be the ultimate puzzle. Any contemporary understanding knows that texts like Chrétien's do not bear a single, totalizing meaning; they are polysemantic and produce complex categories of meanings. The skein of language, wrapped around the skeleton of narrative, constructs perspectival effects and deferrals whose resonance might be endless; so do marginal characters. It is always possible to select out, among multiple semantic potentials, those that respond to a particular perspective. But narrative closure on the axis of linearity is not the end point of narrative. The story ends, but not necessarily its interpretation. The sole gender identity of the reader is not determinative: there is also the attitude he or she adopts vis-à-vis the text. Readers of any gender might resist identification, focusing instead on structural paradoxes to discover the problematization of gender relationships in marriage and chivalry.[60] It is in resisting, not so much identification itself, as any totalizing and exclusive identification, in refusing the passive pleasures offered by self-absorptive reading—including those of erotic voyeurism—that the active reader, tracking the author's structural paradoxes, discovers the form of subjectification that, twelfth century or twenty-first, characterizes the subject of freedom. It assumes the interpretive alternatives presented by the text in paradoxical simultaneity—a paradox constitutive of textuality itself, medieval as well as modern.

The original female fairy character at the *Yvain's* presumed source is split into the haughty, distant seigneur we know as Laudine and the bright, spunky Lunete who manipulates her superiors for their own good: a *soubrette* well known to Molière. Beyond these two, however, we catch glimpses of a relatively autonomous female society—a feminine power structure parallel to men's, within domestic space, with the potential of turning into monarchical tyranny.[61] Lunete is the essential hinge between Laudine's seigneurial domination and the household's female subordinates to whom she distributes Laudine's dresses as the latter's representative. Her role within this semiautonomous structure threatens the male *maisniee* enough to make her the target of their machinations, at the risk of her life. Analogous are the internal workings of the women grouped around the Dame de Noroison, with their mixture of concern, consideration, and restrained eroticism toward the naked man sleeping on the forest floor. These female groups have a narrative density not to be denigrated: they are endowed with enough textual substance to make them more than mere signs of masculine self-negotiations. Nor can one dismiss the three hundred maidens at the Castle of the Worst Adventure as merely male fantasy. It may be a hyperbolic sign of a male author's negotiations of the contradictions of his own society, his personal role in it, emitting a masculine savior-complex. But the point of his rhetoric is "making real" what language can only signify: the despair of women economically and politically enslaved to an extraordinary rate of surplus value expropriation, given in quasi-Marxist terms, that is the signified reality of the three hundred *serves*.[62]

Lunete's manipulations of her superiors for their own good elicits my passionate attachment. A lesser character fascinates as well, arousing theoretical speculation: that anonymous, persistent *representative* of the Younger Blackthorn Sister who unceasingly pursues the Knight of the Lion's trail through dark forests, seeking a champion for her young mistress. An anonymous female character conjoins the problematics of representation with the feminine bond. Secondary, nameless actors are narrative utilities that help tell the hero's tale: that is their functional raison d'être. It is a narrow reading that reduces them exclusively to that function. These female actors overflow their roles and present significations that textualize and assert feminine value: "Chrétien de Troyes narrates from the side of women."[63]

CHAPTER 6

"Marie de France": The Postcolonial *lais*

Identity

"Marie de France" is a battlefield of nineteenth-century constructs and twentieth-century deconstructions. Three works are attributed to her: a collection of *lais*, another of fables, and the *Espurgatoire Saint Patrick*. All name "Mary" as their author. The identification of these three Maries was the work of nineteenth-century scholars.[1] The tag "Marie de France" comes from the epilogue to the fables, where her pride at writing in the vernacular defies thieving clerics from stealing the product of her labor: "My name is Mary, and I'm from France." She's proud of the value of her work: "He's crazy who forgets himself!"[2]

A second stage of the debate was reached in a psychoanalytic denial of the very possibility of a medieval woman having written the texts in question.[3] It is technically true that attributing the *lais* to "Marie" in the grouping and the sequence that is the basis of modern editions occurs in only one manuscript.[4] A contemporary, however, surprisingly unmentioned in the debate, surveys contemporary writers and mentions, after others,

> Lady Mary wrote
> poetry, and composed
> measured verses in the *lais*,
> whose content is not quite entirely true.
> She garners much praise:
> the poetry is loved by all,
> counts, barons, and simple knights,
> they love her much, and hold her dear,

they are enamored of her texts,
and have them read for their delight,
and have them oft retold.
The *lais* also please the ladies,
who listen joyfully, with gratitude,
they follow their desire.[5]

This text does not specify by title the particular poems we know as the *lais* of Marie de France, nor does it provide their order. But it identifies "Lady Mary" as a woman of marked contemporary success and notes her particular appeal to women, to their taste and feelings, especially in the *lais*.

The identification of the three Marys is a scholarly conflation . . . but not an improbable one. There may have been three Francophone women, each named Mary, running about at the turn of the thirteenth century, engaged in forms of writing that stress cultural translation, insist on the duty of remembering the past, all in octosyllabic rhymed couplets. It is possible: it requires that numbers of women were writing at the time and that the distribution of literary talents among women was far wider than heretofore suspected. Identifying the three obeys a logic of parsimonious economy, a sense that leisure, education, the linguistic, stylistic, and narratorial skills displayed, were perhaps fairly rare. An alternative to one Mary is not a male writer, but three different women writers! The Harley manuscript does not identify the *lais'* author as "Marie de France," its order is not sacrosanct, though an excellent case has been made that it is the author's anthology of her own work and that the sequence is her own.[6] But the dismissal of the historical evidence for the woman writer's very existence seems an abrupt male abreaction to feminist claims. As to the variety of her texts, and the capacious multiplicity of the subject it marks, why impose a restrictive notion of unified subjectivity on this medieval woman's experiences of fragmentation?

Women were simultaneously enmeshed in relations of power and marginalized. Their promotions were ambiguous. Louis VII's imposition of "the King's Peace" was problematic, particularly in the anarchic south. Peter the Venerable, abbot of Cluny, said his region of southern Burgundy was "without king, without duke, and without prince." War raged among local chatelains. "Everything is consumed, devastated, soiled by fire, rapine, and murder," says another cleric, imploring the king's help, urging him to consider his kingdom a totalized body, even in areas not formally part of his dominion: what happens when one member of that body withers? Here as elsewhere, a negotiated peace fails. The king proceeds *manu militari . . .*

Toulouse is yet farther. The effort to impose the King's Peace is made: royal messengers and southern prelates promote a generalized pacification. The city calls on Louis: it is his, part of his kingdom, and its population is menaced. The problem is entangled in the feudal problematic of the king's relation to rear-vassals. He takes action in a case involving the Viscountess Ermengard of Narbonne. She wants to establish authority over Berenger of Puisserguier, who has established a new toll on the road between Narbonne and Béziers. On delicate ground, Louis moves cautiously. In spite of Roman law that forbids women to act as judicial powers, he cites the custom of "our kingdom," more generous, which allows women to replace "the better sex" when absent, in the administration of their heritage. Louis proclaims Ermengard's capacity to render justice: "*God made you woman as he might have made you a man*; in his good will, he has placed the regnum of the province of Narbonne in the hands of a woman; by virtue of our authority, let no one be allowed to subtract themselves from your jurisdiction under the pretext that you are a woman."[7] Men remain "the better sex," and yet women's equality is asserted and ascribed to God in the act of creation. The momentary assertion of equality hardly denies women's marginalization. It demonstrates that misogyny was not the exclusive medieval take on women.

Marie de France knew marginalization: to that of gender were added the geographical and the linguistic. Internal evidence of her *lais*, written in French but adapted from "Breton" antecedents, indicates she wrote and lived at least part of her life in England. We know *certainly* nothing of her subject position: she could have been a burgher's housewife, a lady-in-waiting, or a learned nun. She was *probably* associated with aristocratic life, possibly at court: she offers her *lais* to an unspecified "king"—perhaps Henry II, but "king" is sometimes used loosely as an honorific. Since she adapted both fables and the *Purgatory of Saint Patrick* from the Latin, she presumably knew that language. Most probably, she was a noblewoman, perhaps in that difficult position, a solitary woman in a patriarchal world of force and violence.[8]

Her texts often represent cultural, political, and even economic displacement. Falling in love, Guigemar greets his lady with consciousness of his own alterity:

> He dared not declare his love:
> Since he was of a foreign land,
> He feared, if he showed his feelings,
> She might hate and distance him.[9]

Marie renews the tag of the *Eneas—estranges hom, homme d'estranges terre*—thematizing the grief of solitary, friendless exile:

> without friends, a man, a foreigner
> grows sorrowful and grieves in an other land
> not knowing where to seek help.[10]

But self-pity is not at all Marie's game. On the contrary, not only is self-pity absent, her texts view a dreadful historical reality—the savage colonization of the island of England, the destruction of local culture and autonomy—with a haunting transcendence of marginalization into an actively hybrid multiculturalism, encompassing male and female, colonial subalternity and the colonizer. Her textual praxis constructs itself as a site of polymorphous traversals and imaginative equality, an appropriative self-extension to other marginalities. Her self-reflexivity elaborates the interconnections of multiple cultural codes, including a robust sexuality subtending the delicate verbal webs of mysterious texts, which incite theoretical reflection on narrativity and semiotics. Hypothetically, in some suprahistorical sphere, a man might have written these texts, either in France or in England. In the harsh realities of human experience, it is impossible to imagine their subtle put-downs of male phallocentrism issuing from a feather—a phallus—not a woman's.

How Marie acquired the cultural capital of the *ars* of writing (the technologies of letters, grammar, rhetoric, dialectic, and inscription) and developed them into writing in the aesthetic sense (structure, style, symbolic thought, their fusion), we have no idea: her identity, authorial and existential, is entirely defined by her texts. However those acquisitions were made, her strategy within the alternatives of the *ars* can too easily be termed "a woman's choice." Contemporary male writers show a preference for rhetorical *amplificatio*. Marie's texts are not only short, they are often minimalist, preferring the more "modest" *abbreviatio*. The lack of verbal ostentation too readily permits the critical elision of significance. But verbal "modesty" is a complex strategy. The subtraction of verbal rhetoric increases the importance of the remainder: narrative structure and symbolism. Marie's semiosis juxtaposes the dynamics of lithe narrative linearity with the radiating stasis of symbolism.

Texts

Social marginality is a site of cultural exploration where semiotic models are tried, tested, and fleshed out—as in the short, rhymed tales of Marie de France. The conclusion to the *Fables* demonstrates an author conscious of her production, its aesthetic value and its value as symbolic capital, subject to easy appropriation in a culture without copyright. She protects her production as she can, in a world where the extortion of value from producers is the normal way of doing business. Her semiotic reflection is elaborated around the imbrication of narrative and the self-reflexive sign. Such signs traverse Marie's texts, insistent on their enigmatic quality.[11] The texts' "phenomenological gaps" of signification between determinate communication and indeterminacy challenge the reader.[12]

It has been argued that the institution of the title does not exist at this period of the Middle Ages. The repeated internal use of titles in the *lais* offers counterevidence. "Le Chaitivel"—meaning, "Sad Sack," or "Schlemiel"—has been criticized as mediocre, stylistically muddled, having a tedious, disjointed plot, poor character motivation, and a reluctance to fictionalize.[13] In fact, the text's interest is not in narrative. Better than any other *lai*, it demonstrates Alexandre Leupin's point, that "the fiction of the lays is also a meditation on writing."[14] The *lai*'s interest is not in the narrative events, which are summarily recounted, but in the metadiscourse of two characters who survive their own story and assume it as already existing. Not narrative, not even narration, but textualized metaperspectivalism is the point.

The title itself is problematized as an element of signification. The story inverts the usual courtly scene. The knight and titular hero insists he hasn't got it any more, to the lady he loved and loves. It's not intense desire endured in frustration that blocks male potency, it's the permanent flaccidity,

wound-induced in the wars of love, that preoccupies their sole male survivor, when the lady, ruing those wars, comes to visit. Three other suitors
died in a tournament for love of her. It is the lady who prefers numerical
self-glorification, in an argument about the title of "her" story. "Le
Chaitivel" foregrounds her surviving lover; she prefers "Les Quatre
Deuils," "The Four Bereavals," counting her conquests . . . just like a man.
She keeps entertaining him verbally: nothing else is possible. The epilogue
plays with the text's identity, which endows it with an "*état civil.*"[15] Expanding on the perspectivalism already established, the narrator opines
that either title would suit the story, but custom has chosen "Le
Chaitivel"![16] In the debate over the title and identity of the text that constructs their perspectival opposition, the two actors' subjectivities tend to
be submerged. In fact, a complex, ironic chiasmus of cultural clichés is
constructed: the woman counts her amorous triumphs . . . "just like a
man"; the man wallows in his victimization . . . "just like a woman"!

In Marie's most telling texts, the alternatives of self-reflexive symbolism
and narrative content are fused. "Yonec" might be either a first version of
"Laüstic," or an attempt to repeat its success: their intertextuality is unquestionable. A knight becomes the sign of his own presence, in his metamorphosis into a bird (as the hero in "Bisclavret" turns into a wolf). It is
the discrepancy between signifier and signified that signifies: the shadow of
the bird on the windowsill actually announces his presence. By dint of social and sexual intercourse with her new lover, the lady's appearance
changes with pregnancy. Her face signals her new situation, in uninten-
tional communication to her wealthy, older husband. Trapped and killed
(as in "Laüstic"), the dying bird-lover gives the lady a double sign, a magic
ring and a sword (in "Laüstic," it is the lady who gives her lover a doubled
sign), to communicate to his son as instruments of identitarian vengeance.
Signs are integrated into the narrative structure: they serve the story, which
functionalizes them perfectly.

"Fresne" makes use of the same doubled sign construction, but in a
manner that emphasizes its integration into a story of, by, and for women.
Neither sentimental nor gender-prejudiced, Marie limns a spiteful woman
whose resentment encodes the trap in which she will be caught herself, a
trickster tricked by her own trickery. When a neighboring woman has
twins, the spiteful woman libels her as adulterous. But then she bears

twins herself. Against the shame her own dictum would bring on her, one of the newborn girls is cast out and is given the doubled sign—a ring and a cloth. Left at a convent, hanging in an ashtree, she is adopted by the abbess who takes charge of her education and gives her the name Fresne—"Ashtree." Although a nobleman falls in love and takes her as mistress, his vassals insist he abandon Fresne in favor of another young woman of attested noble genealogy, who can give him proper noble heirs—in fact, Fresne's twin sister.

At the marriage, the new wife's mother comes upon a cloth that Fresne has laid out, in the abnegation of perfect humility, on the newlyweds' bed: the cloth that had accompanied her since birth, the sign of her unknown identity. The mother recognizes it, leading to the anagnorisis of mother and daughter, the reward of self-abnegation in the conversion of the evil mother, the accession to real identity, and the annulment that allows Fresne's marriage to her love. Recognition leads to reconciliation: a cognitive closing of the circle resolves the hanging conflict between mother and daughter. Narrative structure reveals a twelfth-century feminism delicately sketching the working of a sisterly collective.[17] Would a man have drawn a world peopled almost entirely by women, acknowledging their potential for evil as well as good, in which a mother-daughter separation is recuperated by the daughter's loyal patience, as constituted by a sorority's collectivity? The problem of signification, functionalized by the narrative as in "Yonec," veers into a specifically feminine problematics with "Fresne," where humility and the mother's correct semiotic reading leads to the reintegration of subjectivity and identity.

The redoubled sign is functionalized in "Yonec" and "Fresne": it is an instrument of storytelling and allows for different forms of resolution. In "Milun," sign structures proliferate and lead more in the direction of a significatory problematics. Milun initially sends his lady-love a ring, to be hung around her son's neck. Fresne's cloth turns into a letter containing Milun's father's name, establishing an authenticating genealogy for claiming the heritage, accompanied by a silken purse furnished with coins: value is thematized both as sign and money. The sign structure here is not just doubled, it is tripled: there is a sign-sign, the ring whose shape is zero but which does signify; the explicatory, discursive text that spells out the sign-sign's meaning; and the purse of monetary signs. This set of signs will be replaced by another. When Milun and his lady-love are separated, they communicate in complicated and cumbersome ways. A courier-bird carries messages back and forth, not a pigeon but a swan. Not a merely functional messenger, it carries letters in its plumage, participating in both ornamental and signifying functions. The narrative naturalizes this messenger of love. The first time, the swan is bodily carried by a human supernumerary. Later, it is starved for days before each occasion, so that hunger impels its flight. Signs proliferate across the narrative landscape, with or without supplement.

The swan (*cisne*) is a *signe*, which the text terms an *[en]seigne* (l. 271): all three words might be pronounced identically. The swan-sign, more expansive than Mallarmé's, bears a complex sign in the form of a letter, signed and bearing the sign of a seal. Naturalizing the sign-messenger counterbalances a willful play of paradox with the dissemination of signs analogous to the proliferating signs whose texture constitutes a text. Narrativity itself becomes the sign of understanding and value. At the end of the tale, the narrative of combat between Milun and his bastard son is itself a sign of the antagonist's warrior excellence, of his *pris et valur*, so that Milun declares: You've beaten me at the joust; How much that makes me love you![18] As with Guivret and Erec, Yvain and Gauvain, fighting is sealed in friendship. In "Milun," combat leads to the son's revelation of his identity, through recounted narrative and signs. Transposing the genders of "Fresne," the play of conflict and signification leads to anagnorisis, reconciliation in love, and the reintegration of subjectivity and identity.

At this point, a distinction has been demonstrated, between a pure sign, a sign signifying nothing but signification—the multiple rings, the white swan—and the metonymic, contiguous series of signs, the missives that discursively explicate the solitary, polyvalent sign. Only in the string of signs, syntactically ordered, can articulated signification arise. The solitary sign alone signifies everything; hence it signifies nothing. Signification requires the analytic differences inherent to language, and only to language, hence pure signs that signify signification per se. They require the juxtaposition of discourse or narration to make sense and advance the anthropomorphic adventures of those pseudohumans called actors or characters.

The exact match of semiotic purity, narrative text, and symbolization occurs in "Laüstic," the achieved fusion of story and the paradoxes of signification. The lady's husband, disturbed by her nightly risings from the marital bed, becomes suspicious of her cover story, that she goes to the window nightly to hear the nightingale sing. The reader knows she converses with the neighboring knight, in an amorous but nonsexual commerce of signs and unfulfilled desires. The "purity" of signification is anticipated by the "purity" of their narrative relationship. When the angry, brutal husband traps the bird, kills it, and throws it at his wife—its blood splatters her chest—she sends the dead bird to her "lover" and recounts the adventure by embroidering its story in brocade—fulfilling woman's function in a patriarchal society. Like Penelope and Philomena, she saves the small ground of independence within the patriarchal marriage by turning the activity which is the sign of her subjection into the sign of her narrative transcendence.[19] The lover will wrap the bird in texted cloth: encasing both within a reliquary, he carries it with him henceforth the length of his days.

Transcendence is achieved through the purity of love and the contiguity of the death of the symbol of their love with its narrative, wrapped in a transposition of religious adoration to a secular, passionate if unfulfilled love affair. The entire text builds toward the triumph of the signifying process over and against repressive male violence: signification itself overcomes the rule of brutal patriarchy so as to maintain love's integrity. Does the lovers' noncarnal love suggest a secular spirituality, displacing the religious opposition of flesh and spirit?

In "Laüstic," the doubled sign structure forms a *mise-en-abyme*: the small syntagm that reflects a narrative's totality. In the representational terms of modern feminism, the tale is regressive, valorizing chastity's transcendence of the carnal. But the woman transforms the natural thing—the dead bird, the instrumental excuse for amorous conversations—into the sign of pure love, attaching its explicatory narrativization. The walls that surround, enclose, and imprison the woman are transcended by wit and ingenuity, as the weave that designates her submission to patriarchal power is transmuted into a play of signification. As with the trickster tricked, a victim transcends the master's power: she uses the powers of signification to overcome death, imprisonment, and separation, in the triumphant transcendence of the secularized relic. Subjectivity transcends the limitations imposed by social identity.

The delicate problematization of the feminine sign in the patriarchal order as its self-transcendence turns into a subtle and riotous explosion of the order of masculine signification itself. "Chievrefeuil" is named after the honeysuckle which, winding around the hazel tree, allegorizes Tristan and Iseut wrapped around each other in the natural "transcendence" of utterly carnal love. This is not a delicately cloying allegory; it resembles rather the analyticity of Chrétien de Troyes's occasional allegories, just more robustly and carnally vulgar. The lovers' brief narrative transcends all barriers by pure sexuality. For anyone who knew the fundamental story—and who, in the culture of the court, didn't know the twelfth century's universal myth of love, of Tristan and Iseut?—their story means the pain of separation, the heart-wrenching comings and goings that occupy the grievous space of adultery, the haunting, burning desire in the absence of the beloved who might satisfy it. The narrative crux is always, how to get Iseut away from her social context with Mark, so that she and Tristan can yield once more to their unending passion.

Tristan, alone in the forest, advertises his presence by waving his stick around, as Iseut passes by on horseback in the forest. Prearranged as a sign of recognition, Tristan's stick is also a sign of his own stick. It leads Iseut to leave her retinue in order to receive his stick in a good roll on the forest floor. The stick is a natural sign of itself. The sign, which normally supposes the absence of the signified, here signifies its presence. Tristan's stick is serviceable, as usual, and that's about all that is in question, aside from the deathless image of deathless love, the honeysuckle wound around the hazel tree as the icon of inseparability, figuring both the transcendence of deathless love and the lovers' limbs wrapped around each other against all effort at transcendence, in words that still resonate:

Not you without me, nor me without you.[20]

But has the great discrepancy been noted, between the imaged inseparability of eternal love and the narrative of Tristan and Iseut? As is often the case, men's utterances, even moving, are unreliable. Here, the lovers, having taken their pleasure on the forest floor, talk the old talk of returning to the king, as if that would finally end the pain. But when it came time to part, both of them wept. The text witnesses their pain, their joy, and the truth of the *lai* he composed later in her absence,

in memory of the joy he'd had,
of the beloved he'd seen,
and on account of what he'd written
just as the queen had said,
to remember the words.[21]

The discrepancy between the narrative and its purported *mise-en-abyme*, becomes a *différance* in the narratee's double reading. The discrepancy between the inseparability of eternal love and the narrative of Tristan and Iseut, inheres in the passage that gives the *lai* its title in free indirect discourse . . . a supposed invention of modernity.[22]

The most vulgar question about men's sticks is their length. The text asks the question, in a manner that confuses unwillingness to countenance the wrapping of Marie's honeysuckle discourse around its gross carnality. Tristan, waiting for Iseut, cut a hazel tree in half, split it square, and inscribed his name with his knife: the queen will recognize her lover's stick. That was the sum total of his writing:

He cannot live without her.
Like the honeysuckle wrapped around
the hazelnut, enlaced and fastened
all around the trunk,
forever they stay together,
but if separated,
the hazel dies quickly,
so does the honeysuckle.
Sweet love, so is it with us:
Not you without me, nor I without you.[23]

The free indirect discourse leaves indeterminate whether it is Tristan's utterance or his author's that is unreliable and indeterminate. Its unreliability is attested by the scholarly debate it has occasioned and the long footnote the editor appends to this passage.[24] The linguistic crux is in the gap between lines 60 and 61. Does the demonstrative pronoun *ceo* of line 61 refer back to the preceding material, so that *la summe de l'escrit* would contain only Tristan's name carved into the stick? Or does the pronoun function proleptically, so that line 62 specifies in addition the facts recounted in the next sixteen lines, that he had sent Iseut a missive, in which he told her how much he missed her, that he could not live without her, that they were bound as the honeysuckle and the hazel tree, "not one without the other"?

The stick is a pure sign of purely sexual desire; the texted representation necessary to elucidate signification may circumcise the man's stick, waving in the air for his lover's recognition. Some apply common sense to the passage: only Tristan's name is carved on the stick, the rest of his message having been sent earlier (by messenger? by Pony Express?). The editor insists that Marie's symbolism is never vague, but that she opts for "concrete and rational precision" (as a scholar should) within a self-sufficient (that is, modernist) text. Therefore, he concludes, Marie had Tristan write the entire message (translated above) on the hazelnut stick . . . at some expense to verisimilitude!

It is, in fact, impossible to delimit exactly the *summe de l'escrit*. The scholarly debate demonstrates that the passage is ambiguous, and that its ambiguity is indeterminable; I add only that it is likely intentionally so. It cannot but puzzle and lead to the reflection that, not only was Tristan's stick long indeed, but that even with the longest "inscription," it could not be brought under control and discipline. Marie's narrative—the briefest of the *lais*—is her hilarious put-down, not only of phallocentrism's deification of the male member, but of the Nietzschean theme of Tristan and Iseut's "eternal return." Is it about always coming back in the endless alternating pattern of presence and absence, or is it about coming again, and coming again, and singing, no matter the singer's veracity or mimetic consistency? It asserts the primacy of the carnal as against the pretense of idealism in the great myth of passionate love. It does so at the expense of verisimilitude: the text is a production of signification, for whose performance narrative is merely instrumental, not a watertight contract of mimetic exactitude. "Chievrefeuil" is both a repetition of the great medieval myth of love and its deconstruction.

Two of Marie's texts—"Guigemar" and "Bisclavret"—address directly the problematic of constitutive alterities: subjectivity's dependence on and grounding in alterity, or the alternative of Otherness and otherness. In "Guigemar," a knight, well-loved by parents and the king who knights him, finds his social insertion in traveling to Flanders, "where there are always combats and wars," a well-formed male with one exception: like Hippolytus, he rejects love. In the course of a hunt, he encounters a peculiar alterity, a complex animal sign: a white animal, a doe by the presence of her fawn, a buck by its antlers. This is not a "real" animal: it is not presented as a "believable fiction" before which disbelief is to be suspended. It is a narrative sign, counterintuitive, counterfactual, complex, and paradoxical. Signaling the alternative between the two genders as totality and interdependence, it faces Guigemar with his lack: the desire for an O/other that would constitute him as subject. His sexual and class identity are given: he lacks the desire that makes a subject and encounters a complex sign whose fiction excludes lack. Only ideology claims to exclude lack. This sign reflects back on Guigemar, as his critical Interpretant. The sign of androgyny, a totality lacking nothing, mirrors the hero's incompleteness in reverse: he lacks lack, the lack that impels desire. His hunter's arrow wounds the doe mortally, but bounces back to wound his thigh in symbolic castration (as with Perceval's father and the Fisher King). A wound (the word *plaie* is subject to multiple repetitions) is essential to the constitution of the subject: the cut constitutes being (see Yvain). The dying animal curses Guigemar: he will not recover from the wound until a woman suffers out love for him, and he for her; until he suffers his lack and his cut.

Desire is not willed. Abandoning himself to the contingency of a pilotless boat, he arrives in the *antive cité*. The local lord is an old man, whose jealousy guards his desirable wife in a room decorated by the text's ideological *mise-en-abyme*. Rather than a "mandatory misreading," its rhetorical organization casts two signifying images as a complex emblem that demands attentive reading in its narrative context.[25] On the walls of her room are portraits of Venus and Ovid, the deity of Love and her opponent, complex signs that wander between visual aesthetics and the literary tradition. They repeat the alternative of the doe-buck, separating them as gyneco- and anthropomorphic figures. Venus shows *how* love is to be observed . . . as an art, a discipline. Ovid teaches how to repress love—exactly what Guigemar had been doing. The alternatives on love are framed as love's binarism: submission or rejection. The Latin poet represents the narrative subject's previous course, the goddess its future alternative. The first is decisively rejected by the emblem of an abyssal narrative, with no *vraisemblance* whatsoever, when Venus throws Ovid's book in the fire, the portrait climbing off the wall and turning into narrative agent against its opposite number.

The painted room in the *antive cité* is an Other World, the equivalent of Jehan's tower in *Cligés*: the location of a passionate but asocial love. The wounded lover and the Other's lady (the lover's Other) live their adulterous love there for a year and a half. The subject has overcome the ontological fault signaled by the white doe. Hypothetically, the initiating lack has been fulfilled. It has been done, however, at the expense of living that love in society. For the rejection of love, the rejection of a sociopolitical insertion has been substituted as lack. The junction of subject of desire and his object is faulty, in an encoding insistent on the interdependence of love and socialization. On this score, Marie and Chrétien are allied against Beroul and perhaps Thomas.

The "reality principle" by which the lovers and their affair are discovered by the jealous husband is not a realistic reality principle. The discovery is *preceded* by the woman's realization that discovery is inevitable: consciousness precedes the event. It leads to oaths of fidelity and passional contracts: neither lover will accept love from any other. These contracts are materialized, symbolized, and narrativized by the knots that each ties into the other's clothing, to be untied only by the one who tied them: both will give their love only to that person who knows the shibboleth. The knots are both sign and instrument of fidelity, hence the ensuing flight from paradise, once the affair is discovered. Guigemar leaves first, the lady follows later, escaping from her prison when she finds her door surprisingly unlocked—a factoid asserted with narratorial imperturbability by a single verse in preemptive mockery of realistic *vraisemblance.*

Similar mockery attends the Meriaduc episode. He falls in love with Guigemar's lady, captures her and blithely organizes a tournament to which he expressly invites the hero. He realizes that his friend Guigemar and the lady of his desire share these peculiar knots, a test for whomsoever they are to love. He introduces them at his castle, both their rival and their Cupid. A fool, or a transparent narrative artifice? A bit of both, and something more. Guigemar's destiny aims at conjunction with a woman. Meriaduc is a good friend and instrument, doing everything required to reunite Guigemar and his lady. But triangular love determines that Guigemar will despatch him in spite of services rendered. Finding hospitality with Meriaduc's warring antagonist, he attacks and destroys Meriaduc's castle and kills him. His friend and rival killed off, he happily leads off his lady friend: the punishment (*peine*) inflicted by the magic doe-buck is ended. Achieving junction with the feminine principle, he discards the society of men through a complicated series of plot turns. It is the same conflict as is faced by both Erec and Yvain: gender and class identities are givens for both, but subjectivity must be found and constructed.

The discipline of love is dual. Ethically, it insists on the fidelity of an exclusive bond and does not tolerate multiplicities. Semiotically, it requires weaving together the signifying modes of the static but complex sign with the unfolding flow of narrative . . . itself a discipline of sequencing, of grasping how "one-thing-after-another" produces an ideational dialectic. But the narrative's cold, concluding words, just before the epilogue, give one the shivers:

> He's taken and destroyed the fortress,
> And killed the lord inside.
> In great happiness he leads off his lady.
> Now he's gone beyond his punishment.[26]

The coldly expedited ending yields nothing to the celebratory pleasure suggested by the well-told tale and its mimetically happy conclusion. Human happiness is not entirely joyous.

"Guigemar" 's trick is the knot of fidelity tied into clothing. In "Bisclavret," Marie adapts the oldest, the most widespread animal metamorphosis, figuring the fears of feral violence in the socialized subject.[27] Much has been made of Marie's use of folktales; she was once seen as a mere adaptor of folk legends and myths. In fact, her treatment of those tales is quite free: their material does not determine her structures or meanings. Hers is the only "literary" text in which the narrator adopts the werewolf's perspective in telling the tale.[28] She redeploys the tradition's projection of civilized fears onto the screen of a monstrous Other, in order to undermine the process of Othering in the creation of subjectivity, by transforming the Other into an anthropomorphic other. The werewolf is a self-conscious artifice, as was the mother-doe with male antlers. The werewolf is proffered, not as diegetic "reality," but as a complex, polyvalent sign in an ongoing discursive exchange: it is not the question of fictive belief that is raised, but that of reading.

The male protagonist alternates regularly between human and animal forms, between his "self" and its Other. The wife's uncomprehending fear of the Other leads her to steal the clothing that is the condition of his return to the human condition: he remains a wolf, unable to rehumanize, until the conundrum is resolved. That is achieved, but not by combat. The king recognizes true nobility even in wolf's clothing, from behavior that signals human subjectivity in spite of bestial identity. Like Arthur in the *Yvain*'s Blackthorn sisters' episode, the king exerts moral pressure on the evil woman to force her confession and the location of the clothing.

"Bisclavret"'s figuration of the subject's inherent splittedness, humanity's monstrous doubleness as *both* socialized *and* bestial, presents an option to those who would address werewolf humanity: address the good, or the evil?[29] The text does not hide the difficulty of the choice. The werewolf reveals human bestiality. Enraged at his wife, he avenges himself by tearing the nose off her face. The gelded nose is an established sign of sexual criminality, such as adultery and bigamy: his wife is guilty of both. Even the wise man who sides with the werewolf considers the act felonious, but the text stresses the appropriateness of the wife's punishment. As in Yvain's mad episode, clothing and language are the signs of properly socialized humanity: mute, nameless nudity signals the wildness that continues to inhere in man, hence the wolf's need to be alone to redress himself: the word "privacy" does not exist in either Old or Modern French, but its encoding is medieval.

Socialization is necessary for the question of identity to even surface; women and power are alternative means of male socialization. Yvain loses his mind, memory, and identity along with his clothing, turning into an animal in human form; Bisclavret loses human form, remains forcibly caught in the inimical form of bestial alterity, but retains memory, identity, and a knowledge of social codes. Both texts address socialized humanity's incorporation of that which resists social incorporation: self and alterity are permanently joined in the human subject. We live with our constitutive Other and project it on the screen of real others.

Subjectivity

In Chrétien's novels, combat is the narrative coin of exchange, transformed from murderous scourge to social utility in serving the weak, the helpless, the exploited. With Marie, combat is less frequent: An embarrassment? A distaste for its endless repetitiveness? Awareness that its use plays into male phallicism? Does the choice of a "female" aesthetic of brevity rather than amplification produce lessened violence? In fact, if viewed with attention, not to the amplifications of violence, but to its occurrences, violence is as frequent in the Marie's discourse as in Chrétien's. A werewolf bites off a woman's nose; she is tortured; an adulterous couple is scalded to death in boiling water; a son avenges his father's death by killing his murderer; various symbolic animals are killed off in wanton violence; a jealous husband hurls a bird whose neck he has just wrung to bloody his wife's breast; female characters endure attempted rapes; a man-bird is impaled on a barbed spike; a thigh-wound stands for castration; a stripling's eager machismo explodes his heart, manuring hilltop grasses, herbs, and flowers with his blood; and so on. Violence is central to Marie's work: along with sexual ambiguity, it nourishes writing.[30] Marie metaphorizes both frequently. The writing subject constitutes itself at the edges of successive cuts: they perdure at its center. These violences are physical in nature; if focus is shifted to symbolic violence, nearly every narrative turn of the *lais* exemplifies it.

Subjectivity grows on internalized violence;[31] identity risks being destroyed by it. Identity, as might be expected of a writer of margins, is crucial in Marie's texts. The structure of "Lanval" is identical to the narrative model of romance: conjunction with the Fairy Princess, her love conditioned on secrecy, is destroyed by revelation of love's secret in self-defense against the queen's wrongful accusations of homosexuality, solicitation, attempted rape, and treason. The Fairy Princess no longer responds to the call of Lanval's desire. He is saved from certain death only by the grace she accords him, after a sequence in which his trial is interrupted by beautiful ladies on horseback arriving one after the other, each not yet the Fairy Princess herself, only messengers of her approach—courtly Johanna the Baptists, a fairy mistress as Christ? When her arrival finally demonstrates that her beauty is indeed greater than the queen's, the lovers are reunited, but with a bittersweet ending. She rides off, taking Lanval with her to Avalon, the beautiful island of the dead: transcendence achieved at the cost of an integrated social identity and existence.

Marie's art of *abbreviatio* is not quantitative merely. It contains as many rejections of dominant cultural models as incorporations: creativity operates by subtraction, division, and inversion as much as by addition. The brevity of her texts does not reduce them to simple, unpretentious realism, or delimit their theoretical import. Are a werewolf, a fairy mistress, a bird-man, or a female saint of abnegation, really "ordinary people coping with the problems of ordinary life"?[32] Her sign-characters track the satisfaction of emotional needs rather than status or "honor," needs that repeatedly lead to alterities of gender and culture, alterities that name so many iden-titarian interdependencies.

Reversing the usual order, Marie's authorial subjectivity is more acces-sible than her identity. Lacking all documentation, she is subject to so many identifications that she obviously has none. Her subjectivity is con-structed entirely in and by her texts, outside any identifiable subject-posi-tion. It is that of borderlines, a marginal individual. Her texts locate her ge-ographically at the Anglo-Norman colonial margin of French culture and semiotically at the borderlines of a male-dominated textual culture. Textual ontogeny displaces and stands for a possible biographical philogeny. Her textual "thresholds"—the margins of prologue and epilogue where autho-rial identity is conventionally given—signal their location at crossings, lin-guistic and geographic, repeatedly invoking the fiction of a prior subjectiv-ity; they construct themselves as those crossings.[33]

Those thresholds most frequently give "Bretons" as Marie's sources. But what does that term mean? It is generally taken to refer to the modern French province of Britanny and its inhabitants. In fact, its meaning is less specific, more ambiguous, lacking the geographical basis it has in moder-nity. Chrétien has "*li Bretun*" identify his hero as Erec, whose kingdom is in Outer Wales (Estre-Gales), though he is crowned at Nantes in Britanny. He and his parents travel from Arthur's court to Erec's land and country, without crossing water, though *the romans antiques* offer many examples of sea voyages. After King Lac's death at Arthur's court in an unnamed town, Erec takes back his land in fealty from the king, who then declares it is time to go "*a Nantes en Bretaigne*" (6495). Erec has Enid's parents join them on the trip to Nantes. Each day, they travel a great distance, they ride a long ways, until they arrive at Nantes—again without mention of a sea crossing, from Arthur's domain to Bretaigne.

The distance from "Brit" to "Breton" is minimal. Bretun and Bre-taigne are derived from Britonnum and could refer either to Britain or to Britanny. Throughout Wace's *Brut*, it refers to those from Britain, but re-tained both meanings in twelfth-century usage. Disambiguation was possible. Marie specifies "*Bretaigne la Menur*," or adds a second geographical encoding: "Laüstic" locates its action near Saint Malo; "Chaitivel" takes place "*en Bretaine a Nantes*." But Marie also confounds meanings, as when she localizes "Yonec" in Carwent (Wales) at the River Duelas (Britanny).[34] "Equitan"'s emphasis on "*cil de Bretaine, li Bretun*," refers to the Bretons of Britanny, but the Nauns whom Equitan rules may refer to a general "Celtic" legend rather than a specific geographical location. "Milun" distinguishes "*Bretun*" from "*Engleis*," but that proves no more than the distinction between Norman and the French in the same passage. Bretan, the language, is associated with Kardoel (Carlisle) and Arthur's court in Logres.

Except where specified, the lexical family *Britaine, bretan,* and *Bretun,* referring to place, language, or people, is undecided between "Britain" and "Britanny," between "British" and "Breton." The distinction that remains stable in the *lais* is its opposition to "Norman": Bretun designates a Norman Other, the conquered Anglo-Saxons or the people of Britanny over whom Norman suzerainty was repeatedly reasserted by military expeditions.[35] The dominant semantic content of Bretun and Bretaigne was not geographical but genealogical: it expressed the notion of the transchannel Celtic unity of a people with a common ancestry, a single lineage. In the epilogue, Wace defines his *Brut* as "the history of the Bretons, and the lineage of the barons who descended from the lineage of Brutus"—whichever side of the Channel (or the Sleeve) they landed on.[36] What they shared in both locations was effective subjection to the Normans: they were the colonized. It is the memory of victims and enforced wanderers that Marie de France honors. It is with the "others" defined by and from her own subject-position that Marie knits a bond repeatedly, in prologues, in epilogues, in the bodies of the *lais* themselves.

In those liminal thresholds, the author defines herself as the site of multiplicities and transgressive traversals. Hers is a "minor literature" in a major language in which everything is political.[37] Although written in French, multilingualism is omnipresent in the *lais*: other languages are named, terms are regularly translated. Marie's thresholds are concerned with the identities of the texts, not with the author's. The author functions as mere shifter, shifting adventure into *lai,* *lai* into poem, Breton into French, always reasserting the duty and necessity of memory: "to remember the words," "to remember lest it be forgotten."[38] Memory is the text's ideology. The first millennium may have been an age of forgetting, a mental clearing of the forest;[39] not so in the twelfth century. A complex dualism haunts Marie's relations to a constitutive past: though disappeared, it engenders identity. The general prologue asserts the extraordinary freedom and creativity of a modernity anchored in memory rather than oblivious erasure. The textual basis of "Chievrefoil," of "Fresne" and "Bisclavret," is literally enshrined in "Laüstic." Subjectivity is a site of constitutive disjunctions, a "margin of hybridity," where cultural differences, temporality, contingency, and conflictuality touch, to construct a "borderline experience" in the cultural and interpretive undecidability of the colonial moment.[40] This borderline experience is a space of encounters "*in-between* colonizer and colonized*": silence or communication, concealment or revelation, essential narremes in the *lais*, make the difference of life or death.[41] It is a space that seeks to transcend identities of class, gender, age, or sex, requiring an extension of the subject beyond the boundaries of self: subjectivity as self-transcendence.

What is remarkable, even heroic in Marie de France's writing, is the appropriative generosity of spirit that extends skill, talent, and knowledge to rescue what can be captured and preserved of the colonized culture. Marie's narrator has an astounding ability to filter other voices through her own, safeguarding both the other's distinctiveness and her own narratorial "I."[42] The gesture toward the other proceeds as a re-creative fusion of personal disjunctions with those of the autochthonous, as authorial subjectivity cleaves to cultural alterity. How to distinguish appropriation from preservation? How to separate out the necessary subjective investment that energizes the rescue of a tattered culture? The wager of writing is to fuse binaries through the injection of new subjectivity. Recognizing the weaknesses of men and the continued dependence of at least some women on those very men, in the frequent vulgarity of both, it repeatedly posits transcendence of anger, resentment, suspicions, into spheres of recognition, forgiveness, or signification. A transcendence cognizant of vulgarity, of carnality and material fact, incorporates them in an equal reciprocity most gently, most nobly assumed.

Marie's recuperation of narratives that acknowledge their ground in other's voices, those of subalterns, models a subjectivity that insists that these scattered fragments constitute a relative but cohesive whole, a complex oscillation between self and Other as a constitutive contradiction: an early colonial hybridity. Her text suggests that one does not simply wait for the Other's arrival:[43] one goes to the encounter to negotiate the differences, in the representation of words if one has the talent, in a dual, coordinate, and always tragic invention of the Other's Real, out of one's own subjectivity.

CHAPTER 7

Raoul de Cambrai: Haunting Violence

F ew medieval texts incite recognition of "the subject of violence" as does *Raoul de Cambrai.*[1] In this monstrous, fragmented epic from the turn of the thirteenth century, form and content take the shape of a chiasmus. The more archaic material of the first section is cast in the later form of rhyme; the more recent material of the second section is cast in assonance, the more archaic form. The text's identity is a constitutive heterogeneity, which devolves from the conjunction of two different kinds of narrative material: cyclical violence associated with epic, women and love associated with "romance." But the women and love of *Raoul de Cambrai* are of a kind *not* found in romance. The poem's fragmentation is usually discussed in terms of scribal or authorial multiplicity, or of genre theory, defined in opposition to an ideal of Aristotelian "unity"—difficult to sustain with medieval texts in general. What counts rather is historic coherence: the text's coherence with itself and with its own historicity. Coherence, here, is grounded both in contradiction and self-*différance*: their cohabitation is one defining element of medieval textuality. Like the *Roland* before it, *Raoul* is a multifaceted text, oriented toward an examination of the problem of violence.

A historical reading depends on two dialectical insertions: in the intertextualities of literary history, and in political evolution. Both incorporate textual Others out of which the text constructs its coherence. *Raoul's* "knighthood and its private wars" are not mere figures of the text's own writing process:[2] they are necessary interlocutors, Others who must be addressed. Their historical quality is not the same as the text's.

Early epic stages the problematic of violence, focusing on the relationship between superior and inferior in the dominant social class, the nobility that included the king. The feudal bond was based in the "fief," an exchange of material value for services between lord and vassal, ideologized as personal loyalty between equals and termed "honor." But both superior and inferior destabilize the system. The superior does not fulfill his side of the feudal contract, to protect the vassal; the inferior is constituted as a subject of mounted violence with a violent character which systemically self-destructs: here, *Raoul* replays *Roland.* Between the two moments of their composition, however, lies the central "invention" of the novel, above all the series of texts written by Chrétien de Troyes, ending with the *Perceval,* left unfinished for unknown reasons. Both date from the early reign of Philip Augustus. Chrétien's text, dedicated to Philip of Alsace, Count of Flanders, is assumed to have been written at his court. No direct influence can be assumed, but the similarities of roughly contemporary texts composed in the same place are perhaps not accidental.

Raoul de Cambrai represents, not simply a linear continuation of the earlier chanson de geste, but a further stage in an intertextual dialectic that embraces other "genres." The initial, "Raoul" section radically denies the idealizations of romance.[3] Male warrior violence does not submit to the female instance: Raoul refuses to heed Alice and incinerates Marsent. The force of *compagnonnage*—straight up, as at the beginning, or inverted, as when Bernier revolts against Raoul—dominates male/female relations. Women, insistently represented, consistently lose out against the homosocial bond and its codes. Its violent dynamic overcomes even the most earnest seeker after peaceful settlements of disputes: Bernier, who repeatedly seeks peace by humbling himself before other Alpha males, himself turns into a pale reproduction of Raoul, impelled to violence before losing himself in the pilgrimage adventure of romance.

An essential (re)transformation occurs at the level of the Destinator. In a major shift from the *romans antiques*, for strategic and structural reasons, Chrétien's texts displace the figure of Arthur, appropriated with heroic refulgence from Geoffrey of Monmouth, reducing him to a secondary function after the vassalic protagonist, often as a figure of ridicule. The king's presence and its effects on the sociopolitical process are nonetheless insistent. It is not a nice or a flattering picture. Some of the late chanson de geste do show the effects of the increasingly "unified order" announced by the *Roland* that Philip II was laying: the institutionalization of kingship; centralization in Paris; and the king's increasing power vis-à-vis the feudal princes.[4] There is little trace, in the "Raoul" section composed at the *beginning* of Philip's reign, of the achievement of the *end* of his reign, more than forty years later. Nevertheless, the king's role is essential to the poem.

Raoul de Cambrai's dialectical reaction to its constitutive tradition denies earlier assumptions: the notion of a good or well-meaning king, or his evacuation from the narrative scene; the willing subordination of Thanatos to Eros; the courtly idealization of woman; the central narrative focus on a positively marked male hero.[5] Instead, the text asserts the harsh effects of royal power; the reinstated opposition of Eros and Thanatos; images of women, focused on this world, who are shrewd, savvy, and carnal and who nonetheless fail to impose their intelligence, understanding, and desire for peace on a male class segment still patriarchal, still violent, still dedicated to war; and finally—*Raoul* goes beyond *Roland* in this—the representation of male characters who, awesome in certain respects, are so flawed as to make the very notion of the "hero" ethically or politically absurd.

The bonds among the male actors are affective as well as economic and political, mediated by the fief. A historian finds half a dozen meanings to the "fief" in this text,[6] but Leupin has grasped its essential narrative ambiguity. Its instability results from its being regulated by two contradictory laws: inheritance by primogeniture, and the sovereign's right to invest a fief that has reverted to him,[7] laws that operate in both history and fiction. What this binarism does not address, however, is the expectation of justice, that the king's award of fiefs will recognize vassalic rights in discharging his right. In fact, royal malfeasance in granting fiefs initiates the disasters of the narrative, with an *agencement machinique* that perpetually rekindles feuds. Royal manipulations of fief are the precondition for Raoul's savagery and Bernier's revenge.

The text leaves no room for doubt: Louis's ill judgments and injustices are the political ground for the narrative's trajectory: first an injustice to Raoul, then another to the descendants of Herbert of Vermandois. Nevertheless, King Louis is not demonized. Each error, each injustice, is made comprehensible in context, as a response to political imperatives. However horrendous its effects, the initiating choice is rational, understandable, that of a human mistake, not a figure of evil incarnate.

All these injustices haunt their victims, iterated specters demanding the satisfaction of revenge. They set the two clans—those of Cambrai, with Raoul at its head, those of the Vermandois including Bernier—endlessly against each other. Spectrality haunts its hosts to the death, without relieving their vengeance of its ethical and political weight.[8] It neither lifts them from the horns of their dilemmas as subjects of contradiction, nor relieves any actor of a burdensome identity or his acts. On the contrary, spectrality haunts individuals precisely because of their identity, because of the fact that they continue as the actor who earlier committed this or that act. The logic of violence is not humane, but it is human, and subject to both ethical and political judgment.

Scenes of the devastation of war are an epic convention. Its agents are men, knightly combatants. The epic's constitutive problematic is male warrior violence. That is the genre's conventional norm. It is a mistake, however, to see the poem as exclusively concerned with the central relation of the chansons de geste, that between lords and vassals.[9] Excessive focus on genre obscures a text's narrative structure and meaning production.[10] *Raoul* introduces a countervailing element into this conventionality. The first major scene of devastation is part of Raoul's campaign to conquer the Vermandois as his newly awarded fief, which leads to the memorable conflagration of Origny at his order. Bernier's mother Marsent is abbess of a convent founded there in her honor by the sons of Herbert of Vermandois; she burns in the furnace of flames along with a hundred nuns.[11] The flames poured out the doors: no one could get as close to the flames as a javelin's cast. Alongside a great marble altar, Marsent is stretched out flat on the ground, her sweet face consumed by fire, on her breast the Psalter burning.

What is unusual about this singular occurrence is not the violence, but its close-up of one victim: the narration zooms in on Marsent and her anguished death. The later narrative exploits and reinforces our memory of the scene, by repeated back reference, in a spectral recurrence that turns the singularity of the event into a leitmotif resounding throughout the narrative.[12] Its repetitions define and affirm Bernier's identity and lead to his murderous revenge: trace, invagination, spectrality, all produce the narrative act. The deconstruction of identity produces an identification of the actor as subject, leaving him or her subject to judgment.

The fact that the victim is a woman is not accidental. The presence of women in this narrative has been amply noted. Their presence reminds one of romance, but they are not migrants from romance. Their number, their importance, the role they play, reveal *an influence* of romance, but the women's character and the character of the love that is narrated are something else. Béatrice, Guerri le Sor's daughter who marries Bernier, is a narrative world away from the ladies of romance: no false timidity, no hesitation in self-analysis, no problematization of dominance, none of the complexities and subtleties of *fin'amors* or courtly love: she assumes desire and sexuality unhesitatingly and with anticipation.[13] Meeting Bernier at her father's castle, she directly asks his name. She falls in love with the man dressed in silk and immediately calculates "how to get him," whispering to herself:

> Lucky the lady whom this man were to choose, for he has a
> tremendous reputation for knighthood; anyone who could hold him
> naked in her sheets would find him worth more than any living
> thing. . . . Anyone who was allowed to kiss and embrace him would
> find it better for her than meat and drink.

If she can manage it, she'll have "her arms around him by nightfall."[14] A bit later, she tells her father she wants a husband for her body's pleasure.[15] She rejoins the narrative functions separated in the *Yvain*, between Laudine as the site of desire and power and Lunete as the instrumental manipulator. She does so as a new feminine type, neither epic nor courtly, neither timid nor shy. On the contrary, she is a dialectical rejoinder to these oppositions.

That occurs in the second major part of the text, however, which may be a continuation dating from the later part of Philip II's reign. Those later parts of the text develop themes already present in the first, "Raoul" section. That contains no love interest comparable to Béatrice and Bernier, but it does field two female figures that are imposing in their own terms and who stage a particular relationship, that of mothers and sons. Has it been noted that this relationship is not only crucial to the "Raoul" section, but that it is redoubled there? Mothers and sons here have complicated relationships, as do the sons.

The female presence is established in the second laisse, which announces four major characters, including Lady Alice—*la gentil dame au gent cor avenant* (l. 38), emphasizing her nobility. She recurs in successive laisses.[16] Nor is her presence merely a matter of linear frequency. She performs a particular narrative function, the cognitive one of political sagacity. She recognizes, as her son Raoul does not, that King Louis's grant of the Vermandois is a dangerous trap: it will result in Raoul's own death. Her political understanding is prophetic. It is not that she had read the poem she occurs in ahead of time—as a poststructuralist turn might have had it—but that she grasped the king's political strategy of divide and conquer. She also demonstrates susceptibility to the same rage as her son when she pronounces a malediction. Warning Raoul of the danger the Vermandois grant represents, she adds rules of behavior: that he not destroy chapel or church, kill the poor, take booty, or pillage.[17] These are reminders of the Peace of God legislation and condemn Raoul in the reader's eyes retrospectively. He is enraged. Alice, rehearsing her services as his mother, curses him: "Let God who judges everything not bring you back safe and sound and in one piece!" She will regret immediately having pronounced the curse, but the malediction is pronounced. It correctly predicts Raoul's death at Bernier's hands. Similarly, the abbess Marsent shows courage and skill in negotiating a truce with Raoul, without recourse to any but moral force, as well as will and religious dedication in choosing not to escape from the abbey in flames. Both mothers are women of strength, courage, independence, political sagacity, able and ready to negotiate even from positions of weakness. Joining their representation to that of Béatrice, a new female *representamen* is being constructed.

Alice and Marsent resemble another mother, being written at about the same time: the mother in Chrétien's *Perceval*, who, at the beginning, voices a harsh critique of the very knighthood that is the object of her son's quest. Her condemnation shadows the entire text: if the mother's presence in the narrative is short, her absence remains present throughout Perceval's adventures and casts its spell on Gauvain's as well.[18] All three mothers are presented in binary opposition to knighthood, though in different ways. As Perceval's mother dies at grief at his departure, so Bernier's mother dies in grief at the hands of her son's lord—a fused fraternal and paternal figure.

The earlier account of the horrific scene of Marsent burning to death at Origny was incomplete. The text does not proceed only by "objective" narration of the event, though this would be normal narrative technique in both epic and romance. It introduces an observer on the scene, Marsent's own son, Bernier, vassal and companion of the feudal lord who orders the attack on the town. Bernier rushes up, sword in hand, only to be forced back by the intense heat, to watch his mother burn and die in the flames. There is a dual narrative object: the mother as victim of raging feudal violence, the son who watches her die helplessly, her killer's feudal vassal. The violence is observed and implicates the observer.

This was the most memorable scene for medieval audiences, who did not mystify mother-son relations.[19] Perhaps the blend of desire and fear, of envy and hatred, which infuses and culpabilizes the boy-mother relationship according to Melanie Klein,[20] is partly satisfied by the revenge Bernier will take. Has it been noticed that when he kills his lord Raoul, Bernier kills a father-figure in symbolic completion of the Oedipal triangle, an infraction whose culpability will haunt him the rest of the narrative? What the scene certainly establishes is the structure of the perspectival observer: the mother's son, who observes an inverted primal scene, integral to the narrative's ulterior trajectory.

Implication is not limited to Bernier. In staging so memorably the son's gaze on the dying mother, a shameful fact,[21] the text also inscribes the reader's own voyeuristic and epistemophilic gaze: as Bernier observes his mother, the reader observes Bernier observing his mother. The audience is implicated in his shame: the original medieval audience, and we ourselves. Readers perceive Marsent's torture both directly and as mediated by Bernier's torment: violence compounded by violation. The function of the perspectival observer is recursively reenacted by various narrative actors: not only Bernier observing his mother, but also mothers observing their sons err and judging their behavior. The poem stages submission to scopophilic desire repeatedly. With its aural equivalent for an oral audience, scopophilia is inevitable not only in cinema but also in literary communication: what is striking is its recursive staging in the text itself.

It is insufficient to consider Alice and Marsent narrative "material," as "motifs" or "themes." They perform a particular structural role, that of observer. Even as victims, they establish a "point of view," a "perspective" from which to view the narrative. De-idealized woman becomes the narrative observer and the judge of male violence. Her gaze is turned on the men whose violence kills, and sometimes kills the women themselves.

Readers are not forced to adopt their perspective: it is offered, a choice for the audience. Perhaps that's why it has been missed, or repressed.

Marsent's spectral trace works through to *Raoul*'s and Bernier's ends. The final haunted reference to Marsent's death occurs toward the end of the text, in a passage that fuses the work of memory, guilt, and moral indeterminacy. Bernier, beset in battle, prays:

> "Lord God, Father," said noble Bernier,
> "Never was I so fiercely attacked by any man.
> Some sin has caught up with me here;"

First he regrets having taken revenge on his lord:

> "I was mad in killing Raoul
> he reared me and made me a knight."

Then he reverses field to counter guilt:

> "Holy Mary, what have I said?
> He burned my mother in Origny church,
> he wanted to rob my uncles of their vast lands,
> he wanted to exile and shame my father
> how could I not kill Raoul?
> God judge me, if I acted in wrong."[22]

The indeterminacy of perspectivalism and the moral ambiguity of life under a hidden God are presented hauntingly. Bernier's identity is precisely to be the subject haunted by the moral indeterminacy.

Medieval perspectivalism is varied.[23] One technique is the introduction of allegorical figures, not as agents of the narrative action, but as interpretive signposts for the surrounding narrative diegesis. Another is discursive commentary by agents who function as interpreters of the narrative action. A third technique, the most important to *Raoul de Cambrai*, consists of simply implanting a character who does triple duty: as participant, as observer, and as commentator, representing not only a personal "take" on the action, but a *point* from which a narratee can *view* the action as it unfolds. The arrival of Blancandrin in Charlemagne's camp in laisse 8 of the *Roland* leads the text to pass in review the Frankish warriors according to recognizable class distinctions. In the *Perceval*, the mother's denunciation of knighthood provides a *perspective* from which to *view* the narrative as bearing far more complicated meanings than the narrative subject himself can grasp. In *Raoul*, female observers function as loyal spouses, but also as predictive commentator linking past and present, and as enunciators of negative sanction on male characters. The scopophilic sacrifice of a mother to the male nexus of politics-and-violence transcends its narrative frame to implicate the narratee, reverberating through the later narrative as a crux that offers a privileged optic from which to view the poem as a whole.

The perspectival structure itself is polyvalent. It may have some utility for a postmodern historiography. In fact, the process of adaptation has already begun. Jacques le Goff's monumental *St. Louis* (1996) limns a somewhat different image of the king according to each category of documents inscribing the king's figure. It presents a fragmented, and though Le Goff does not say so, an example of postmodern historiography. Another is Gabrielle Spiegel's *Romancing the Past* (1993), directly pertinent to *Raoul de Cambrai*.[24] Spiegel recounts Philip II's relentless manipulations of his relations to successive counts of Flanders as part of a general strategy of expanding the king's territory by weakening his vassals' hold on their own lands and annexing what he could, by hook or by crook, by peaceable means or warfare. His technique was time honored: destabilize the environment, undermine the nobility's autonomy, divide and conquer, sow conflict among opponents so as to weaken them. The king was pitted against Count Philip of Alsace. Between the two Philips, the "Vermandois Succession" was a central stake[25]—as in our poem—affecting marital strategies and financial resources. The intense struggle broke out into open hostilities, leading to the count's humiliation: he lost all practical authority over most of his county. By 1192, his lands were split five ways. By 1196, the king's maneuvers led practically the entire Flemish aristocracy to rebel. According to a contemporary chronicler, "There was scarcely any baron in this march of Flanders who was not against him." The violations of a hypothetical trust between king and subjects led to the violences of "open rebellion."

The intensity of the conflict was proportionate to the stakes. Flanders was one of the most successful of the twelfth-century principalities, with a solid economic basis in the transformation of raw materials from England into finished textiles for resale throughout Europe—especially at the fairs of Champagne—and a highly centralized node of state formation: its submission and acquisition was a major triumph for the king and helped finance his successful campaigns against his Angevin and Flemish rivals in 1204 and 1214: they were key to his ultimate triumph, which led to naming him "Philip Augustus."

Raoul de Cambrai does not show the initial institutionalization of the French state. What it shows instead is a king who misuses his right to award fiefs and arrange vassalic marriages in ways that sow discord and dissension among his vassals, plunging them into conflicts that deploy the constitutive characteristics of the aristocracy, not just in Flanders, but throughout France. What *Raoul* shows is a fictional royal strategy analogous to Philip II's divide-and-conquer technique, but seen from the opposite side, the reverse of the king's point of view. The poem is not narrated from the perspective of a wily, cunning, successfully centralizing kingship, or its idealization for that matter, but from the perspective of a subset of vassals who are its victims. The dreadful narrative is not the constructive side of state formation, but its deleterious effects on those who would have hoped to stand in its way so as to retain their independence precisely from that state. It is a counternarrative to the creation of statehood in France, the feudal narrative of a feudal class losing ground before the advances of the monarchical state.

The *Pseudo-Turpin* appropriated the monarchically inclined *Song of Roland* for the ideological purposes of the Flemish aristocracy against the king's hegemonic reach.[26] *Raoul de Cambrai* is a far more ambitious dialectical response to the sequence of twelfth-century vernacular textualities, revised and rebutted from the perspective of a complex, feudal subject position, decidedly noble, but incorporating both male and female points of view. It refracts the disintegrative effects of the king's divisive strategies, through the prism of local historical memories. As a contemporary chronicle puts it: "The virus of these past passions creeps still today in the men's viscera of the Vermandois and the Cambrésis."[27] The Flemish nobility is only a local metonym for a larger class in a "France" that is yet no more than a tentative ideologeme, a class fundamentally threatened by the expansions of monarchy. Those expansions transformed the chanson de geste from its earlier cultural dominance into the marginality of a "minor literature."[28] That problematic is what gives, not Aristotelian unity, but semiotic coherence to the poem's heterogeneities.

Neither textual narrative nor the narrative of history follows a simple, linear logic. Both are internally complex: they integrate heterogeneous instances. Different kinds of historiographical praxis are needed. One is a perspectival history, in which the perceptions and actions of specific groups, operating within the horizon of a social totality, are seen as relatively autonomous agents or subjects. The recent argument over whether the medieval period was or was not violent is not a tempest in a teacup— the major shape of medieval history is in question. But the resolution to the question will come not as a choice between the two terms of the binarism "violent versus nonviolent," nor simply as a delicate verbal compromise adjusting the two terms, but by a recognition that activities that seemed a profoundly objectionable violence to some segments of society, were a perfectly ordinary and appropriate performance of noble duties and entitlements to others.

PART II

GOVERNANCE

CHAPTER 8

Representation in State Governance I: Literacy

The birth of "the calculable man [dates from] that moment
when . . . a new technology of power and a new political
anatomy of the body were implemented in the formation of a
disciplinary society. . . . The individual is no doubt the fictitious
atom of an 'ideological' representation of society; but he is also a
reality fabricated by this specific technology of power that I have
called 'discipline.'"
Foucault, *Discipline and Punish*

T his chapter's goal is more modest than a synthesis of modern research. It suggests a model, in the recorded practices of the late twelfth and early thirteenth centuries, of those structures, practices, and processes that inscribe the state as the Other of this book's subject. The evidence for the practices of governance in England and France during the process of state formation is fragmentary, but touches key nerves. As governance is institutionalized through bureaucratization and administration (a questionable distinction), its dependency on literacy expands: literacy incites both governance and its evidence. But governance is not identical with the state. As Friedrich Engels noted, the state "has not existed from all eternity. There have been societies which have managed without it, which had no notion of the state or state power."[1] Tribal organization, or an empire that trades tribute for protection, is not a state. The state is a particular, historical form of governance, "a human community that (successfully) claims the *monopoly of the legitimate use of physical force* within a given territory," in Max Weber's classic definition.[2] In addition to force, the state also proceeds by ideology,[3] as well as by discipline. These—the state's prostheses—result from the size of the polity's territory, which imposes on the governed a relation of representation.

Size is integral to the state: size affects internal functioning. Its medieval beginnings require a partial shift of focus, to forms of governance smaller than what register as the "state" in modern codes. At all levels, however, the body politic was modularized, separated into discrete units by a process that resembles fragmentation but is in fact its opposite. War and finance were essential concerns, which required representative agents of control, organization, and profit extraction, as well as practices of general surveillance, and the control and accountability of the agents of representation. Discipline pierced even "private" life on landed estates. All these processes participate in complex subjectifications; they require subjects and produce them by the very activities that use and control them. Subjects are constituted by ideology, disciplines, and concrete practices: subjectivity is hypothetically a closed circle. Cracks and slippages occur, opening it to some degree of freedom.

That ideology inheres in fiction is readily understood today; discipline associates rather with claims of truth. Both model subjectivity and address the subject's imagination. "Ideology" indexes the political import of texts that hover between the truth and fiction, straddling the fence, marking a space of fluctuation between the two: both may inhere in the same text, in various ways and in different proportions. Both served the voracious medieval hunger for domination (*dominium*) that percolated at all levels, from the lowliest chatelain to the highest prince, in town as well as country. Its concrete historical forms and institutionalizations were only exceptionally theorized before Aquinas. Most Latin discourse regarding governance is framed by moral and theological problematics that little hampered the practice of medieval princes. John of Salisbury's *Policraticus* legitimizes tyrannicide, but along with other contemporary theorists disregards the burgeoning bureaucracy.[4] Although religious problematics and a classicizing style obscure the import of his work, its theoretical importance and its influence on Machiavelli are underestimated by modernist scholars.[5] But its registration of political and economic processes is cast in a complex paradigm that does not answer fully to the historical processes instantiated by other documents.[6] Men at court talked politics, economics, finance, weighing persons and policy alternatives, structuring social processes and institutions in ways that manipulated the social realities they governed. Their talk and thought went mostly unrecorded. Governmental secrecy was as prized in the twelfth century as in the twentieth. Beyond that, those with the requisite intellectual training had been cast as theoretical subjects in an episteme of moralo-theological values rather than political practices. Praxis did not find adequate accounting in discourse. Clerics invested their reflections on government with "intellectual generality" more than administrative detail.[7] With one major exception (Machiavelli), we do not have a medieval theory of the praxis of medieval politics.[8] The description and history of medieval politics cannot be made in purely medieval terms, since these are lacking. This history cannot be historicist, in the narrow sense.

The Principality

Governance in the twelfth century is exercised at two major levels beyond the local: the principality and the nascent state. A handful of medieval principalities survive as curiosities, thanks to their diminutive size: Monaco, Andorra, Liechtenstein, and Luxembourg are the quaint survivors of an earlier scale of political organization. As central power first disintegrated and later reconstructed itself in new forms, the principalities were a major locus of governance.[9] They came into existence in various ways. Some devolved from the disintegration of centralized Carolingian power, as its regional representatives assumed effective power directly.[10] Others were cobbled together by the combination of previously independent castellanies, like the Bourbon principality of imposing progeny, whose founders raised themselves from local lordships.[11] Champagne resulted from the sudden accession of Eudes II in the early eleventh century to the counties of Troyes and Meaux on the death of a young cousin. The resulting agglomeration of counties, churches, and domains possessed no unity other than the person of Eudes himself; he came to be known as "le Champenois."[12]

The noun "France" was one of uncertain content, referring ambiguously both to the king's principality, the small Ile-de-France, and to a larger, vaguer entity in which the king wielded little effective power. The former was a mere 2,600 square miles, one-eighteenth the size of modern France: half the size of Connecticut.[13] In ordinary usage, "France" bore the more restricted meaning: the king's own principality. By the twelfth century, it was surrounded by more powerful principalities: Anjou, Normandy, Flanders, and Blois-Champagne. Royal strategy was to prevent alliances by these powers against the king. Farther off lay Britanny, Burgundy, Aquitaine, Gascony, and Toulouse.[14] England was the product of early European colonialism after 1066, an offshoot of the Norman principality.

The principality was ruled by a "prince," the Machiavellian figure; the term appears much earlier, in John of Salisbury's *Policraticus*, and even in the Carolingian period. It applied to the king, as well as to the counts or dukes who ruled principalities like kings. *Principatus* derives from *princeps*, a compound of *primus* and *capio*: he who takes first place as the head. The essential characteristic of the prince is that he is first, the leader or chieftain. The term was used of any man of importance, even the leader of a robber band.[15] He is "first citizen": no one precedes him, no one is above him; he exercises sovereignty. Later, the notion of the "prince" would transcend the concrete individual. In the late sixteenth century, the prince was defined as that "organism governing the state, whether it be one of many persons, a few citizens or all."[16]

It is in this functional sense, of the prince as sovereign, one who commands and governs without an effective superior, that the term appears in the *Policraticus*. Referring to emperors and kings as well as officials of lower jurisdictions, including ecclesiastics, *princeps* denotes a function, not an absolute rank. In the vernacular, it is rare: terms such as count or duke, seigneur and baron, are used. Beaumanoir uses *baronnie* as a synonym for principality. Rather than a manner or form of government, *principatus* stresses primary authority, the fact of sovereignty, a governance submitted to only theoretical superiors.[17] Such claims implied competition with the king. The count of Anjou asserts the autonomy of his principality as against the king's authority, just as he claims quasi-royal power.[18]

Machiavelli in the Twelfth Century

Paradoxically, the theory of the principality's governance was elaborated only after the principalities had passed their peak in France, when their incorporation into the state was already well under way. There, they were an active part of history; in Italy, they still promised hope. Machiavelli's *Prince* is usually taken as a meld of abstract theory and classical reference to theorize cynically realistic statecraft, a miraculous work of individual genius at the threshold of modernity, signaling a radical break and the "Renaissance." This historiography is obnubilated by the ideology of individualism that cleaves to it as a vampire. Without detracting from his brilliance, Machiavelli allows for a different reading, less miraculous, more comprehensible. Citing Dante, that knowledge depends on retention of past learning, he asserts that his work on principalities should interest especially a new ruler.[19] Special attention is paid to issues facing the new ruler of a new principality, lacking the prior structures, political and mental, that frame political practices. It does not detract from Machiavelli's stature if, in addition to being deeply grounded in classical history and the "first theoretician of conjuncture,"[20] he is read as reflecting on the practices of the historical past: the medieval past.

Machiavelli compared the Italian present, its uncertain opening on an undefined future, to the accomplishments of a neighboring state that had seemingly resolved some of the problems of nascent statehood. France was a composite kingdom produced by earlier annexations of principalities: Burgundy, Brittany, Gascony, and Normandy.[21] It was "one of the best-ordered and best-governed modern kingdoms," among whose "countless good institutions" was Parliament, restraining the arrogance of the nobility and favoring the people.[22] *The Prince* was about the statecraft appropriate to the principality.

Before being a manual for the cynical statecraft of Europe's future, this work was a theoretical reflection on Europe's medieval past.[23] In its identification of the state with the prince's public personality, it answers to medieval practice in the most frequent medieval polity: not the empire, not the "nation-state," but the principality. This most famous and ill-reputed work of political theory is regularly mistitled by modern editors. In the manuscripts, its title is not *De Principe*, which could mean *Of the Governor or Ruler*, but *De principatibus: Of Principalities*.[24] That is how Machiavelli himself refers to it in his letter to Francesco Vettori: "my treatise on principalities."[25] If medieval theory consists in a centuries-long effort to establish a moral discipline of governance *against* the practice of *dominium*, that may be because the latter was, not in theory but in cold, hard facts, very much what the medieval prince faced and practiced. Like the Machiavellian prince, the medieval ruler of a principality faced a world constituted neither by morality nor by established rules of governance. It was a frequently chaotic world in which power did not automatically devolve from a post or a role, but had to be constructed, husbanded, and preserved.[26] Machiavelli, studying the practices both of the near and distant pasts, deploys an attitude and a method of reading the discourse of *historia* far closer to medieval practices than to the modern,[27] in order to grasp the specificities of governance as the manipulation of power outside the paradigms of moral theology. That specificity is essential to grasping the political and administrative evolution of the twelfth century. In France, before the king found his kingdom in the concept of the regnum, governance preceded the state at the level of the principality.[28]

The principalities do not look like modern states; they do not operate at the scale of modern states, hence the difficulty the modern gaze has in recognizing them as states. They were an administrable polity of a size appropriate to the initial phase of the recentralization of power after the castellans' revolution of the late tenth and early eleventh centuries. Smaller than modern states, principalities nevertheless rediscovered, established, and imposed the essential parameters of statehood: territorial definition, a relative control of violence, internal bureaucratic organization, the development of "police" oriented toward the general welfare of the *res publica*, and "foreign" policies that included the encouragement and protection of commercial exchanges. Like later rulers, princes were concerned with the creation of governable populations, integrated in a totalized polity: "It is not the well-being of individuals that makes cities great, but the well-being of the community."[29] It is at the reduced geographical proportions then available that these parameters of statehood developed. Within determined territories, princes acted like kings in their own realms. Their principalities were "statelets."[30]

The two levels of governance, principality and state, were porous. Both England and France became states after being a principality (the Ile-de-France) or the colonial offshoot of one (Anglo-Norman England). These two levels were ruled by men whose marriages connected them with large, marital, and informational networks. Techniques and procedures migrated rapidly across territorial boundaries and political levels. The avidity for power/knowledge was immeasurable. The same constitutive dimension of territorial space, the resulting mediated structuration of governance, its internal coherence, countered the distinction between principality and state, clearer to historical hindsight than to twelfth-century politicos or theoreticians. The rulers of principalities acted like kings within their own domains: they were, after all, "princes."

The major principalities shared one trait with each other and with the state: size sharply differentiated them from the feudal *châtellenie*. There, the chieftain of the fortress lived in the presence of his warrior knights and could dispense justice to the population he ruled. The size of principalities precluded a permanent face-to-face relation with vassals and subject populations as the basis of governance. Early rulers responded with peripatetic, itinerant courts that brought the sovereign into periodic contact with vassals, enabling rulers to live off their dues in vassals' residences according to a traditional hospitality that bracketed the binarism Derrida unexpectedly tries to save, of gifts and exchanges[31]—a perambulatory rulership that proved inadequate.

The principalities incorporate the rule of a territory whose size, though imprecise in delimiting geographical frontiers, precluded rule by the ruler's direct and personal presence to the governed, even though governance was identified with the ruler's person: a fortiori the eventual state.[32] In the principality, as well as in the newly colonized space of England, the new spatial dimensionality that defines the modern state was determinative. It separated ruler and subject populations with a distance that defines the state as a state of absence. Expanded territories, too large and complex for itinerant rulership, came to be ruled from a mobile central point, defined by the physical presence of the prince and his itinerant court. A new mode of governance developed in which continuous rule of expanding territories from a central point was added to rule by itinerancy. Power in absence was the new mode of governance in the principality. That had been true, of course, of the Roman Empire, its Carolingian version, and the papacy. But circumstances, responses to space, and the quantitative suffusion of that space differed. This spatial dimension led to the invention of and reliance on new modes of information and control—defining elements of the new state. Present states represent developments of eleventh- and twelfth-century beginnings.

Semiotic Mediations in Representational Governance

Because of its new dimensions, power was exercised mediately. Presence in absence is the domain of the sign and representation. Representation can be defined as "the maintenance of presence by the mediation of the envoy," a definition equally functional in diplomacy, semiotics, and religion. The fact that it adapts a formulation of Bruno Latour's notion of transcendence[33] signals the identity of the process of political representation with that of religious transcendence: What else are Moses and Jesus but envoys or signs mediating God's absence? Hence the simultaneous congruence and competition of religion and secular power, both constituted by the same process. Another perspective might be that humanity divinizes its processing of political power by attributing it to God. Nascent Christianity's (re)claiming of the process would then be derivative of the Roman Empire's empire over known civilization. As against the immediate physical presence of the castellan (however deceptive such corporeal presence proves), state governance, to be effective in the absence of the source of authority and legitimacy, depended on the complex function of the *lieu-tenant*, one who holds a particular place (of power) in the absence of another, one who holds that other's place. It is on this possibility of governance in absence, making power permanently present in spite of the sovereign's physical absence, that the twelfth century capitalized, (re)inventing a form of governance, different from the face-to-face polity of the Greek polis, the face-to-face *dominium* of the fortress, and the tributary distances of the Roman Empire. This new form of governance was not elaborated for the sake of a nation-state that did not yet exist. It took shape as a practical orientation toward solving immediate political problems. We still live in its aporetic constructions, in the era of fictional simulacra and representative government. Power was projected across distances that precluded the physical presence of the sovereign by representation. The *lieu-tenant*'s projection of the absent power of the Subject *is* representation, sans elections. The medieval principality and the later form of state that the Middle Ages constructs hinge on the elemental function of the sign, making present a signified that is itself absent. To distinguish it from the electoral government typical of modern democratic states, call it "representational governance," as opposed to "representative government." In its multiple forms, medieval governance, like the modern, constructed itself on a regime that combined representation with force. The necessities of distantiated governance make of the state a violent semiotic state.

The requisite *representamina* took two primary forms: human and nonhuman. The first were *lieu-tenants*, the agents of power. Man is a sign, *dixit* C. S. Peirce. Agents were both signs of an absent power and powers themselves. They were the first "subjects," submitted *and* empowered. The nonhuman are texts, collocated signs of men that are not men themselves: texts of power, literacy, and numeracy, performative representations. Literacy, to modernity, is a cultural matter. In medieval culture, it was political, an instrument of governance.[34] Its signs include the ideological representations we call "literature": they too were signs and representations of power, texts in a fuller and more dangerous sense than the exsanguinated usage of modernism. Complex, polyvalent, and aporetic, their ideological charge remains largely unmeasured. Oddly enough, that is equally true of governmental documents. Many exceed their functions as goal-oriented representations. Representation, in the means available to humanity, is inherently unreliable, with a large, inescapable quotient of indeterminacy. That is why, in spite of gross differences between fiction and a charter, for instance, a governmental survey resembles a charter as a historical document resembles fiction.

Michel Foucault differentiated feudalism, governed by laws of reciprocity, from the twelfth and thirteenth centuries' administrative state, with its principles of regulation and discipline defined territorially, and from the modern state, focused on population instead of territory; he placed the first explosion of government in the sixteenth century.[35] History "on the ground" was not so schematic: elements of all three forms of governmentality were active in the twelfth century, in the initial explosion of governance that begins modernity. The governance of political economy implies both the extraction of surplus value from the subject population and a certain solicitude for its welfare. Both require information. Surveillance and control are the business of police, in the modern sense. "Police" in the seventeenth- and eighteenth-century sense is not restricted to the enforcement of laws. It is identical with "the science of government," with "the science of happiness," and, I would add, with a cultural politics: "sciences, education, good order, security and public tranquility" are its objects.[36] "Police" was the orientation of the state toward the welfare of its population as a whole. Sovereignty, discipline, and governance aim at the population: the police is its "essential mechanism."[37]

In spite of his critiques of humanism and Marxism, and a focus on the disciplinary practices by which "civilization" "normalizes" people, a utopian strain suffuses Foucault's historiography of the state. The rhetorical topos of the golden age undergirds his text: an older, solicitudinous pastoralism provides an implicit, contrastive critique of carceral contemporaneity. There is also a methodological fault, inherent in a purely discursive methodology eager to differentiate itself from the Marxist tradition. It consists of addressing theoretical/ideological discourse without inquiry into its relation to practice. One loss of certain forms of "theory" was the possibility of calling an assertion a lie, a possibility based on the comparison of language with a referential other. Acknowledgment of the profound, constitutive ambiguity of the state, medieval and modern, is required: the state has become both the necessary vehicle for large-scale ameliorations of human life, such as peace and general welfare, and a major source of cruel oppression and devastation.

Modularization

The spatial dimension of the new polities required their systematic subdivision. Modularization, characteristic of modernist design, architecture, and painting, was fundamental to medieval civilization. Erwin Panofsky pointed to modular construction in gothic art and scholasticism, a view confirmed by examination of a single architectural site and expanded to a far more comprehensive conceptualization of medieval architecture.[38] It was a basic technique of novelistic construction.[39] It also characterized political and administrative practices, as revealed in the "police" of one principality particularly noted for its commercial role.

An early expression of the state's ambiguous solicitude was the commercial policy of the counts of Champagne. Agricultural production in Europe, the production of wool in England, its weaving in Flanders, the cutting of timber forests in the north of Europe, the weaving of silks around the Mediterranean, the harvesting of spices and the production of armaments and horses in the Near East, all produced commodities to be exchanged. From Russia and the Scandinavian countries in the north, from England and Flanders in the west, from Spain and Italy in the south, from distant countries of the Near East, sometimes relaying products from China, merchants brought wares or samples for the international trade that formed the apex of the European exchange-system to the markets of northern France. One was the king's Lendit Fair outside of Paris. More important were the year-round fairs in the towns of Champagne.

Most had as origins local or regional fairs, but underwent major expansion in midcentury, to become "the basic economic fact of the western world."[40] With two fairs annually at Troyes and Provins, and one each at Lagny and Bar-sur-Aube, a merchant could find a site for selling and buying commodities, for bargaining and exchanging monies, in Champagne at any moment of the year.

Each fair was a relatively autonomous, six-week module, defining annual temporality commercially:

Lagny: January, February
Bar-sur-Aube: March, April, May (beginning)
Provins: May (end), June, July (beginning)
Troyes: July, August
Provins: September, October
Troyes: November, December

Each fair was internally structured by a set sequence of temporal modules, identified by different commodities and commercial processes:

1. Entry period
2. Cloth sale
3. Leather sale
4. Financial settlements.[41]

Time and exchange were structured by modularization.

The organization of commercial exchange was more than encouraged by the counts of Champagne. A number of requisite conditions were objects of comitial attention. Medieval coinage, issued by multiple local lords, varied enormously in value, reliability, and availability. A coinage of sterling quality was required as monetary standard for international exchange. The count of Champagne issued the famed *provinois*, which came to be respected throughout Europe for consistency and value. It was the currency of reference in the count's markets, where coins from all over the known world were traded by money changers sitting at simple wooden tables. The flow of monies and goods required protective policing, especially during the final period, when books were balanced and all financial accounts, deferred until the end, were settled. Policing was provided and overseen by Wardens appointed by the count; their reputation stretched across the continent. Finally, the growing fairs spawned profitable subsidiary institutions, such as hotels for transient merchants, categorized by national origin.

External policing was trickier. Travel was not secure. Brigands, unemployed mercenaries, haunted the forests. Merchants on the way to and from the fairs risked life and goods. A travel document—the *conductus*—was developed as a pass, guaranteeing protection of the merchant and his goods to and from the fairs: it enjoyed a continental reputation. The count's power guaranteed the safety of merchants and their caravans. When a merchant on his way to Champagne was robbed while crossing the king's demesne, the count wrote the Abbot Suger to obtain financial settlement for "his" merchant. In effect, the count became the diplomatic representative of the merchants who patronized "his" fairs, even when they were outside his principality. It was profitable for all concerned. The French nobility was never unconcerned with money and profits: participants in fairs were to be protected as major sources of income, for the sake of the principality's population and its prince.

The transformation of regional markets in Champagne into international fairs and their extraordinary success was neither accidental nor "organic." It depended on the prince's will and power.[42] The fairs' schedules, locations, structures, and sustaining practices were directed by the count for the benefit of his population, his vassals, and himself. In an early form of mercantilism that married aristocracy with the profits of commerce, the count relocated some fairs, established subsidiary contracts with local institutions, splitting the profits with them. He used the fairs strategically to compete with the king's fair of Lendit which Suger wanted to develop, even at the cost of blocking the development of fairs elsewhere in Champagne.[43] His policies fused concern for the welfare of subjects enriched by commercial activity, a sophisticated politics of population welfare, and self-interest. "His" fairs were not only "the most noteworthy and commercially the most important in medieval Europe"; they formed "the center of commercial activity of the western world."[44] That was not the blind workings of economic history. The counts' consistent policies demonstrate a sharp understanding of the interrelationship of sovereignty, economics, and security: of "police." Sales taxes on goods, other taxes on money exchanges, shared organization of services like the hotels for foreign merchants built by local ecclesiastical establishments together with the count, and numberless other techniques of extracting secondary and tertiary profits from the commercial exchanges of the fairs, secured the fusion of ideology and crass self-interest: their profits were substantial. As with feudalism, justice and financial punishments were profitable. Henri the Liberal contracted with the monks of Saint Ayoul in Provins to share the profits of justice: the monks would retain three-quarters of the profits, the count generously reserving only one-quarter for himself.[45]

Surveyance

Mercantilism is only the most obvious aspect of a developing political economy. An essential component of the new governance is the cognitive machinery set in place to feed the informational thirst of the drive for centralized totalization. The count of Champagne had begun to take a global view of his lands;[46] that vision required information.

Nothing is more characteristic of late modernity than awareness of incessant surveillance.[47] The postmodern state and its late-capitalist civilization enforce a regime of fragmentary existence on its subjects while subjecting them to totalizing surveys of behavior and habits. The accumulation of huge banks of information on the population as a totality and on each individual in particular, legitimates a generalized, empirically justified paranoia. Surveillance in the twelfth century was less efficient. It lacked the clusters of radio and television towers that service power centers such as Los Angeles and Merida, projecting discipline and law enforcement to surrounding regions. It did not account for individuals uniformly, as do modern taxation and polls. It focused on the social modules of specific collective units for war and finance. Of special concern were the estimates of surplus value and military resources. In spite of substantial differences from the modern, "surveillance and control" was practiced by agencies of medieval governance. Even the technique characteristic of late modernity's information gathering was widely used. Its deployment peaked at a particular moment that marked a historical crux, during the third-quarter of the century. Taking a slight linguistic liberty, I refer to a form of control as *surveyance*: surveys, formulated at court, were implemented in the field by agents of power. They are representations, like contemporary "fictional" texts.

Governmental and estate surveys were not new.[48] Surveys since the Carolingian period project the paradigm of "modern" social science: the numeralized, supposedly "objective" representation of modularized social reality, serves to manipulate it in the interests of power, implementing narrative programs of governance. Their techniques were never completely lost or forgotten. But their rise to eminence, their sudden multiplication at a specific point in history, suggest that they responded to a new need: surveys had become crucial to governance. If numeracy had its origin in commerce and the international banking practices of the "money changers" of Lombardy and the Levant, its techniques were quickly adapted by government for the interdependent purposes of war and taxation: the governmental numbering enterprises of the central middle ages, from Domesday on, owed part of their origin to "some ruler's desire to sponge up liquidity."[49] Surveys implemented a politics of cognition and manipulation, equally apt for violent warfare and economic expansion. They became a form of normalized relations between the state and its subjects. Their subject was not yet a citizen-consumer. Nevertheless, he was subject to *surveillance*: "a watch kept over a person, etc., esp. over a suspect, a prisoner, or the like."[50] Like Althusser's subject, the twelfth-century subject lived on the receiving end of the state's interpellation.

The great ancestor of the genre is *Domesday Book*. No comparable survey was undertaken in the Middle Ages. Other surveys, less monumental, have their own interest, however. Several dealt with the connection of state and warfare, seeking to determine the prince's exact military resources. The earliest known survey of knight service came from Norman Italy, at mid-century (1149–50).[51] But since it was England that pushed state structures to their utmost development, we start with English and Anglo-Norman surveys. The first date from the early twelfth century: insofar as such distinctions are valid, surveyance first occurs as a "private" manorial activity, before central government adapts it.[52] That second step occurs exactly a century after the Norman invasion. In 1166, Henry II undertook a military survey, the first "fully *comprehensive* survey of knightly enfeoffments."[53] The *Cartae baronum* of 1166 asks the question: How many knights are available, in all and from each of the king's major fief-holders?[54] Epics claim that tens of thousands of warriors fight and fall in battles; the survey's figures are more modest. The 1166 survey lists a total of 7,525 knights in 313 entries. Each entry is a subsidiary module, differentiated from the others by geography and by its available military force. Many barons owe only their own service. Of the more powerful, only two claim more than 200 knights: Cornwall and Gloucester. A dozen number between 100 and 200 knights. The religious house with the most knights is Peterborough, with 63.83 knights.[55]

The *Cartae baronum*'s importance is dual. English knighthood operated under the system of scutage, a term with two etymons: *scutum* (shield) and *skot* (contribution, the individual share of a bill). The pun makes the point: money payments could replace the actual service of knights, making the connection of finance and war pellucid. The survey's information was bivalent. The commutation of military service and money made each the other's signifier. This systematic commutability, however, undermined the ideology of knighthood, lending "an air of unreality to the whole system of tenure by military service" known as vassalism.[56] Before Marx, the cash nexus undermined the cohesion of the dominant class and its "feudal" political system. That will shock only to those who credited the nobility's claim to disinterestedness: in fact, the feudals' seigneury constituted a violent, noneconomic mode of economic exploitation. Even its castles were an early form of capital investment.[57] Beyond that, the survey of 1166 has political importance. Not only did it secure oaths of the knights' allegiance to the king before his planned departure from England, it also marks the beginning of a new period in English feudalism. It asserted the principle of the king's claim to the allegiance of knights, even when these were subordinate to intermediary lords.[58] The state established its preeminence over the feudal system, employing the feudal tie itself to undermine feudalism.[59]

In 1172, pursuant to ducal writ, a comparable survey was undertaken in Normandy: the *Infeudationes militum*. The *Cartae baronum* had surveyed military England in writing. In the Norman case, major barons assembled at Caen in person and were required to state before justiciars how many knights each owed the duke's service and how many knights each had in his own service. After the assembly, the information was deposited at the Norman treasury in Caen. Those attending numbered 1,846, a figure that probably represents only about three-quarters of the Norman enfeoffment: the real total was perhaps closer to 2,500—numbers comparable to the knights under the command of other princes. The survey showed that the duke could claim the services of about 600 knights.[60] The bishop of Bayeux had the largest number, 120; he owed the duke the service of 20. Again, few barons had more than 100 knights. Alençon had 111, owing the duke 20; Giffard 103, owing the duke none; Tancarville had fewer than 95 knights, owing the service of only 10. As in England, the numbers are small; many holdings owed only 1 knight's service or less: the landholder himself or his purchased replacement.[61] Each knight was a unit of military violence, bearing a heraldic banner and a mounted dollar sign. The representations of the *Cartae baronum* of 1166 and the *Infeodationes* of 1172 demonstrate the fusion of military and financial values in representation.

English administrative practices have been the most extensively studied, but the Continent serves up analogous representations. Catalonia's efforts are more systematic. A survey was commissioned in 1150 and carried out the following year by Bertran de Castellet, a knight who traversed the domains accompanied by a scribe, convoking and interviewing local notables and bailiffs, recording their declarations under oath. The survey was complete, extending beyond the central domains into their peripheries; it ignored only the count's urban holdings.[62] Around 1150 as well, Roger II, the Norman king of Sicily, undertook a survey of his feudal resources, all those who could contribute to his defense, those who merely held property in his domain, and those who owed military service: the *Catalogus baronum*, compiled from declarations of tenants. The original was updated by Roger's successor in 1167–68, with additional information drawn from royal chamberlains and constables. It catalogues 1,400 men who responded; the entries are arranged according to constabularies, counties, or other great lordships throughout Norman Italy.[63]

In 1172, the same year as the Norman survey, a similar census was drawn up in Champagne. It is more than a symbolic accident that, at the very same court where the fantastic adventures of Arthurian knights appear in fictions whose representations both idealize noble life and offer its critique, another mode of discourse and another kind of textuality occurs within the same temporal frame. Although in the Latin of officialdom, it addresses similar facts of secular noble life. The document is the *Foeda campanie* (The fiefs of Champagne), the first list of feudal vassals drawn up for a French secular lord to survive. It details the count's fief-holders, their fiefs, and the military obligations they owed the count.[64] Together with the other surveys, its very existence marks a major cultural and sociopolitical phenomenon of historical importance. Such a list exists in Latin only as the result of a process, analogous to the texts we call "literary." A cleric, in the count's service, trained in Latin and the technologies of writing that define medieval "literacy," produced the list, as the adjuvant of a narrative Subject desirous of that object, perhaps as a celebration of power, but also for its instrumental uses. Producing the *Foeda* was an instrumental narrative program, subordinate to the desire for an ulterior object of Value. The list stands for, and is a way station on the road toward, some other object of value.

Lists are associated with the earliest forms of writing; they are characteristic of early "literature." Some of the earliest lists are not "literary," but administrative, commercial, and political.[65] Writing, of lists and other sorts of documents, is more than a useful tool; it becomes a necessary means in the elaboration of a certain kind of polity.[66] The list marks the accession, not only of a certain class to new forms of power and to new desires, but also of a well-established class of men, the great barons who were "princes," to a certain kind of self-consciousness, which cast their principality as an object of cognition separate from their selves. The surveys recognize the principality as a domain of organizable resources. Beyond a celebratory function, the new, somewhat strange object of desire—the list of vassals— also envisaged pragmatic effects. In spite of obvious differences, the *Foeda Campanie* and the contemporary romances of Chrétien de Troyes incorporate and signify an identical, complex phenomenon in different ways. Both propose a coherent representation of a relative totality, a totality that cannot simply be labeled and written off as "the County of the Count of Champagne," merely the referent of the *Foeda*. Both texts announce and bring something new, a feature that marks the civilization we inherit from the Middle Ages.

The represented totality is coherent, as is the text that represents it, first of all, in being constituted by the bond of vassalism. It is constituted in and by the relation of domination and subordination. It totalizes the fief-holders of the count of Champagne, some 1,900 of them—a number close to that of the contemporary Norman survey. It systematically specifies the degree of each fief-holder's allegiance to the count and the amount of military service owed him. All persons listed in the *Foeda* owed military service, but only about 41 percent owed castle-duty: the others apparently owed service only in case of outright, major military hostilities. The *Foeda* is also systematic in that its registers do not merely list the fief-holders helter-skelter, or according to some meaningless principle of textual organization such as the alphabetical. Instead, fief-holders were assigned for administrative purposes to specific castellanies and were listed accordingly. Twenty-six such castellanies were dependent on the count of Champagne in 1172. A hierarchical organization of the County of Champagne thus details the allegiance and services of nearly 2,000 mounted warriors for administrative purposes through the intermediary step of the castellanies, in spite of the fact that not all the knights were dependents and fief-holders of the count. Even the great private lordships of the area, not actually within the count's castellanies, were nevertheless attached to them for administrative purposes.[67] The force of the administrative hierarchy that relayed the will of the count overrode the principle of feudal independence.

The *Foeda* not only represents a totality, but a totality that is a complex whole, including differentiated and relatively autonomous subunits subject to intermediary principles of organization: its modules. This description of totality fits the text of romance as well, which also represents the diegesis of a differentiated social totality, according to a complex system of modular subordinations. The novel's episodes are more subtle, more finely tuned and analytic than those of the *Foeda*—as well as more enjoyable to read! Although focused on the nobility, it includes elements of the population disregarded by the survey, such as women, hermits, shepherds, and weavers. It also fields differentiated social units—the noble family and household—and the functions of economic production and distributive justice. It is more comprehensive, examining the effect of ideology on the subject, who traverses the totality of secular social instances in the diegetic universe of his narrative.

Survey and romance clearly comprise important differences, linguistic, formal, and discursive. But they share essential characteristics. Both represent; both represent a social order; both represent the same social order and its values, and do so at the same time; the same segment of the social order is primary, the dominant noble class, reaching for the administration of society as a whole. That social class is itself segmented by successive levels of hierarchy. Both organize their representation in the modularizations of castellanies and episodes. Thus, this description covers both the text of "high culture," the "literary" work of art, and that which belongs to a historical political anthropology, the instrumental document of power and finance. It traverses different levels of culture, different epistemic disciplines and institutions. The two contemporary texts were both produced under cultural conditions of restricted literacy, at the same court, perhaps by the same personnel: there is no reason to exclude the novelist from the chancellery that organized and carried out the survey, as there is no way to demonstrate that he took part in it. Another writer, the contemporary *trouvère* Gautier d'Arras, was a political administrator close to Philippe d'Alsace and Thibaut of Champagne, to Marie de Hainaut, Isabelle of Vermandois and Marguerite of Flanders, who spent time at the courts of Louis VII and Frédéric Barbarossa. He figures in sixty acts datable between 1160 and 1186.[68] Cultural, political, and bureaucratic functions were not rigorously exclusive. The same individual—the writer as bureaucrat—could mentally migrate and manipulate two orders of discourse belonging to different languages, different modes of textuality, and different cultures. Once the difference between novel and survey is acknowledged, their complex identity can be seen. They are each other's interpretants, differentiated representations, each a version of the real, on the interplay of which a representation of reality can be constructed as a Real—understanding that such reality is always a conflicting construct, never a unary given, and always a hypothesis.

These surveys represent relative totalizations: they represent a specific part of the body politic, its warrior elite, from the totalizing perspective of a superior power, count, duke, or king. The French monarchy undertakes its first systematic census of all the fiefs in the kingdom, noting the services due by each individual, during the reign of Philip Augustus.[69] The king is the Subject of the *surveyance*; the knights are its subject in the sense of topic. Their value or meaning is fungible, equally military and financial. This complex, partial totality implies a conceptualization of the body politic in the relative autonomy of its parts. They are autonomous, but only insofar as they relate to each other in the totality of the prince's perspective. Their textuality is essentially utilitarian, "an instrument of seigneurial control . . . over men."[70]

Etienne de Fougères: The Book of Social Categories

Surveys and romances establish relative totalities: the totality of a particular quadrant of society. The task of comprehensive social totalization was not abandoned. It was pursued by verbal rather than numerical means, starting with the traditional categories of the three orders.[71] Originally a reassertion of episcopal privilege and power as against the violent irruption of the low-level nobility, it became the most durable sociology of the Middle Ages, enduring until the French Revolution.[72] The first vernacular "estates" text was written by Etienne de Fougères, a distinguished official of the chancellery of Henry II Plantagenet, collaborator of Thomas Becket and Geoffrey Ridel, whose career led to the bishopric of Rennes. The *Livre des manières* dates from his episcopate, 1174–78.[73] The first text of its kind, it was not the last: at least ten more survive.[74] The bishop unhesitatingly casts himself as lawgiver, with the customary disdain for the values of this world, and formulates moral and behavioral rules for all segments of society, excepting monks. Imposing discipline on lay society, he adopts the vernacular in its marked discourse, verse in monorhymed octosyllabic quatrains. The treatise partakes of three discourses: the moral epistle, sociological analysis, and "literature."

The author belongs to a privileged elite sustained by the peasantry:

> We must cherish our men,
> For villeins bear the burden
> From which we live, whatever our status,
> Knights, clerics, and ladies,[75]

and sketches the ideology of the three orders:

> Clerics pray for all,
> knights unhesitatingly
> fight for honor
> and the peasants labor.[76]

Even this early in estates literature, however, the totalizing division of society into three orders is deconstructed by additional categories. After the clerics, knights, and peasants, further sections on burghers and women appear to adjust ideological conventions to incorporate new social realities.[77]

The order of discourse constitutes social reality as its Other and reacts to it as if it were another text in an intertextual relation. The bishop ends by confessing his own sins, an exemplary Everyman on the way to a universal prayer for God's mercy, entered into a colophon that bears the simulacral "signature" of *mestre Esteinvre de Fougieres*.

This text's literacy is not functionalized by direct military or financial utility. The totalizing representation of its sociological analysis provides a moral mirror to all on the way to individual salvation. The "signature" inscribes the author's subject position: he is a *mestre, magister* (teacher) and master who insists on the sanctity of tithes and the preeminence of clergy among the three orders. If this "Book of Social Categories" is not, like the numerical surveys of the same period, an instrument directly linked to raising taxes, it does reassert the power of the dominant classes, particularly the clerical: it is a class document. The connections among power, taxation, and totalizing representation, whether the totalities are absolute or relative, are intimate.

Domesday Book

Literacy operates simultaneously in the celebratory and critical modes of romance, as well as in the documentary, administrative mode of the survey. What is its effectivity, however? How does literacy actually function in social context? One scholar thinks it creates "textual communities."[78] Historical documentation suggests another response.

In 1085, two decades after the Norman Conquest, external invasion and internal rebellion threatened the newly conquered island country of England. Imminent danger revealed an alarming lack of reliable information about the country, as the king assembled a massive and costly mercenary army in northern France. An immense survey followed, concurrent with a reassessment of the Danegeld, the Anglo-Saxon tax on land.[79] William's avarice was well known; his military campaigns were costly. The new survey aroused terror and perhaps violence among Anglo-Saxons. Their aristocracy had been eclipsed by William's reign, who replaced it with Normans, Bretons, Flemings, and others auxiliaries in the invasion. Its clear, practical, totalizing list of holdings proffered a statement about power in England in 1086. It was composed with remarkable speed.[80] Discussed at court at Christmas 1085, it was nearing completion in September 1087. It proved to be a unique and unequalled document: *Domesday Book*.

Its purview was extraordinary. Earlier surveys existed, but no census so vast or detailed had ever been undertaken.[81] A minute inquiry into the extent and value of the royal demesne and of lands held by the tenants-in-chief," its "inquest," or *inquisitio*, records an extensive *descriptio* into the whole wealth of England, actual and potential.[82] All England south of the river Tees was divided into separate circuits. For each, a panel of three or four royal commissioners was appointed, to visit each shire in turn, interviewing local juries and representatives from each manor according to a planned program of inquiry. The process is described at an early stage:

> Here follows the inquiry concerning lands which the king's barons made according to the oath of the sheriff of the shire and all of the barons and their Frenchmen and of the whole hundred court—the priests, reeves and six villeins from each village. They inquired what the manor was called; who held it in the time of King Edward; who holds it now; how many hides there are; how many ploughs in demesne and how many belonging to the men; how many villeins, how many cottars; how many slaves; how many free men; how many sokemen; how much woodland; how much meadow; how much pasture; how many mills; how many fisheries; how much has been added to, or taken away from, the estate; what it used to be worth then; what it is worth now, and how much each freeman and sokeman had or has. All this had to be recorded thrice: to wit, as it was in the time of King Edward, as it was when King Edward gave the estate, and as it is now. *And it was also noted whether more could be taken from the estate than is now taken.*[83]

An Anglo-Saxon parodies the survey's exquisite thoroughness. The king

> had [England] investigated so narrowly that there was not one single hide, not one yard of land, not even (it is shameful to tell—but it seemed no shame to him to do it) one ox, not one cow, not one pig was left out, that was not set down in his record.[84]

It was a survey, then, of present holdings, in the historical context of each estate at specified stages of its past, with a burning question for the future. A king with great military needs asked: Could more taxes be wrenched from the soil and its people?

The *descriptio* is not only immense, it is monumental. It gives an impression of timeless finality. Folio after folio lays out in uniform columns whose neat headings and rubrications make its totalizing logic immediately perspicuous. "Everything about it looks final."[85] Its survey of the landed wealth of England is created through a modular hierarchy of existing governmental structures, feudally arranged: boroughs, royal land, and then tenants-in-chief. "In its totality and in its survival there is no precedent in medieval Europe."[86] Totalization and finality were traits noted by the original recipients of the message.

Its information-gathering aspect was essential. It was performed in a tumultuous historical context, the violent redistribution of land after the Norman Conquest which amounted to a far-reaching "tenurial revolution," a violent discontinuity in landholders, "which more closely resembled a free-for-all than a centrally sponsored program of colonization."[87] The modern scholar comments laconically: "Private enterprise played a significant role in the formation of post-Conquest fees."[88] Some consider it an exaggeration, but for current opinion, *Domesday* indexes a vast, violent, and extortionate redistribution of lands by Norman lords.[89] Within twenty years of Hastings, old lordships and kindreds were destroyed, England's tenurial fabric shattered.[90] Orderic Vitalis observed the process from Normandy:

> foreigners grew wealthy with the spoils of England, whilst her own
> sons were either shamefully slain or driven as exiles to wander
> hopelessly through foreign kingdoms.[91]

Domesday may have been the product of an "astonishingly efficient" royal administration; it was also based on the willing collaboration of the new landholders. Had these barons not cooperated with the king's representatives, they could have brought the projected survey to a standstill.[92] They had an interest in its completion. It served as a legal register of titles. For many of them, it may have been the first representation of their holdings to confirm them. It was a political confluence that served both nobles and king. It warranted noble lands newly pirated by the Norman invaders. It served royal interest, establishing the principle that all land was held "of the king," hence subordinate to him. It provided the information required for the king's revenues.

Domesday Book is not a survey of direct military resources: it does not inquire about knight-service. It emphasizes value, both as fact and a potential source of further extraction. The closest parallel is the *Usatges* of Catalonia, intended to restore control over the old comitial domain and related to the augmentation and stabilization of the count's credit in view of future military campaigns in Occitania. In Catalonia as in England, literacy is an instrument of control and discipline that serves the gathering of finances to prosecute wars.

These surveys, ordered by princes and kings of their holdings, were not isolated occurrences. There were others, such as the *Gros Brief* (1187) from Flanders, or for that matter, the earlier Pipe Rolls of England. They instantiate the generalized use of literacy throughout Western Europe for information gathering about resources and regularizing records of official acts.[93] Literacy constituted the bureaucratic state. Social realities—economic, military, political—were mediated by paper (or parchment) work: writing constituted social reality. "Communities" produced by the textualities of literacy may be imposed on what the French call the *contribuables*: those forced to "contribute" the monetary signs of their labor for exercises of violence, domination, and oppression, even unto programs of extermination of heretics or works of welfare.

French Royal Surveyance

The French monarchy focused on paperwork and surveys later than the Anglo-Normans and other French princes. Twenty or so years after the *Foeda campanie*, the monarchy awoke to the importance of record keeping after the loss of its treasury and records at Fréteval in 1194. The incident led to a conscious, deliberate policy of saving documentation—the birth of the bureaucratic spirit in France! Archives became sedentary, remaining at the Palace on the Ile de la Cité, its originals transcribed, successive redactions adding information, revising their structure, setting aside blank folios for later additions. There was awareness that surveyance was an ongoing, long-term process, each stage subject to later revision. Each revision marked its self-consciousness by improvements in the organization of the registers, facilitating their use for information retrieval.[94]

The collection of charters marks a new royal consciousness and a new model of what "France" might be. Kings wanted to know their kingdom and its resources. The interest in money led to a search for a totalizing view of the kingdom. There was even a sense of the enormity of the task. One region, the *châtellenie* of Poissy, was treated as an experimental laboratory for testing measures of the quantitative resources of the kingdom. The registers of the *Scripta de foedis* were exercises of analysis and classification intent on imposing the royal will.[95] The king's counselors were not satisfied with a military account. The exact number of men to be counted on for armed service was important and included both vassals and the obligations of towns. But the counselors also wanted to know the contours of the kingdom as a whole, asserting sovereignty, incorporating new conquests, doing so with precision and attention to the legitimation of claims. The new vision is that of a larger and a more unified country: "A civilization was in the process of being born, but it was not an easy thing."[96] The kingdom was still imagined as an enormous seigneury, but a realization that sovereign kingship is something other than feudal leadership began to appear. The king is not a count, he is somehow above the feudal hierarchy. He needs literate administrators more than warriors. After Philip Augustus, his grandson Saint Louis will create an "administrative chivalry," whose members earn noble privileges.

CHAPTER 9

Representation in State Governance II: Agency

The disease called man . . . [was] a declaration of war against the
old instincts . . . an animal turning against itself. . . . It occurred
as a break, a jump, a necessity, an inevitable fate, against which
there was no resistance and never a spark of resentment . . . the
fitting of a hitherto unchecked and amorphous population into a
fixed form . . . starting as it had done in an act of violence, could
only be accomplished by acts of violence and nothing else. . . .
Such is the origin of the "State."
Nietzsche

S urveys provided information. Its obtention and use required
agents, men in the field. At both ends, human *representamina*
were required to make flesh the principle that "Man is a sign." These man-
signs represented a prince or a king, central power in the multiple fields the
Subject could not occupy simultaneously. Making himself present, at least
to great nobles, was a ruler's major preoccupation. His peripatetic trajectories were relayed by agents permanently in the field. Sheriffs in England
and provosts and bailiffs in France played key roles in bringing power to
bear on polities too large or distant to remain directly under the ruler's
eyes. These representatives of a centralizing, absent power were subjectivized first: the general population came much later.[1]

The representation of central power by field agents was not invented in
the twelfth century. The *missi domenici* of Charlemagne, the very counts
and dukes of the empire, had functioned as estate managers who provided
the foundations of power for central government.[2] Governance relied on regional administration. Under the Robertians, a viscount represented an absent count in half a dozen counties.[3] A major difference between earlier
agency and that of the twelfth century is quantitative: the later period suffused the body politic with royal agents to a degree previously unheard of.
To carve up the relatively small principality of the Ile-de-France into over
sixty territorial subunits, each overseen by a permanent official, answers to

a new conceptualization of governance. A permanent presence-in-absence is established that lays the basis for later bureaucracies of state. If the medieval suffusion of the body politic is not as totalizing as the modern, it turns in that direction. Another difference is the use of commoners in such roles, even when supervising nobles—a practice that scandalized contemporaries. A crucial epistemological difference is that of historical continuity. The earlier model is cut off by centuries of devolution: twelfth-century governance develops in overall continuity beyond the French Revolution. Eighteenth-century revolutions occur within the state form, not outside of it.

Sheriffs, provosts, and bailiffs, as agents of power, perform many of the functions of lordship: surveillance, justice, law enforcement, and taxation, nourishing central government, gathering incomes "from cultivated lands, woods, meadows, and fisheries, as well as from mills, ovens, presses, marketplaces, and commercials stalls . . . revenues derived from property": fixed and proportional rents, arbitrary payments, tithes, land taxes, patronage fees, and other customary dues.[4] The Middle Ages was imaginative in many areas and multiplied occasions for extraction of moneys from the body politic. In England, where all land was held from the king, all men could be thought the king's signs. Some held power by delegation, in the place of the king: the sheriffs. Sheriffs are *reeves* of the *shire*, its administrators. Their Latin name defines their function: they are *vicecomes*, "viscounts" who hold the count's place, or the king's: they are lieutenants. The same is true for the vernacular term, the *prévôts*. Their name derives from *prae-positum*: the one who is placed in the place of another. Lieutenancy was recognized and analyzed by the languages themselves. Agents were men of *presentment*, making present an absent power. The royal *prévôts*, drawn initially from the castellans of the Ile-de-France, had originated with Philip I around the turn of the twelfth century.[5] At the beginning of Philip II's reign, thirty-five *prévôts* administered the king's domains. Their number increased. By 1202–3, there were forty-five, who held jurisdiction over sixty-two *prévôtés*.[6]

Metacritical Verification

The instability of representation is early remarked: the medieval state is well acquainted with its problematics. Representation, textual or human, is made of signs, hence inherently unreliable: signs are made to lie with.

When the signs are human, a question always arises: to what degree does the agent represent his superior's interest, to what extent does he betray it, through incompetence or in subverting the lord's interest for the sake of his own? The possibility is particularly strong under the system of "farms," in which the agent is paid a proportion of the amount collected. The fiduciary issue is doubled by a political question. To what extent does the agent spare his principal the anger and resentment of the population; to what extent does bad judgment or a malevolent character poison the lord's relations with his population? The meanings of texts and documents are notoriously unreliable, a fortiori in scribal culture: the practices of human agents of power even more so.

Diplomacy illustrates the problem. For diplomatic agency to be effective, the diplomat must be given some latitude, a degree of independence. He must be given the power to negotiate on his feet, in the absence of the principal's immediate control. Villehardouin recounts that crusading barons holding a *parlement* at Compiègne sent ambassadors to Venice to negotiate for transportation. They were given "full powers to act in all things just like their seigneurs."[7] Such broad powers of representation were *plena potestas*, giving agents *carte blanche* within limits set by the principal's welfare and knowledge of the issue, in principle setting the latter's consent to the conclusion of the business.[8] Clearly, such delegation requires confidence both in the ambassador's ability and trustworthiness.

In other circumstances, medieval political practice expends substantial efforts to counteract the indeterminacy of representation. One method of supervising the king's agents is the special commission of inquiry. In the same year as the promulgation of the *Cartae baronum*, the Assizes of Clarendon charged the English sheriffs with making searching inquiries on criminal suspects through juries of *presentment*. The inquiries of the king's representatives could override the rights and privileges of local lords—the radical aspect of the Assizes to contemporaries.[9] As in knightly allegiance, fidelity to the king overrode fidelity to lower, more immediate lords. But that was not the end of the affair: follow-up was established. When Henry II returned to England in the spring of 1170, a commission was established, known as the "Inquest of Sheriffs," inquiring into malpractices of local government since Clarendon.[10] The inquest into the royal agents melded an *inquisitio mirabilis* into the "whole financial exploitation of the country": like a feudal seigneury, an entire country could be conceived of as a source of exploitation, depending on agents to respond to the "insatiable appetite" of governance for information. The orderly political machine of an enlightened administration depends on knowing the state of the population, whether for war, taxation, or commerce: "To be exercised, power needs to know."[11]

The inquest of 1170 marked a major shake-up by the central government of its representatives. The inquest, carried out by barons operating as circuit judges (*barones errantes, justiciae errantes*), concerned more than sheriffs: all representatives of the king were targeted, clergy as well as seculars: "archbishops, bishops, abbots, earls, barons, sub-tenants, knights, citizens, and burgesses, their stewards and servants." Many sheriffs were sanctioned with fines; some were dismissed. But an increasing number were men of the court, familiars of the king's household (*domus regis*), *curiales* well versed in the needs of royal governance and the "force of things," trained to the idea of administrative efficacy and centralized administrative control; the attraction of profits from their charge remained strong. Sheriffs and itinerant justices were largely the same persons at different stages in their careers. "Revolving doors" redistributed men between the two categories. Some of the sheriffs dismissed in 1170 were reappointed later; they were usually harder on their subjects after than before.[12] Central government turned the screws on its agents and through them, on the populace they administered. The sheriff, as sign, was a performative at the junction of different worlds: centralized authority and the local practices of sociopolitical enunciation, meaning and the "reality" meaning constructs as a product of various Reals, thus containing the seed of its own deconstruction. Making present the powers of an absent king demonstrates the separability of king and power. The arbitrariness of the sign, the instability of representation, ultimately desacralizes kingship, the church, and meaning itself.

More elegant, less injurious methods of verification and control developed in France. One is doubling. Agents of the count of Anjou undergo a sudden spurt of growth after 1056: they often appear in pairs.[13] The famous wardens of the Champagne Fairs were appointed in pairs. The king's *prévôts* and *baillis* (bailiffs) and other officials also worked in pairs.[14] Reciprocal observation is a means of verification. Control was also institutionalized in more imposing ways. Philip II emitted an ordinance on the eve of his departure for the Third Crusade in 1190. The *prévôts*, by that time, are well established: their functions are assumed. The document, however, mentions another class of officials, the bailiffs, virtually unknown earlier.[15] Their duties included supervision of the *prévôts*, appointment of locals to advise the latter, and the assizes, monthly sessions to hear pleas and record fines. Commanded to protect churches, distribute royal alms, hold inquests to develop information regarding the king's rights and resources, they rendered accounts three times a year in Paris on the profits of justice and other royal rights. The status difference between the two ranks of officials was marked: *prévôts* are identified by location; *baillis* by name. Mostly knights, their assignments were frequently shifted, discouraging them from putting down roots, impeding collusion between officials and the populace. The *baillis* were a second, supervisory level imposed on the original *prévôts*, differentiated in terminology, number, and responsibilities. Their substitutability, the identity of their functions, reveals an increasingly layered and hierarchical bureaucracy.

A far more complex form of institutional supervision developed in England, in governmental oversight of the sheriffs as tax collectors. A remarkable system verifying and controlling their "returns" was devised and put into operation at the Exchequer—the Treasury. A. L. Poole's contribution to the Oxford History of England was titled *Domesday Book to Magna Carta, 1087–1216* (1951). The two texts are among "the most famous documents of English history, unparalleled in Europe": they mark their epochs and frame the growth of the nation, the medieval initiation of the state itself, which will cover the face of the earth in the nineteenth and twentieth centuries. Literacy, numeracy, and the earliest forms of state organization see the day together.[16] Succeeding generations appealed to *Domesday* and the Great Charter as monuments only slightly less authoritative than the Bible.

The importance of both documents was felt in their own day. *Domesday* ushered in the whole series of surveys noted above. Without the attendant pretense to "scientificity," they resemble modern polls and the modern census in procuring categorical, numerical, relatively totalizing representations of the territory under governance, its population and resources. At its beginning, the state is already aware of the political utility of

numeracy, its potential of summarily totalizing representation, and its unreliability. This consciousness is exemplified in the subtle, complex system
of verifying the sheriffs' accounts of their farm of the fief. Begun in
1176–77, completed by Easter 1179, the *Dialogue of the Exchequer*, was
roughly contemporary to the English and Norman surveys, to Etienne de
Fougères's moralizing survey of his social formation, to Chrétien de
Troyes's *Yvain* and the *Foeda campanie*.[17] It represents a different aspect of
administering the new civilization, and in a different region. Tied to Anglo-Norman institutional processes, it is a disquisition on the functioning
of one institution: the Treasury. It is a remarkable text, weaving a witty and
worldly wise discursive intersection of heterogeneous cultural strands. Its
attention to institutional minutiae reveals much about the state and its cultural framework. The author was well qualified to depict the Treasury:
Richard Fitz Nigel was the bastard of Nigel, bishop of Ely, himself treasurer of England before his son. Richard was a member of the *regis curia*, a
justice who heard civil pleas, canon of St. Paul's, archdeacon of Colchester,
dean of Lincoln, elected bishop of London in 1189. He may have had a
hand in designing the process he describes. In the midst of a turbulent and
often chaotic court, the Treasury was "the gyroscope that kept the whole
structure of government and administration on an even keel."[18]

De scaccario dramatizes its process, fusing historical event, dramatic
structure, the awesome deployment of the power of monarchical officialdom, around a spatial territorialization. It is cast in the traditional form of
a dialogue between student and teacher. At one point, *Discipulus*—a sharp
student—asks why the table around which the action occurs is called the
"exchequer." *Magister* responds that it resembles a chess board: it territori-
alizes a *conflictus* in which every participant - like a chess piece—has a
specified place, position, and role, centering around two officials as the essential antagonists: the treasurer and the sheriff. The Exchequer is a table is
a chessboard is a prop in a theatricalized political ritual. An inherently conflictual narrative is spun around this prop.

The Exchequer formalizes and standardizes the audit of the king's collection agents, his sheriffs. The extended metaphor or allegory to chess designates as noble play the most serious, grubby business of governance outside of war. It does so with false implications. In chess, white and black are
equal forces, differentiated only by the advantage of the first move. The al-

legory implies equality between the two primary participants, the treasurer and the sheriff. In fact, the superiority of one player, the subordination of the other infuses the entire procedure. An agonistic narrative is constructed and performed under false pretenses . . . as the text specifies. The sheriff is not the king's equal, who might beat his monarch by playing the game shrewdly enough: he is the king's agent, called to account, and the only question is whether he has obeyed the rules established by the king for the king's profit in order to produce the king's wealth. The overriding purpose of the process is pellucid: "The duty and aim of all [in attendance] is the same, to secure the king's advantage [*regis utilitati*], without injustice, according to the appointed laws of the Exchequer."[19] The dependence of rule on revenue, of kingship on finances, is noted in the work's dedication. Doing quick obeisance to the powers ordained of God, it quickly segues to "the worldly wealth which accrues to kings by virtue of their position." The power of princes "rises and falls as their portable wealth flows or ebbs." Kingdoms are governed and laws maintained by prudence, fortitude, temperance, justice, and other virtues . . . but on occasions, money is indispensable, no less in peace than in war. The Exchequer's rules are not arbitrary: they produce the necessary cash flow for the king's glory.[20] The sheriff is essential to this flow as collection agent, the Exchequer as a process of verifying his work in high-level accounting.[21] The misleading reference to the noble entertainment of chess is purposive. Its allegory is a trick of ideology, in the older sense too readily derided as "vulgar" Marxism: ideology as interested misrepresentation. It disguises the exercise of power in its essential subterfuge: in the extraction of surplus value from the population.

The Exchequer was not a place housing a department of government; like the court of which it was a specialized extension, it was an occasion.[22] Beside the treasurer and the sheriff, others sit at the Table: the marshal, chamberlain, constable, chancellor, justiciar, the bishop of Winchester, whose task it is to observe and decide on the outcome of the conflict. They are judges, assisted by technical aides: an assayer, a calculator, a secretary. In addition, against the norms of the Exchequer, a place is reserved for one Thomas Brown at the king's insistence. The monarch's personal representative? He sits next to the sheriff, at the small end of the table reserved: Does their spatial contiguity represent a team? Or an ideologeme?

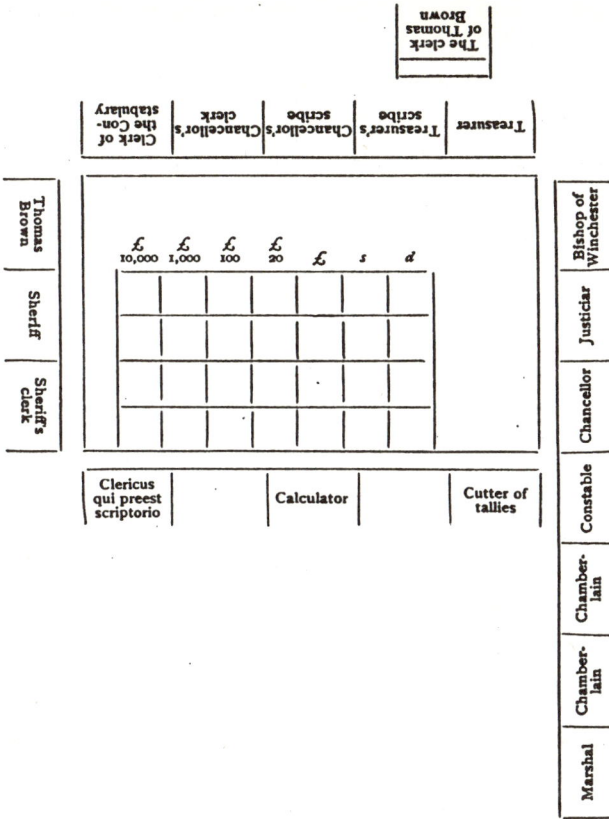

Diagram of the Exchequer[23]

The table itself is both a concrete, real-world physical object, and a highly complex sign, which organizes an institutional and theatrical process and casts each participant into a particular role. That signifying function endows it with effectivity in the world of political and financial reality.

The table also functions as an extended abacus, allowing not only arithmetic calculations but cultural translations. It is an arena in which forces of power, wealth, and culture play across the divides of a governmental hierarchy, between Latin literates like the chancellor, and those of vernacular orality like the sheriff. Special codes bridge these differences. The sheriff was a layman, ex officio illiterate.[24] Since he could not be informed of his financial status on the basis of written, archival records, his financial position was recorded and made "legible" to illiteracy by wooden tallies. The tally-cutter had a place at the table. Notches were made in a stick, which was then split in half: one side was given to the payer, the other to the payee.[25] The *tablabacus* is arranged so as to render its financial verifications and transactions intelligible to the layman—the sheriff—in spite of his presumed illiteracy.

If the Exchequer is a meeting place between the cultures of literacy and orality, its description is very much the product of sophisticated Latin literacy. *De scaccario* is a study in financial semiotics, inscribing the multiple codes at play to address the issue of value. The tallies are described in detail: their size and codes of inscription. Description of the accountant's code for distributing the coins before him leads to a major theoretical development, in which the arbitrariness of the sign becomes a scholastic allegoreme of human nature, acknowledging both social mobility and the permanence of social classes while melding realistic and nominalistic views of signification. A penny can serve as a counter (= signifier) that stands for a penny, a shilling, a pound, a hundred pounds or a thousand (= signifieds), depending on the "accidents" (semantic markers) that are added or removed by the accountant. So also,

> any common man, who is essentially a man, and can be nothing else
> may, if the President will to add some worldly 'accidents,' rise to the
> top, and as the wheel of Fortune revolves, be thrust down again to
> the bottom, without changing his nature, however much he may
> appear to be changed by his rank and estate.

The variability of individual wealth is presented according to several codes: the scholastic, deploying notions of substance and accident (a low-born man remains nothing but a plebeian throughout his life, whatever changes the accidents of wealth may bring); the literary topos (the wheel of fortune records the changes as unforeseeable); and the coinage code (the value of the man is figured by the value of coins). But the value of a coin used as a counter depends on its position on the *tablabacus'* grid. The essentialist bases of human nature and social structure are asserted in their integrity, no matter the individual variations that the production of wealth or history may cause. At the same time, this integrity is deconstructed by the principle of arbitrary signification, necessary to the financial process and its representation.[26]

Even "deeper mysteries" are hidden in the processes of the Exchequer, holy mysteries. In processual complexity, a hidden harmony operates. Its imposing rituals, the sometimes harsh effects of its judgments, are but a figure of that other "strict account," to be revealed "when the books of all are opened, and the door shut." The Exchequer's accounting is an analogue to the ultimate accounting on the Day of Judgment. Periodic financial accountings are regularly analogized to the Final Judgment, terrorizing those subject to their procedures in the rulers' benefit. The treasurer's responsibilities are said to be grievous, they cause him much anxiety—are we in Kafka's *Castle?* His dictation has to be precise. No mistakes are allowed: "The authority of the Roll is such that no man is allowed to dispute it or alter it, unless the mistake is so obvious that it is patent to all." Once the Roll is written and the Exchequer rises, only the king can alter it . . . as only God alters the book of life and death.

Metacritical self-reference is endless. The Exchequer generates internal systems of verification of accountability. In addition to the tallies, archival doubles known as "counterwrits" (*contrabreve*), are retained by the chancellor, the treasurer, and the chamberlain, as dispersed evidences of the writs issued. Thomas Brown makes his own copy. As fixed payments, earlier inscribed in the account books, are made, they are cancelled by a stroke through the middle to note payment has been made: the code is specified. As a process of verification, the Exchequer is itself a double articulation by definition, institutionalizing the principle of communicative redundancy.

This self-reflexivity inserts the institution itself in a larger social, political, and historical text. Right after the Norman Conquest, the king drew no money from crown lands, but only victuals, each commodity being contributed in appointed measure. The officers concerned knew how much was due from each estate. But that source of value left a major gap: the cash required to pay his knights (*stipendia vel donatiua militum*). So the king drew money for that purpose and other necessary cash expenses from the profits of his judicial jurisdiction, from voluntary payments made by individuals for privileges, and from cities and towns whose business was not agriculture but commerce. Thus a differential distribution was established. Payments in kind provided for feeding the court, but cash, essential for military enterprises, was obtained in other ways. Agriculture, on the one hand, and on the other, judicial fines, the sale of privileges and confiscated lands, and what was in effect taxation of town commerce, provided for victuals and liquidity respectively. The king acquired a reputation for greed and venality, selling off lands ripped from owners for sale to the highest bidder. According to the monk known as the Peterborough Chronicler, "The king gave [land] into the hands of the man who offered him most of all, and did not care how sinfully the reeves had got it from poor men, nor how many unlawful things they did."[27]

The mix of barter, monetary taxation, and accounting requires "translatability" between codes, from one mode of gathering value to the other. For enough wheat to bake bread for a hundred men, one shilling was allowed; for the carcass of a grazing ox, one shilling; for a ram, a sheep, or the forage of twenty horses, four pence. Interchanges between different cultures, codes and systems of exchange, mix repeatedly to constitute the country's fiscal and economic life. The arbitrariness of the sign, and the resulting exchanges between systems of value, is implicit and presupposed throughout, allowing both ambiguity and forgery.[28] The polysemousness of "*thesaurus*" (treasury) requires explanation. "Treasury" means coined money, gold, silver plate, or changes of raiment. It is also the place where the treasure is kept. As a storage space, it includes the king's seal and various forms of accounting archives: *Domesday Book*, the Roll of Demands ("the Writ of Farms"), the Pipe Rolls (yearly accounts), and a multitude of charters, countertallies, rolls of receipts, royal writs for the issue of treasure, "and sundry other things which are needed for daily use while the Exchequer is sitting."[29] Documents produce instability.

Ambiguity, long recognized in medieval literary studies, was the widespread awareness of a general culture. Forgery is not only a concomitant of a culture of literacy, it is a permanent concern of all institutions based on literacy. The scholar acutely supposes that the sheriff, who has the summons in his hands well before the hearing, might alter it. No, says the master, that won't work: exact copies of the summons are made and kept, so that a falsified version would be identified. Literacy may occasionally provide the basis for a community of interests: it is also an instrument in the ongoing conflicts among individuals, classes, and the state. Literacy bears and produces conflict as well as community.

Administration, information gathering and tax gathering, the agents of officialized bureaucracy fanning out over a territory to be ruled, a pastoralized version of policing, all are alternate sides of the administrative Moebius strip of twelfth-century governance, doubling a sentimentalized version of "manorialism" as defined by obligations and reciprocity. These characterized relations within the nobility only, as it extracted surplus value unsymmetrically from the peasantry, in support of the activity which was its ideological raison d'être: the prosecution of war. This too, feudalism shared with the nascent state.

War and Philip Augustus's State

War in textuality presented faces of heroism and devastating destruction. It was itself subject to multiple disciplines: strategy, logistics, finance, etc. Any major human activity responds to multiple frames of inquiry: serious interest in the object itself (the real), as apart from the object of a particular discipline (a Real), requires transdisciplinary study.

The numbers of fighting men in medieval armies seem remarkably small to modern eyes. An expeditionary force of 80 knights and 140 mounted sergeants was considerable in the twelfth century. Knights were served by at least three horses and one squire; mounted sergeants had 1 or two horses. Such an army could mean a total cavalry force of some 300 men and 400 horses.[30] In France, around the end of the eleventh century, the royal army has 300–500 knights. A few years later, it has grown to 700 knights. A bit later yet, the king's avant-garde, by contrast to Roland's supposedly small rearguard of 20,000, numbers only forty.[31] At Bouvines, in 1214, Philip Augustus amassed about 1,300 knights, along with perhaps 4,000–6,000 auxiliary foot sergeants.[32]

Small numbers mean that relatively small changes in the forces available made a substantial difference. Behind the numbers, an equally important question is: What brings the men to battle? What drives, what bonds, what ideological values and what material rewards activate men to fight at the risk of injury or their lives? Feudalism was supposedly characterized by an intense personal relationship of reciprocal loyalty between vassal and lord, a political and military relationship that shaded into a familial one. This personal bond precluded, in the opinion of one great medievalist, even the idea of an army of hired soldiers.[33] In England, for a century after the conquest, the system of knight service and castle guard, supplemented as necessary by the *fyrd* or militia, sufficed to satisfy the demands of modest wars, enabling the monarchy to survive without unduly straining the vassals. Although household knights were paid wages for their service, throughout this earlier period "the feudal army remained the ultimate defense of the land," the monarchy depending on the loyalty of individual barons and their knights.[34] Military needs were largely met by "unpaid" service. The volume of production and exchange was low: grants of fiefs, productive of value and sustenance, sufficed.

The feudal arrangement suited a time when money was scarce and land plentiful: vassals were most frequently rewarded with a fief, usually land with peasant labor power attached. This disregards, however, the economic motive of the fief itself, a motive that eventually led men to contract multiple, potentially contradictory homages for the sake of profiting from multiple fiefs. As a hierarchical political arrangement, the fief blended with quasi-familial bonds, a doubling that produced loyalty and strengthened the connection. As economic capital, plural allegiances were a logical increase in available resources. As they allowed vassals to pose objections to actually performing the feudal service expected, loyalty was undermined. What originally strengthened feudalism (its tripling of political, economic, and familial dimensions) undermined it later.

With increased liquidity, overlords were relieved to seek out the services of mercenaries eager to fight for cash, avoiding the troubling complexities of feudal ties. An entire society was transformed into one based on money, rents, and taxes. The feudal levy was superseded by an army chiefly composed of men paid to fight. The transformation was not easy. The finances of war were of "startling magnitude." A war economy was imposed: direct taxation of incomes, price controls, import and export licenses, the regulation and supervision of certain industries, requisitions, currency and credit controls, increased borrowing, the organization of a customs system, regulations against trading with the enemy, even the use of a blacklist. War finance brought into existence a bureaucratic state, able to pay for a war effort on a vastly greater scale and different in kind, in conjunction with rapid economic expansion beginning in about 1180.[35]

The shift of exchange into a money economy increased incomes, enabling princes to amass huge treasuries. Only fragmentary records survive for the French monarchy, but they suggest an impressive fiscal harvest.[36] In 1202–3, the king's regular revenues had increased by nearly three-quarters since the beginning of the reign in 1180, and by half in the twelve years since 1190. These figures exclude extraordinary incomes, such as the confiscations of Jewish moneys and property in 1179 that financed Philip's military adventures in the 1180s. Jews who had earlier resided in the king's domain resettled in Champagne and other territories neighboring the royal domain, the king depriving himself of the considerable income available from the Jewish community. By 1198, feeling the pinch, he returned to his father's more tolerant policies. A pact with Champagne allowed Jews to reenter the royal domain: the two princes pledged to respect each other's Jews, to guarantee their money lending, and restricted their operations to their respective territories. Jewish communities were treated as capital: mobile, replenishable, and proprietary. The financial exploitation of Jews alternated expulsions, confiscations of property and returns, special forms of taxation, and the installation of officials in each city to evaluate the accumulations of Jewish funds as part of a general surveillance of "credit controls."[37] Other extraordinary sources of funds included "mulcting the church." When the pope levied an interdict in 1200, Philip confiscated the properties of the bishops who respected it. Combined with large feudal reliefs, these measures produced a substantial surplus for the treasury that financed Philip's war efforts after 1202—including Bouvines.

The French army seems small to modern eyes, but it was permanent, independent of feudal service, and fully funded from the royal treasury. Expenses included salaries of foot soldiers, mercenaries, and mounted knights, as well as strategic shifts from specific garrisons to other theaters of war. Some 65,931 pounds were spent on the Norman invasion, another 17,100 pounds elsewhere. Major additional expenses were incurred in fortifying towns and building defensive fortresses.[38] Their costs are not calculable on the basis of available documentation, but were considerable. In spite of ongoing warfare, outlays were far lower than income. Expenses amounted only to 28 percent of total revenues; local government cost only 12 percent. This left a surplus of over 60,000 to 77,000 pounds: half to three-quarters of total receipts. In addition, the profits of a war tax brought in at least 27,000 pounds. This left Philip a surplus of at least 90,000 pounds.[39] Such sums sustained the war effort, allowed for considerable freedom in planning military expansions, and became themselves a strategic instrument.

Cash was the essential sinew of war and power. When Rufus died in 1100, claimants to the throne and their supporters "rode like hell" in a race for the keys to the treasury: its moneys were convertible into military force for the mastery of England and Normandy. The crucial role of money in warfare explains the savage punishment Henry ordered for English money-coiners in 1124, who had issued coins with a silver content of scarcely one-third: Henry's knights, paid in these coins, complained to the king that they could buy nothing with them.[40]

"Battle" and "war" were differentiated. *Werra*—whence both "war" and *guerre*—was a seasonal adventure, an annual depradation, a regular economic harvesting, one form of argument among others, a brusque incursion for booty and pillage. War per se settled nothing, but existed in a continuum with words, alone capable of settling matters by discussion and oaths. In this sense, "war" was part of the peace process. "Battle," the *praelium*, was something else: an ordeal, a judgment of God, which forces heaven to choose: a sacred oracle.[41] Battles were desperately risky business: a few minutes of confusion or panic could destroy the patient work of years.[42] They were avoided. Henry II did not fight a single battle. Philip Augustus fought only one: Bouvines itself, and that only when it became unavoidable.

Other strategies were preferred, which did not involve the risk of defeat. If the numbers of troops was small, their perceived devastation was very large: that devastation was strategy.[43] Its least costly form, as William the Marshall, famed exemplar of "the courteous knight," makes clear, ensures that wars are "directed against the poor and labouring people and against their goods and chattels."[44] If the early medieval economy consisted of ravish and seize (*ravir, prendre*), medieval warfare can be summarized as "*ravir, détruire*" (ravish, destroy). For Vegetius, the great strategist of antiquity, logistics and supply were primary: "secure . . . provisions for oneself and . . . destroy the enemy by famine. Famine is more terrible than the sword."[45] War's devastations of the civilian population are not a sign of chaotic anarchy: they are strategic and intentional. Violence is not anomalous: it is willed and functional.

Destruction and harrying may reduce a land and its population to obedience; they cannot hold it. Successful rule is based on castles.[46] The castle was a multifunctional unit: administrative center, base for offensive and defensive operations, and seigneurial residence.[47] Garrisons were often small—nine to twenty-four knights are numbers frequently mentioned—too small to stop the incursions of an invading army. Castles were often built in strings, on naturally high points or on artificial mounds, as observation outposts, units of territorial surveillance sited to observe and report on hostile movements.[48] Their systematicity was one of surveillance and warning more than territorial control. In the urgencies of war, they could operate as independent military units.[49]

As the technique of construction shifted from wood to stone in the course of the twelfth century, the cost of construction soared. Richard I, far from romantic and impetuous, was methodical and given to careful preparation.[50] In 1197–98, he spent the "fantastically large sum" of about £11,500 on the construction of Château-Gaillard, overlooking a turn of the Seine.[51] Occupying a strategically commanding position, it was logistically ideal. The fortress and the town of Les Andelys at the river's edge below formed the advance base from which to conquer the Vexin. Men and supplies could be sent upstream from Rouen on long river boats built for this purpose, or they could travel by road, a more direct route that crossed the twisting Seine twice, at the bridges of Pont de l'Arche and Portjoie. Richard's construction of bridges, residences, and castles along this royal and military road between Rouen and Les Andelys, reveals a planned, logistical supply network, based on communications and geography.

It also implied construction specialists.[52] Sudden transformations in military architecture at this time are revolutionary. Territorial conquests, the maintenance of new frontiers, led to new requirements. Philip Augustus created a corps of engineers who developed a new military architecture. One document lists over a dozen men, mostly titled *Magister*, thought to be charged with fortification architecture in widely scattered regions.[53] The architectural innovations of the period are explained in part by study of Vegetius, in part by the analysis of classical ramparts and fortifications. These constructions were part of a coherent policy of staged conquests, the occupation of conquered territories, and subsequent population control. Policies regarding castles were similar on both sides of the Channel. In England, the castle, all but unknown in Anglo-Saxon times, became a chief instrument of Norman colonization. After the conquest, the countryside was dotted with castles built by William I and his followers.

Once built, castles require further expenditure. They had to be manned, maintained, and defended. Even in the eleventh century, planning was annual and quite specific. Each of the three towers in the castle of Vendôme was to be guarded year-round by one watchman, two others walking the perimeter. The guard was rotated on a monthly basis; in a year, sixty men were required. In April and May the guard was supplied by the count; in June, July, and August, by the burgesses of Vendôme; the remaining months were covered by seven of the count's military vassals.[54] Architects, construction crews, the provision of timbers and cut stones, the development of logistical supply routes and communications among a series of castles, furnishing troops to man them, to feed them and their horses—these represented multiple disciplines, major financial investments, and organizational ventures.

Another huge military cost was the increasing dependence of rulers on mercenaries. Their increased use changed the nature of the discipline of war, rendering it yet more devastating.[55] Romance heroes are sometimes referred to as *soudoyers* (whence "soldiers"), but the real thing had poor press. Their small bands were particularly destructive: they were accused of killing, stealing from the poor, and being sacrilegious. Captured alive, they were readily exterminated. Nevertheless, they were highly desired by rulers. So long as they were paid, getting them into battle where and when desired was easier than interminable negotiations with recalcitrant vassals manipulating multiple feudal contracts and loyalties. Losing mercenaries was less damaging politically than losing vassals. Beyond ideology, the distinction between paid mercenaries and knights rewarded by fiefs is secondary: both did battle at someone else's orders in exchange for returns of value. Money facilitated the process. Mercenaries were an integral part of "the medieval military revolution."[56]

De scaccario frames its exploration of the Treasury with rhetoric about the necessity of money in peace as well as war, but demonstrates the ubiquitous need to finance war:

> Money is no less indispensable in peace than in war. In war it is
> lavished on fortifying castles, paying soldiers' wages and innumerable
> other expenses, determined by the character of the persons paid, for
> the defense of the realm.[57]

The platitude proves a point: the state's need for lucre in all seasons. Its necessity in war is the common understanding. In modernity too, the military budget is sacralized, enemies or no. For the sake of war, the state develops bureaucratic structures that haunt it in peace. The history of the development of state structures of administration in France and England is intelligible only in terms of the pressing needs of war finance on an entirely new scale.[58]

The combination of war, taxation, and the bureaucracy that made both possible, proved highly successful for Philip Augustus, belied by the ideological representations of the king. At the beginning of his reign, as a young man, he was portrayed by Alain de Lille as the alternative to the failure of the Plantagenets.[59] Philip was the new man, inaugurating a golden age of love and peace. The Capetians were said to excel in qualities the Plantagenets lacked: the simplicity of daily life, affability, avoidance of blasphemy, chastity, modesty, and the peaceful exercise of power. Their emblem was not a wild beast, but a flower, the *fleur de lys*: probity, moderation, elegance, and lightness of touch, as opposed to the tyrannical, vulgar, extravagant, and gloomy nature attributed to the English monarchy.

Bouvines was the culmination of lifelong strategies and campaigns. In three years starting in 1203, Philip embarked on an internal *reconquista*, multiplying the territory actually controlled by the French crown outside the Ile-de-France. He aimed first at Normandy, the traditional enemy of the French crown now controlled by King John; militarily the strongest and the most aggressive principality in France. Philip first attacked and won Château-Gaillard and the string of secondary installations that supported it. The region gave way readily: Rouen surrendered in June 1204. The conquest of Normandy was already a brilliant success. Philip went on to the great fiefs of the Loire Valley and Poitou, taking Poitiers and investing the fortresses at Chinon and Loches; they surrendered the following year. A two-year truce, reached at Thouars in October 1205, stabilized Philip's conquests down to the river Loire for the time being.[60]

The climax came a decade later, on a Sunday in Flanders, at a *lieu-dit* Bouvines. It was the Lord's day, when Christians were enjoined to avoid the sins of money, sex, and spilled blood. Thousands of Christian warriors transgressed the Law under the command of two Christian kings, Philip II and Otto of Brunswick.[61] Major powers had joined in alliance in opposition to Philip's conquests: John of England, Otto of Brunswick, Renaud of Boulogne, Ferrand of Flanders and Hainault, and many others from the Duke of Brabant to the mercenary captain Eustache le Moine. Before the event, Philip withdrew his son Louis from the Albigensian crusade, renounced the invasion of England, and reconciled with his wife, Ingeborg of Denmark.[62] The Flemish plateau banked by marshes between the Empire to the east and the Artois to the west, was very much Philip's own country, the heritage of his first wife.[63] He arrived first, and placed himself in the center of the field, facing the enemy coalition. After the rituals required for a true *bellum*, the armies reconnoitered by feints. During the battle itself, each of the opposing kings in turn was unseated by enemy troops, to be saved only by his household knights. Eventually, the Empire retreated, leaving the French victorious, having captured some 130 knights, including twenty-five bannerets and five counts, all held for ransom.

The battle was acclaimed as a historical event throughout Europe. Contemporary chronicles underscored its importance, a refulgent signal of royal success. In spite of the monarch's monumental disinterest in historical and literary patronage,[64] his triumphs were celebrated in a 9,000-line panegyric in Latin on the model of the *Aeneid*, the *Philippide* of Guillaume le Breton, apparently during the king's life.[65] It links Philip with Alexander and Julius Caesar, in a monument glorifying the unity of nation and king.[66] Not only was Bouvines the first victory of a Capetian king in *bataille champel*: it brilliantly affirmed Capetian legitimacy. God had favored the Capetians, granting a decisive victory and vindicating the king's rights over baronial rebellion as feudal overlord. As against the German Otto, depicted as a Roman emperor and imperialist invader, Philip was a *rex christianissimus*, defender of the church. A leading supporter of pope and clergy, he represented the established order against Otto's imperialist scheme for world domination.[67] After Bouvines, nothing stopped the expansion of the royal domain, or the exploitation of subjugated provinces such as Flanders. In the entire kingdom, no principality was any longer in a position to rebel. An expanding bureaucratic organization, the country's stable centralization and sharply increased resources had laid the basis for Philip II's victories. Starting as the leader of a principality somewhat more eminent than others by reason of a royal title, he defeated the united forces of England and the Empire, tripled the land surface subject to the monarchy, gave France Paris as its capital, and laid the foundations of the centralized state it would become.[68]

His triumph, however, was also the triumph of a new sociopolitical organization and its ethos. The *Philippide* opposes the feudal nobility's loyalty to ancestral honor as an aristocratic order trapped in its false consciousness and internal contradictions, as against the ethos of commoners as bureaucrats: careful planning and management. Bouvines is not only the triumph of the French against rebellious barons and an international coalition, it is the triumph of "the bureaucratic state over the feudal aristocracy."[69]

Philip's reign was crucial in the history of France. It represents a major shift in the conceptualization of the state: a personal power exercised over men is transformed into power based on an increasingly unified territory.[70] These military-political triumphs were accompanied by emerging elements of a discursive royal ideology, scattered ideologemes that would be coordinated into the coherent theory that dominated the West later in the thirteenth and fourteenth centuries.[71] Their scattered fragmentation impels divergent interpretations. The ill-defined concept of regnum that Philip had inherited was restricted to the king's feudal domain: Suger had equated it with the Ile-de-France, excluding Normandy. Philip was called "King of the Franks" (*rex Francorum*), not yet "King of France" (*rex Francie*). Although the royal registers begin to observe an incipient distinction between domain and kingdom after 1204, it is not until the reign of Philip the Fair that *regnum Francie* (the Kingdom of France), begins to be clearly distinguished from the royal domain. The concepts of *kingdom*, of *France*, of an *imperium* that might legitimate dominion over England as well as France, did not change in spite of Philip's victories on the ground.[72] Whether as discursive ideology or a theory of kingship, Latinate intellectuals produced only ideologemes, not yet a coherent ideology.[73]

More odd is a marked ideological absence. Philip's disdain for jongleurs and popular entertainments is well known. Until well past his death, in spite of an anonymous prose translation of the *Philippide*, history in the vernacular flourished only far from the royal court, under patronage of the aristocracy, its perspective on historical events quite different from the royal. When the monks of Saint Denis, some fifty years or so after the events, translated Latin histories into French, it was in a dialectical relation to earlier vernacular historiographies. Half a century after Philip Augustus laid the bases of the bureaucratic state on territory newly expanded by conquest, the necessity surfaced of addressing the aristocracy in the language of its own class, on the topic that produced its identity.[74]

The vernacular poets of the chansons de geste contemporary to Philip's reign continue to work the discrepancy between violence and legitimacy initially explored in the early twelfth century, identifying a scandalous and persistent cleavage between the levels of power and violence of king and vassal.[75] Violence loses legitimation, and the political hierarchy is undermined. If the texts reveal nostalgia for the certainties of past and established hierarchy, they view it as unrealizable in the actualities of secular politics.[76] Their perspective is that of a nobility whose status and value are being sapped by contemporary monarchical progress. It is colored by their historical location *after* the burst of cultural creation of the twelfth century. The *jongleurs* of the early epic, the writers of the *roman*, had prepared a textual terrain in which multiple perspectives incorporated contradictory ideologies. Nostalgia was one possible reaction. But other reactions, more "realistic," prevailed. As against a traditional view, the Middle Ages were eminently practical. Praxis often developed beyond the reach of ideology or theory, which caught up only with the delays of uneven development. Some searched out the invisible lineaments of God in the firmament; on the ground, the institutions of state that house political governance developed apace, in an aggressively ravenous creativity that blended bloodthirstiness, hunger for wealth, a drive for power, and a realm of symbolic fictions we are only beginning to decipher as addressing and implementing this evolution.

Subjectifications of Governance: Ideology and Discipline

Two early categories of subjects were functions of a centralizing but absent power: those who apply violent force in the name of that power, its military and police force; and the functionaries of bureaucracy, who furnish its cohesive glue. Max Weber said that the state claims a monopoly of the exercise of violence, and that bureaucracy, though peaceable, exercises power in a form that is "practically unshatterable."[77] Although nowhere near their full fruition, both forms of state power undergo a turning point in the twelfth century.

"Knighthood" and the categories of bailiffs, provosts, and sheriffs, stewards and reeves largely overlapped. But the historical distinction is quite real: the problematics of knightly subjectification are explored primarily in the ideological texts of novels, vernacular symbol formations of narrative fictions that offered imaginary identification and deniability. The power of their pragmatic effectivity incompletely sensed, these could seem just stories, entertainments of the rich and powerful: as popular culture's vernacular "appendages" to the scholastic arts, they were hardly worth serious attention. Their deniability enabled the work of civilization to be performed with relatively little interference from official, Latin ideology. The distrust of these texts by church authorities was well grounded. At first, they did not go beyond occasional denigration. Secular vernacular ideology in the mode of fiction successfully disguised its long-term potency. Later efforts, in the thirteenth century, rewrote the narratives in religious garb.

Much the same is true of the pendant development of disciplinary subjectification. The church provided both the model of an official bureaucracy and its personnel.[78] Clerics trained as masters of *artes* and *disciplinae* were employed in courts that spawned the burgeoning bureaucracies which were "the most crucial phenomenon of the modern Western state."[79] Its beginnings left little trace among the theorists who lacked both a vocabulary and a conceptual framework to inscribe the new phenomenon.[80] The most noteworthy exceptions are the critical satires of courtiers by John of Salisbury and Walter Map.[81] The disciplinary process in which the agents of governance were given marching orders, instructions from the center of power on the duties they were to perform—their job descriptions as it were, the procedures to be employed, their ethos—has left no documentation. Government has never acknowledged the balance of terror and pastoral care its agents exercise. What remains are complaints, correctives, and even one self-analytic description by a former thirteenth-century *bailli*: Philippe de Beaumanoir's text.

At one moment of his varied reflection on power, Michel Foucault made a sharp break with the tradition that identified power as devolving from the state. He asserted the omnipresence of power in all exchanges, its local character outside the structures of state, and its existence on both sides of the state divide. The positive point is incontrovertible. Unfortunately, making that point led to slighting the state and an imbalanced perspective on power. In the medieval case, rather than a sharp opposition of categories, continuity among levels of the exercise of power are the rule: the kingdom is conceived of as a seigneury, the subject is not distinguished from the vassal, and king, noble, knight, husband, and father all devolve as ideological simulacra of God.[82]

The discipline of power initiated in the twelfth and thirteenth centuries for French and English agents of princes and kings was a first stage of sub-jectivation. Did the imposition of discipline seep into the larger society?

In fact, the management of households was another locus of discipline. Not the commoners' peasant or burgher households, but that of great no-bles. The notion and practices of discipline jumped from the Latin school tradition to the apex of the political structure and then wended its way down the hierarchical social structure. The English king's household is brought under discipline with Henry I, in the *Constitutio Domus Regis* (1135–39).[83] A century later, around 1240–42, the English philosopher-bishop known as Robert Grosseteste (c. 1168–1253), teacher, translator from the Greek, chancellor of Oxford, metaphysician of light, epistemologist who opened the intellect to sense perception, theoretician of infinite ag-gregates, best known for his innovations in scientific method and as-tronomer, composed a set of "*reules*" for the countess of Lincoln on "how to manage and govern her lands and household" (*de garder e governer ter-res e hostel*). A rubric immediately follows this incipit, which promises that whoever keeps to these rules "will live well and comfortably from his demesne, sustaining himself and his people."

Grosseteste's *Rules* were the first vernacular treatise in estate manage-ment and accounting. They were written for the use of one particular no-ble on an estate of many manors. Other works of the same type followed, in French or in English, written for a larger public; a few were then adapted to the Latin of clerics. The best known, composed in the last quar-ter of the thirteenth century, are the anonymous *Seneschaucy* and Walter of Henley's *Husbandry*. A little verse, inserted into some versions of the *Seneschaucy*, states their general promise:

> If a man's eager to know
> governance of land and keeping accounts
> this book can teach him
> how to act in all matters.[84]

Self-help tapped a substantial interest in the literate public. One lawyer whiled away his time in Flete prison by conflating Walter and the *Seneschaucy* around 1290: his work was dubbed the *Fleta*.[85] Accounting was popular: one text appears in thirty-five versions, rewritten so extensively as to preclude the scholarly amusement of constructing a stemma.

These texts are remarkable. Seneschals had previously appeared as major administrative officers of royal and princely domains: the necessary conservatism of that function made Keu a butt of fashionable humor in Chrétien's novels. The governance of principalities and kingdoms required complex systems of representative agents covering their territories France and England. Similar issues recur at all levels. The *Seneschaucy* addresses the question, how to manage and improve manors governed by administrators. Successive chapters deal with the *seneschal*, the *bailiff*, and with the *provost*: the same terms are used for the administrators of private domains as at the highest political levels.[86] At the end of the brief treatise, two other crucial figures are discussed: the auditor, who reviews the profitability of the enterprise and its finances; and the lord of the manor, also subjected to a certain discipline. In between, behavioral discipline is extended to a remarkable social depth within the manor. The functions of the hayward, the carter, the plough-keeps, the cowherd, swineherds, and shepherds are discussed; even the dairymaid and her duties are given a chapter! All the personnel of the manor, its lord, its administrators, officials, each of its productive functions, is sketched out in the dos and don'ts of their tasks in descending hierarchical order. The focus is on personnel, the performance of specialized functions. Theory's suffusion of the manor is total.

Walter Henley's treatise is more literary in form, more analytic in focus. It takes the form of a sermon delivered by a father to his son. After a religious and moral prologue, it addresses questions of management, specifically those concerning the bailiff and the provost. Then come the techniques of corn farming, including ploughing, sowing, and the harvest, costs, and how to increase fields. It then shifts to stock farming, cattle, pigs, sheep, and poultry. A fourth section contains brief comments on finance (buying and selling, keeping accounts, arrears) and is concluded by an epilogue.[87] Walter knows the *Seneschaucy* and follows it on some points, but organizes his work differently. Although his primary concerns are with production, personnel is not disregarded. He urges hiring, not on the basis of parentage or appearance, but by reputation, loyalty, and knowledgeability or skill in husbandry. Men are to be chosen from one's own tenancy: if they do anything amiss, damages are more easily recovered. Servants often loiter: they must be supervised daily so as to counter their "*fraude.*" The bailiff must know everything they do: anything untoward is to be reproved and corrected. Redoubled supervision is recommended at this level also, albeit more informally. Buying and selling should be done in the presence of an honest man or two, who may bear witness if necessary. Accounts should be drawn up by a trusted man, and one should beware that servants and provosts often

> make merchandize of theire maisters money for theire owne gaine and not for the gaine of their maister; and that is not faithful (*loialtie*) dealing:

let such money be taken out of the hands of the servants![88]

Grosseteste's *Rules* have no such obvious scheme of organization: a subjacent dialectic may be detected, at most. Their style and conception differ markedly. The philosopher recommends an initial, totalizing inquest of each manor, including all rents, customs, usages, bond services, franchises, fees, and holdings, as well as all its moveables and immoveables.[89] Once a baseline is established, the countess is to address the seneschal before witnesses who are her friends. In all courtesy, he is to be entreated and commanded to keep her rights, franchises, and property whole, to increase it, to send all income without fraud or "disloyal reduction" to her personally; and to do the tenants no harm through violent or tyrannical means (*torcenuse demaundes*): formal inquiry will follow reports of such acts.

The bishop's text reads like a skeletal outline, to be committed to memory and developed in actual delivery . . . a script for the countess! She should also address the material conditions of her demesne, estimating the production of corn so as to know how much to apportion for bread, how much for alms. The year should be planned out ahead of time, sojourns allotted to different manors according to seasons and available resources, so as not to drive any one manor into debt by the expenses of her residence. Checks on productivity are to be carried out in great secrecy. After a year, when manor accounts have been rendered, in great secrecy, with one or two most discrete and faithful men, earlier harvests are to be compared with present production: so will you measure the performance of your servants and bailiff and correct matters as necessary.[90]

Behavior is controlled. Supervise your servants and order frequent examinations (*enqueste*) of their behavior, to see if any are "disloyal, ignorant, vile, indecent, habitually drunk, and not useful." Such people should be turned out of the house, as well as those who "create strife, discord, or disagreement. . . . All ought to be of one accord and of one will, as one heart and one soul." Miscreants and troublemakers are not desired: harmony shall prevail, in the key set by the mistress of the house. All guests, secular and religious, are to be received promptly and courteously by all members of the household.[91] The servants' clothing as they wait on table, the manner of serving at mealtimes, the servants' behavior toward friends, both in the master's presence and in her absence, are prescribed.

The last two rules are fascinating. Rule 22 instructs the countess to be courteous and agreeable to her bailiff and her servants, to inquire openly and forthrightly as to the development of stock and plowing. Grosseteste is concerned, not only with her acquisition of information, but with the pragmatic effect her questioning will have on those who serve her: your knowledge, your understanding will be *mut plus dute*, much respected or even feared. The relations between mistress and personnel are not merely a matter of command: they are to be politic. The lady is to manage her own behavior in view of its effect on the servants. Her image is an ideologeme, manipulated to communicate a desired effect on the servants.

And finally, a small detail: Forgotten and added on, or a concrete example of a major principle? The countess is to forbid her people from eating dinners and suppers outside the proper dining hall, in either hidden corners or their rooms: much waste comes of this, and no honor *a seyngnur ne a dame*. The countess is to behave affably toward her people, to impress them positively, even as she seeks to control the details of their in-house behavior in enacting the double rationality of economics and nobility: to prevent waste and protect honor, the profit motive and the feudal ethos both. Discipline is a rationality; it responds to complex cultural values. In this case, the countess is to draw a line impeding the development of a private life uncontrolled by her discipline.

There is some question as to the intended audience of such texts.

Would great lords of manorial estates, like the countess of Lincoln, with sufficient lands to employ the large and costly staffs indicated, have the time or inclination to take the active, detailed role in farming their manors posited by these writers?[92] In the case of small estates, their lords would likely find themselves overstaffed and overextended. Would the bailiffs and the provosts or reeves be worth hiring if they needed such book learning? To what extent was the newly formalized discipline of estate management similar to modern armchair travel? To what extent was the formalization of a new discipline of life itself a sign of that discipline, a sign of the disciplinary dynamic at the heart of the new civilization? A reproduction and politicization of manorial life according to the highest model?

Discipline and Ideology: Constitutions of State

The twelfth century sees momentous changes in political governance, changes constitutive of later European history. Individual rulers achieve a preeminence formerly unknown, thanks to accumulating wealth, manipulations of networks of reciprocity and patronage, and military action. Old techniques of governance acquire new importances, to the point of creating a new civilization, equipped with new institutions and new modes of thought. From its very beginnings, the state acquires the twin branches of its Janus-faced ambivalence. The creature of war and taxes, Leviathan also enacts pastoral solicitudes of a different kind of "police," the welfare of the population. Its trunk is the expropriatory process, which feeds the two branches competing for nurture: war and welfare.

The state did not spring full blown, as a coherent totality, from the shrewd minds of Henry II and Philip Augustus suddenly imagining its structures and offices, functions and bureaus, which they then concretized on the ground. Before Machiavelli, even the idea of the state as a unary totalization of land and people is rare. Nevertheless, there are indices that the modern, abstract, and unitary notion of the state began to take form during their reigns.[93] The kingdom of France comes to be conceptualized as "a single *seigneurie*, directed by a sovereign chief, peopled by subjects increasingly endowed with a sense of national unity."[94] The *res publica* represents the kingdom as an ensemble of material wealth, "superposed on the king." It is not far from the modern notion of the state as a *personne morale* whose juridical existence transcends government. *Francia* starts to designate territory beyond the Ile-de-France: the whole kingdom under Capetian domination. Expressions like *regnum Franciae* and *rex Franciae* replace *regnum Francorum* and *rex Francorum*, to signal a new conceptualization of power. Kingship exercises power, expecting obedience to an authority no longer conceived of as only personal, but territorial in a sense that includes the population: *status regni, status reipublica,* and even more: *status regis et regni.*

In England, Henry I's general administrative and legal reorganization after his conquest of Normandy in 1106 was soon followed by the effort to raise a huge aid for his daughter's betrothal in 1110. This conjunction is linked to the sophisticated accounting reforms that ultimately produced the Exchequer as a permanent financial bureau and the central organ of government.[95] Philip II's police of the realm included practical interventions: clearing Paris of mud and smelly garbage; chasing merchants and prostitutes from the cemetery of the Innocents and walling it in; building a central market—the original Halles—for commerce. Other aspects of "police" are less admirable. Teachers of "false doctrine" on the Ile de la Cité were burned at the stake: "By iron and by fire, the king decontaminated."[96] Even before Louis VII's death in 1180, Philip seized Jews in synagogues, canceling all Christian debts—he claimed one-third for himself, extorting 31,000 pounds, one and a half times the kingdom's annual revenue—before releasing them. "Police," anti-Semitism, and the king's crass self-interest were identical. Even in less offensive circumstances, the pastoral "police" of a kingdom is rarely disinterested. A healthy, well-fed, properly housed populace for which employment is available, will prove more productive than the same population weakened by disease, hunger, and homelessness. Increased productivity in turn produces more surplus value to be raked off by the state. Concern for popular welfare and extortion of its labor are identical. All depends on the political values in play—on ideology.

Ideology inheres in all forms of representation, directly or indirectly. Representation takes multiple forms: the textual and the human are two. Literacy and bureaucracy become the links of power, education, and culture. Agency becomes a key function of governance. For some, this includes literacy, calculation, letter writing, and record keeping. Others have roles better described as enforcers. Agency at first is largely drawn from the nobility; later, commoners are used as well. Bureaucracy appears. The need for bureaucrats fuels the "twelfth-century renaissance," as the social function and programmatic content of educational institutions undergo revolutionary change. Schools adapt their pedagogy, from preparing clerics to training administrators. Medieval M.B.A.'s now spend less time reading the traditional corpus, reducing classical textuality to the formulae of grammar and rhetoric in order to accede more rapidly to the techniques of letter writing and argumentation, more useful in the practices of governance. The state constructs itself in representation well before the creation of representative assemblies and popular elections. Its bureaucracies, first subordinated to existing feudal practices, fused the military, financial, and personal in tight intimacies of representation, evolved out of rulers' manipulations of complex, existing power relations and structures to their own advantage. Like Derrida's *Internationale* rather than Marx's, it developed "atop the networks it combats, using the adversary's own instruments."[97]

At first fused with the king's personal feudal domain and court, its bureaucratization did not observe Weberian norms of depersonalization and routinized specialization.

Toward the end of book I of *De scaccario*, the master takes a historical view of his project and defines the role of literacy in the composition of *Domesday Book* as an instrument of domination. Its survey legitimated property claims. Beyond that, its pragmatic effect was awesome. Writing in Anglo-Saxon culture had been secondary. Now, it recorded and represented the country, its land and people in minute detail, within the physical volume of a book: the book encapsulated the land. It was seen by natives, the colonized people of the conquest, as awesome, not only because their labor, their dues, their very existence were transformed into writing, as in the Book of the Day of Judgment itself, but also because exactly like that other Judgment, its judgments, once written, were unalterable, irremediable. The text represented submission as irrevocable, fixed in the permanence of writing. *Domesday* was an inquest: it fixed, spelled out, and signaled their doom, like stone images of Christ in majesty.[98]

This effect was precisely the intent attributed to William the Conqueror, who had not benefited from the stock account of the communitarian benefits of literacy. *Domesday* meant domination to the native population, their subjection, because in fact, William had so willed it. After the conquest, the king had

> decided to bring the conquered people under the rule of written law.[99]

The conqueror, having subdued the country militarily, now imposed the yoke of law on his conquest. Cobbled together from previous juridical systems, this law by which the people was subjected to the new masters was to be *written*. Daily life was subjected to literacy as a totalizing discipline. The terrified reception of *Domesday*, as the representation that doomed people to irrevocable subjection, was a perfectly correct reading of its "author's" intent.[100] Terror was an instrument of state policy from the first.

The church offered one model of the inherence of terror. Its "final judgments" of the damned were scattered across the countryside on tympanums and capitals of churches, particularly those associated with pilgrimages like Congues on the road to Compostella: one such image is reproduced on the cover of this book. Many others were to be found, at Autun in Burgundy for example. Its western portal, illustrating the Final Judgment, is deservedly famous. Within the visual discourse of the damned is inscribed the metadiscourse of the "author," though whether "Giselbertus" or Stephen of Bagé the bishop should be considered the sculptor is open to debate. Whoever the "author" was, word-games were not beneath him. Below the tympanum which represents the damned, a legend is carved:

> LET TERROR TERRORIZE THOSE BOUND BY TERRESTRIAL ERROR:
> OBSERVE THEIR FATE IN THESE IMAGES' HORROR.
>
> *TERREAT HIC TERROR   QUOS TERREUS ALLIGAT ERROR*
>
> *NAM FORE SIC VERUM   NOTAT HIC HORROR SPECIERUM.*

In the church before the nascent state, terror is an instrument of governance and control. Villon, in the ballad for his mother, will reinscribe the ideological practice. Its discursive and literate violence recycles the physical violence it attempts to control.

Violence was hardly dispelled by literacy, numeracy, or state governance. Literacy and numeracy are instruments. Their systematicity may be arbitrary and independent of reality, they may imply and facilitate certain modes of thought, but they are never neutrally employed. They are ambivalent social instruments, whose value is determined in particular uses. Literacy and numeracy are inherently no more "humanistic" and culturally desirable than they are inherently the tyrant's oppressive instruments. They are technologies, used well or ill. Alone, neither brings the *pax et justicia* so earnestly desired by so many.

The military and the church, analogously organized in hierarchy, admired or feared, are the historical sources of the "discipline" that is one mode of subjecting individuals to the state.[101] But force, like the new prince, is present-in-absence. Even in the disciplined state, violence is always an offstage potential. Feudalism's knights were the historical antecedents of Althusser's repressive apparatus, the instruments of organized terror. Practically speaking, however, that is an expensive method. It is not a method applicable to a general population, except in wartime or by totalitarian regimes. It is supplemented by representations with ideological value. The state, besides its preoccupation with violence and self-aggrandizement, also concerns itself with the interests of the people, their health and welfare. The population becomes the object of the state's solicitude, all the more convincing when wrapped in a religion which captures the holy terror of the sacred with symbolisms of peace and the pastoralism of the shepherd and his flock. Persuaded that its submission is divinely willed, that in exchange it receives salvation, protection from external dangers, and the solicitudes of power for its social security; its peace, health, welfare, and wealth; a population may more readily yield its substance to power's tax agents.

The *dependency* of the state on a population engaged in peaceful, productive pursuits, once it becomes the focused object of governmental attention, can produce an increased *independence* of the organs of government from the population in which it is embedded. That is the first paradox of governance. Angevin government, though "arbitrary, unreasonable, unjust and harsh," was nonetheless better than government in other places and at other times: "The crown imposed *discipline*, but it required *disciplining* itself."[102] Discipline is not only an instrument of state control, it is also an independent, systemic force, acting on and through the various instances of the entire sociopolitical culture. It produces a disciplined civilization that trumpets its freedom as an absolute.[103]

Ideology and discipline are differentiated in the subcultures of different social groups. The peasant's includes continued peaceability in the service of productivity; the knight's retains the potential for violence, submitted to the orders and commands of superior authority; the monk's is tailored to psychic subjugation, self-abnegation, and devotion to psychic instances. The newer religious disciplines of the twelfth century disseminated a mental technology appropriated from the monks, literacy and interpretation, but practiced by individuals living in the world—secular canons—or even at court, bureaucratic clerics. Jacques le Goff's "intellectuals of the Middle Ages" were early examples of Gramsci's "organic intellectuals."[104] In the secular world, their subjectivity was not simply equated with subjection. Only in the later Middle Ages, under Louis XI, would a concept of sovereignty based on the Roman *imperium* transform vassality into the unquestioning obedience of subjection.[105]

Official, instituted ideology was a monopolistic practice cast in a secret language, protected from inquisitive eyes and argumentative subjects by its inaccessibility to the overwhelming majority of the population. Church Latin protected a cultural enclave that excluded most of the commonality and lay nobility. For those not of the church, it was a form of universal disenfranchisement. Not that ideology within Latin clericality was uniform. It harbored political critique even before the political was established as an independent discursive domain. Such critique, however, proceeded by subtle adjustments and subtractions from a stock of traditional arguments as much as by overt affirmation, in a shared intertextuality sensitive to nuanced omissions under surface conventionalities.[106] Merely learning Latin as an instrumental, communicative language would not open its wealth of cultural capital. Linguistic proficiency was not equatable with cultural competence.

In any case, practical politics in princely courts was likely too crude for such intertextual delicacies. Vernacular ideology worked in discourse more accessible to the realities of knighthood, capturing crude desires and violent behaviors to subject them to the discipline of social utility. It operated by a stock of representations, images, and narratives, to which the warrior

Imaginary could staple its own terrors, desires, and hopes. The vernacular is the skein of daily experience, the intellectual architecture of its construction. Not acquired through institutional disciplines, schools, churches, or authoritative professions, it was not mediated by learned rules and technicalities; nor does it aim necessarily at clarity or precision.[107] From a Latinate clericality's perspective, the vernacular is the realm of the unforeseeable, the disseminations of potential counternarratives. It is the vehicle of the plebs' obduracy, offering a continual play of resistance to dominant discourse, sparking dynamics of dissent, intervention, and strategies against and around hegemony's integrative assimilation . . . even the development of oppositional systems of value. The vernacular's role and status are crucial to comprehending particular conjunctures in bilingual cultures. Absent prose discourse, ideological representation initially proceeded in the symbolic forms of poetry and narrative decried by the church. Lyric poetry, epic, and the novel constituted the ideological domain of the formative period.

PART III

IN STATE

CHAPTER 10

Problematizing the Subject:
Rose I

L ike his forebears, Philip Augustus did not patronize vernacular artists. Perhaps a matter of personal taste, it was certainly also a political choice: the crown's close alliance with the church precluded such patronage. The net effect is a peculiar discrepancy between the growing centralization of the monarchical state, and its exclusion of a lay, vernacular culture and ideology from royal support. That discrepancy itself is related to an epochal contrast. The process of subjective construction and elaboration characteristic of the twelfth century is generally a positive enterprise, expanding on the mirror of princes tradition. Late texts like the *Perceval* and *Le bel inconnu* are exceptional, looking forward to the problematization of subjectivity in thirteenth-century narrative: thus Guillaume de Lorris's *Roman de la rose*, a generation into the new century, and Heldris of Cornualle's *Silence*, a generation or so before its end. The juxtaposition of the two suggests the distinction between the subject and its identity.

The experimentalism of medieval textuality is nowhere better exemplified than in the intense sensorial rhetoric with which Guillaume de Lorris teases out a coherent, ambiguous dispersal of sense and the senses—particularly olfactory and visual—in nearly apprehensible meanings that seduce and elude the reader. The lover discovers a fountain in an orchard. At the bottom of clear water, among small pebbles, the crystalline mirror is suspicious: one stone or two, irradiating the orchard with the rainbow of colors? The entire garden is reflected there, but unreliably: it can't be seen all at once, one has to shift positions "to get the whole picture." So it is in reading this poem: the crystal(s) are its metaphorical *mise-en-abyme*; they mirror the effect of the text that contains them. Its internal referent, what it is about, the story its language tells, shift continually under one's gaze, a cognitive *moiré* propelling interpretations of ineluctable ambiguity. If Chrétien de Troyes and Marie de France define the modernism of the twelfth, Guillaume de Lorris signals a thirteenth-century postmodernism.

The status both of text and authorship are dubious. The very existence of the supposed author is questioned. His only trace is in the discourse of his "continuator," Jean de Meun, who says that Guillaume died before completing the poem. Was "Guillaume de Lorris" Jean de Meun's invention, palming off a text of his own, perhaps from his youth, as the initial fragment?[1] The existence of two authors paralleled the fragmentary nature of the first (short) and second (long) parts. But the fragmentary nature of the initial fragment also has been called into question and read, however implausibly, as a finished work.[2] This section is designated as *Rose I*, without prejudice. Its coherence will be our major concern. Arguments about authorship characterize our ignorance of medieval authors and are unimportant outside an ideology of "individualism" in which the figure of the author, as idealized subject, supposedly "guarantees" the work. The medieval text is "guaranteed"—as if any text were guaranteed!—by an appeal to tradition, often fictitious, invented on the spot for the purpose, and understood as such. Many texts are anonymous. Even when we possess a name, we usually know little more. Textually, "Guillaume" exists only insofar as Jean gives his name. That the proper noun "Guillaume de Lorris" is ipso facto fictive, however, stretches modern certainties too far. Even if "Guillaume" is a self-attributed pseudonym of Jean's, even if their identities were the same, still, the author of *Rose I* was not the same writing subject as that of *Rose II*. Authorship may reduce to identity; the enunciatory subjectivity is radically other.

The *Rose Novel* delves into love with intense exclusivity. There is no other topic but love, except, of course, its doublet poetry: they are each other's equivalents. Nevertheless, *Rose I* is not a mawkish, allegorized narrativization of past love poetry. The past is crucially important, in its omissions or elisions as well as in its positive continuation. Above all, the poem's brief exploration of love, together with its apparently unfinished state, have endeared it to modern readers put off by the intellectual gigantism that medieval readers relished in Jean de Meun. Jean's totalizing incorporation of the earlier work a generation or two later was *the* medieval bestseller for centuries. Even in the sixteenth century, the poet Clément Marot translated Jean's *Rose* into "modern" French for contemporary readers, as Chaucer had earlier done for the English. They loved length in those days and had the stamina to treasure its rhetorical transformations.[3] Yet, the modernity of Kafka, Beckett, and Borges prepares us somewhat for Guillaume's experimental sophistication . . . as Proust reconstitutes a dimension that ought to rehabilitate Jean.

Reading *Rose I* starts by recognizing its constitutive rejection. What is rejected is not a mere "literary" tradition within the conventionalism of medieval aesthetics, but a textual world constructed as diegesis of social reality. *Rose I* turns its back on the narrative tradition of knightly violence. Earlier, knightly predation gave specific, historical form to narrative's conflictual axis, in the political explorations of epic, in the political glorifications of history, in the civilizing attempts to coordinate Eros and Thanatos in "romance." The issue of violence was far from dead at the time of *Rose I*: see the cyclical *Vulgate Lancelot*, where the very virtues of knighthood bring about its self-destruction in *La mort le roi Artu*. *Rose I*'s constitutive gesture excludes violence from love.

The Peace of Love's Subjectivity

An earlier Marxist reading of *Rose I*, anchored in the assumption of social mimeticism, saw it as the nostalgic idealization of a chivalric aesthetic ethos, at a moment when the realization of chivalric ideals had become impossible, feudalism being pushed ineluctably toward introspection. Its Edenic framing of chivalric courtliness lay beyond a renunciation of all political, military, social function—any historical meaning. The aesthetic morality of knighthood survived, at the price of extruding itself from historical time.[4] Such a reading locates the text as a feudal class document: nothing is less certain. The textual machinery derives from the aristocratic twelfth-century novel tradition. But the *je* of the poem gives himself no social rank. He depicts himself as leaving a town—*la ville*. Some nobles resided in cities, but that was hardly typical. More telling is the fact that what is subtracted from the *Rose Novel* is precisely the warring function that, as the noble class's real social performance, was an integral ideological element. As a chivalric text, the *Rose Novel* has everything to recommend it, but the essential: a warrior on horseback.

Warrior violence, even in its submission to love, is elided in the *Rose*

Novel. Only love's desire remains, rather than "honor," to propel the narrative. The interdependence of Eros and Thanatos is broken: only Eros remains, as the dualistic problematic of "romance" is evacuated. "Romance" had been class specific, in both lyric and narrative. Its very success in establishing a new cultural domain of secular vernacularity made its *Stoff* available for the self-explorations of other classes. The young lover, leaving the city of an early spring morning, to explore a countryside that might derive from the gardening practices of either noble textuality or that of town dwellers, could just as readily have left a merchant household or a banker's home, as the town *hôtel* of a noble family. Codes, dreams, conventions, migrate across the walls of class.

Culture had acquired a new relative autonomy from preexisting structures, but one that was only *relative*. Medieval culture always marked indebtedness to constitutive traditions and a social presence that was both content and context. It was autonomous, not as an absolute, but *in relation to* some prior capture, and *in relation* to its social cotext. The indebtedness to aristocratic traditions of poetry is proudly displayed in *Rose I*, even as it opens a new textual domain. So is another and contradictory indebtedness, to the religious tradition. Personifications of the virtues and vices, common in the Latin clerical tradition, had recently been adapted to vernacular textuality. Throughout the thirteenth century, allegorical battles multiply, conjoining personifications in battle order with a narrative of personal adventure in teaching religious morality.[5] As with feudal genealogy, tradition is adapted by subtracting its originating rationale. Personifications now are grouped in certain ways, but in abscission of any religious morality. The forms of religious hermeneutics are captured for secular cultural reinvention: a secular deontology fused with erotic self-gratification.

The underpinnings of the appropriated traditions, their connections to historical political development, are evacuated. The framework allowing this evacuation is strategically selected from a third tradition. The dream vision allows for elision of the cultural *vraisemblable*, bypassing normative representational expectations while developing a principle of coherence of its own. That principle recasts narrativity itself. Before that, the text's rhetoric dialectically counters the freedom obtained by and for the dream vision and reasserts it simultaneously. Dream-freedom will be warranted by cohesion with reality, but with inversion of their usual relationship: reality follows vision, confirming its "truth" yet relegating "reality" to the dreams' tailwind. Dreams have a reputation for mendacity, but the enunciating "I" asserts their meaningfulness: *songes est senefiance*, a word both weighty and polysemous, occurring in grammar and rhetoric, in philosophy and theology.[6] It designates verbal maneuvers of indirection, tropes that signal meaning "covertly." Before Freud and Lacan, the language of dreams has the same ambivalence as poetry, alternating between signifying modes. At night, people dream

> many things covertly
> later seen overtly.[7]

Dream is one form of poetic language: their rhetorical structures are identical.[8] The "I" of the poem wants "to rhyme the dream." Nothing in the dream did not later materialize just as the dream had recounted.[9] The "dream" strategy allows the freedom to assert a truth contrary to "truth," making the dream as prophetic as it is free in invention: dream and the unconscious ignore the principle of noncontradiction. Dream rhetoric asserts textual independence from dross history, veridicality, and logic at the same time. It does not refer, since its putative reference lies in the future.

The dreamer dreams himself awake and leaves the city for an early morning walk to hear the new season's bird-song. At an enclosed orchard, on the outer wall are painted portraits of negative qualities: Hate, Crime, Low Class, Covetousness, Avarice, Envy, Sorrow, Old Age, Hypocrisy, and Poverty. Not only the images, but their narrative location produce meaning: these qualities are excluded from the society reconstituted within the walled orchard. The lover is allowed to enter: he is burdened by none of these conditions (though the text fudges on "poverty"). The wall marks the inner/outer category as constitutive. The remainder of the text will deconstruct it.

Entry to this new society is conditioned on leisure: Oiseuse is doorkeeper, a personage of ambiguous fame, whose Latin etymon (*otium*) signifies political and mental peace as well as a soft and lazy negativity.[10] Her role as doorkeeper underlines an unexpected "realism": not the reproduction of social reality, as in the nineteenth century, nor medieval philosophical realism, but a cold judgment of social necessities: a certain leisure, financial ease as well as mental *disponibilité*, are required to play the game of love, or to play love as a game. One does not play at love by earning a living through manual labor, but by participating in the figure of perfect harmony available to a closed society that operates by exclusion, hierarchy, wealth: the dance of the *carole*, the ballet of social elegance whose circular shape constitutes the equality of the elect. This is not a world of unmediated gratification—dream makes room for anxieties as well as wish-fulfillment—but it is a world (re)constituted entirely around the single value of love. Nothing in the garden does not bear on love. Nothing exists in the world of the garden except by reference to love: all things reflect love, hamper or further its fulfillment. Negativities exist, but only as negations of love's centrality. It is a totalitarian world of ontological and exclusive eroticization.

Along with politics and history, identity also disappears: the anchoring of the individual in the structures of society. Identity depends on two processes: (dis)identification with binary others, and the location of the self on a universal social gridwork. The very possibility of representing such processes is eliminated by the regime of *Rose I*. Identities in the ordinary sense are erased. The narrative's subject is nothing but a *je*, of which we only know it is young, male, and knows something of the courtly tradition. The object of the narrative refers to a woman, a rosebud. The dreamt and dreaming subject, the rose as object, exist merely as origin and destination of a narrative action, which alone makes sense of the figures it deploys.[11] But that narrative is one of singular indeterminacy. Identity and alterity disappear along with the known political and historical world. Together with singing birds and burgeoning springtime flowers, qualities act throughout, dancing in harmonious pairs.

Identity disappears, but subjectivity spreads like an oil slick over the textual surface. Emile Benveniste identified the pronoun "I" as the individual's entry into language. In *Rose I*, "I" subtends the entire discourse. Other entities are accorded status as discursive subjects, but the reader never doubts that the discourse before him is enunciated by a single speaker. Other than its age and gender, that *je* is defined only as the subject of desire, and the narrative efforts to gratify it. Desire for the rosebud subtends the entire text as its narrative axis. Narrativity has replaced poetry as love's constitutive other. The pronoun's narrative invites the reader to assume both.

There is a story then, somewhat odd, whose rhetoric is odder. The endlessly repeated *je* grounds the discourse, not as autobiography or autobiographical fiction, but as the playfully self-conscious simulacrum of autobiography: in the subject's anonymity, the subtraction of all individualizing traits of identity, the "I" simulates the conditions of autobiography—which does not yet exist in the vernacular—even as it eliminates its basis.[12] This simulacrum of autobiography and fiction poses the most fundamental questions of subjectivity and identity presupposed, not only by autobiography but also by actual language use. The simulacrum problematizes subjectivity, in the very act of creating it as an embodied subjectivity. Outside conventionalized descriptions, primarily of idealized icons of cultural beauty, medieval literature (except the fabliau and *Renart*) assumes more than it portrays the body. Epic heroes are tall, barrel-chested, and emanate presence, but little more. Yvain's body has little density, other than the wound that marks his identity: by the cut, the man is known.

Embodiment does not derive from any self-description. Rather, the body functions as the vehicle of a surprisingly wide range of sensory perceptions: the body is a medium making its synesthetic sensorium available to the reader. Sight is assumed and constitutive in narrative, particularly in relation to identity. Here, it records, in addition to the portraits and the personages of the dance, dimensions of space, shapes, depth, and color with a concrete specificity rare in medieval texts. Sound flows from the birds both outside the garden and inside, and instills a strong desire to enter. Once *je* does so, their song is identified with poetry and hence the text itself:

> The birds furnished
> A great, a sweet and pleasing service,
> lais of love and courtly sonnets
> warbled in their songs,
> some high, some low.
> Joking aside, their song's
> sweetness and melody
> regreened my heart.[13]

It stresses that lowest, most animal of the senses, the most evanescent of sensory experiences, the sense of smell. The rose's

odor spreads throughout,
its sweetness
fills the entire space;
and when I felt it so perfume,
I felt no desire to return,
but was eager to take it.[14]

Synesthesia of sight and perfume alleviates sorrow; smell and touch transport the subject.[15] As memory, they overwhelm the subject:

When I recall the kiss
which perfumed my flesh
sweeter than balm
I almost faint
for my heart still encloses
the sweet savor of roses.[16]

The subject is coterminous with corporeal sentience. Slipping into the sliding signifier's proffered textual identifications, the reader is in for a prime sensorial exploration, one which reconstitutes an Edenic wholeness of corporeal integrity. Not so the object: it possesses not even the illusory wholeness of the pronominal subject. Rather than constructed by a narrative quest, it remains passive, reactive. It lacks identity, as does the subject, but without the integrity of a subject engaged in narrative action, or the corporeality that devolves from a sensorium engaged.

The erasure of identity dispels the alterity that grounds conflict. Conceiving of an interlocutor as Other, it is thought, ipso facto turns that other into an enemy. If "Othering" is circumvented, perhaps war and violence can be avoided. Absent identity, alterity disappears and with it the very possibility of identifying an antagonist. The poem's disintegration of identity responds to the idealistic desire to substitute love for conflict, Eden for a world of violence. Its vision evacuates the condition of possibility for conflict: it is the first Utopian novel in modern Europe. Perhaps that is why Jean de Meun, a shrewd, realistic, and materialist thinker in the line of Aristotle, Spinoza, and Marx, criticized its illusory quality.

Narrative and Reflexive Subjectivation

Rose I draws on multiple textual subsystems: (1) the *locus amoenus*, the Garden of Pleasure that figures a terrestrial paradise; (2) the trap of love, with its God of love, his arrows, a key for the treasure of the heart, the ideology of love, the rhetoric of the rose; (3) the actantial system of the psychomachia, its warring personifications recast from religious morality into an amoral secular deontology of amorous satisfaction.[17] This heavy intertextual load could readily fly off into centrifugal anarchy. It is held together, quasi magically, by that powerful narrative form, the quest. After an initial, discursive prologue, its first major episode, the qualifying test, is redoubled: disidentification with the negative qualities excluded from the world of love by the portraits on the outside wall is followed by the second qualifying test of a potential identity, that of Narcissus. Both proffered identifications are denied.

At the Fountain of Narcissus, the lover is installed as the full-fledged narrative subject, constituted by desire. Seeing the reflection of a rosebud, the lover assumes his narrative program, oriented to its obtention as his object. At this point, he—like Yvain before Laudine at their first interview—lends homage to the God of Love as his feudal superior. His thirteen–count decalogue is the Destinator's ideology, and names the Adjuvants to see him through hard times: Hope, Sweet Thoughts, Sweet Talk, Sweet Looks, and above all, Fair Welcome. Having gathered his troop of supporting forces, the subject encounters his opponents: Dangier, along with Gossip, Shame, and Fear. Ambiguous are new adjuvants: Reason and Friend. Together, they approach the object of desire—the rosebud—and obtain a kiss. This first success is immediately transformed into disaster. The opposing forces imprison Fair Welcome, the lover's link to the object of his desire, in a rapidly erected fortress. Without Fair Welcome, the lover cannot accede to the lady's favors. He is left to plaintively apostrophize Fair Welcome, as the fragment ends.

Is it possible to read the text just outlined as "a finished work," an autonomous whole self-sufficient unto itself? For all its ambiguous complexities, this text responds to what was once called a unitary inspiration, but the postulation of a proximate ending defines the limits of modern imagination more than medieval practice. True, Fair Welcome is now imprisoned in a fortress, but since the lover has glommed on to the rose with desire at fever pitch, why defer aesthetic pleasure beyond conquering the rose in short order? Three major reasons exist to believe *Rose I* is incomplete: Jean de Meun's assertion of its incompleteness; the fact that the poem never fulfills its reiterated promise to state its own meaning; and most tellingly, the narrative frustration of the quest pattern. These reasons are

most convincing: they undermine the argument of the fragment's wholeness. Perhaps Jean de Meun was right, not only in asserting that *Rose I* was
incomplete, but in the demonstrated length required to complete it.

The Fountain of Narcissus is a key moment in the poem's narrative
structure. It is hyperbolic to claim that the lover had lived nothing previously, but there is truth to the notion that his story really begins at the
fountain.[18] There, the lover assumes his narrative, by an act of disidentification: he rejects a proffered image as a self-image. Only a subject is capable of that de-negation of identity: the poem's *je* acquires subjectivity by it,
marking the sophistication of medieval narrative and its understanding of
subjectivity. The episode of the fountain is structured as a triptych: the
Fountain of Narcissus, the Fountain of Crystals, and the Mirror of Love.
Each successive section rewrites the preceding, the whole exploring the
problematics of representation.[19] The first panel is bipartite. A beautiful
fountain, identified by an inscription at its upper edge, is the place of Narcissus's death. A metacommentary (or the fountain's indirect free discourse)
briefly retells the story of Narcissus and the nymph Echo.[20] Pride leads him
to disdain Echo's love, *une haute dame*. She dies of vexation, demanding of
God that Narcissus of the savage heart be destroyed by such a love as finds
no doctor—invoking the convention of love as illness and the beloved as
doctor—to teach him the grief of true lovers refused in such vile manner.

In the second section, Echo takes revenge. Narcissus falls in love, not
with himself—this Narcissus is not a narcissist, any more than Oedipus
suffers from the Oedipus complex—but with his reflection, his *ombre*. He
goes mad and dies in short order. One modern reader finds this abridged
revision of Ovid uninteresting:[21] it answers neither to classical memories or
post-Freudian expectations. Another cites this text to assert that, for the
Middle Ages, Narcissus is the universal model for noble love.[22] But the
poem's lover rejects that imposition. Myth is one form of the fictive referent of fiction: originally, a shared, collective fiction. The Freudian reading
interprets the myth of Narcissus as a narrative of universal pertinence, but
texts are not merely symptomatic formations: they always interpret and
distort the myths they retell, whether in a psychoanalytic context or not.
Texts also interpret and distort the elements they take from their culture to
reconstruct themselves. The lover in the *Roman de la rose* retells his own
story. At first, he is first afraid to look into the fountain: he fears for him-

self . . . until he remembers Narcissus. That reassures him. He can approach the fountain, without fear of ill effects: it had been madness to distance himself.[23] The point is not rationalization, but the disjunction between the mythic narrative of Narcissus, and himself as "reader in the text." The lover is not Narcissus. The myth—the story of Narcissus—is the referent; the exemplum of the Fountain is the *representamen*, the narrative sign; the lover, as interpreter, produces the interpretant. The ground is the experience of love. So far, there is no basis on which to either accept or reject identification. Something more is required. An element is missing: that which gives the basis for judgment of the relationship between self and exemplum. How can the lover be so sure of rejecting Narcissus as an image of himself?

Temporality is essential. The myth of Narcissus allows no room for self-knowledge,[24] but the lover acts as if he already possessed something lacking in Narcissus. What he already knows, in fact, is the story of Narcissus.[25] Temporality generates disjunctions, too readily disregarded. Autobiography generates two instances: the subject of the past, and the present narrator. *Rose I* subdivides these further. Four have been specified: the dreamer, the young man who walks into the garden, the slightly older young man to whom all the events of the dream subsequently happened, and the narrator who addresses their stories to the reader;[26] the last constitutes a fifth level of subjectivity. Moving down the instances from the original dream toward the present narration, we move farther away from the primary identificatory process of dream life. Rather than fuse any of these with Narcissus (a sixth level of subjectivity), it would be wiser to respect the narrative's own distinctions by yet another instance of subjectivity: the author, whatever his name or identity, the subject of the text. These instances are not collapsible if one wants to track their production of meaning, but they may prove endlessly recursive.

Each instance marks a different subjectivity. All differ, at least potentially, from Narcissus. The myth of Narcissus, as reinterpreted by its exemplum, does not form a mirror of self-knowledge signaling a danger to the subject. Modern psychoanalytic "Narcissism" is quite irrelevant to the non-Narcissus, the *I* of the poem in question, as well as to the Narcissus recounted by the exemplum: the story of a young man who is betrayed precisely because he does not recognize the image with which he falls in love as an image of himself. It is precisely because he understood that he could not accomplish his desire (to love another? to make love to the *ombre* afloat under the surface of the water?) that Narcissus dies.

The mythic narrative of Narcissus turns into a negative exemplum, rejected as not representing the lover or his possible narrative. Identification has two forms: positive and negative. A reader may positively identify with a narrative character . . . or not. The first reaction is quasi automatic: it is the primitive reaction, ridiculed at least since Aristotle made fun of an audience member who jumps up to warn a dramatic actor of an impending turn of events. Conjunction is assumed as the normative reaction: that's what a positive exemplum counts on, teaching a moral lesson via a psychic identification with a narrative actant. The negative reaction of nonidentification, the statement: "That's *not* me!" is more sophisticated. It is the reaction which says: I understand the story, I compare it to myself and what I might do in similar circumstances: that, however, is *not* how I would react, that is *not* what would happen to me. That disjunction defines the subject as the interruption of the effect of a rule by a subject submitted to that rule.[27] The aesthetic distance of twelfth-century narrative, incorporated into the palimpsest of fiction, both defines and reaffirms the reader's moral and aesthetic freedom.[28] The story of Narcissus is not that of the *Rose Novel*. Rejecting the narrative that would lead to the fate of Narcissus, the lover becomes the subject of his own narrative program. Embedding does not mean going to bed with.

The second stage of the fountain's narrative substitutes for the exemplum its condition of possibility, the representation of representation. It rewrites the first in the direction of both greater danger and philosophical amplitude: the wider net is more dangerous. Part of the danger is the worst of all dangers for an interpreter of language. The language itself is contradictory: a modern editor throws up his hands before a "practically insoluble problem."[29] In a detailed, crisp, limpid, and precise ecphrasis of the clear and ever-flowing waters of the fountain, running in separate channels that feed the surrounding thick green grass, the passage gives a self-contradictory account: medieval hyperrealism etched by Escher. First, it speaks of the lover's seeing two crystals in the depth of the flowing waters; then, it tells of a single crystal that reveals the entire being of the orchard.[30] One crystal, or two? The question is pregnant in several ways. It is pertinent to the number of crystals themselves, and to their pragmatic effects. When the sun sends down the clarity of its rays, more than one hundred colors appear in the crystal. Such force inhabits the crystal that the place—its trees and flowers and whatever adorns the orchard—appears in it. The crystal(s) is/are an ultimate representation: all things enter in the sign, refracted, reproduced, represented in their own image (*ombre*), in their own shape and color. As *speculum*, the mirror is a totalizing representation of all existence, with one caveat. Crystal as universal signifier can represent the totality of its closed-off world, but only in a two-step. Whatever position one occupies while looking into the crystal(s), only one half of the orchard is seen. To see the remainder (*le remenant*), it suffices to turn, though here again, there is ambiguity: Is it the lover who turns, or is it the crystal(s) that turn(s)? To "see" the images in the crystals is to "read" them: Isn't the two-step a formula for reading, possible only in its doubling in rereading?

An ordinary hermeneutic sees the crystals as the eyes one would see reflected in any mirror: one's own. That is not how one of the most famous of troubadour poems saw it. Bernart de Ventadorn fused the Narcissus myth with the image of the beloved's eyes as mirror, and himself with Narcissus.[31] Guillaume de Lorris separates and opposes them. The exemplum of Narcissus is not relevant to him, but the crystals that reflect the entirety of the world reflected, his lady's eyes, that is the real danger, the *miroërs perilleus*. Looking into that mirror, Narcissus saw only himself and died from it. Indeed, no one looking into this mirror has protection, feudal or medical, to prevent seeing what leads to the path of love.[32] The crystals are not safer than Narcissus's example. But they are different.

Difference is key. Erotically speaking, a vertical distance of only two or three feet separate crystals from rosebud. The textual difference is greater. Between the moment the reader is informed of the crystalline reflection of the garden's totality, until the narrator explains what he saw in the refractive surfaces, a rhetorical development intervenes that is far from the detailed specificity of the garden described. It has to do with the powers of the crystalline mirror. No one who looks into it is protected. A new rage attacks its victims, where neither sense nor measure count: here there is pure will to love (*ci est d'amer volenté pure*. l. 1584). Hence the name, the Fountain of Love, about which a number of people have spoken in the vernacular and in [Latin?] books (*en romanz et en livre*. l. 1597).

This passage is rhetorical, emphatic, and puzzling. It occurs between crystalline eyes and rosebud, whose distance is determined visually and narratively. Having differentiated Narcissus and the narrator, the text juxtaposes them again. Describing in precise detail the functioning of the crystals, it develops what had lightly been touched on as a simile (l. 1553), the theme of the mirror, the Old French term which translates the Latin *speculum*: the mirror as encyclopedia, the summation of all knowledge.[33] The mirror is repeated, then qualified as perilous, the source of new rage, sown with Cupid's seed.[34] Puzzling, a bit mysterious: one hopes to catch the drift. The text promises it will deal with the issue later: the reader will hear the truth when "I" expound, describe, and comment its *mistere*.[35] The narrator emphasizes his mystery, promising to clear it up . . . later. In a peculiarly self-negating moment of proleptic history—after the discovery of the fountain, but earlier than the present, thus simultaneously past and future from different perspectives—he notes that the mirror betrayed him: he would never have gotten mixed up with it, he would have avoided its traps, had he known its power and strengths. This, just before he discovers the love of his life, the single bud among the rosebushes. After exemplary limpid clarity, confusion and mystery set in, as religious terms like "martyr" and "mystery" mark the intensity of secular love. The rhetoric promises clarification . . . later, but the narrator's promises are lies: whoever he was, whatever his identity, "Guillaume de Lorris" never did explain himself or his text.

He does tell a tale, however. Staring into the crystals, the lover spied a thousand things, so many things a wide-angle image must have registered, one that implies a substantial volume between the mirror's eyepiece and the objects reflected. Among these thousands, a hedge of rosebushes appeared. The lover went toward them. When he approached more closely, their delightful odor penetrated his deepest heart. The description occupies dozens of lines, until he discovers the single rosebud he falls in love with. The textual distance between crystals and rosebud, between eyes and sex, marks another distance, one that makes modern readers distinctly uncomfortable. Medievals, more accustomed to the artificialities of language, had less difficulty with them. If I have spent some time on this particular textual crux, it is not for its erotic character alone, which is quite real. Its careful organization, its emphatic rhetoric, its willful confusion of prior distinctions, combine to mark a major disjunction, by comparison to which the earlier subjective disjunctions are minimal. It is the disjunction, within a given, highly coherent narrative, of the two functions of language, signification and representation. A text organized as representation of a love affair, even allegorical, between a young man and the lady of his desire, would take a different shape than *Rose I*. Depending on what was to be done with that narrative *Stoff,* varied structures were available, from the rather loose compositions of Beroul and Thomas, through Chrétien's highly organized narrative structures, to contemporary experiments with the complex forms of interweave. Other allegories assume a more demanding referentiality and remain closer to an originary narrative than Guillaume de Lorris's text. *Rose I* opens a space between signification and representation, toying with their separability.

Jean de Meun's *Rose II*, toward the end of the century, uses the (dis)guise of the by-then largely obsolescent intellectual structure of allegory, for a different purpose. Exactly contemporary to the vernacular maturation of prose discourse, Jean deploys a brilliant exploration of the allegorical structure, not as prose theology but as poetic discourse. In the expansiveness of its many personifications, its poetic discourse constructs a multiplicity of perspectival subject positions vis-à-vis the problematic of love, in multiple discords with each other. *Rose I* develops a complex layering (a *feuilleté*) of subjectivity within internal space. The construction of that "internal" space is the central feature of its structural experiment. The inner/outer category, integral to mental life both as a positive, legal, and ethical construct and as an illusion that Jean de Meun might also have denounced in calling for its deconstruction, is a standard topos in twelfth-century textuality. No other text in the Old French period constructs an inner space comparable to *Rose I*.

The question is, inner to what? A mental space between signification and representation, it retains reference to the experiential while producing meanings not anchored in recognizable experience. The latter remains pertinent but marginalized, at the edges of the text, occasionally concretized, held at a distance by the text's elaborate constructions of a significatory reality. The text reminds us, from time to time, of its representational potential. Rather than tell an anthropomorphic story, it does something else. Its continual maneuvers establish and sustain the parameters across which is woven an oscillatory interiority. It is a mental space. Is it a psychic space? Does it constitute subjective space, as might exist within a given individual? It certainly does not "represent" subjective space, since such space does not exist in anterior secular reality.[36] But in textually constructing such space, was *Rose I* doing the ideological work of its polity by creating a model of subjectivity, defined as inner space, on which ensuing subjects could model their own subjectivities? Does it imply that the model of subjectivity that pertains to the centralized, disciplinary state is a reader's subjectivity?

Between the first two panels of the triptych operates, not a principle of equivalence, but an intertextuality that constructs a difference in focus. That difference is comparable to the different views of reality obtained by shifting positions in front of the crystals. Depending on one's position toward the transparently reflective surface, they produce different images. The surface stays identical to itself, but the images struck off it differ. The same is true for the surface of the text and the different readings produced by the readers' differing positions vis-à-vis the text. The reader's zoom lens may focus on the crystals themselves, in a literal reading of the subject's pursuit of the rose and Fair Welcome's imprisonment in the fortress. This focus will strike most readers as odd, since it postulates as literal what would be metaphor or simile in ordinary language ("My luv is like a red red rose"), and deploys the anthropomorphic framework of narrative onto a discrepant object and secondary characters. It cathects gynecomorphic desire with an inanimate object and attributes capacities for narrative action to entities that are not anthropomorphic agents. The discrepancy between the framework and the objects leads the reader to refocus the lens by treating the object and the secondary characters as "symbolic," which allows for their redefinition by reference to a "normal" reference, the social relationship between a man and a woman. But the surface of the text does not allow for that "translation" consistently. While certain moments allow and indeed encourage the effort at redefinition, at treating textual givens as referring to another scene, others don't, blocking the effort at "translation." As a result, the reader is shuttled back to the "original" text in its literal meaning.

Reading *Rose I* consists of a continuing shuttle between the two parameters of meaning, roughly similar to a medieval "realism" that takes the qualities of the personifications as real and a nominalism that considers them as mere nouns to be traversed in getting to the narrative. Neither is entirely satisfactory, each "saves" the other at moments of discrepancy. That shuttle constructs an intermediary space, a space of incompletely coded correspondences. It is, then, in the space constructed by that shuttle between phantasm and reality that "I" progress toward a postulated object of desire. Insofar as desire—*d'amer volonté pure*—is thought of as internal, the space through which the subject of desire travels is constructed as an interior space. And since it is the space through which travels the subject of desire, it is subjective space.

And yet, the object of erotic desire is external: the other . . .

The Dangier of Woman's Body: Pulverizing the Object

The construction of subjectivity in the name of "civilized" peace incurs substantial costs. Various choices—the tradition excluded, the topic selected, an imagery of sensory gratifications—suggest an idealized diegesis of peaceful harmony. The subject, lacking marks of identity but inscribed by the universal shifter "I," presents the reader an easy assumption of textual subjectivity. The subject "feels" whole, even if analysis reveals unsuspected divisions.

The object's identity, however, is not merely erased: it is pulverized. The other—the lady, admired, desired, sought out in the garden—is fragmented and fetishized. The reduction operates in two modes. One is the metaphoric, metonymic, and symbolic reduction of the lady to a rosebud. Some have denied the erotic reference of the rose. The rose may be Rose, the narrator's lady; it may be the lady's love that the lover seeks; but the rose cannot be a representation of the female genitalia, "unrepresentable" in any case.[37] Why should Guillaume de Lorris or the modern medievalist be held responsible for the transgressions of Georgia O'Keeffe or Judy Chicago? In no way can the slow opening of the rosebud's petals represent the glistening labia opening with arousal. It is generally agreed that no single key delivers a univocal "translation" of *Rose I*; there is also agreement on the suppression of its most obvious reading, the erotic and most fetishistic metonymy of all. Jean de Meun may reach the "scabrous" stage of writing, but hardly courtly Guillaume de Lorris, oh no!

At moments, the rose is Rose. At others, the rose is Rose's love or the lover's love. At other moments yet, the burgeoning rose petals are the lady's sexual lips, opening responsively. Always, of course, the rose is a rose is the rose. The rose also has nothing to do with the woman: it is the symbol of the lover's desire, of the lack that impels him toward the rosebud. The rose is the metaphor more than metaphoric for the object of desire, however conceived. But metaphoricity disappears in the totalizing substitution of the rosebud for that object. The rose is the polyvalent signifier that, tantamount to the object of desire, takes the meaning appropriate to whatever context is imposed. In the totalizing effect of memory—a crucial theme— all aspects differentiated in immediacy are fused: its "I" is objectified and derealized simultaneously.

The second reductive mode is analytical. Anthropomorphic narrative actors—"characters"—disintegrate into qualities that, rendered as autonomous and independent, act like characters. Personifications pick out qualitative aspects of psychic functioning, staging the shifting motions of feeling and passion as the drama of interacting agents. The reductive analysis of personification negates the representation of persons. Yet the actual functioning of the text is the opposite of its supposed "abstraction." "Fair Welcome" (*Bel Acueil*) is the lady's social grace; *Pitié* is closer to "sympathy" or the German *Mitgefühl* (the meaning it retains until Rousseau) than its modern English cognate "pity." *Franchise* connects to the tribal freedom of the Franks, their legal and characterological "nobility": hence the signifier's slide into meanings like "sincerity, openness." These, along with Shame and Fear, are all aspects of the lady's person, as the lover approaches, parts of her psyche:[38] the intervention of Venus marks the awakening of her desire. Partial representations of the lady's psychic life, they result from psychological analysis, fetishistic at worst, yet linked metonymically to the lady's own subjectivity, as embodied in a person. She may be the lover's object of desire, but as a narrative agent, she has her own subjectivity, whether presupposed or textualized. The fetish retains a connection to the total person its metonymy distorts.

As their variety is examined, however, the "personifications" become profoundly ambiguous. So does narrative, after Venus's intervention obtains a kiss for the subject, willingly delivered by the lady. New agents expand the field of personifications and forces arrayed against the lover and his desire. Badmouth and Jealousy suddenly enter the scene. The lady has no triangular reason to be jealous of the lover. Jealousy is a general social phenomenon: others who observe the progress of the relationship become jealous of its participants. Jealousy expresses its resentment by spreading evil Gossip about the lover and the lady: Badmouth. A simple, recognizable drama of court life stretches under the allegory. It is not the drama of romantic triangles.

The drama of representation is another matter. The personifications that represented partial aspects of the lady's psyche are now juxtaposed to personifications of a different status. As general social processes, Jealousy and Gossip are not anchored in individual persons at all, whether the lady or another. Rather than aspects of individual psyches, they represent multiagent social processes: more than one person is involved when gossip spreads. Some personifications are aspectualizations of individual psychological reactions; the ontology of others is in a larger social sphere. And then there are the personifications that denote neither individual qualities nor social processes, but philosophical "accidents" or circumstances of life, such as Old Age and Poverty, painted on the orchard's outer wall, and Leisure who admits lover to the garden. Finally, and most paradoxical from a theoretical perspective, some "personifications" are persons. Reason bridges the gap between a social rationality and the reason of the individual, but Friend and the Old Woman are narrative encounters of a third kind. They are, in fact, exactly what their names state, character-types who define a human category. Friend is a friend, Old Woman is an old woman.

Trying to conceptualize these personifications as "acting abstractions" (*abstractum agens*) is beside the point. The text's narrativity, its transformation of an intertext, and its conception of subjectivity are far more radical. The traditional psychomachia is symmetrical: two armies arrayed against each other fight it out until one obtains victory. In *Rose I*, a fundamental dissymmetry[39] unbalances previously equilibrated forces and the possibility of suspense their [near] equality provides. A first set of negative values is simply excluded from the diegetic world: those painted on the outside wall. Most personages within the garden belong to the troop of the God of Love. A smaller number present obstacles to love's progress. They share one trait with their antagonists. The existence of all is defined entirely by their relationship to the lover's project. None of them—Gossip, Jealousy, Shame, Fear—has any existence outside the lover's potential narrative trajectory.

The coherent diegesis of the terrestrial Eden is defined by its exclusion of any quality, circumstance, or character not defined by its relation to Love, whether in support of or in opposition to its progress. All existence within the orchard is defined by Love. Furthermore, although an abstract spatial representation of the garden is possible even to its very corners,[40] the narrative trajectory and the personages encountered are all oriented by the subject's progress. No male narrative in European literature will be so entirely subjective, until Samuel Beckett's novels. If the narrative is centered on the subject, and the subject possesses the illusory wholeness of the first-person pronoun, the object is fragmented and fetishized. The subject's wholeness is guaranteed—superficially—by the questing first-person singular pronoun, driven by desire and assumed by the reader's identification; the object is rent by personifications and by its reductive symbolic representation as "the rose." So persuasive is the poem's organization around a quest, its sensorial description of the orchard, its subtle tracking of interpersonal tropisms, that the object for the sake of which the text's narrative is supposedly created disintegrates into dispersed fragments at the subject's approach.

The Big Noise of Politics

Rose I rejects the noisy world of politics, even in its courtly refinements, taking refuge in complex maneuvers of dream, idealization, and sensory overload. Yet reading complicates the text. An incomplete survey of political terminology picks up some fifty lexemes, many recurring more than once. A partial but substantial sketch of medieval society is implicit in terms like *seigneur, chevalier, sergent, païsanz, vilain, cuvert, poesté, conestablie, vassal, sooudoier,* and *sougiez; ban, covant, garantir, homage, pleges, regne, servir,* and *se rendre; guere* and *gerroier, forces et vertuz, forçoier, traïre, traitre* and *traïson, prison, recreandise, malvestiez, gonfanon;* and, of course, *fortrece* and *Dangier.*

The spatial dimension of the narrative reproduces, with hallucinatory hyperrealism, the social space of an orchard. The same is true of the narrative's reproduction of the political codes of its time, at both the verbal level and that anthropomorphic level where narrative organizes the diegesis of the text. In spite of the initial rejection of war and politics, that component of the twelfth-century romance paradigm returns in the very notion necessary to narrative development, that of an obstacle to the satisfaction of desire. Obstacles are the essence of narratives. The impediment in *Rose I* harks back not only to earlier adventure novels but also to epic warfare. Fair Welcome's imprisonment in the newly constructed fortress lays the narrative basis for ulterior—though unwritten—episodes of the fortress besieged. The idealization of a harmonious, peaceful society, disciplined by *Amor*'s deontology and the rules of music and dance, gives way to a representation of affect and desire as conflict, rage, and war.

The war party is led by an odd personage named Dangier. The term will eventually give modern French and English "danger," but its medieval meaning is broader and more imposing. The actor is a most peculiar creature, seen from an inimical perspective: ugly, ill tempered, a lazy guardian who takes pleasure in threatening those he guards against. Large, black, bristling; eyes red as fire, wrinkled nose, a hideous face, screaming like a madman (2904–9); standing on his feet, nasty and angry, holding a thorny stick (3139 ff.); he lifts his head, rubs his eyes, shakes himself, wrinkles his nose, rolls eyes, and swells up with anger (3713–16). Like Calogrenant's villein, Dangier marks the borderline between animality and the lowest reaches of the human: the peasant, as seen by those who exploit and depend on the peasantry . . . or possibly a guard dog!

What is such an intensely negatively charged description doing in an idealized landscape of amorous passion? First, Dangier figures precisely as obstacle to love's fulfillment. He is the grimmest obstacle, which explains the rhetorical negativity that attends him. This functional description does not explain, however, why Dangier should be put in charge of Fair Welcome's imprisonment. What sense does Dangier make, in the social narrative of love? What would Dangier respond to in the mental world of Love, alongside his cohort of Fear, Shame, Jealousy, Badmouthing, Gossip? Both the personification and the common noun appear as *dangier*. Uses of the latter may tell us more than study of literary parentage. There is little direct indication, in the text, of the word's primary set of meanings. That is political. A synonym of crown, power, and lordship, of lands, possessions, inheritances that transmit power over others, its best translation remains the cognate of its etymon. It comes ultimately from Latin *dominium*, through an intermediary *dom(i)niarium**: "domination," "lordship,"

---

* In philology, denotes a hypothetical form.

"rule," "ownership," indicate the meaning it retains in Shakespeare: "You stand within his danger, do you not?"[41] It was key to a theoretical struggle between secular politics and the church: Did anything other than ecclesiastical sanction raise secular political communities above their origins in "brigandage and usurpation"? In medieval Latin, it expressed the feudal conception of ownership.[42] In French, it readily metaphorized power: love's, God's, or humans'.[43] The meaning modulates to violence, force, and strength, to arrogance, insolence, and presumption, as well as to eagerness and appetite. One specialized use is oppositional: denial, refusal, resistance, or impediment are often the meaning, in phrases such as *faire dangier de* or *a*, and *mener dangier*. So in *Rose I*, the God of Love, using his arrows, weakens the lover and demands surrender:

> Vassal, you're captured, there's no point
> turning aside or defending yourself,
> don't *fai dangier* to surrender . . .
> Whoever *moine* [show, demonstrate] *dangier* against
> someone he should flatter
> and entreat is crazy.[44]

After power and domination, the word acquires a secondary force as resistance, both oppositional and interpositional, in line with Dangier's appearance. He appears first after Fair Welcome's initial fright at the lover's request for possession of the rosebud and Fair Welcome's refusal to separate the bud from the rosebush; he threatens to jump the lover and chases the latter away. "Plucking the rosebud" does not translate readily into a social or erotic relation of lover and lady (unless as plucking her virginity), but Dangier clearly represents a psychic function which withdraws the lady's warm welcome when the lover becomes too eager for favors.

The lover seeks advice from Reason and Friend, rejects the former and embraces the latter, who recommends mollifying that side of the lady opposed to the lover's advances. Thanks to this strategy of flattery and the interventions of Franchise and Pitié, Dangier moderates his position, allowing the return of Fair Welcome. So charming is the latter that the lover thinks he has moved from Hell to Paradise! The rose has swelled a bit, not yet opening to the point of revealing its seed among the petals, but relations with Fair Welcome—social relations with the lady—go swimmingly: the lover requests a kiss. Chastity opposes the grant: a kiss is a down payment on the rest. The conversation continues, kisses continue to be deferred, until Chastity's antagonist arrives on the scene: Venus, desire always at war with chastity. She addresses Fair Welcome . . . the lady's desire engages her social side and conquers it: the kiss is granted, unleashing antagonistic forces. Badmouth, Jealousy, Fear, and Shame are aroused. They build a fortress with a tower to imprison Fair Welcome; Dangier is reprimanded, who comes into play after and because the lady feels fear and shame. He runs about the garden—the world of love—closing it off. Jealousy hires all the masons, contractors, and landscape architects of the region to build the fortress with meticulously detailed realism. Jealousy adds a garrison. Dangier carries the keys. The fragment ends with Fair Welcome's imprisonment in this hastily erected fortress: only a siege can free him.

Dangier throughout plays a reactive, self-protective role, pitted by social forces against the lady's own desire. He displaces the welcome that greeted the lover earlier, as the lady's awakening interest renders her fearful, even ashamed of her own desire. It is an intensely socialized view of a woman's reaction, based on an image of woman desired by patriarchal codes, a world away from the robust sexuality of the fabliaux. It is not that distant, however, from Lunete's manipulations of Laudine: woman does not drop her guard easily, but retains self-control even against her own desire. Dangier represents that function of self-control, the internalization of domination that allows autonomy and self-rule within the individual. It is self-governance, violence against one's own desire, control of the individual both "inside" and "outside" the individual psyche: outside as ideological codes of society legitimating violent extractions of value from labor; inside as the individual subjectivity constituted by those ideological codes.

Dangier is the psychic link between individual and social worlds, simultaneously in- and outside that psyche. Dangier is the key to civilization as developed in the Middle Ages: the self-discipline requisite for the "policed life," under monarchy and republican forms of government, which require active self-discipline and self-governance of the citizen. Dangier, self-domination, is the internalized form of the state, overlapping with the function of the superego, ferocious against the self. Its ugliness is a projection of the narrative subject's trajectory, impeding his progress toward the object. Paradoxically, since the object's desire responds to the subject's, the object interrupts the flow of desire between them. Asserting her own subjectivity, she interrupts responsiveness. Subjectivity, among other things, is the ability to say "No" to desire. The incompletion of the young male lover's quest leaves the female subject in command of the field—herself, herself as subject, ugly Dangier as the lady.

I imagine our author, male or female, more likely young than old, talented but inexperienced in the ways of the unconscious, returning to the manuscript one day to realize, upon rereading, that the text betrayed its own constitutive gesture. The negation of violence and politics by subjective privatization had entailed the deconstruction of subjectivity, its fragmented and aspectual (re)constitution, and their fetishistic narrativization. This new level of narrative subjectivity retained traces of its origin in the subject, the fetishes that populate the "allegorical" landscape continually teasing us with hypothetical reintegration in the subject. In spite of their fragmentation into scattered identities strewn across the fictional landscape, in spite of the endlessly divided subjectivity, the political unconscious, rejected and repressed, had returned. In the heart of the country of love, the central fact of politics—domination—had reared its villainous ugliness. As a corollary of this return of the repressed, the ultimate indeterminacy of the text also turned against itself. The permanent hesitation in the status of the personifications—aspectual images or independent agents?—negates a condition of possibility of subjectivity itself, an identity to house its problematic congeries of contradictions. In the place of the subject, it leaves only *d'amer volenté pure*: the pure desire of love, the pure will to love. That purity itself dissolves the subject, as the *Rose Novel* demonstrates. On rereading, the author abandoned his uncompleted text and never took stylus to parchment again . . . until reborn as Jean de Meun!

CHAPTER II

Problematizing Identity:
Silence

I f Guillaume de Lorris's *Rose* unsettles the binarism of subject and object, *Silence* plays games with identity. Paradoxically, a new medieval text came into existence in 1972, when Lewis Thorpe published the *Roman de Silence*.[1] Outside of one textual study,[2] it received little critical attention until the problematics of contemporary gender theory made the medieval narrative of cross-dressing more accessible to moderns.

An initial wave of criticism divided its attitudes. One tendency opened the "miraculous and enigmatic text" to an adventurous exploration of the relation between language and sexuality, and the "extreme lability of the sign," particularly with respect to the problematics of reference and sexual difference.[3] Its indeterminacy begins in the very first line, which names its author as "Master Heldris of Cornwall." Both its denotative elements are ambiguous. The place-name may refer to the English Cornwall, or to a French hamlet, La Cornuaille, near Nantes.[4] The otherwise unknown author is designated as a male; but some of the text's *effets de réel*, its appeal to textual strategies that are often the recourse of the marginalized, suggest a feminine element behind the masculine designation, reiterating its protagonist's role switching.[5] A recent article suggests using queer theory to read *Silence*.[6] The other critical tendency insists on the text's conservatism, its linkages of essentialized nature, naming, sexual difference, and inheritance, countering the artificial transgressions allowed by a simulacral order of representation. *Silence* is viewed as being "about the search for ancestral property and a proper name," positing linguistic propriety as integral to a natural order. "Viciousness . . . is a rhetorical concept designating incorrect usage (barbarism and solecism) . . . and a confusion of genders." The text continues the medieval misogynist tradition.[7]

Indeterminacy is a staple of theory. Even so, the spread of interpretations here is remarkable, from "rah-rah feminism" to "boo-hiss chauvinism."[8] Respect for the text's ambiguity, a categorical rejection of indeterminacy, are both argued.[9] The dissonance of interpretations often disregards the narrative articulations of *Silence.* Jumping from the verbal integument directly to textual meaning eludes intermediary dimensions of meaning. Multiple structures shape a single text: identifying the narrative also signals other structuring factors. A pluri-vocal text may be perspectivally organized and scatter in its semiotic landscape signposts of reading, markers to indicate, not precise meanings to be extracted, but the kinds of questions to be raised. The disciplinary specialization of "literature" that modernity factitiously imposes on the Middle Ages is reluctant to allow that the linkages among a text's semiotic levels are political in nature. Disciplinary scholarship impedes knowledge.

*Silence'*s narrative is bipartite, according to the same generative principle as Chrétien's *Cligés,* a model in multiple ways. *Silence* starts with the parents' story, Cador and Eufemia, too timid to speak their love for each other except after reciprocal teasing and coaching—just like Alexandre and Soredamors. They eventually declare their love and are married with the king's good will. Because of a bitter conflict between two other counts, however, the king has outlawed matrilineal inheritance. Although Eufemia, the daughter of the count of Cornwall, is excluded from the decree's purview, it could affect the family succession. The text then transitions to the story of the hero(ine). When Eufemia becomes pregnant, Cador decides that if the child is a girl, it will be brought up as a boy. This turns out to be the case: the father's plan is followed. The child is brought up by faithful subordinates. It wears man's clothing, trains as a battling knight, takes a man's coloring from the sun. It is called Silence; the text refers to her as "he": I will use s/he. In adolescence, s/he runs away from home with two jongleurs, learns their craft, so that Silence sings, and eventually winds up at the French king's court, admired and loved by all. Silence returns to England, where the queen falls in love with the handsome, polished young "man," declares her feelings, and invites Silence to a liaison that the reader knows would be both adulterous and lesbian. Silence refuses, the queen is enraged (as was her counterpart in "Lanval"), and switches Silence's letter to the French court: Silence delivers a letter that demands her own death. The conscience of the French king impedes the treachery, however, and Silence eventually returns to England, helps save the king from a rebellion, and confronts the evil queen again, who is eventually denounced by Merlin. At the end, Silence is reconciled to the identity of her sex and marries the king of England: the novel ends according to the traditional "happy ending" formula, at some cost to representational complexity.

Cross-dressing was one of the irregular activities related to sex and gender that caught the church's eye, before the modern invention of sexual binarisms. Scripture was cited to forbid men and women from wearing each other's clothing.[10] An early-fourth-century council was concerned not only with deviant sexual preferences, but with the practices of "holy transvestites," women who wore men's clothing in order to gain admittance to ascetic, male monastic communities.[11] In general, however, cross-dressing was of minor concern to canonists and decretalists, though Gratian, who paid scant attention to sexual offenses among the laity, reproduced without comment an earlier conciliar condemnation. Among early decretalists, few commented on the practice. Stephen of Tournai distinguished between respectable women wearing male dress to protect their chastity and transvestitism meant to facilitate sinning. In the thirteenth and fourteenth centuries, it was condemned but rarely prosecuted. When Cypriot knights fought tournaments dressed as women, they were treated as peculiar but not criminal. Until the time of Joan of Arc, it was not high on the church's targets of deviance, not in the category of heresy, Judaism, prostitution, or even monastic homosexuality. Indeed, a woman taking on the guise of masculinity, as in the case of Hildegund von Schônau, could be thought praiseworthy.[12]

Gender roles had already been problematized in vernacular texts. A female figure performing as male warrior appears as early as the mid-twelfth century: Camille, in the *Roman d'Eneas*, where Turnus's funereal *plainte* stresses her gender anomaly.[13] In spite of undoubted misogynistic and homophobic currents in medieval culture—too readily taken as normative—various theories of sexuality were current.[14] Furthermore, the structures and trajectories of particular texts are not mere exemplifications of general cultural codes: text and culture enter into dialectical relations with each other. Camille's death is a pendant (*lo contrepan*) to that of Pallas: the woman warrior is the structural equivalent to the male.[15] Her burial becomes a famous descriptive set piece.

Adjutorial Allegory

Silence poses major challenges to interpretation, concerning issues of gender, truth, and the biopolitics of inheritance. This challenge is imbricated with a structural and historical problem: the reading of allegory. Allegorical figures appear, apparent escapees from a world of philosophical realism in which the words "nature" and "nurture" textualize ideational entities taken as "real." That is how they are proposed in traditional allegories of the virtues and the vices, as far back as Martianus Cappella, as a figure of combat. Superficially, *Silence* continues the tradition. "Nature" and "nurture" appear to posit an exclusive disjunction: two antagonists are engaged in a zero-sum game, a verbal transposition of knightly conflict that one must win, the other lose. But that assumes the binarism of allegory and ordinary discourse, which is, in fact, a modern artefact. Modern editorial practice differentiates between ordinary words like nature or nurture and their allegorical uses by capitalizing them: "Nature" and "Nurture." Medieval inscriptional codes were less explicit, less categorical, less binary, demanding that medieval readers be more active in construing texts and negotiating textual indeterminacies that modern editorial practice disambiguates. The binarism "noun versus allegoreme" is modern. Allegorical discourse formalizes the appeal of the medieval individual to the universal, which is always implicit. The ideology of the exemplum institutes one meaning per tale. Otherwise, medieval texts rarely try to specify a single, univocal meaning.[16] Instead, they give local interpretations or deploy markers to signal the kinds of questions to be asked of their narratives.

"Allegory" is a vague and general term. Even Borges dismissed it as an "aesthetic mistake."[17] More recently, it has been identified with reading in general.[18] Even in a medieval context, it stands for a variety of figures, all forms of self-reflexivity requiring that words be read in other than their most obvious and literal sense. Rhetorical turns—a local irony or sarcasm, the ironic citation of a proverb, an overly polite formula—are moments of discursive style.[19] At the other end of the allegorical axis are two interpretive structures. One is the hermeneutic that, since the Jews and the Greeks, is pressed into service to save ancient texts after a major cultural change, ensuring their survival in spite of shocking discrepancies with new moral codes: the *Book of Job*, the *Song of Songs*, preserved in spite of a restrictive priestly morality; Homeric texts, alienated by a moralizing Platonic critique; or the Hebrew Bible, appropriated as a whole by the new cult of Christianity. It is often assumed that such theological use of allegorical reading imposes totalizing closure on the entirety of the text. Nothing is further from the truth: even in biblical interpretation, the deployment of allegorical levels is selective.

The other interpretive structure is allegory as a double writing, extending the principle of metaphor to an entire text. Guillaume de Lorris's *Rose I* retains an ambiguous indeterminacy between an apparent narrativity and its "literal" reference to an ideational world of psychic love—the willful oscillation between "realist" and "nominalist" philosophies of the sign. Structural allegory appears in the often vengeful adaptation of Christianity by Dante Alighieri, anything but a moralizing spin-off from Thomas Aquinas. Fiction, in the Middle Ages as in modernity, is not bound by morality, philosophy, or theology.[20]

Occasional local ironies do occur in *Silence*; so does a system of narrative cross-references, as in *Cligés*. Repeatedly, however, a third type of allegory is deployed, an *adjutorial allegory* as self-reflexive refraction. Recognizing narrative as a primary generator of meanings, it sets out discursive signposts to guide—not determine—the process of interpretation: the text's metadiscourse is a nondirective self-glossing. An early example was the allegory that, in Chrétien's *Yvain*, interrupted the combat of Yvain and Gauvain, fighting as champions for two sisters struggling over an inheritance. Their identities hidden by armor, the two buddies' fight to the death contains an allegory of Love and Hate inhabiting the same inn: an allegory of ambiguous friendship and split subjectivity. How can two knights, the best of friends, fight each other to the death? Was Gauvain really Yvain's friend, urging him to abandon his new marriage, with disastrous results? Beyond its immediate episodic context, the allegory also questions the relationship between Yvain and Laudine: love or hate? More generally, social relationships are queried: neither term is restricted to personal meanings. The local syntagm reflects on the entirety of the text, and more.

This early instance of the principle of adjutorial allegory occurs between allegory as stylistic localism and a totalizing compositional structure. A discursive passage, attributed to a textual figure that is fictitious within the diegetic frame, can develop a conceptual framework through which a reader might view the narrative. Such figures appear and disappear as personifications, leaving the scene once again to the anthropomorphic "characters," pseudopersons taken as "real" within the regime of truth which constitutes the fiction, after having illuminated the scene from some perspective not immediately given by the narrative or the actors. They develop overtly fictive subject-positions that project sideward illuminations, aspectualizing the narrative from implicit perspectives. They build the principle of narrative-as-problem-of-interpretation into the narrative itself.

The allegories of *Silence*, though stressed by the text, have been ignored or treated dismissively. The allegorical principle is built into *Silence* before the personifications actually come on the scene. Cador and Eufemia are inching toward intimacy in private conversation. He explains the king's reward for vanquishing a dragon: a fief-and-wife of his choosing. He coyly implies he has already chosen the one woman his heart is set on, by refusing the next best three alternatives:

> But in the kingdom there's not three [women]
> I'd even consider,
> If *the one* is denied me . . . o beautiful Eufemia.[21]

And the narrator comments:

> Beautiful Eufemia, that's *the one*
> Which Cador's heart gloms on!
> Eufemia *glosses* "the one,"
> But doesn't dare assume it,
> For she hasn't the daring,
> To *gloss* it onto herself.[22]

In self-glossing, the text turns back on a word just pronounced to elucidate or comment on it—a rhetorical technique well established in twelfth-century vernacular textuality. What is new here is its insistent self-naming: it insists that it is *glossing*, overtly declaring its appropriation of a technique of religious hermeneutics. It is not only self-reflexive, it names its self-reflexivity and names its source.

Nature does not occur in the prologue entirely centered on social morality. Her opposite number, *noreture*, does not appear in the first half of the narrative at all. *Nature* occurs incidentally during the first part of the novel, both as a common noun and as an occasional personification. Thus at the bedside of Silence's birth, presented dramatically by the narrator, who has left the baby's sexual identity a mystery until now:

> Now I'll turn back to the child,
> To show and clear up
> Which it was, male or female.
> My lords, it was a girl.
> In her, *Nature* shows her craft . . .
> *Nature*, with her great powers,
> Addressed the child, and took great pains,
> Saying: "Now I want to create a powerful work."[23]

Nature creates the child as an *ouvre forcible*, but the enunciator opts for a culinary and class-determined simile. Her creation is compared to the sifting of flour through a sieve or colander, separating it from the coarser bran, so that no straw, chaff, or husks—reserved for pigs—make their way into the extrafine white flour. Silence is processed like "a valiant man, whom nature wants to create in majestic art."[24] Lurking behind this culinary differentiation lies a class distinction: fine white flour is coded for the nobility.

Nature's creativity continues, following Alain de Lille's *De planctu natura*. One might say that, in creating the beautiful girl child, "Nature broke the mold." What nature does say is that the mold she chose from thousands was unique and would never be used again. The rhetoric of the girl's creation goes on for nearly two hundred verses and leads to the announcement to king and court that a son is born (ll. 1795–1974)! The countess later tells her husband in private:

> You have a daughter,
> She's the most beautiful creature
> That ever nature made in this world.[25]

Only in the second part of the novel do the major personification allegories occur, arguing about Silence's "nurture." *Nature* appears first, the creative demiurge of totalizing perfection, but capable of ill temper and of a mixed creation, which results in a lowly man (*le bas home*, l. 1851). The low-born can have high character, however, and nobles can be sullied and tricked by vile hearts: the lowly but honest exist, will exist, and have always existed to carry out great deeds (ll. 1849–60). Genealogy does not determine moral quality. The theme of mixture, of crossings, a both/and structure, first appears in terms of social classes, allowing for great achievements among the lower classes and a nobility that does not live up to its heritage. *Silence* belongs to a tradition that imposes morals on nobility.

A striking discursive mixture also occurs, which confuses the levels of language and reference in a postmodern manner. Nature's intent effort in creating Silence includes an internal monologue that distinguishes between material, craft, and the resulting work, emphasizing the beauty to be produced. Nature ends with self-satisfaction: after all, she says, "my skill has to surface sometimes" (l. 1885). The formation of the extraordinary creature follows the order of a literary portrait, enumerating individual features of the face and body from top down: nature "writes" ears and eyebrows (ll. 1904–44). Nature's creation follows the textual order, creating the subject of the future simulacrum. Narrativized gender transgression is integrally linked to the order of representation. Nature follows art—or *is* "Nature" art?

The narrator reaffirms the girl's unique and extraordinary beauty. When the count sees her, he greets her with unreserved joy: he would never want to exchange her for a boy, a remarkably "liberal" attitude, given his concerns with problems of inheritance. Even a feudal noble, preoccupied with the biopolitics of lineage, is sentimentally overwhelmed by a baby daughter's beauty, in spite of the political problems she causes him. The upbringing and education of the child—its nurturing—is given over to an odd couple, unmarried, a faithful seneschal and a loyal woman cousin of the count's. They follow Cador's instructions to bring up his daughter as a son. Nature, tricked and deceived, her work turned upside-down, notices they have transformed her daughter into a son. She is insulted. They act as if *noreture* was worth more than her own craft: nature's own discourse introduces her defining, binary opposite, cast as her antagonist. Nurture is an integral element in nature: *norir, norisce, noreture* retain a primary sense, nourishment as the provision of food, especially for an infant. Nurture's nature is a metonymy: food is a necessary part of a larger process of education and general formation of the person—her subjectivation—in which the social remains grounded in the carnal.

Nature the artist complains that her great effort at creating a work of extraordinary beauty is being disguised and ruined—in full cognizance of *mouvance*, twelfth-century artists were intent on preserving their work from alteration. She is incensed at her work's disfigurement and projects a conflict of power between herself and nurture. Narrative is inherently conflictual. For the narrator, the conflict concerns power (l. 2296): many a man acts against nature because others force him to or because he dares not act otherwise. This is not a natural weakness (*natural faintize*), it is fear that rules him. Away from fear, his "heart" puts its stamp on him, insisting that a thousand marks gained shamefully are worth more than honor's penny. A realistic calculation leads to a direct contradiction of Mies van der Rohe:

> More is worth more than less.[26]

Men will act well for years, following good habits inculcated by nurture, in spite of vile nature, and repent their good works only later, their villainy plunging them once again into crime:

> A little bad nurture
> Worsens a good nature more
> Than long training in acting well
> Can improve a vile heart.[27]

Nature continues to lose ground. The child learns to wear clothing against "its nature" (l. 2360), learns to read and stay housebound rather than wander off, reveal its nature, and betray nurture. In the space of a few lines, the text deploys an imposing vocabulary to designate nurture's educational aspect: *doctriner, estruist, enthice, doctrine, ensegne*, doubled by *apresure, aprent* (ll. 2375–89). In fact, the child, who may have read Foucault's history of subjectivity, teaches itself:

> Il meïsmes se doctrine. (l. 2386; compare also 2389)

Knowledge is *science*, and conveniently rhymes with *Silence*: rhyme is poetry's ultimate moral accolade! But the child's studies go well beyond its age and extend intellectual education into deontic formation: the child is unequalled in goodness as well as in knowledge. Silence is being formed as subject by a discipline, an art in the medieval sense, simultaneously cognitive and moral.

Is it a *pointe*, a passing manner of speaking, or a paradox, that this marvel of learning, whose morality and intellect equal its beauty, acquires these virtues, not by any effort of study, but by its own good nature, which devolves to it from its origin or birth (*orine*: ll. 2384–86)? Does the text, which has so strongly developed and praised nurture, undermine and deconstruct it by this reference to the child's "nature," its genealogical heritage? Does it point in the direction of indeterminacy in the fundamental paradox the text explores, the relation of nature and nurture? Or does it assume that both nature and nurture go into the constitution of the individual subject? The text, whose style is straightforward, loosens some rather substantial intellectual hares.

When Silence reaches the age of twelve—the age of puberty and physiological changes unmentioned in the text—nature directly and strongly criticizes her behavior. It is a strange thing, she says, to see Silence take pleasure in acting like a man, going in the wind and burning sun, for "I have a *speciäl forme* [mould], with which my two hands formed you." Nature endowed Silence with the beauty of a thousand others, women who are now in love with her [as a man], but who would hate her if they knew her real identity. It is a great big ugly thing she does, to adhere to such "nurturing." Quit the forest, the jousting and hunting, hide yourself back to the chamber and to sewing, is what the custom of "nature" wants. "You are not Silent*ius*," brusquely declares nature, signaling masculinity in gendered Latin.

The response bears more than passing resemblance to both Hamlet and modern philosophical and gender discourses:

> I never heard of such a thing!
> Silencius! so who am I?
> I'm called Silencius, I think,
> Or I'm other than I've been.
> But this I know well, by my trusty right hand,
> That I cannot be other!
> Thus am I Silentius,
> So I think upon't, or a nude nullity.[28]

Silence rejects being other than s/he is: no Rimbaud s/he, even as the reader remains conscious he's a she, she's a he. Nullity, in medieval codes, neighbors nudity. Clothes do not make the man, but constitute him as a recognizable social identity: the pun on *nus*—"nothing" or "nude"—makes cultural sense. For Silence to be undone of the male identity signaled by

the name Silencius, implies being denuded of clothes, identity, and inheritance. Material interest goes into Silence's inner argument and is named
as such:

> Then he reflects
> That nature argues sophistically:
> Since the ending in -*us* goes against usage,
> If the name is not Silentius.
> It's proper to go sewing
> Just as nature argued,
> For such uncultured ways must not
> *For the sake of a fief's inheritance* adopted be.[29]

Nurture comes on the scene, and Silence explains her desire to follow nature's advice, invoking social customs and God. The tables are turned: it's
nurture's turn to be angered.

The two allegoremes engage in their first debate. "I have completely
un-natured the child," nurture claims, and insists her work be left alone,
threatening and chasing nature:

> All told, I can nurture
> A bad man from a noble child.
> I'll undo your narrative account.
> Nature, begone in your disgrace![30]

A declaration of war is close, symmetrical to nature's creation of Silence.
Nature granted Silence the beauty of a thousand women; nurture threatens to make a thousand people work against their nature, undoing nature's
work, before chasing her away in shame. Allegory resolves into the black-
mail of threatened violence.

The personifications are lost from sight for more than 2,500 lines. They
return briefly for Silence's knighting at the French court. S/he has achieved
widely recognized social status. At Pentecost, when s/he is seventeen and a
half years old, the French king—acme of the social order—knights
him/her in Paris. In celebration, a joust is held in a field next to Saint Germain: Silence wins the prize. Never was a woman less timid in doing battle, remarking the paradox of the female knight after Camille: anyone who
saw Silence jousting like a knight,

> Could really have said that nurture
> Can work wonders over nature,
> In teaching such practices
> To a soft and tender woman.

A knight unhorsed by Silence would have been shamed to learn it was

> a woman, soft, tender, faint-hearted,
> With nothing manly but a tan,
> The clothing and bearing of a man,
> Had knocked him down with a lance.

The text insists on its fundamental paradox, the assumption of a male identity and practices by a subject sexed with female organs. Neither is identity absorbed by sex, nor vice versa. The paradox remains lodged in the narratee's mind through frequent reinforcement.

The nature/nurture issue is generalized by being displaced from Silence. When s/he returns to England to help defend the king against a rebellion, the old problem with the queen recurs. New advances, rejection again, once more anger: the queen manipulates the king so that he sends Silence on a mission impossible: capturing Merlin. In fact, it will be solved with a little advice and slight culinary effort. In a wasteland, close to one of Merlin's haunts, an old man emerges, who explains how to trap Merlin: with honey, milk, wine, above all roast meat to tempt the magician out of his vegetarianism. "If humanity remains in him he will come to it" (l. 5955 f.). A doublet of Merlin? Does Merlin formulate his own transformation? The double displacement, from Silence to Merlin, from vegetarianism to noble carnivorousness, anticipates the recent juxtaposition of subjectivity with "carno-phallogocentrism" that, as Derrida points out, is essential to all politics: leaders eat meat![31] The smell of roasted meat rises in the smoke of Silence's outdoor grill and wafts its way to Merlin's nostrils. He turns toward the meat, but nurture protests. How easily are flouted those who nurture people. What nourishment and labor I give, nature steals in a day. Admitting the taste for meat as *nature d'ome*, Merlin should have put it behind him, having long eaten grasses in the woods. What does he want? Greens and roots are his food (ll. 5997–6010).

Nature and nurture form a culture of complaint. Nature complains of the number of nobles bastardized by nurture, who denies the accusation, reversing responsibility:

> If a man is noble in body and evil in heart,
> If he acts shamefully, what can I do?
> Neither he nor I can do anything,
> But Nature can, who started this.
> A man who wants what's shameful,
> I don't want him, but I can't prevent him.
> But you nurture him to shameful action,
> Since he doesn't care to act the good . . .
> To a man who holds to honor,
> I teach no dishonor.
> For every man who's bad by nurture,
> A thousand are bad by nature. (Ll. 6017–28)[32]

The discussion turns theological, circling around the biblical narrative of the problem of evil in Eden, in a set piece that bears its own surprises. At first sight, it contains little that is remarkable. Nature caused Adam and Eve to sin, says nurture. Not so, sayeth nature. God created man in his own likeness, the Devil's nurturing occasioned original sin, from which are born envy and avarice, stinginess and gluttony, spitefulness and criminality. Depart, and never return (ll. 6045–87)! At nature's discourse, nurture pales: relinquishing her place, she leaves nature triumphant. Allegory folds back into theology. This sense of a "natural" fit blinds us to a negative fact that obtains its full significance only in context.

In a sophisticated rhetorical culture, intently aware of its constitutive traditions, points of argument can be made negatively, by abscission, as well as by positive assertions. Omission of an element known to be integral to an argument can be as significant as a direct counterargument.[33] Here, an element integral to the misogynous tradition is elided. Culpability for original sin is usually attributed to Eve, with Adam a victim of her and Satan's conjoined manipulations: the disculpabilization of men proceeds by dumping guilt on the women who are Eve's image. This maneuver, conventional in the misogynous tradition, is noteworthy in the present case by its absence. Eve is mentioned twice in the entire poem. Cador, considering the possibility of a female child, cites the creation of Eve from Adam's rib.

Instead of reinscribing female secondariness, however, he cites it to assert woman's equality in the unity of marriage. Eve was made from Adam's rib so that the two would be of a single substance and of a single will. Both should be united in will, joy, and sorrow. In man and woman exists great commonality, for they share substance.[34] Marriage cements commonality, so that they are one in blood and flesh:

> C'uns sans et une cars deviennent. (l. 1719)

During the allegorical debate between nurture and nature, Adam and Eve figure as the original parents from whom all descend. The only differentiation is the first victim of evil: it is not Eve seduced by Satan and turned into his instrument of evil, but rather Adam as nature's victim. The apple is assigned to Adam who ate of it as the first man. Again, it was Adam who sinned, because of nature. When le diables, l'enemis comes on the narrative scene, it is Adam he deceives with the fruit (ll. 6030–80). The stress, the emphasis by omission and rewriting, is unmistakable. Eve is mentioned twice, both times in a positive light. Adam is foregrounded as the target, victim and agent of evil, consistently replacing Eve in the narrative of the Fall. "Heldris de Cornuälle" disowns the misogynistic discourse of his narrator, who has succeeded in deceiving modern readers unaccustomed to the subtleties of medieval hermeneutics. Having overcome nurture by rewriting misogyny—a rewriting of the conventional story that turns it inside out—nature chases off nurture and proceeds to beat up on Merlin so mercilessly that he yields to carnivorous desire, grabbing and attacking the roasting meat.

Nature returns briefly later, when Silence confesses her story to King Eban, explaining her nature—her sex—as what had to be kept secret. When the king forgives her, granting his protection and friendship, the queen, caught in the trap she had set for Silence, is drawn and quartered. Silence, now dressed as a woman, has her body refinished by nature so that no traces of manhood are left. In the conventional happy ending, the king marries Silence, power united with the beauty of nature's most gorgeous creation. Her parents come to the court happily, leaving only an author's epilogue to conclude.

The confrontation of the allegorical figures has been followed to its narrative conclusion in the politics of culture. The conclusion occurs within the terms of the conflictual allegory. One of the two opposing figures wins, the other loses, as in any zero-sum game. For the sake of this ending, nature defeats nurture: Silence discards "his" habits and usages and returns to her identity as sexual female. The narrative conclusion may be abhorrent in the context of modern feminisms, not to mention gay and lesbian liberation movements, all intent on the self-assertion of gender as against genetic sexuality, but the text is perhaps not quite as orthodox as it has been painted, not quite as imprisoned by a supposed essentialism. The "happy ending," contrary to a presumed unitary medieval misogyny, allows a strong assertion of the inherent value of woman, as heroine and as the typological Eve. The principle of exclusive disjunction is deconstructed by *Silence*, as it had been in the *Charrette* and *Partonopeu de Blois*.[35]

Narration as Thirdness

Personifications present arguments, differing voices that course through an ideological realm, rhetorically elaborated. Where the allegory of conflict only presents the clash of opposition, *Silence* attempts to elaborate a principle of thirdness similar to Chrétien's semiotics of episodic structure, but by different means. Where Chrétien introduced the series of beneficiaries who index a totalized society that includes the subject, "Heldris de Cornuälle" introduces the principle of thirdness in ways that retain a profound ambiguity.

Along with nature and nurture, a physiological figure with claims on both is introduced. The "heart" is not only a physiological organ; in Old French it marks the site of psychic life, of need and desire, of intentionality and willful decision making. Doubled into *cuer* and the emphatic *corage*, it straddles the distinctions between the physical and the moral, between nature and nurturing:

> The *heart* is a creature
> Of marvelous strange nature. (l. 2667 f.)
> A man who knowingly dishonors himself is mad. Such a man,
> . . . if his vile *heart* makes him act
> so that he cannot pull back from it,
> then he is a serf, and his *heart* is lord,
> Behold! when such a *heart* masters man![36]

A question of dominance, of lordship, is at work here. The heart is a superior instance of decision making, where the freedom of individual will asserts itself among besetting forces. Sometimes, it functions as "conscience" (ll. 2667 ff.), sometimes as victim (ll. 2322 ff.), sometimes as figure of dominance in conflicts.

Another "third" occurs with a third personification, in addition to nature and nurture. When the two figures squabble as to Silence's gender, *reason* enters to address Silence. Her argument has everything to do with her nature. "Reason," in Old French, is not the abstract power of reasoning—logic or dialectic—but an eminently social reason, a socialized intelligence working in recognizable norms. Reason sides with *noreture*: abandoning nurture's teaching would be tantamount to suicide, she says, pointing out that if Silence follows nature's injunctions, she stands to lose her inheritance. Reason's argument—brief, "objective"—carries the day. Silence reflects on the temptation to reject her upbringing, of refusing her male habits for the sake of a woman's life, and decides against it, on the basis of recognizable social "reason."[37] Men's lives and customs are better than women's:

> Miols valt li us d'ome
> Que l'us de feme, c'est la some. (l. 2638 f.)

To choose *us de feme* would be to choose inferiority. Silence decides she is a man, not a girl, chooses not to lose a great "honor" (the word often means "fief"), nor exchange it for a lesser one, nor give the lie to her father. Whatever nature does, never will I enact the uncovering (*descoverture*); Thus, the voice of reason, within Silence's consciousness.[38]

Both "heart" and "reason" are fundamentally ambiguous. Though possible thirdnesses, they straddle the division established by the allegorical figures they are called on to transcend. Their presence underlines the character of the nature/nurture opposition. These two allegoremes present different, contradictory aspects of human comportment. To transcend their opposition would retotalize a moral, psychic, and social world their opposition rends. The attempts to resolve their contradiction, from the theoretical point of view, are failures: their opposition as narrative antagonists allows for no subsumption. Taking nature and nurture as opposing characters in a drama of representation leads to an unresolvable narrative conflict.

Taking them as semiotic signposts may produce a different "ending." There is more to the narrator than traces of orthodox misogyny lead one to suspect. The high point of Silence's social ascension is her recognition at the French court, ratified by the king himself, and her triumph at the accompanying celebratory joust. The highest diegetic instances ratify Silence's construction of her performing subjectivity. This is arranged by the author, but the narrator gets his say as well. In a passage already cited, he acknowledged that "nurture can do a lot against nature." Now, he comments directly:

> Do you know what my heart says?
> Blessings on the man of daily goodness!
> Good acts erase base births,
> And lead to a courteous life.
> Good behavior uses life for good,
> Rejecting baseness.
> Many a man's dishonorable daily,
> Who, with a taste of honor
> Maintained since childhood,
> Would have eluded lowliness.
> He cannot help acting shamefully,
> His practice fits his lessons.
> Silence regrets nothing
> Of his practice, but loves it well.
> He's valiant and good as a knight,
> No king or count engendered better.[39]

Ethical rules acknowledge but override Silence's unrepentant deception. Before her confession, King Eban says of Silence, "You've been very valuable, a good knight, courageous and worthy; no king or count engendered a better one." After her confession, he adds, "Silence, you are wholly loyal. Your loyalty's worth more than my royalty" (ll. 6579–81, 6630–32). If the narrator earlier acknowledged he was not above adding a bit of lie to the truth of his tale, he insisted on preserving truth itself: for I must not mute the truth.[40] From narrative structure, its diegetic ratifications, and the narrator's own words, one can only judge that Silence's moral achievement in constructing the performance of a (false) identity is as admirable as the beauty with which nature endowed her.

The entire narrative trajectory confirms how much nurture can do against a "natural" sexual identity. The text insists throughout on the protagonist's ambiguity—not vague imprecision, but the simultaneity of opposing values, structurally identical with paradox. Evading this ambiguity means falsifying the text and losing its essence.[41] The text continually plays with its narrative paradox, overtly, repeatedly specifying it is a woman who is acclaimed for achieving the height of virility as a heroic, knighted warrior: no illusionism here! More telling, it plays with the structure of language, transgressing ordinary gender agreements, continually referring to a woman disguised as a man as "he." In spite of the naturalization of gender through its identification with sex, the text insists on the priority of gender even against linguistic norms, in its extraordinary lability of pronominal reference.[42] Throughout, the narrator keeps reminding the narratee that Silence is a "she," continually referring to "her" as "he."

Beyond these subdiscursive games, the narrator insists on a metadiscursive say, on voicing discourse as a subject. S/he introduces commentary with a rhetorical question, and deploys emphatic verbal forms. For "heart," *corage* appears, rather than the more ordinary *cuers*; for habit, or the customary manner of being, *usage* replaces the more common *us*. Not surprisingly, they rhyme (l. 5165 f.). And the answer to the rhetorical question—do you know what I really think?—repeats the simple, ethical maxim:

Bons us a qui bone vie uze. (l. 5169)

That is, good actions define good life, not natural birth or a lowly condition (*vilonie, viltance*). The narrator, in the whirling complexities of his/her text, comes down on a simple and direct rule: an ethic of behavior, overriding the circumstances of gender and genealogy, determines the judgment of value. Silence enjoys a calm conscience, regretting nothing of his/her transgressive behavior, become habitual by a social calculation. In the diegetic conscience of the text, cross-dressing's misrepresentation is neither crime nor sin. The text differs from both cultural norms and morality. By linguistic practice, narrative construction, and direct moral discourse, it shows sympathetic approval of unorthodoxy. Normative social, cultural, and moral codes are flouted: praised be the hero(ine)'s shuttle between nature and nurture, so sayeth "Heldris of Cornuälle"! Which does not preclude psychic conflictuality, the medieval originality of allegorical personifications. "Nature versus nurture" names a conflict in Silence's psyche. The terms not only "reflect" psychic turmoil: the entities in psychic battle are larger than their mental container, which they enter in continuum with their larger, social existence. The subject is constituted by the conflictual intersection of multiple codes whose continuity extends to a realm independent of it, to which the latter remains "passible."[43]

The Monsters of Subjectivity

The personifications of nature and nurture are semiotic signposts. The same is true for "characters" in general. Narrative actors provide aspects of complex systems of signification, adding specific perspectives within a subtle set of refractions.

In the first half of the narrative, Cador obtains wife, fief, and social ratification by conquering a dreadful serpent—the "oniric animal par excellence" of romanesque art, iconographically diabolical, frequent in popular and folkloric legends.[44] The dragon in *Silence* owes something to this tradition, but even more to its intertextuality with *Tristan et Iseut*. Huge, it spews murderous venom and flames, breathes light-blocking smoke, and gobbles up the king's men (ll. 345–72). Terrifying, it indexes the hero's knightly heroism when he attacks and kills it. As in the Tristan story, it also provides the occasion for Eufemia/Iseut, who possesses the secrets of medicine, to care for the wounded hero after the dragon's death. The dragon is a narrative element: obstacle, occasion, and means by which the heroic subject attains his goal. But it is also one of a complex system of figures, allegorical and representational both, whose reciprocal refractions produce meanings and signification. By opposition, identification, and modification, characters define each other and the protagonist. Their paradoxical names recall that they are mere constructs, figures of an active, generative textual system. In a bipartite text, a double system is at work: one within each of the two parts, and another across the binary division, as narrative parallelisms establish cross-references and equivalences across the binary dividing line. In *Silence*, part I, the dragon is the primary antagonist. In part II, the primary antagonist is the queen, who (as in "Lanval") offers herself in adultery to her husband's virtuous vassal, is rebuffed, and vengefully accuses him of attempted rape and homosexuality. Eufemia is an admirable wife; Eufeme is a moral monster, metaphorically as venomous as Cador's dragon.

The dragon of part I has no human identity. It bears no relation to humans, save one: introjecting them by eating, it absorbs their meat and their being. Perhaps that's why "the dragon" takes different anthropomorphic forms in part II: Eufeme and the polymorphously perverse Merlin. Thanks to Eufeme's manipulations, Silence tracks down Merlin, (re)converts him to carnivorousness, and brings him back to court. Hairy, he is shaggy like a bear, speedy as the deer. Although a man, he's very like an animal, a version of Chrétien's wild man, a deconstruction of the borderline between the animal and the human, the natural and the cultural, the domains of nature and nurture. Merlin the magician problematizes the dual nature of *humanité* (l. 5955).

Merlin's return to meat signals reconversion from his animal nature to the human. Meat is also the food characteristic of nobility: culture, nurture, nobility, humanity itself, are class-tagged, as against the peasantry, identified by noble codes with the state of nature, animality, beans, and greens. Medieval textuality is far more honest, more "realistic" in its recognition of a necessary materialism, than the modern.[45] It assumes the interdependence of "humanity" and class structure. "Heldris de Cornuälle" and Chrétien de Troyes are closer to Marx than to Derrida on this point. They proleptically recognize the pungent critique of deconstruction and delight in the linguistic possibilities it rediscovers. They remember as well the material force of history, as it impinges on the endless *différance* of language, catching the individual in the toils of subjectivity and the necessity of choices.

Merlin is also a monster . . . a kinder, gentler monster, one of medicinal laughters, speaker of hidden truths, a kindly, truthful, morphing trickster: the opposite of Silence's silence, insistently self-identical in her false identity. Or perhaps, if we remember that the character changes, Merlin is Silence's model. It is after s/he has brought him back to court, that his laughter reveals the truth about Silence's monstrous enemy, who also avoids language: Eufeme, whose "circumlocution" consists of vengeful lies. Queen Eufeme, Eufemia, and Silence, are all named in the tradition of Saint Alexis, whose father was Eufemien: an alexical hero, speaking neither to those who seek him nor to his family son of circumlocution, his virginity keeps silence.[46] Silence is as Silence keeps. S/he also keeps silence, keeps to the father's decree, but for a secular purpose: to retain his inheritance. Paternal obedience and material wealth are the operative motives, in contradistinction to the saintly one beyond language.

Who, finally, is Silence? Alexis may be silent because he is a saint; Silence is silent in spite of and against woman's clichéd volubility. The name, like so much else, is paradox. In certain cultures, identity connects the individual to an essence of being: the propriety of naming supposedly guarantees the individual's proper insertion in the "natural social order."[47] But medievals often named themselves, and texts toyed with plots of anonymity, pseudonymy, and false identity. Names are a resource for permutations of signifying potentials. In *Silence*, the name designates, not an essence, but an unorthodox strategy of covert language aimed at eluding the legal injustice of that "natural social order" that claims to generate the grammatical-gender order. In modern social science terms: "There are very tangible benefits to be gained from constructing oneself as a particular sort of person and interacting with others in specific sorts of ways."[48] Silence mediates between two hypotaxic figures, father and king, set in conflict by this text. "Silence" is the successful "barbarism" and solecism, rewarded not only by her father's inheritance, but by marriage to the king and universal diegetic approval! Insofar as "S/silence" names a materialist strategy to counter the king's misogynistic decree to preserve an inheritance, it is successful beyond calculation. In a literature that delighted in the structure of "the trickster tricked," *Silence* reversed the reversal into "the trickster rewarded," as *against* a sociopolitico-grammatical orthodoxy.

Two systems of value circle in this text: the conservative system of misogynistic orthodoxy; and another that shifts the focus to the worldly calculations of necessity and survival that drive the narrative. The intersection of these two systems of value constitutes the split subjectivity of Silence: *Silence ot le cuers diviers* (l. 2681). The protagonist knows turmoil and psychic contradiction. Having decided not to reveal her secret gender but to remain the *vallés* dictated by the strategy, Silence yields the site of discourse to the narrator. Never was there such *abstinence* (from speech?) as Silence's, as s/he endures contradictory thoughts and doubts, painfully mulling large thoughts over and over again, tormented by ideas endured and suffered.

Every day, he was ready to counter
What his heart wanted.
Whoever strives against his own will,
Will often suffer pain.[49]

Silence's subjectivity is split in the debates between nature and nurture, not to mention heart and reason, figures of psychic processes as well as autonomous actors. At the level of language, the Latin heritage of Old French allows the subject to be marked morphologically: "*je*" rarely needs to be lexicalized, except for emphasis or clarity. But in the last four hundred lines or so of *Silence*, *je* makes an emphatic number of coordinated appearances, as if the narrator not only insisted on manipulating a notion of split subjectivity, but drew attention to it as well.[50]

The "I" of Silence shuttles within the terms of constitutive contraries, contradicting her noble heritage by running away from home with jongleurs, learning to out-sing and outperform them until they are jealous. Silence learns to speak as another, performing others' speech and song, to earn twice the money as the "authentic jongleurs." Peculiarly, it is Merlin who allows Silence's multiple returns to identity: daughter to father and mother, subject to her king, to her "natural" state and vestments. Merlin, both animal and human, is the one who sees but does not speak, does not speak but laughs, whose pre-Rabelaisian laughter communicates truth. He is the (re)converted forest animal, bear and deer as primitive vegetarians, to a split *humanité*, a far cry from later, idealizing "humanisms."

Nature d'ome, of Merlin and Silence both, is one of contradiction. *Silence*'s strategy of duplicitous silence is never questioned by the text, by any of its characters save nature, or by the narrator. Its materialistic rationale is an unquestioned social reason. The text apparently approves the subject's performance, yet a theme floats throughout with enough insistence to make one wonder. The narrative's ideological premise is retention of a material inheritance, which figures as *grant honor*, as *droiture*, as *fief* and *iretage*—as noble value.[51] The desirability of worldly goods, the status they produce, the social and material value of landed wealth, are unquestioned. Yet the prologue harshly condemns the vice of avarice. Moderns associate it with middle-class values, but medievals saw ample evidence of noble avarice. The prologue considers manure preferable to moneys amassed in the strongboxes of the nobility—kings, counts, knights (ll. 2651, 2487, and 2545). The king's decree disinheriting all women responded to a mortal conflict over noble claims of inheritance:

> Greed robs many a man of his noble freedom
> And more: when he bites,
> It makes him trot to death.[52]

What shall we think, then, of Cador's summary of his strategy:

> If I succeed, she [Silence] shall be rich?[53]

What is the relation of this *covoitise*, the construction of a factitious life for the retention of wealth, power, and status, with the *Avarisse* of the prologue? What does Silence think of it? Explaining to nurture that nature has persuaded her to adopt the *us de feme* (l. 2558), Silence invokes the saying that God "dispenses his bounty to each creature according to its nature":

> Was ever woman so tormented
> By vile fraud so deceived,
> As I by *covoitise*?[54]

Silence inculpates herself of covetousness, close enough to avarice and greed to raise a question about the rationale for the entire strategy of deception: the material value of a great *honor*. Silence as knight is a living mendacity, in the service of the same material values as those that are objects of *avarisse* and *covoitise*. The narrator approves of the strategy, recounts it with evident sympathy, and disapproves of the fundamental value it incorporates. Self-contradiction? Undoubtedly. Narratorial incompetence, or fascination with the forbidden? Doubtful, given the text's intensely self-conscious reflexivity. Distinction between narrator and author, as suggested by recent critics?[55] More likely, but the exact territorial divide between the two is hard to trace in a culture where an author is likely to have read his text out loud to an audience. Above all, the medieval vernacular text is a site which attracts and deploys contradictory systems of value and keeps those polysemous, contradictory values in play for the reader to meditate. This text does not boast of the classical unities, or the fictive semantic unity of the theoretical exemplum. Contradiction is the form of logical coherence that defines a semiotic text.

Again, who is Silence, or "what"? The subjectivity its transvestitism constructs and the value systems it introjects are irrevocably split and contradictory—short of the happy ending, believe in that who will: a dose of camp here is not inappropriate. The unitary subject is the most transparent fiction of all. Silence is not silent: the actor speaks. Silence speaks; as jongleur, Silence sings. But the name denies both speech and song. Silence is a barred sign, marking a space that should be specified, but is not. Silence speaks, but only to a special kind of listener, accustomed to challenges of unspoken meanings: a narratee / listener / reader trained in the tradition of Chrétien de Troyes. *Silence* speaks to one whose attentiveness, earlier caught by puzzling texts, has embraced the discipline in which the sonic-scopic eroticism of textual interpellation are formed to intellectual acrobatics. The performative subjectivity constituted by *Silence* can only be that of a paranoid reader, the attentive decipherer of the individual voices playfully aspectualized by the concrete text.

The premise of *Silence* is materialistic. For Georges Duby, the novel's sociological basis was the fantasy of a subclass.[56] Inheritance was ever the nobility's obsession. Only when gender intrudes overtly is criticism of social materialism in the form of inheritance voiced. The text rewards the hero(ine)'s strategy by having her accede to a kingdom to which neither her father nor the text had never laid claim. "Silence" is never given another, more "proper" name, nor does any serious "quest" drive this text. It consists of a character with a simple ideology (obedience to the paternal injunction to retain paternal property), putting aside a "natural" sex-based identity for a "nurtural" gender. "Silence" is also the strategy of anomalous identities living under oppressive regimes of the Other as the rule of the Same. All major female characters are punningly named for an avoidance of language that nonetheless speaks in the text: not only Silence, but Eufeme and Eufemia both—the conventionally evil female, the traditional idealized female—all avoid *and* engage language. The transvestite here is the leading edge of a local women's cohort whose members, set into oppositions by the narrative, share a fundamental commonality: all live in hostile territory. Insofar as we all speak an Other's language, the transvestite figures universality. Merlin laughingly convicts a world of five characters (king, queen, her lover disguised as a nun, Silence, and himself) as equally guilty of comparable trickeries:

> There not a one of us
> hasn't tricked one of the others.[57]

He "uncovers the truth," using the same term "silence" had used in pledg-
ing never to do so: *descoverture.*[58] The revelation of Silence's sex leads to a
simulacral closure that attends the happy ending, one that lies according to
rule while retaining some truth, the narrator's *vertés . . .* despite little lies
added to his tale (ll. 1660–69).

That truth is a critique of the notion of signifying propriety, a demonstration—more than six thousand lines long—that the connections within
the sign, between signifier and signified, and between the sign and its referent, are purely conventional and arbitrary. You can call a girl a boy, by
saying so and by dressing her as a he: the "real identity" of nature will be
signified or "covered" by the social gender imputed to the individual, by
the birth announcement and the nurture that instills the discipline of masculinity: how to perform the social gender of masculinity. One sidelight of
this text is to reveal, so insistently it has been missed, that the *male* gender
is not a given, from which the female is a degradation: being male is a social construction of nurture just as much as being female. It is constructed,
it is learned, even when the subject is female. The reader of *Silence* witnesses the social construction of gender, from beginning to end!

Corporeality is not to be denied. That sexuality, as distinguished from
gender, is seen as irrevocable, does not impinge on the social construction
of gender: no errors of Silence's reveal her "true nature," no slip signals the
truth of her sexuality. Her social construction of male gender is universally
convincing and could continue indefinitely, if not for Merlin's second
sight. Transvestite role-playing fuses identity and subjectivity without a
crevice or a gap. In performance, the body makes no claims, gets no attention: it is absent, except as negation of that identitarian subjectivity. Silence is a walking cliché of knightly behavior, to which the asserted body
gives the lie. The unitary subject is a perfect performance, insofar as it is
a successful lie.

Silence legitimates a walking lie, entirely successful, which earns universal approval within the text. It is a textbook example of the arbitrary nature of the sign, linked to the arbitrary nature of gender, inversely hooked
to the determination of sex. Of sex and gender, which is the signifier,

which the signified? The arbitrary bar between the two sets the ordinary linkage in doubt. The space of that doubt opens the freedom that devolves from interrupting the determining social codes of gender. The sign is made to lie with, especially when an inheritance is in question. The subject is pliable, before authority and the material force of history, and wins against them. The sign erases gender and creates it, as a decisionary criterion to social status. No one will argue with that. Or at least, no one does, in *Silence*. Its subjectivity is fused with its perfect performance of the lie, the liberation of the subject from a restrictive political edict and socially determined gender codes.

Slavoj Žižek speculates that "personification" is "the necessary reverse of 'reification'": as "capital becomes the capitalist," things are treated as persons. The entry of personification allegory into the field of vernacular literature in the thirteenth century might be read as an inverted sign of the period's nascent capitalism.[59] However, *Silence* is not a text to ground political philosophy. Whether Merlin is carnivorous or vegetarian, whether Silence or silence is male or female, whether the character of woman is glossed into disappearance as Eufemia or Eufeme, would be serious issues for people caught in the toils of real-life decisions. In *Silence*, they are matters to play with, in a domain of nonresponsibility whose ideological openings are engaging without engaging text, narrator or author—whoever that may be. Whether such indeterminacy leans toward conservative or "progressive" positions is itself a question. The lability of the sign is prima facie apolitical.

The politics of history may construe it differently. The poem's moral and political indeterminacy, what can be called the "libertarian" attitude toward transvestitism, contradicts the notion of an oppressively rigid binary distribution, theologically determined and operative throughout the Middle Ages. In a deontological chart of the necessitated, the forbidden, and the allowed, cross-dressing, especially by women, occupied a place of indeterminacy: monks wore dresses, and women might reject their sexual identity! On the one hand, it was available to saints and laity alike as a technique of circumventing the social role of serving as men's sexual object; on the other hand, it was also subject to condemnation. The practice occupied a realm of social indeterminacy and defined a marginal individual freedom of avoidance within an established patriarchal hierarchy. It allowed the subject to disaffiliate from sociosexual identity.

That playful indeterminacy did not prevent the instrumental capture of cross-dressing as a major accusation against Joan of Arc at her trial. What had previously been indeterminate was suddenly construed, for political reasons, as moral and theological turpitude. Structural analysis—à la Lévi-Strauss or A. J. Greimas—reveals a surprising degree of identity in the two narratives of Silence and Joan. Both are born female, both are mandated by father-figures (the father Cador, God the Father) to preserve a territorial heritage (a fief, France) by "passing" as males, cross-dressing and engaging in warrior pursuits. Both are extraordinarily successful at it; both are acclaimed by their contemporaries; both hear voices (nature, nurture, and angels). Both return to female dress at the end. One might even extend the analogy by suggesting that while Silence marries the king of England at the end, Joan, in the brutality of her execution and sacrifice, marries the King of Heaven as the savior of France, or more exactly, the Creator of the as-yet-inexistent community of the nation of France, just beginning to be imagined.

In both cases, cross-dressing circumvents the ordinary gender distribution by virtue of an optional choice. It is a mode of "passing" in a domain recognized as the Other's, selected as a political stratagem to achieve material ends: saving or constituting a patrimony, a kingdom. It is a strategy which enables the disadvantaged, the subjected, to subordinate gender to the materialities manipulated by politics. Joan's effort to take advantage of indeterminacy, as others had done in text and historical reality before her, for political purposes, provoked the political parody of justice, implicating ecclesiastical and lay authorities both, of her trial. Parody of gender roles can have burdensome entailments.

CHAPTER 12

Subject and Community:
Adam's "Congés"

The experimentalism of *Rose I* and *Silence* veers from the aristocratic codes of the twelfth century, oriented toward political unification. The texts to be examined in the coming chapters dislodge themselves from the "modernism" of that cultural tradition as new social classes surface into textuality. None of the texts would claim to start absolutely afresh, wiping clean the slate of the past—that would be too close to modernity's naïveté, but all introduce new practices of subjectivity through radically new developments in the forms of ideology, including political discursivities of theory and prose. Cultures of the urban—defined by commerce, the university, bourgeois intellectualism, political administration, early forms of gender and national identities, and fraternal identification with the excluded—fragment any putative unity to claim cultural space alongside the continued development of twelfth-century aristocratic and clerical cultures: a late-medieval postmodernism. A handful of texts has been selected for case study, *exempla* of a new kind of history: simultaneously literary, cultural, and political.

Adam de la Halle's texts negotiate a personal fate in terms of the specific, singular locality: the commercial and banking city of Arras, in the late thirteenth century. That negotiation structures the medieval dialectic of the individual and its alterities: the intimate other, the community as a complex, even conflictual whole. Addressing the city of Arras, it disengages a notion of community from a new middle-class perspective, whose subject is defined by doubled hybrid bastardy. The father is a "bigamous" cleric, a man of the church also defined by relations with a woman who is either an adulteress or a widow. The son's own life is torn between marriage and the desire for further study, blocked by impecuniousness. From this complexity, Adam constructs community as relative totality.

Three poets of Arras constituted a lyric subgenre: the "Congés." "*Pitiez*" is the first word of the first poem of our collection, the leave-taking of Jean Bodel, probably written around the turn of the century, about halfway through the reign of Philip Augustus.[1] The word is highly ambiguous from our point of view, but such ambiguity is sometimes created by modern distinctions. As language grows more analytic, it establishes new distinctions and loses others. New words mark multiplying distinctions. Words and meanings pullulate where monovocalism reigned. Analytics replace large areas of poetic meaning in a symbolic episteme.[2]

Piety? Pity? Or merely pitiable? *Pitiez* repeats the Latin polyvalence of *pietas*. Does it bear something even more ambitious, on the order of strength the term has in Rousseau: empathy, *Mitgefühl*? Here, the most precise translation might be "distress, a miserable state":

> *Pitiez*, whence I draw my matter,
> teaches me to take pleasure in this
> that I speak on my matter.

Pitiez is that state of misery which arouses compassion in others, perhaps leading to the piety of theological charity. It draws on the human potential for identification with an other in a face-to-face encounter and for whom something in human nature leads us to assume responsibility: the basis of Emmanuel Levinas's ethics.

The distress of Jean Bodel and Baude Fastoul was leprosy, the terrifying illness, devastating, incomprehensible, and uncontrollable: the AIDS of the Middle Ages. Its terror assimilated other frightening diseases such as syphilis, made its victims untouchables, forced to separate themselves from the socius.[3] The poet-enunciator's ritualized leave-taking in a verse form associated with death—that of Hélinand's *Poem of Death*, ca. 1195—is the *mythos* of the three poems. Their subgenre struck a chord in Arras, open to the nonpoetic externalities of individual mortality, dismembered temporalities, and the collective to which an appeal for psychic survival is made: a concretized socius.[4] Arras was part of the intense economic machine of Flanders. Does a particular consciousness of the interdependence of subject and collectivity arise from this historical context, the specifically urban commercial context at the origins of modern capitalism and the bourgeoisie?

The poems also touch on something more profound in the human condition. The ritualization of departure addresses what is painful in separation, both to the one who leaves and those who remain behind. The individual loses part of his identity: an Arrageois outside Arras, he will lack the physical, geographical ground of identitarian being. The collectivity loses the principle that it is not only composed of, but constituted by, the totality of its individual members. On both sides, violence is being done and endured. The ritualization of departure parries the sense of loss, of threatened disintegration and fragmentation, for both socius and individual.

Adam de la Halle's leave-taking is occasioned by something less dramatic than leprosy, but more important for subjectivity. He leaves the collectivity of Arras to return to the project formulated in the *Jeu de la feuillée*, to complete his studies in Paris. In the play, lack of funds blocked his project, as his father declined to pay for his education. Here, a series of father substitutes does the trick. The poem thanks a series of individuals whose generosity found outlets in partying and providing a subvention for the poet's study. But the collectivity is ambiguous in several ways. Mentions of "Arras," some mentions of "*vile*," signify a totality: the entire city, its entire population, are meant by Jean Bodel and Baude Fastoul (ll. 13 ff., 25, 145). In Adam de la Halle, disjunction is stressed more than by the other two poets. His collectivity is split along several axes.

Town and gown are topographically distinguished in a split one can see even today in Rouen, for example. The *cité* is the smaller ecclesiastical enclave, the *vile* is the larger, more populous industrial and banking center. The split between town and gown is geographical and horizontal. The text harbors two elites. The love-elite, signaled by terms such as *amans, Amors, amie*, goes back, through *Rose I* to the courtly texts of the twelfth century (ll. 11, 49, 61). Another elite is that of the boon companions, drawn from the patriciate which ran the city.[5] This second elite is the central one of the poem, commanding its center and running close to half the poem's length (ll. 73–144, 71 lines out of 156).

The collective subject is split, then, along three axes: the geographical, which comports economic, political, and cultural dimensions; the society of heterosexual love, defined as in *Rose I* by adherence to the single value of love not merely as an affective value, but a social and a moral one as well; and that of the homosocial bonding among the exclusively male component of the well-to-do burghers of Arras, dedicated to dinners, drinking, and good works such as funding fellowships for the deserving unfortunate of their own class. Those who fund Adam's future are substitute fathers, as he himself recognizes.[6] Their revels and fine dinners are a disappearing custom. The grass has been mowed close, their elegant pleasures have seen their basis cut. Those who've pulled so much to shore and dried the fisheries commit a mortal sin.[7] The other split in the collectivity is temporal, defined by a former wealth whose economic base has been undermined: exactly what the *cité*, the ecclesiastical enclave, was doing to the *vile*, the commercial center of Arras.

What of the individual who says "*je*," between enunciator and collectivity? We are all constituted as individuals by our collectivities. How far does belonging go, in the case of Arras and Adam? A simple onomastic accident: Adam de la Halle was also known as Adam d'Arras: Adam of Arras, Adam who came from Arras, Adam who belongs to Arras. In any case, it was not as a poor beggar picked up in the streets as an object of gratuitous charity that Adam received value from the good burghers he salutes and thanks. He was not quite one of their own either. Adam belonged to a class of men between the class of wealth and power, on the one hand, and peasants, journeymen, day laborers in town or in the country, manual laborers in general, on the other. That intermediary class frequently furnishes writers and intellectuals. His father Henry was a "bigamous" cleric, a *clerc bigame*: though a cleric, he had had relations with more than one woman (legitimate or not), or married a widow. This was a category of ambiguous social status, benefiting from both marriage and ecclesiastical immunities, such as exclusion from local taxes. They had a poor reputation, in public opinion and among town powers, which held that their married status undid the protection of ecclesiastical immunity and rendered them subject to taxation. They were also a headache for the church hierarchy and the frequent object of papal legislation, impelled by the tendency to separate church and secular society.

Adam was a son, then, of hybridity, a zone of mixtures of status and culture. He maneuvers, in the *Jeu de la feuillé*, to escape being tarred with the brush of "bigamy," but does not escape the internal divisions of subjectivity. Indeed, the pattern of his life is that of a shuttle between two states, that of *clergie* and that of town poet of love. As a student, he was a cleric. As a young man, he fell in love, which meant quitting the clerical state. This ushered in—he says—the most joyous, the most content, the sweetest life outside of paradise (ll. 49–52).[8] Adam means marriage. The portrait he draws of his wife, Marie, in the *Jeu de la feuillée*, inspires the conventions of lyric and narrative poetry with a breath of experienced reality. Convention, in those lines, shares its *littérarité* with a representational value of lived experience.

Two stanzas of the "Congés" inscribe this love. Stanza five is addressed to love itself; the following stanza is addressed to his wife, with a spousal tenderness unusual in medieval poetry: *bele tres douche amie chiere* (l. 61). It rehearses the sorrow with which he leaves her, assuring her of continuing love: she will remain the treasurer of his heart (cf. twelfth-century imagery of the beloved as possessing the key to the lover's heart) even as his body wanders elsewhere (cf. the twelfth century's paradox of present love and absent body). His body will go seek out *engien et art*, craft and discipline, elsewhere. And with a usurer's contractual calculation, common in Arras, he assures his wife of her part in the increase of value to be accumulated, making his talent fructify by tripling or quadrupling his value, just as a farmer leaves a field lie fallow for a time, so that it may be more productive later.

This rationale for abandoning a spouse makes the one abandoned inspire the abandonment. For the sake of love, he left clergy. In the state of love, in its service, he acquired a sense of value, of *courtesie*. From this experience of love, he takes the will and desire to regain reputation and value (*los et pris*). The syntax is fairly contorted, the contorsion of an aporia. The text lays responsibility for his choice of leaving on the shoulders of love or lady (the identification of love and beloved is standard in courtly lyric) without saying that by living in love and with Marie, he had lost the values it and she inspired. He wants to regain what he cannot acknowledge having lost because of love.

The transfer between different categories of life is both rhetorical and moral. The shift from one culture to another, from one language to another, from one status to another, combines unhappy separation with the desire to assert continuity, a continuity that shows up only in terms of the personal relationship with his beloved. There is no indication of possible return in the stanzas addressed to the various boon companions of drinks, dinner, and carousing in Arras. Only with her, whom he leaves with heartfelt repetitions of reinvented conventions, does he look forward to a reunification.

One disjunction is that between the theme of separation in sadness from the woman he loves and the themes with which he starts the poem. The opening lines of the poem look forward not only to François Villon, two centuries later, but to far later modernities. Time, consciousness, and loss under the whip of necessity are the stuff of the first stanza. Time is metonym for life, lost and wasted, now mourned: it must, in the future, be better spent—shades of Villon, Shakespeare, and Proust. This is also the constitutive structural disjunction in Augustine and Rousseau: the selfhood that is lost as consciousness turns into memory to retrospect the evanescence of pleasures past. Time is experienced as personal destiny. However time was being used, whatever the activities, some degree of self-consciousness, some element of awareness, always urged him to refuse pleasure, *pour tendre a venir a honnour*: in reaching to approach honor (l. 6). Still, he spent time's flower in a world of wastage . . . he was forced to it by a power of lordship: Love's lordship? Let lovers forgive him the error of his ways.

It is not characteristic of Adam to assume responsibilities. Aside that moral point, however, there is a psychic structure of some importance: a consciousness that urges the individual to an ethical value it calls *honnour*. The word is both familiar and odd. As the ultimate value of both epic and romance, it is quite familiar to the reader of those texts. The warrior-knight's honor requires a material base, hence a fief to furnish investment in armament, weaponry, and horses, and a performance of his function with those instruments, with courage, skill, and loyalty. How these values transfer to the urban son of a *clerc bigame* is puzzling, however. Is there an "honor" befitting a burgher-merchant negotiating and carrying out commercial contracts? A cleric living in the world, finding the correct balancing act between other-worldly values and sympathy for those living fully in the *saeculum*? A poet-jongleur-experimental-playwright voicing disparate value-systems in the very acts of composition and performance? The question is all the more perplexing, because Adam's best-known work, the *Jeu de la feuillée*, is a particularly "open work," juxtaposing a variety of human experiences and relationships with little concern for ideological reconciliation.

Honor is a sliding signifier, empty of meaning except for the positive marker: the space of meaning borne by the sign, the signified, is nothing but the (+) of social approval, which devolves by social codification on those words that reflect or incorporate the supposed values of the socius. "*Honnour*," here, is "the good," undefined, except by the implication of the individual in the honor of the city—an implication of both meaning and subjectivity. The courtly conventions of the love stanzas bear a new paradigm, amorous and ethical. Rather than the impossibility that produces frustration and transcendence in the noble lyric of the twelfth century, love among thirteenth-century city burghers entails the pleasure of satisfied sensualities, tenderness, weighing of career alternatives, and a daily morality of manipulation in the place of violence upon self.

Only one of its native sons, "contaminated" with yet other values, could pen this jeremiad against the city:

> Arras, Arras, city of discord
> And hate, and bad-mouthing,
> You were once so noble!
> They say you're being renewed,
> But unless God brings back the good,
> I see none to bring you peace:
> Heads and tails [that is, money] are too beloved . . .
> Elsewhere I'll hear the word of God:
> Here there's nothing but lies.[9]

The aporia is patent. Honor, the good, devolves from the collectivity, but how shall "honor" devolve from a collectivity that has none? Given over to love of money and hate of others, given over to the evil uses of language that cannot but shock the poet, the text suggests Arras follows after Sodom and Gomorrah and justifies the poet's casting his lot with Lot.

Disjunctions are the poem's drone, its walking bass. Disjunction, experienced as the loss of something so precious it is essential, both as possession and as loss, is the topic the poem addresses. It does so, without the overt theatricality of the dramatic *Jeu de la feuillée*, without the bombastic rhetoric of the poem whose form it adapts, Hélinand's *Vers de la mort*, but with the formulaic conventionalisms of a subgenre: an urban thirteenth-century rap. Adam's poem still enjoys the luxury of a ritual civility lost to the cultures of atomized individualism, civility that derives from the city:

civitas. Earlier medieval textuality features the extraordinary civility with which Roland, struck by his companion Oliver, blinded by the blood pouring into his eyes, asks his friend why and how he could have struck him so. Yvain and Gauvain, suddenly recognizing each other in judicial combat, abandon the fight, each calling the other the victor. What happens only on the field of justice and death in the epic and the novel is recast as social ritual in the northern French town of commerce, in all three poems of leave-taking, in the repetitiousness of social formulas, whether as the result of the dread, untreatable disease of leprosy, or by career choice.

For Adam, his choice is made. He is leaving to return to his studies. But he cannot merely hop a train or plane, and not only because the technology is lacking. A social technology requires something quite different from a modern departure. Tender as that may be in performance, one person leaves, others stay; all may be saddened, but the roles are clear: one leaves, others stay. In Arras, even in corrupt Arras, things are different. The discovery of the individual in the twelfth century had not set the individual against community, as in modern society. On the contrary, it emphasized the location of the individual in a corporate group, the integrity of their interdependence. The new self-awareness defined that self in terms of likeness, of models, of the imitation of types.[10] Social diversity was expressed in the ideological constructs of corporate metaphors that provide models for individual self-recognition, not as a unique singularities, but as a social type embodying specific models. The social culture of Arras here represents the generality of human cultures, as against the anomaly of the sociologies of modernization: the radical opposition of the individual and society is exceptional.

The individual cannot just up and leave, whether by choice or mortal necessity. In either case, the disjunction is marked by the ritual of leave-taking. A *congié* is not "goodbye," brusque or kind, thoughtless or considerate. A *congié* is the leave that is given by those who remain: it is a ritual of reversal. The individual leaves the collectivity only with its permission. The ritual does not "paper over" a loss incurred. Its recognition switches something around. While the individual has made the choice to leave, he or she does so only as a member of the collectivity. The individual "belongs" to the collective in a strong sense: as being "possessed" by it. In asking its leave to leave, the individual retains both his or her own integrity and the collectivity's. Its loss is erased, insofar as it gives its permission. And so, surprisingly, is the individual's. The *congié* is the social ritual of leave-taking that absorbs and transmutes the violence of leave-taking. Adam structures it as a ritualized reinvestment of constitutive splittedness, in both himself and the collectivity, so as to produce an assertion of wholeness, of integrity, which is also a meditation on the social condition of subjectivity.

The subject opens the question and attempts to shove it aside, in the opening line: "However I have used my time." The abstract concept of time is wrapped around the issue of a judgment to be performed on one's own life. His mind—*conscienche*, as in modern French, covers both conscience and consciousness—always led him toward the best, he says, in the effort to attain honor. *But* he weeps for lost time, whose flower he spent in worldly amusements. *But* the power of lordship—*forche de signeur*—forced him to it, and all lovers will hold him excused of the error.

Judgment is made from some point of futurity. Time is the potential for action, to be engaged or lost at the time, to be judged later. If "conscience doth make cowards of us all," it is insofar as a position of future judgment is interposed between the subject and the act. Speaking of one of his interlocutors—the last, as it happens—Adam invokes this temporal structure. May God grant Colart Nasart the employment of his time, so as to be valued when he's old:

> Evening is witness to the day.[11]

Time metaphorizes the subject's potential of taking action and provides the structure of judgment. What is to be judged at the end of the day is the honor attained, the quantity of value accumulated:

> To be of value in the distance.[12]

This may look like a particularly commercial conceptualization, appropriate to Arras. In fact, the nobility did not think of the value of honor otherwise: it is quantitative, it accumulates and is counted and judged at the end of the day.[13] The distinction between nobility and commerce, between commercial and nobiliary values, was a crucial ideologeme for the nobility. As ideological values often do, it tended to deceive. But burgher codes mix the sentimental, social, agricultural, and financial codes with which Adam bids goodbye to his lady-love, identified with the sweetness of life. The wise processes of ecological agriculture harbor the same principle of increased social value as interest in the bank. The fact that the same code of value operates in all three fields, that it is implicit in the social codes of the time, implies an analysis of value per se.

Having set the goal, the means become the issue. Arras is an unlikely place to increase honor. But it is his place: the identification of the subject with a particular geographical location, specifiable on the representation of a map, is a mark of settled civilization that sets it apart from the nomad. That identification makes departure difficult. And yet it is a necessity:

> I have to go out of my place.[14]

Hence the ritual of the "Congés." Leave-taking is something that language allows the subject *to take*.[15] In one place, the verb is switched. When the text addresses the best man of Arras, Symon Esturion, the language changes. Rather than being *taken*, leave is being *asked for*. Syllable count and internal rhyme have something to do with it, but the verbal change is informative semantically. *Congié*, first of all, means permission, authorization, objects more appropriately requested than appropriated. *To take one's leave* is an idiom; *to ask for one's leave* is not only more literal, it is more revealing of the actual structure of the relationship between the interlocutors. The request formally places the interlocutor into the position of authority that makes the choice to grant the request or not. The request grants decision-making power, recognizing the interlocutor's autonomous superiority. Alterity is acknowledged, at the moment of dislocation between self and other. That dislocation is inherent and necessary to the self's new autonomy. Radical individualism does not yet exist: its ground is being constructed.

Alterity takes several forms. Indeed, its major forms structure the poem. The autonomy of the self, its departure already decided, nevertheless required, if not (re)constitution, at least reaffirmation. In leaving his place, the subject is off to a place not his, which will test his mettle. The ritual leave-taking is polyvalent. Its performativity faces both the self and the peopled place he leaves. The first alterity addressed is Arras. The city is totality, the world of the place that is the "speaker's." It is addressed in that peculiar rhetoric of make-believe, the apostrophe whose very function is to (falsely) presentify: the most intense and essential linguistic form of all. The first stanza has the intimacy of overhearing an intimate monologue. The second contrasts with rhetorical grandeur, that of a raging biblical prophet:

> Arras, Arras, City of discord
> Of hate and badmouthing.[16]

Once you were noble, now they claim renewal is here, but only God could overcome your love of lucre. Here are only lies; salvation's truth lies elsewhere. Let's go hear the Evangels elsewhere. . . . The totalized Other is evil, the evil of its "soul" and reputation . . . its *los et pris*, its raison d'être. Jeremiads against love of lucre did not start with Marx, nor were they restricted to the church in the Middle Ages: in the thirteenth century as in the nineteenth and twentieth, poets, writers, students, engaged in the rejection of lucre and its cultural powers. The industrial manufacture of woven goods that makes Arras's worldwide reputation, its agility at financial deals, express and nourish the love of money that feeds incipient capitalism. The opposition of money, commerce, and capitalism to human values is not of recent date.

An allusion to the golden age topos recurs briefly. The city was once noble, but internal division opposes its two parts. Arras shares the frequent polarized structure of medieval cities and towns. The urban agglomeration is divided into the *ville*, deriving from the classic villa—both the noble house and its surrounding agricultural development—and associated with residence and productive labor; and the city, deriving from *civitas*, sometimes used for old cities thought to have been Roman. In English as in French, *la cité* retains its associations with the structures of governance, the state, law, and citizenship. In London, the City is associated with the practice of law. In Paris, the Ile de la Cité is both the center of government and of the bishopric. In Rouen, the cathedral was planted in direct, linear opposition to the center of labor and life, of commercial and agricultural exchanges. In Arras, city and town are separated by a small river, the Crinchon. *La Cité*, west of the river, is the ecclesiastical domain, containing the cathedral, the bishopric, various other religious institutions, and a relatively small population. To the east, much larger, completely surrounded by defensive, turreted walls, *la Ville*, with two market places, nine parishes, a dozen churches, and the renowned Abbey of Saint-Vaast.[17] The split was not simply that between the commercial life and vernacular culture of the burghers, as against establishments of the church. Burgher life in the town was amply provided with religion. The opposition is rather between the full, totalized life of the townspeople, including religious practices, and the central, administrative organs of the church as an institution of power.

The opposition is a strong one. Adam provides a thumbnail historico-political sketch of one urban dialectic: the *ville* goes downhill, from which the *cité* becomes prosperous.[18] The town's degeneration has been the city's advantage. Like any subject, the poet's Other is divided, and conflictually so. But the poem's primary interest is not in their opposition. It is rather in the burgher town, where all its citizens once strove toward honor (127 ff.). Ambiguously, the poem recalls the burning flames of games and holidays (ll. 130 ff.): Fires of joy, or of hell?

Arras is cast in the role of Other, with a complex topography and class history that leaves it as the incarnation of evil in the present. However lost the city may be, some ambiguous hope may glimmer yet in the next stanza, thanks to the

> *bons reniés*
> A cui je voiel prendre congiet. (ll. 27–29)

Even though Arras has lost its way, nevertheless . . . and then "reading" stops and dual semantic paths appear, depending on which of the two substantives is taken as noun, which as adjective. The italicized phrase may be either "the good men rejected" [by the city], which is the editor's reading. Or it may be an oxymoron: "the good renegades," friends as boon companions in drinking and revels. "Good renegades" is not inappropriate. But the ambiguity persists, an unresolvable pun.

Punning continues in the next stanza, with its play on *lais*, four times at the rhyme: leave as an active verb, *lais* as a poetic form, *lais* as an adjective meaning ugly or ignorant, taken as a noun and referring to the population of Arras, and finally *lais*' return as an adjective: ugly, repulsive. . . . The punning is neither accidental nor ornamental. It inscribes an essential trait of writing and the poetic manipulation of linguistic polyvalence, as conceived in vernacular practice and Latin poetics. This is the stanza in which the subject identifies himself as the poet who produces songs, music, and stories, recognizing he is no longer a tyro, but a poet of some achievement getting on in years.

The subject is located between the city and its ambiguous population of the ugly, the stupid, the greedy, and "the good renegades" who know how to live. Having identified itself, it turns to the most intimate alterity, in two quite remarkable stanzas. They are remarkable not only for the intimate ekphrasis, the tender loveliness and lived intimacy already noted, in some of the most tender love lines in medieval French. Literary history already knows well that this love poetry is a continuation of antecedent conventions. Both conventional yet infused with a new tone, recycling established codes and bringing a new, vibrant specificity, a remarkable meld of the Other and the other. The concrete corporeality and sentience of the woman is recognized and incorporated in a rehearsal of traditional codes that reverses their terms. Traditional codes allow for recognition and representation of something radically new and individual in and by the text. It is one of the more delicately admirable demonstrations of the working of ideology, in which prior values and their vocabulary envelop and constitute a lived reality with a directionality that depends entirely on the particular circumstances of an individual destiny.

At this point, oddly enough, the text returns to the distinguishing rhetorical figure of its subgenre. It names particular individuals in the city, the *bons reniés*, as those who will grant the subject the permission to leave he requests. Naming them, it recalls particular social traits associated with them, or recognizable habits—though it is always difficult to know whether such traits should be taken literally or by antiphrasis, contextual knowledge perhaps turning an overt meaning upside down. Symon Esturion, Baude and Robert le Normand, the brothers Pouchinois, Jakemon and Peter, Robert Nasart, André Hauiel, Robert Nasart, Giles the Father, Joyful John, and Colart Nasart, these proper nouns designate specific individuals. If reference elsewhere depends on sense, here sense *is* reference. If nouns elsewhere name categories, here the category is of one and the reference is radically unique. Proper nouns pick out specific, particular, concrete existents: even at this distance in time, partial lives can be reconstructed on the basis of documents.[19] They are major financiers, magistrates, men of power and wealth who lend large sums of money to the nobility: the town's patriciate. They participate in the Other of the *ville* at a level of command, even as they shimmer with textual individuality. That refulgence, which for us derives from scholarly habits of footnote hunting, was an immediately coded supplement to a famous name at the time his reputation was alive. It was part of the name's encoded meaning.

A radical individualism, a radical otherness, is impossible. The other is never seen, felt, or imagined, in a total absence of the Other's encoding. The self is inconceivable without its constitutive alterities. These draw on the general cultural codes in which each individual participates, and on the experience of the concrete other who is a goal, a posited reality behind the shimmering codes that link object and subject. That interdependence of self and other, of subject and cultural ideology, is the subject of Adam's leave-taking. Their opinion, their evaluation, their judgment counts. That is why the distinction of the last stanza is so crucial. He reassures the people of Arras that he is no less loyal toward them in taking leave, but addresses those false prophets (*faus devin*: l. 148) who deride his project. For he will not be as they judge him when talking in their cups. Instead, he will pluck a disdainful heart and will be strong, powerful, and straight when they lie supine, drunk, or dead:

> quant il gerront souvin. (l. 156)

The literal meaning is first: *souvin* < *supinum*, stretched on one's back, hence secondarily dead; or *souvin* = *sous vin*, under [the influence] of wine. While they are flat on their back, he will be straight, presumably upright and strong. In the future past anterior, he will have been seen to have given his detractors the lie, to have used well his time, to have learned *engien et art*, to have produced the *cant*, the *son*, the *lais* of which he bears the potential. Future time will legitimate the wastrel of past time.

The last stanza gestures toward a generality, "all those of Arras" to be left. Before that, the text insists on concrete, specific forms of alterity. The social ritual of leave-taking binds the community together in wholeness after the subtraction of one of its members. It binds the individual to the memory and consciousness of his place of origin. Both are restored to wholeness, by the ritual that licenses the individual's departure. Did the departure threaten a loss of some part of subjective identity? The subject rehearses the different forms of alterity that constitute it as subject: the

Other as city, the other as intimate paramour, others as mirror images of generosity and friendly kindness. By the end of the leave-taking, the subject has regained the strength of wholeness to assert its self in futurity, as against the badmouthing of anonymous doubters. The social ritual of permission to leave reconstitutes the individual as a relative autonomy.

In leaving, he tears the sheet of personal existence from the sustaining communal body. Separation is a form of death to the city's collective form of being. The poet eternalizes the ritual of leave-taking on the living sheet of parchment, the skin of a dead calf or sheep. Living tissue of a dead animal, he inscribes on it the *points de capiton* to suture its life, the community's, his own. His rivets suture the three sheets of existence: poem, collective, and self, with proper nouns marked with the seme of / reality / well beyond the *effet de réel.* They signal individual referents in the social body. The individual, his character, occupation, wealth, history, financial value, his traversals of the streets of Arras, all will have been part of textual decoding in the Arras of the thirteenth century: a wealth of information that contemporaries attached to the name, now mostly lost. What is left is the marker "real." It is, of course, only a marker, a seme. But as a marker, it is real.

The dying nail themselves to the skin of the living. The "Congés" of Arras are hardly the first use of proper nouns in medieval literature: they are frequent in troubadour texts. But the "Congés" use them in a particular way. As with François Villon later, the cascade of proper nouns rivets their signed poetic skein to the life of the collective left behind: the proper is nailed to the common.

CHAPTER 13

The Subject on the Subject: Philippe de Beaumanoir

S ubjects are constituted by ideology, an aspect of all cultural artefacts and processes. Ideology must be in a language understandable by the individual to be subjectivized: Latin was ineffective in transforming mounted-warrior Franks. Generally, ideology is more effective, in proportion as it presents the individual to be subjectivized with representations that resemble the representations already present in his or her imaginary. There may be a human craving for difference, but same-to-same is the name of the ideological game when it comes to reproductive efficiency. "New" ideology is more effective as it fuses with already existing ideology. The first cultural revolution was the association of the vernacular with writing, still marked as cultural product by being cast in verse. The next cultural revolution was the "invention of prose." Peculiarly enough, the ever-present medium of ordinary communication had to be "invented" in order for it to be recognized as a cultural entity. Neither cultural revolution was an overnight affair: both stretched out over generations. The creation of prose as an ideological vehicle for prosaic analytic discourse ran parallel to the exploration of increasingly overt vernacular ideology in verse. Poetry as vehicle for ideology burgeoned, even as experimentalism in prose ceded to triumphs of writing. The thirteenth century was key for both.

Prose is a technical term notoriously difficult to define beyond a negative notation: the absence of metrical rules and a rhyme scheme. As verse does not equal poetry, so prose does not equal discourse. They are different objects of knowledge. Discourse, for Foucault, covers all social use of language. Its use here is more limited. Discourse is an institutionalized language use, less given to figural speech than poetry, often aiming at precision and relative directness, with a peculiar ideological history. Its first ideology was "truth," which developed into the analytico-referential as the normative discourse of disciplines.[1] Academics, lawyers, doctors, business executives, all use the disciplined linguistic form of discourse initiated in the late Middle Ages, marked as a practical vehicle for information and conceptual manipulations. Its oral version has the written form as referent. Early forays into prose led to the constitution of a vernacular discourse of politics, opening the possibility of popular participation in political processes.[2]

Early bits of vernacular prose occur in the ninth-century Oaths of Strasbourg and in the eleventh-century prose prologue to the *Vie de saint Alexis.* In spite of the continued dominance of Latin for institutional purposes, vernacular prose is used for cultural and legal purposes. Shortly after the Council of Troyes in 1128, the Rule of the Templars is translated into Old French for new recruits.[3] The record of a land transaction between 1156 and 1158 survives in French.[4] Slightly later, laws attributed to William the Conqueror are written down in the vernacular.[5] At the turn of the century, customary laws of Normandy are collected.[6] The crusade chronicle of a barely lettered knight appears around 1202, a perspectival pendant to Geoffrey de Villehardouin's high-level account of a diplomat and general that emerges only a few years later.[7] The first prince to use French prose systematically was the count of Champagne, who grants franchises to certain cities such as Troyes (1230) in French: the royal chancellery follows in mid-century.[8] Private vernacular charters appear.[9] Customaries are composed in French, such as those from Touraine-Anjou (1246) and the slightly later *Usage d'Orléanais,* both recycled in the *Etablissement de Saint Louis.*[10] This inscription of customary law, rather than the introduction of Roman law, may count as the great juridical event of the reign of Louis IX.[11] Prosifications of chivalric fictions proliferate in thirteenth-century rewritings of the twelfth century's versified novels, attempting to dominate and deconstruct the represented violence of warrior practices.

The Pseudo-Turpin

The introduction of a new cultural technology and its concurrent ideology did not go without textual problems. The first effort to construct prose as institutional discourse occurs in the reign of Philippe Augustus. Twelfth-century ecclesiastics had equated vernacular verse with fiction, and fiction with lies that are at best a waste of time and at worst a corruption of Christian representation.[12] Even a poem like Chrétien's *Perceval*, thought "religious" by some modern scholars, is seen as composed of lies, in pretending to report on events that had not in fact occurred; by not conveying instead the spiritual truths desired by the church, the simulacral accounts of such fictions distorted the proper function of language.[13]

Curiously enough, the new claim to the truth of prose appears as an ideological tool of resistance. A prose vernacular historiography takes root, making claims of veridicity as against verse history.[14] Its claim of truth is an ideologically motivated argument, justifying the Flemish aristocracy against the growing centralized power of the king. That historically localized ideological argument established the modern assumption that prose is the most appropriate vehicle for referential veracity.

The self-legitimating, authorizing topos of the new medium was the equation: prose : truth :: verse : lie. The prologue of a lost prose history of Philip-Augustus survives . . . in verse:

> So I'll tell you the account,
> unrhymed, which rightfully recounts,
> just like Lancelot's book [the *Vulgate Lancelot*]
> where not a single word is rhymed,
> the better to tell the truth,
> and speak without falsehood;
> for (hi)story can't
> be rhymed without adjustment
> of lies to fill in the rhymes.[15]

Justifying prose in verse signals the historical shift paradoxically: it looks forward and speaks backward.

Among the first texts of the new veridicity is a French translation of a Latin forgery that appropriates the *Roland* for local ideology and politics, claiming its author, Archbishop Turpin, despatched by the Oxford *Roland* at Roncevaux, as the battle's sole survivor.[16] Half a dozen different versions were produced between 1200 and 1230. The issue of veridicity is directly addressed in the prologue.[17] As against other versions of Charlemagne's conquests, here you can hear the truth about Spain according to the Latin of the history which Count Renaud had sought out . . . among the books of my lord Saint Denis.

Renaud had the text translated from Latin into romance in 1206:

And since rhyme chooses to dress itself up with words collected outside the history [itself], the count insisted that this book be without rhyme according to the Latin of the history which Turpin, the archbishop of Rheims, treated and wrote just as he saw and heard it.[18]

Rhyme had codified the vernacular as a marked cultural form. It had institutionalized Old French, differentiating it from ordinary vernacular usage, giving it the status of a cultural form. This is rejected now. Rhyme hunts words outside the strict requirements of (hi)story's veracity.[19] Translating Latin prose into rhyming French would mean inserting words superfluous for a strict translation, undermining the value of an eye-and-ear-witness account. An extralinguistic truth claims to be conveyed across two relays, linguistic and temporal.

Truth is not merely referential. A "larger" concept of truth is invoked: moral, political, and performative. The story will reinvigorate the political world, its strength and the heart of its political system (*li cuer des seignorages*), and tell us how to behave before God and in the world. It climaxes in a class ideologeme:

Car vivre sanz honor est morirs.

The final word goes to *honor*, the banner of the nobility. Class interests drive this antihistory. Flemish nobles were patrons of the *Pseudo-Turpin*, summoning religious and class values against the encroaching powers of Philip Augustus's expanding state.[20] The self-legitimation of prosaic truth is born of political conflict. "Truth" is an ideologeme, in a contest for aristocratic cultural and political survival against the looming forces of monarchy. Philip decisively defeated these Flemish aristocrats at Bouvines in 1214, but the ideologeme loosed upon the body politic by their self-defense survives.

This definition of the text's ideological value as self-legitimation, while unquestionably valid, is not quite adequate. The themes of charity for the poor, the hypocrisy of the religious orders, the freeing of serfs whose servitude was caused by evil seigneurs, all reiterated in the text, overdetermine the Flemish polemics against the French king. They synthesize free-floating ideologemes critical of the present order, in constructing a would-be hegemonic ideology. The *Roland*'s epic grandeur is subverted; so is the logic of subordinating the feudal nobility to Emperor Charlemagne. Implicit in this appropriation is a strong criticism of the chanson de geste and the heroic ideologization of monarchy. The condition of its receivability was the figure of Turpin, whose identity guaranteed the self-legitimizing veridicity of the prose account.

The installation of prose as the regime of discursive truth caused structural problems for its enunciator. The ideological claim of "truth" is based on two indexical claims: that it is an eyewitness account, and that the eyewitness is Archbishop Turpin. The archbishop wrote his account on the spot, by night or by day, as moments of leisure allowed, noting the events of the day.[21] A recurrent phrase (later appropriated by Christine de Pizan) textualizes this duality as a leit-motif: the apposition *je, Torpins*. Since Old French allowed the subject to be marked morphologically and normally skipped the personal pronoun, the phrase is a rhetorical choice. It insists on the claim of a reportorial eyewitness, even alternating in close proximity with the third person. In one paragraph, two uses of the strong form (= *je, Torpins*) frame several uses of the first-person pronoun *je* alone:

> After that we arrived together in Vienna, and *I, Turpin*, remained there suffering from wounds and blows which *I* had suffered in Spain. Then *I* prayed Charles and entreated him on the love he had for **me**, that he let **me** know the day of his passing if he passed away before **me**, and *I* granted him *I* would let him know mine if *I* passed away before him. *I, Turpin*, the archbishop, thus remained in Vienna.[22]

No formulaic convention of first-person pronoun + proper noun exists in vernacular narrative, but that coupling occurs in the social practice of the notary, performed by ecclesiastics since the fourth century, which proliferated until Philip the Fair claimed it as an exclusive royal monopoly in 1302.[23] Notarial practice, combining dual functions as scribe and witness, authenticating and legitimating written texts, is paradoxical in a narrative. The subject is grammatically split between alternating, multiple functions.

Turpin *redivivus* is simultaneously (1) the observer who witnesses the events thanks to (2) his participation in them as a narrative actor, (3) the subject of the Latin narrative and after it, (4) of the French translation, (5 and 6) their respective scribes, and (7) the authenticating notary. Levels of subjectivity multiply, even as the actor's identity across these levels grounds the claim of referential veridicity.

Keeping track of these levels became a problem. In the prologue, Turpin is introduced in the third person as the archbishop of Rheims who wrote the Latin (hi)story just as he observed the event. He occurs in the third person at the end of the text, with regard to his death and burial. The same occurs within the body of the narrative. Charlemagne crosses mountain passes at Aspre, "Turpin the archbishop and the others manned the rearguard." Charlemagne then recalls the promise to alert Turpin of the emperor's impending death. Again, it is not to "me" that Charlemagne sends a messenger, but to " *Torpins l'arcevesque*": " *il le nonçast Torpin.*"[24] When Turpin is designated in the third person, the nonperson, the impersonal form appropriate to a reporter of history, who is the enunciator, if not Turpin?

Twelfth-century fictional narrative had ample experience in distinguishing different subject positions in the language of its texts and did so systematically without the kind of "error" Johannes falls into. The *Pseudo-Turpin*'s pronominal trouble devolves from the new criterion of "truth" at work in the Old French text, which places the author/narrator in a double bind. The third-person singular is most appropriate to the function of the narrator: neutral and objective, sans the passions and interests that beset participants. But the most convincing narrator is the eyewitness whose "being there" was recognized in medieval historiography as authenticating: the first-person pronoun, the "I," is the necessary form of witness.

The two legitimating assertions of historical truth conflict: the neutral, reportorial observer, as against the eyewitness participant. Ordinary rules of consistency in writing suggest a choice: either "he" or "I" will do, though with different effects. But the *Pseudo-Turpin* is not an ordinary narrative: one of the first to try out the new mode of writing, it performed a forced experimentalism. The textual subject found himself before an undecidable actorial role choice in attempting the new mode: to speak as witness; to speak as historian. He syncretized the two by appropriating a formula from the practice of a neighboring discipline. Disregarding existing conventions of narratorial intervention, appeal was made to an established institution, one whose business was secular veracity.

Subjectivity's difficult exploration is more readily pursued in fiction than in "truth." The domain of fiction has a specific kind of veridicity, defined neither by empirical factual reference nor by appeal to spiritual values. Some truths require the mediation of fiction and of poetry, even perceived as lies.

Jean de Meun: The Verse Discourse of Political Idealism

During the thirteenth century, one ideological avant-garde promulgates prose as the vehicle of discourse. Another continues to use verse. Jean de Meun's still perplexing experiment with perspectival discourses in his "continuation" of the *Rose Novel* continues to use demotic octosyllables. His vernacular rewrite is cast in a hoary textual structure, a polyvocal allegory of personifications with little relation to religious hermeneutics. Its rhetorical structure has been tracked by an exhaustive analysis that still oversimplifies, by disregarding the structural polyvalence of rhetorical figures.[25] Hypothetically, this totalizing structure should guarantee the semiotic coherence of the text, running more than 21,000 lines. As in Guillaume de Lorris's text, the conversation is about love, but its view of human love is much broader than *fin'amors*. The form shifts, sapping narrative drive with a wide-ranging multiplicity of perspectival effects, a series of rhetorically developed "mirrors," all fragmentary, in the multiple contradictions of an art of juxtaposition. Their serial brilliance overrides the potential coherence of textual hierarchy. Around 1270, Jean de Meun textualized human life as relative, perspectival, and contradictory, in a text whose fragmentary ideologemes are radical or even revolutionary in content, postmodern in form.

A generation ago, a survey of medieval prose unhesitatingly cited "Jean de Meun's anti-feminism."[26] Today, a study of Western misogyny begins by citing one of "the many anti-matrimonial tirades" of his text; Christine de Pizan is said to have been "the first to take the side of women against *Jean de Meun's anti-feminism*."[27] Key to this view is the famous tirade, nearly one thousand lines long, attributed to a jealous husband. Is its unquestionable misogyny the author's, as Christine claimed? Are character and author to be differentiated? The tirade is embedded in the longer discourse of the lover's Friend, which aims to convince the lover of a particular perspective on love.[28] The question is layered: Why does Friend cite the misogynous discourse in his own? Is the Jealous Husband the Friend's mouthpiece? Is the Jealous Husband the narrator's mouthpiece? The author's? The Jealous Husband defames women:[29] Does the citation of his discourse for purposes of condemnation infect the poem as a whole by synecdochic contamination?

The issue is not a (post)modern imposition on a medieval text. On the contrary, it was identified in the course of the fifteenth-century *querelle des femmes*, which was also a debate about text analysis. One of its participants, Jean de Montreuil, criticizes those who attack Jean de Meun, accusing them of misunderstanding Jean by reading superficially, "*by bits and with no concern for context.*"[30] Does the significance of an enunciation vary according to context, the speaker, and the speaker's role in the narrative hierarchy of a fiction? This technical question does not reduce to an opposition of "pure form" against the political valence of "social pragmatics."[31] A contemporary feminist points out that the ironic mode allows for citations and references to earlier traditions that are not only not assertions, but which flout the original epistemological and moral hierarchies.[32] A citation can be used and turned against its own ideological content. The conflict is one between opposing social views that give different ideological weight to different values, not a claim of transcendent aesthetics or humanism.

Not only *is* the Jealous Husband misogynous, he exists in order to exemplify misogyny: that is the reason for his presence in the text. After he beats his wife, Friend calls him *cis fos vilains jalous* (l. 9391): this insanely jealous lowlife, whose flesh should be given to the wolves. His discourse is cited as a negative exemplum, behavior that solicits a negative judgment: it is meant to be judged negatively. Far from being endorsed, misogyny occasions condemnation. Friend goes farther. He analyzes misogyny so as to identify it not only as an identitarian gender issue that affects women: he reveals it as a political issue. He stresses a point integral to modern feminism: the intimate, the familial, are political. Husbands who punish, abuse, and beat their wives, criticizing them as foolish and crazy for dancing and listening to younger men, husbands who try to establish mastery (*mestrie, mestrise*) over their wives, they are at fault, they themselves cause the end of love by conjoining two things that cannot live together, two things that exclude each other: *amor et seignorie*, love and lordship, love and domination (ll. 8419–24).

Ending the Jealous Husband's tirade, Friend glosses his own rhetorical procedure: "I have given you an example [of a man] who makes himself lord of his wife" [*qui se fait seignor de sa feme*] (l. 9395). This is a fundamental mistake, a categorical error. Even a mere reversal of roles is a mistake. Neither man nor wife should dominate, neither the man

> making himself lord of his wife,
> nor, in turn, should [the wife] be a lady,
> but *his equal and companion*,
> as the law conjoins them,
> and he himself must be *her companion*
> without making himself lord or master.[33]

Gender domination is irreconcilable with loving marital relations, promulgated on principles of equality and intimacy, excluding any hierarchy. With domination over another person, love must die: love can live only when the heart is free and unencumbered.

The husband's tirade brings home a point: it makes the political intimate. It exemplifies misogyny, but it does more: it casts misogyny as a form of political inequality. Egalitarian love was typical of the Golden Age: people lived in natural simplicity, wearing hairy leather and drinking plain water instead of sherry or claret, before property or political rule. There was no king or prince, no culpability or theft, when all were equal and private property was sought by none.[34] All were equally wealthy, all loved each other loyally . . . then was love without lordship.[35] *Amors* refers to erotic and marital sexual relations. It is also a diplomatic term, illuminating human relations in general: "politics" in general, or collective life at any level. *Amors* is the ideologeme par excellence: *both* intimate and political.

How was this Golden Age of collective equality lost? Friend responds in a brief personification allegory, a recursive imitation of authorial discourse. It rehearses the old allegory of vices and virtues, with a twist. A troop appears in mounted attack, lance at the ready, composed of *Barat* (greed, ruse, treachery, ostentatious elegance), Sin, and Bad Luck. Dissatisfied with sufficiency, they are joined by Pride, Covetousness, Avarice, Envy, and all the other vices that pulled Poverty out of Hell (ll. 9528–36). From Poverty descends Larceny, spreading discord, contention, and war across the earth, ripping from its entrails metals and precious stones, which people then desire enviously, for—as in *Silence*—

> Avarice and Covetousness
> have lodged in men's hearts
> the burning desire to acquire property.[36]

This acquisitive ardor caused men to abandon the Golden Age:

> They have not ceased doing evil since,
> and turned false and treacherous.
> Henceforth they grasp property only,
> cutting apart even the earth, . . .
> the strongest taking the most.

Along with property, politics enters the scene:

> They chose the most ignoble among them,
> The most crooked there was,
> The biggest and the toughest,
> and made him lord and prince.[37]

A scholarly effort to defang this radical discourse claims that egalitarian ideas pervade medieval political thought:[38] that rather strengthens its import. In fact, the *Glossa ordinaria* held a contrary opinion: Jean de Meun was attacking conventional ideas, perhaps aiming at Thomas Aquinas.[39] Is vernacular poetry an inappropriate place to argue theology?[40] So be it: medieval poetry is full of transgressions. Jean's Friend takes a position on the theological debates of his time, transgressing genres of discourse. A historian of theology considers Jean's ideas, even in romance verse form, "revolutionary."[41]

The narrative and rhetorical organization of discourse reveals a complex perspectivism that not only illuminates persistent interpretive errors but also opens vistas of interpretive possibilities for readers of vernacular, secular texts. Jean de Montreuil was correct: Christine de Pizan's attack on Jean de Meun's supposed antifeminism was based on the superficial reading of a text fragmented into decontextualized bits. The attribution of a negatively marked character's trait to the author runs counter to basic principles of reading, known in the Middle Ages and today, as well as to common sense. Misogyny is the topic of the text, exemplified by a tertiary figure of ridicule, cited as an error of human behavior, self-defeating in terms of the desire for intimate happiness, revealing the fundamental evil that besets human society: acquisitiveness. Misogyny exemplifies the thirst for domination, expressed not only in the institutions of private property, differential wealth, and political domination, but in intimate relations as well. Its counterpart is Jean de Meun's version of primitive communism: universal equality, common property, reciprocal loyalty, and trust.[42] For Marx, the first form of property is tribal, corresponding to an undeveloped stage of production: hunting, fishing, cattle raising, or agriculture.[43] Pastoral or migratory community appears spontaneously and forms into a clan for the communal appropriation and utilization of land held in common, each person a proprietor through membership in the clan, each individual a link in the text(ure) of community.[44]

Jean's hypothetical reconstruction of primitive human history reaches back farther than Marx's. Before hunting or fishing, cattle raising or agriculture, there was simple gathering:

> Scarcity reigned,
> People were not so delicate,
> In dress or food.
> They gathered acorns in the woods
> Instead of bread, or meat, or fish,
> And searched out among bushes,
> Among valleys, plains and mountains
> Apples, pears, walnuts and chestnuts,
> Buds and mushrooms and plums,
> Raspberries, strawberries, the red berry of hawthorn.[45]

Like some modern anthropologists, Friend thought "primitive" life, not a laborious scramble for survival, but easy and varied: he differs from Marx's concern with the labors of production. Nevertheless, a past diegesis sketches out an ideal future society, a utopia of equality without property, domination, or violence.

Friend is a protofeminist: Is Jean de Meun? To what extent was Christine's devious attack on Jean de Meun, which also attacked the relative autonomy of textuality, motivated not only by her own protofeminism, but by the politicization Jean brought to the issue of women in society? To what extent was the "Quarrel of the Rose" not only a femino-textual skirmish but also a conservative, ultraroyalist counterattack on a hugely popular progressive, materialist intellectual and writer?

Discursive Subjects of Representation

The great prose novels of the early thirteenth century invent an artistic prose discourse of the first order as of around 1220–30. Half a century later, two roughly contemporary works mark the triumph of a secular discourse of veridicity: Brunetto Latini's *Book of the Treasure* (before 1266),[46] and Philippe de Beaumanoir's *Coutumes du Beauvaisis* (1283). Brunetto was a notary, a technical discipline of writing that overlapped with law, scribal functions, and authorship.[47] The *Trésor* vernacularizes the encyclopedic "mirrors" of knowledge that already number more than twenty titles, climaxing in Vincent de Beauvais's *Speculum maius*,[48] adapting the Latin *speculum* to a vernacular, bourgeois world whose ultimate values are economic and political. Highly successful, the work survives in seventy-three manuscripts.

Having dealt with personal self-governance according to ethics and *iconomike*, the author addresses politics,

> how the city is to be governed. The city is nothing more than a
> people, assembled to live according to one law and under one
> governor. The highest discipline in governing a city is rhetoric, the
> discipline of speaking; for without speech there would be no city, nor
> any establishment of justice or human collectivity.[49]

Language is integral to governance, its use fundamental to collective life. Brunetto transfers not only information but also the very idea of disciplined knowledge as a classification of phenomena, for a middle-class lay public.[50] His "truth" is not that of ecclesiastical *specula*. Theology is subtracted, politics and rhetoric occupy one-third of the book. Large sections of the classical heritage and clerical culture are made available to a public clerics considered "illiterate" because non-Latinate. Insofar as knowledge, understanding of the world, and intellectual discipline ground the subject, Brunetto's text is a sine qua non for lay commoners as political subjects in a city.

Philippe de Beaumanoir's *Coutumes* is oriented more toward the prince a *bailli* serves—at least at the surface. With previous experience in royal administration, Philip was made *bailli* of Clermont in 1279, a post his father had occupied before him. He later served Philippe IV as seneschal of Poitou and Saintonge, then as *bailli* of the Vermandois, Touraine, and Senlis. He was a career civil servant. His role was precisely key to state governance, as "representative" or "lieutenant" of power. His purview is superficially narrower than Brunetto's; yet, his world is similar. His book represents, not a totalized secular culture, just the customary laws of the county of Clermont. Such laws underwent constant change under normal political pressures: his work is valid as a source of information only for the deictic period of its writing.[51] His customary follows upon others; more would follow throughout France. None equaled Philip's in thoroughness, in style, in the subject's investment in writing the polis, nor in his sense of the complexity of human situations. It is the first medieval legal anthropology, prefiguring the discovery of modern anthropologists from Marshall Sahlins to James Clifford, that the anthropological study of one's own culture is not only feasible but even a duty.

In characteristic self-reflexivity, the text announces its self-limitation by title and date: "Here begins the Book of the laws and customs of the Beauvaisis as they were current at the time this book was made, that is to say in the year of the Incarnation of Our Lord .M.cc.IIIxx and three."[52] The writer, hoping for salvation, composes a book by which those who wish to live in peace can learn how to defend against lawsuits, how to know right from wrong according to the customs and usages of the region: right and wrong are assumed to be social, variable, and relative. From this region himself, he undertakes to preserve its rights and customs, by order of the high lord and very noble Robert, son of the king of France, count of Clermont. His book will enable the region's inhabitants to enact the commandment to love one's neighbor as oneself and will please the count, who will learn how to ensure observance of the customs of his county, so that his men and the common people (*li menus pueples*) can live under him in peace: the subordinate teaches his superior the county's custom and justice. It will record the memory of judgments enacted during our lifetime. And though the author does not count on understanding the meaning of [his own] book, he hopes its *sens* will be completed by God: humility marks the indeterminacy of a legal text! He expects that his judgments as *bailli* will be confirmed by the customs of the Beauvaisis, but defers naming himself as author until the end of the book, lest his effort be less prized because of his identity.[53] Is Philip playing coy, does he recognize a conflict of interest, or is he appropriately modest before an understanding that the *sens* of his book broaches the *sens* of collective life on earth?

After the prologue comes the book's "division," the table of contents, enabling the reader to find the topics of interest to him: a new discipline of the book flourishes in the thirteenth century.[54] This discipline, making the book a good and reliable subject of the new state of cognition with allegiance to truth, does not preclude fictional exercises throughout. Veracity in recounting the customs of the Beauvaisis repeatedly leads to the fictional narrative excursions of *exempla*: the referential truth of prose is repeatedly transgressed, as Peter, John, Walter, or William saunter into the text to exemplify problems of interpretation. They do so frequently, so that when a seemingly specific "Peter" is cited (Pierre de Thiverny, in conflict with the town of Les Haies over bovine trespass: he objected to their habit of sending animals to pasture on his land) *this* "Peter"'s reality is doubtful.[55]

Does it matter? Witness the murder that occurred on the road from Clermont to La Vile Nueve en Hes, where a man was killed by a single blow. A butcher who had dined with the man the previous evening was arrested and interrogated. He agreed that if he lied, he would be judged guilty; if he was truthful, he would be freed. In fact, he was proved to lie regarding the road he had taken, on which the crime occurred, according to the testimony of Peter, John, Walter, and William. The butcher was condemned; before being hung, he admitted the crime.[56] The narrative has all the earmarks of a real occurrence: What of Peter, John, Walter, and William? The principles are what count, the laws of customary justice. Whether the narrative is "hard" in all details, whether the witnesses are "real," makes little difference, no more than the "truth" of Montaigne's anecdote of the peasant-thief from Armagnac: what counts is the principle exemplified by the narrative, its meaning. History and exemplary fiction both produce signification: *its* truth is what is properly in question. That ambiguity defines fiction.

Philip's first major chapter is on the character and function of the *bailli*: the enunciating subject. He produces a theory of subjectivity as representation. The chapter is bipartite, displaying the interdependence of an actant's qualifications and his narrative program: first the ten qualities required of the *bailli*, then his functions. The bureaucratic system of values differs from the religious, the knightly, or the courtly. Not *caritas* or faith, not courage or loyalty, not largesse or *mezura*, is the bailiff's primary virtue. That is prudence, after which come devoutness, kindness, patience, courage and energy, generosity, obedience, knowledgeability, managerial capacity, and "best of all," *loiautés*, "honesty." The bailiff must feel honest love, not like serfs who love their seigneurs out of fear.[57] Nevertheless, he must have the courage to anger the powerful in conflict with the poor man.[58] Two kinds of courage are distinguished, prudent as against foolhardy (*l'uns sages, et l'autres fous*). Forethought requires preconsideration of the effects of actions, a protonarratological talent.[59] No greater contrast exists to bureaucratic calculation than foolhardy courage (*fol hardement*).

The subject of representation is normally caught up in the conflicts of others, requiring his judgment in the encounter of contradictory codes. Philip grasps the deontology of medieval violence. Vengeance is a mode of justice: that is why it is a problem. Justice and violence, as the Middle Ages knew before Walter Benjamin, are inextricably linked. Vengeance must be swift and proportionate, an example of behavior toward the lord and his representative. Vengeance leads to an essential understanding of "representation," one implicit in Thierry's argument at Ganelon's trial in the *Roland*:

> For the *bailli* as long as he is acting in an official capacity [*tant comme il est en office de baillie*] represents [*represente*] his lord's person; and for this reason a person who offends against the *bailli* offends against his lord.[60]

The *bailli*'s representation is Janus-faced: it looks both ways. Whoever offends the representative offends the principal: the *bailli* represents the count. He is a sign facing two interpretive codes, a signifier with two signifieds, each in a different diegesis. He is the site of their encounters, translations, and the negotiations between their constituted worlds. This structures a new kind of mental space. The phrase "*tant comme il est en office de baillie*" divides subjectivity. The representative, in the course of performing his duties, "stands in" for his seigneur, his lord, as his "lieutenant." But "representation" is a limited situation. There is a limit, temporal and moral. There are times when the *bailli* is no longer his lord's representative and agent. On those occasions, he does not benefit from the protections of representation. The subject is split: he is himself and the subject of his lord, loyally obedient and identified with that lord.

Another quality required by representation is what Philip calls "shrewd ruses" (*soutil engieng*), which allow him to succeed without damaging others; this quality is paired with knowing how to count. The *bailli*'s overall principle is clear: he is to avoid reducing the value of the lord's property by negligence, and he is to increase the value of that property without doing harm to others. Being "calculating" is precisely the point: counting and accountability are essential. To avoid blame and harm, better know how to count.[61] The same subtilty enters into the examination of witnesses, when functioning as a judge. A subtle examination can lead to knowledge of the witnesses' hearts and opinions, allowing clarification of the truth value of their evidence.[62] Experience of the world, self-understanding, combined with shrewd interrogation, may lead to understanding the other's subjectivity. The imaginary analysis of narrative possibilities is an essential technique of governance.

The *bailli* is totally obedient to all the lord's orders and interests, with the single exception of one particular kind of case. That exception distinguishes the subject from subjection. In one kind of case, the *bailli* is required to act against the Subject who has constituted him as representative. Total obedience to the lord is demanded, *essieutés les commandemens pour lesqueus il pourroit perdre s'ame s'il les fesoit*:[63] except for the orders on account of which he could lose his soul if he enacted them. It would be no excuse toward God if the bailiff knowingly did wrong at his lord's order: better he should resign than commit a conscious wrong. But this exception does not apply in all cases. The bailiff does not question his lord's orders in cases of property, or for other matters. It is—the point is repeated—only in one category of cases that his judgment intervenes. Only when a man's life or mutilation are at stake (*essieuté mort d'homme et mehaing*)—mutilation being a frequent form of punishment. In matters of permanent corporeal punishment or death, let the bailiff rather leave the lord's service, "for that lord is not good to serve who pays more attention to act willfully than to preserve right and justice."[64]

The bailiff's code of obedience to the lord is opposed to the probity that allows salvation. The relationship of representation is in question, precisely because the representative questions his principal, the subordinate questions the superior—as in the Oaths of Strasbourg. In such a conflict, the individual becomes a subject who chooses between two values in contradiction with each other. One code constitutes the subject in a function of political, juridical, and financial representation. The other code, determining the salvation of the *bailli*'s soul, is a universal principle. The difference is marked by Henry V's distinction: "Every subject's duty is the king's; but every subject's soul is his own" (*King Henry V*, IV:i) The *bailli* might lose his soul because of an unjust punishment that is irremediable. The decision entailed by the *bailli*'s role requires the interruption of a constitutive code by which the individual is made into a subject.[65] The representational subject is constitutively split, precisely as a subject: his constitutive code is to be interrupted on specific occasions. A religious principle may supersede his institutional role of representation: only the subject can judge whether or not it does.

This split is not accidental, nor is the subjectivity of the official laid over a more basic and "socially undetermined subjectivity."[66] The identity of the Christian who hopes for salvation is prior to the subjectivity of the bailiff; the subject who is the bailiff is not. Designating an individual as bailiff is what lays on him the simultaneous hypothecs of loyalty to his seigneur *and* independent judgment of that lord's orders, with the possibility that he will not obey his lord "loyally." The subject is two subjects, loyally obedient, potentially disobedient, as he decides between two determining codes. He is placed in that position by his designation as *bailli*.

The contradiction of constitutive codes is uncomfortable. It enforces freedom, costly in emotional, material, and political terms. Curiously though, the thirteenth-century bureaucrat's responsibility is given more of this uncomfortable freedom than is granted his early twentieth-century descendant by the latter's theoretician. Max Weber allows the modern bureaucrat no freedom at all: "The honor of the civil servant is vested in his ability to execute conscientiously the order of the superior authorities, exactly as if the order agreed with his own conviction. This holds even if the order appears wrong to him and if, despite the civil servant's remonstrances, the authority insists on the order."[67] The historical evolution from the Middle Ages to modernity, in this case, reduces freedom and individual responsibility rather than expand them.

Cognitive ability and self-reflexivity are required of the *bailli*. Governance of men requires understanding them, which devolves from experience of the external world, but from self-knowledge above all. The *bailli* must know himself (*especiaument il se doit connoistre*). This gives him understanding of his lord's will and behavior, as well as the *bailli*'s own household, the provosts and sergeants under his supervision. Only with such knowledge will he be able to act rightly and inform his subjects (*ses sougiés*) of the law. He will be able to terrify the warlike, so that the peaceful can live in peace (*si que li pesibles vivent en pes*). Knowing himself, knowing what kind of man he is, he will be an *essample* to put other men on the good path, and sustain the office of *bailli*.[68] The subject's self-textualization as a model, from the *Saint Alexis* and the *Roland* to Philippe de Beaumanoir, is the means of performativity.

The subject is not merely implied. Beaumanoir regularly uses *sougiet* without hesitation, as a term well understood. His usage sometimes entails the sense of absolute subjection to a superior.[69] In an eerie forward loop, he addresses the structure of subjectivity in the same carceral context as Shakespeare and Foucault.[70] Should a suspect released on bail from imprisonment have his bail returned? Yes, if held in the subjects' prison (*en la prison des sougiès*), under the authority of the sovereign, where he is clearly located as *subjectum*, in the passive subjection of an object of law and power. More interesting is the paradox that melds submission and agency in necessary interdependence. "Subject" no longer refers to the accused, but to jailers and judges. These *sougièt* should not accept gifts or favors from those detained for criminal causes: as subjects, they must give straight justice. The subject—*li sougiès*—in whose prison the accused was kept may have done the prisoner wrong, out of hate or because he demanded the return of what he had given or agreed to give.[71] Such subjects are acting as agents of the suzerain: subjectivity as agency. They act under the supervision of the count's representative, his *bailli*, in the recursive process of representation that marks the alternation between submission and agency.

A different form of conflict awaits the *bailli*, when faced with a case that opposes the lord to his subordinates and subjects. In such cases, the *bailli* submits the case to the judgment of the lord's men: the count must deal with his subjects just as his men deal with their own subjects.[72] The principle of recursivity is close to that of substitutability: both inhere in representation. If necessary, the *bailli* or provost can appoint *accesseurs*, who replace either in their duties. Care must be taken in the selection of those substitutes: the principals are blamed if their lieutenants act wrongly.[73] The principle of substitution is simple: the same criteria apply as for principals. Replacements must be men who could themselves be appointed as *bailli* or provost. Those not worthy of being provost or *bailli* must not be put in their places.[74]

Philip's customary justice reaches for impartiality. It attempts to be impersonal and invokes being *sans amour et sans haine* toward any of the parties.[75] The *bailli* cannot be both judge and advocate, both judge and a party to a case.[76] If the *bailli* is plaintiff within his own jurisdiction, he should appoint another judge in his place. The issue of fairness touches ideology. Philip's political ideology is the ordinary conservatism of the bureaucratic state agent, strongly opposed to the progressive phenomena of his period: labor organization and the communes. For the *bailli* of Clermont, these are criminal: plots, alliances against lords or against common good, which call for the most strenuous punishment.[77] Workers conspire to stop working at current low wages, demand pay increases, agree to not work for less, decide among themselves on sanctions for those who do not join their alliance.[78] The language is different, but the issues are recognizable: unionization, strikes, and the treatment of scabs. Such workers' tactics contravene the common good, for they impede commercial deals, since each craft would seek greater pay increases than reason and commonality can accept: in other words, widespread unfair pay raises. The seigneur or other lords must throw their hands at all participants in such an alliance immediately and hold them in a harsh prison. When they have been in prison a long time, additional fines can be imposed.[79] The techniques of labor organization, the strategies of labor in conflict with wealth and the powers of justice and force ranged against it, are ancient . . . or at least medieval! From tenth-century Norman peasants to thirteenth-century towns in the Beauvaisis, labor organization leaves traces of oppression.

Communes are noted. Many cities have been destroyed, many lords shamed and disinherited, when the commons of a city or several cities together, make alliance against their lord, hold out against him violently, take his property by force, or lay hands criminally (*vilainement*) on their lord or on his people. As soon as a lord realizes that such an alliance has been organized, he must seize the participants by force, punishing them by a long prison term, ransoming them according to their wealth. If he can learn the identity of the leaders, hanging them does no harm, for they threatened shame on their lord, who can claim they were traitors: all participants deserve death, since they are all obviously traitors. If no one has been killed, if it pleases the lord, he can just seize their property and keep them imprisoned for a long time. And it is a good thing to do: others who observe it will be taught a lesson.[80]

Philip's account of the genealogies of serfdom is oriented toward the legitimation of servitude, but his comments reveal a fundamental ideological contradiction and bad faith no less common in the Middle Ages than in modernity. Men, he says, fell into serfdom by various accidents of history. Those who did not answer promptly enough a summons to the army; those whose gifts and exchanges so depleted them so that they fell prey to malice and the villainy of heirs; those who sold personal property of land (*allods*) to their lords, exchanging freedom for money. In other words, serfs, whose condition everyone agrees is miserable, had it coming, because of their own acts or their forbears': the victim bears the blame of his condition. The very existence of serfs, however, requires explanation. By all these ways did servitude come into existence, for according to natural law each person is free—*selonc le droit naturel chascuns est frans*—but natural freedom is corrupted by practices.[81] It seems universally understood that all are free by nature, but that certain social practices and structures that contradict that natural law (*droit naturel*) must be explained away and legitimated. The ideologeme of universal freedom by natural law comes wrapped in the self-legitimating account of its loss . . . but it is formulated and transmitted. That initial steps in the establishment of ideological discourse should be conservative is not surprising: progress is often conservatively wrapped. Discourse becomes more than the translation of political struggles or systems of domination: it is itself a power to be struggled over. It is both that for which one struggles and the means of struggle.[82] Initially, its written form belongs exclusively to those in power and requires complex readings.

The *Coutumes du Beauvaisis* establishes French vernacular discourse as an institution, reporting on sociojuridical practices of ideology and subjectivity. It shares with the discourses of modern disciplines assumptions explored by Timothy J. Reiss as "analytico-referential discourse."[83] A-RD claims a referential truth outside and independent of itself. It became normative throughout Europe as of the sixteenth century and spread throughout the world, anchoring the scholarship of all academic disciplines in referential truth and adequacy. Although Beaumanoir exemplifies A-RD, he readily shifts into inventions of narrative fiction as an appropriate mode of communicating principles taken as true. The disjunctive shift, unproblematized, is easy on the reader; it is aporetic nonetheless. Philip's A-RD dating from the thirteenth century is partial: his text, like most great texts, is a hybrid, compounding alternations between A-RD and something else not adequately described as a "discourses of patterning" or resemblance, found in the Middle Ages, the "Renaissance," and the discourse of Lévi-Strauss's "savage mind." This coexistence questions the assumption that discrete modes of discourse model a sequence of exclusive stages in the history of thought: first the discourse of resemblance or patterning, then analytico-referential discourse, then its incipient disintegration.[84]

The presence of A-RD in the *Coutumes*, three centuries "too early," suggests another possibility: the inherence of different discursive modes in language itself, their simultaneous coexistence, one or the other coming to dominance in a particular sociocultural environment. This dominance differentiates an institutionalized dominant discourse and occulted discourses:[85] it does not necessarily erase other modes. Culture, language, the practices of the several arts are not unitary monoliths. Different discursive modes may operate in cultural, social, and political simultaneity, constructing different mentalities in the same socius, the same polity. Access to occulted practices is through their texts when available, through indirect, often hostile, indicators when not.[86]

Beaumanoir inscribes the discipline of "policed" living according to constitutive rules of behavior—its customary laws—as a reflexive anthropologist examining the functioning codes of his own polyvocal culture. He is the institutionalized subject of modernity's disciplined society—a self-reflexive case of what Gramsci called the "organic intellectual." The adjective "organic" does not mark political approval. It designates an intellectual created by a rising social class for its own purposes in all domains: economic, social, political. The "organic intellectual" is a specialist representing "the primitive activity of the new social type" coming into existence.[87] His intellectuality is organic insofar as it consists of the critical elaboration of the intellectual activity which shall found "a new and integral conception of the world."[88]

The new class Beaumanoir instantiates is that of the aristocrat-turned-administrator, representing the nascent state, still in monarchical form. This new conception of the world, developing over the succeeding centuries, turns each subject of the nascent state into an instantiation of the state, the state's representative to itself, to the world, and to the multiplicity of its subjects. Beaumanoir, as bailli, records and publishes customary laws: the discipline of behavior in the administrative state. The bailli of Clermont precedes Althusser's distinction between the state's repressive apparatus of coercion and its ideological apparatuses geared towards the production of hegemony. As judicial enforcer, he is the state repressive apparatus. As student and publicist of law, he produces a legal ideology which may enable people to avoid the repressive state apparatus by obedience to that legal ideology: by becoming its subject. Knowing the law, the subject can avoid its infraction; he also learns the resources available to him as agent. The bailli's first subjectivation, however, is his own. He is constituted as subject by the discipline of his function, which he himself establishes. It enables the subject to represent the interests of the institution that authorizes him, the count or king, the principality or kingdom, both early forms of the state. Constituted by the institution, he also marks its limit. A circumstance may arise which forces him to choose not to represent his constitutive authority, but require him to betray it. That is the option "out," the self-desubjectifying option presented as a matter of conscience. Subjectivity always cohabits with the possible violence of its self-destruction as subject, in the negation of its constitutive code. In the name of another subjectivity, and its ideology.

CHAPTER 14

Ideologies of Subjectivity: Christine de Pizan and Alain Chartier

T he cultural creations of the later Middle Ages were performed in the face of towering disasters: the Black Plague, the Hundred Years' War, protracted economic downturn, external invasion doubled by civil war, popular uprisings both urban and rural, sometimes leading to paroxysms of rebellion savagely repressed. War is endemic: truces are "abstinences from war." The ideology of just war is sharply reduced: war is just when led by a king in the name of the state. Attacks are launched on Sunday or on other holy days when defenders will be at church. "Mortal war" lacks all rules. "Warrable war" (*guerre guerrable*) or "good war" (*bonne guerre*) appear in the fourteenth century and then disappear in the fifteenth, as rape and arson come to be tolerated.[1] Wars become national and *therefore* "mortal." Victory is sought at any price; death in the field of honor is valorized. "Warrable war" is swept from memory by an early version of "total war."

Horrific violences are juxtaposed to marked advances in the practices of representation, ideology, and subjectivity. The invention of vernacular prose allows more universal communication within the structures of the nascent state. Previously unrepresented classes of the population enter the realm of institutionalized political discourse and power, as the burgher class burgeons with the growth of capitalism. Around the turn of the fourteenth century, representative assemblies are institutionalized: the parliaments in England and France initiate the history of political theoretical discourse in the vernacular.[2]

Philippe de Beaumanoir inscribes the theoretical necessity of the subject's great "Nay!" Christine de Pizan exemplifies it and does so paradoxi-

cally. She stages the first translinguistic identitarian debate to attack patriarchal misogyny, aggressively rejecting the ideological devalorization of
women and providing women with a counterideology. She has been called
the first professional author, the first author *tout court*:[3] "Here, in a true
sense, is the first author, and the author is a woman."[4] Frequently cited,[5]
this remark elides the fact that what we "know" of Christine is mainly her
own, extensive self-textualization. The subject constructs herself in her
texts: documentary controls on her self-presentation, as author or person,
are rare.[6] "Christine de Pizan" 's historicity and her subjectivity are almost
entirely textual. Her practice of ideological subjectivation, by contrast,
seems utterly self-conscious.

Christine's iconization in the genealogy of feminism labeled her "the
first feminist" and credited her with the first analysis of cultural gender
bias, aimed at reorganizing knowledge and rewriting history.[7] But her bi-
ographer and editor viewed dubiously attempts to portray her as "the fore-
runner of modern feminists in her defense of women's rights": she gave no
thought to liberation and made no mention of equality between the sexes.[8]
If "feminist" implies theorization, a concrete program based on the relation
of female to other subjects and to the power structures of her polity, to the
economic processes in which she is imbricated, to the cultural values that
permeate her own (un)conscious, the pickings in Christine's writings are
slim and run counter to most modern feminisms. A simple iconoclasm is
not in question. A more balanced, less adulatory focus on textual, cultural,
historical, and political specificities might be salutary.

The representation of women in Christine's texts is partial. Working-
and middle-class women are mentioned but not represented in the *City of
Ladies*. Prostitutes are human, but should change profession and take up
honest work.[9] Women are asked to rejoice in the perfection of this new
"City of Women" constructed entirely of virtue, as their refuge and ram-
part, on condition they live honorably, in virtue and modesty—terms
whose patriarchal origin is patent. Single women are recognized only as
virgins or widows. Married women are to accept submission to their husbands. If their husbands are good and reasonable, they should be thankful
for having received the greatest gift on earth. Those with average husbands
should be grateful for not having gotten worse. Women whose husbands
are "cruel, mean and savage" should accept their fate, try to overcome their
husbands' vices, and lead them back to "a reasonable and seemly life."

Even if these women cannot reform their husbands, their souls acquire merit through patience. In all cases, women are to accept marital submission, no matter how vicious or perverse, fleeing passion and affairs, to live for reputation, honor, and virtue. Does the continued imposition of upper-middle-class patriarchal codes on women in general constitute feminism? "If feminism implies a political movement . . . it is nonsense to broach the subject of feminism in Christine de Pizan."[10]

Far more certain than her purchase on "feminism" is Christine's cultural achievement in ideological creation. She is one of an important group of late-medieval writers who endowed Western culture with the universal medium of political and ideological discourse. Her contribution is revolutionary in at least three ways. She participates in the historical moment that invents a new mode of vernacular ideological struggle, that of prose discourse oriented toward the *hic et nunc* of political problematics. She does so as the first vernacular Leninist ideologue, in direct response to the revolutionary question: "What is to be done?"[11] Some of her ideological discourse directly targets the (re)constitution of female subjectivity, repeatedly insisting on the connection between her own subjectivity and the political.

(Re)constituting the Female Subject

In the twelfth century, except for John of Salisbury's *Policraticus*, "the political" is not yet a separate discourse. Political topics are normally mediated by religious biblical codes.[12] Only slowly does the political acquire relative autonomy, as the state develops more articulated structures and practices. As institutions appear and formalize political conflicts and decision making—the assemblies of Philip the Fair, the normalization of English parliament—"the political" appears in its own right. That is when vernacular, political discourse of ideology begins a continuous history lasting to our own time.[13] Christine de Pizan was hardly the first political writer in French, and her feminism may be problematic. She unquestionably launched a discourse on how women are seen by society and by themselves—an ideological discourse that still resounds. Abruptly, she placed the question of women on the rulers' political agenda. Her efforts garnered recognition and respect from contemporary writers and beyond. For Martin le Franc, she is "valiant Christine."[14]

Christine's key text today is the *Book of the City of Ladies* (1405).[15] Its first section has frequently been commented. The moment of interruption when Christine's mother calls her daughter to dinner—a highly symbolic moment from the perspective of modern feminism—has been privileged.[16] But interruption precedes that moment as structure and as textual event. The section is composed as a triptych:

> a. on [not] reading (anti)ideology
> b. a "natural woman"'s reaction
> c. the apostrophe to God.

Its disjunctive structure sets—oxymoronically—a female clerkly scene.[17] The religious is a "cleric-being-replaced": connotations of the clerical are filtered, leaving book knowledge and the technologies of writing, minus the religious connotations. The woman as writing subject who is an "artist" in the medieval sense is immediately established: a student of past greatness. The repetitions of life constitute a habitus: *usaige, exercice de ma vie, frequentacion, plusieurs volumes*, as well as *estude de lettres*. In her *celle*, with many volumes, she labors at the task of collecting the weight of authorities. The *auctores* are authorities for study; the poets, mere appendages since Hugh of Saint Victor, offer lighter amusement and relaxation. The turn from authors toward poets is already a significant interruption: Christine began her career as a vernacular poet.

But from the very beginning, another kind of interruption has always already occurred, a radical disjunction with official medieval culture. A woman acts like a monk, an intellectual cross-dressing with transgressive implications of status and hierarchy. A woman reads, not as pleasurable relaxation, nor as a conventual nun, but repeatedly in the exercise (*le exercice de ma vie*) we call "professional." Like all medieval authors, Christine recycles cultural conventions and transforms their codes. The fact it is a *she* who invokes and transforms the cultural heritage remains a radical interruption of norms: Marie de France is probably lost from sight two centuries later, the multiplicity of learned nuns has not changed cultural norms, nor will it until Christine's *celle* is transformed into Virginia Woolf's "room of [her] own." Woman, as subject of intelligence, knowledge, and creativity, is always already the interruption of patriarchal culture. The secularization and feminization of knowledge are always begun again.

Looking for a bit of light reading, she browses through the *Lamenta-*

tions of Matheolus, recently translated into French. Its translator, Jean le
Fèvre de Ressons, found it so offensive he disowned his own translation.[18]
Her reading is interrupted by mother's call to dinner, in a "radical intru-
sion" of female nurturing on the traditional masculine reading scene. This
may not merit the mystical associations food could have for medieval
women.[19] Christine's religion is conventional and politic, but the moment
reiterates multiple strands of meaning: disjunction per se, the female principle, and the distance between Matheolus and his fated reader. Con-
fronting Matheolus again the following day, she interrupts herself once
more: its topic is so unpleasant, its content nothing but lies, the style so
poor . . . the reading breaks off, the bad book abandoned for higher, more
useful study. Matheolus is not one of the great *auctores*, but irritation by
mediocrities is recognizable. In spite of herself, this unimportant, libelous
work catches Christine's attention and gnaws at her. It arouses in the heart
of her being (*en mon couraige*) awe and amazement: *grant admiracion*.[20]
Not "admiration" in a positive moral sense, but the recognition of something remarkable as monstrous.

Skimming Matheolus, Christine is a subject in dramatic confrontation
with a dominant ideology that brutally denigrates her: what constitutes
subjects denies her value, her claim to existence as a subject. The confrontation is aporetic. "Matheolus" can be discarded—the book is poorly
reputed, nothing but a "satire"—but not its foundation. An entire tradition, all philosophers, poets, and orators, share the same opinion: "The behavior of women is inclined to and full of every vice."[21] This is the thesis
Christine's entire book rebuts. It states the negative ideologeme, the evil
pearl around which the *City of Ladies* is constructed, less as affirmative
feminism, attacking rather its presupposition: a rebuttal of the basis of
misogyny.

The double bind is constitutive of the tradition. Misogyny, the ideology of early Christianity, and monasticism, directly contradicted an alternative biblical tradition, as well as other religious ideologemes.[22] All God's
children are equal, potentially good before their Creator. But woman lives
under the pall of a radical desubjectification. A confrontation of contradictory codes of value interrupts the ordinary, reproductive function of ideology. The condemnation of her sex reverberates, forcing self-examination as
a *femme naturelle*: her character, her conduct, women she has known of all

classes who have confided their most private, intimate thoughts, all are addressed. It is an experiential argument, citing "princesses, great ladies, women of the middle and lower classes"—a prolepsis of those addressed by the *City of Ladies.*

The encounter the book stages is not that of misogyny with experiential reality itself. The real, as experienced, is always represented by a Real, staging an encounter within the psyche itself, hence always already ideological. The entire *City of Ladies* amplifies this encounter of contradictory ideologies, its narrative reality rooted on the terrain of the subject's psyche. The event may occasion profound fear, eventually turning into cutting, assertive and polemical violence.[23] In a first phase, however, the negative ideology of misogyny wins. The author accepts the judgment of "so many famous men," about her own nature and that of the women she knows. Men all agree that women are inherently full of vice. Although this contradicts her experience, "I relied more on the judgment of others than on what I myself felt and knew."[24] The cognitive loop by which the subject bows to regnant ideology and submits to its judgment is well known:

> I finally decided that God had formed a vile creature when He made woman.[25]

Christine traces the origin of self-hatred:

> I detested myself and the entire feminine sex, as though we were monstrosities in nature. . . . I considered myself most unfortunate because God had made me inhabit a female body in this world.[26]

Official ideology overwhelms an individual's grasp of lived reality. Generations of self-castigating women turn in the wake of that involution; so did victims of the Moscow show-trials. Dominant ideology generates hatred of the category constituted as Other, internalized as self-hatred. The structure of the experience is identical for the colonized, for the enslaved, for women, for serfs, and undocumented workers . . . until and unless their self-knowledge is—somehow—reinforced. Conscious reality alone does not trump ideology.

The third panel of the triptych apostrophizes God. In exploring the problem of evil, it comes close to inculpation of the Creator. The argument is actually a backhanded affirmation of woman's necessary goodness. How can God create anything that is not good? Whatever woman's nature, it was given her by God. The argument slips off, from God's creation to misogyny's repugnance of women. The real inculpation is not of God, but of those who hold the misogynistic ideology so strongly as to make even its questioner regret her sex:

> Alas! God, why did You not let me be born in the world as a man . . . ? . . . I considered myself very unhappy that God had made me be in this world in a woman's body.[27]

The discursive function of the rhetorical figure of apostrophe is the same as personification in narrative: it presentifies absence. In construction, the apostrophe of God serves as Christine's prolepsis of her own personification allegory, its triune female divinity a feminized secularization of the Christian Trinity. Christianity is one rhetorical resource among others, a source of discursive authority that works by "contamination."[28] It also juxtaposes two figurations of the divine—male versus female—which, given Christian theology, constitute an aporia. The writer textualizes herself as a subject so split she cannot but reproduce the negative judgment of herself she recognizes as false on the basis of personal experience, what hypothetically might be the most solid foundation of judgment . . . but in fact is not. Empirical reality, in the matter of self-representation, is too weak. It leaves the subject no other option than the lamenting apostrophe to an absent Subject. At the end of this section, Christine presents a subject in the radical sense, abjectly subjugated in total submission. Knowledge of reality is inadequate to counter the totalizing negative judgment of culture's dominant ideology.

The project of the *City of Ladies* is to remedy that abjection. Christine is selected by a female trinity of Reason, Rectitude, and Justice to build an enclosed city, but only for *ladies*, not for women: *la cité des Dames*, not *la cité des femmes*. Only those who observe standards of behavior for "ladies of good repute" will inhabit the city. Women adjudged evil, dissolute, and perverted are monsters in nature, black, dirty, and uneven stones to be discarded and excluded from the city.[29] As a female trinity replays the Christian Trinity, the *City of Ladies* replays Augustine's *City of God* and anticipates Rabelais's *Abbaye de Thélème*, which assumes all inhabitants are of good birth. The city as the idealization of human life is a countertradition to the orchard as ideal landscape. That topos, marked by exclusion, was a favorite of aristocratic narrative. Its counter is a political icon, demanding attention to issues of inclusion and exclusion, of social mixture and cohesion, and to questions of governance. The citizenry is culled, morally, socially, politically. Women of all classes are cited, but a selection is to be made. Only women of upper middle class and noble morals, mores, and values will be admitted.

The city—this is the reason Christine has been chosen—will be built in the field of letters (*ou champ des escriptures*). She can supply what was missing in her own, personal confrontation with the negative mirror image of herself as a woman: a counterideology. The *City of Ladies* is tautologically built and written in the field of letters, because it narrates (hi)stories whose ideology will constitute new women subjects. Disregarding the new tradition of prose as the discourse of truth, Christine returns to the twelfth century, when writing in *roman* overrode the distinction between fiction and history. Her stories mingle literary personal reminiscence, mythology, and invention in the service of the greater cause: the production of exemplary ideology for women subjects. Some follow tradition, some strongly contradict the heritage: what counts is performative potential. Henceforth, women who read Christine's text will be endowed with what she was lacking in the confrontation with misogyny: a positive ideology, built in the field of letters, as the counterideology to support and confirm their judgment as to their own nature and moral worth: that they are *not* "inclined to and full of every vice": that on the contrary, in every field of endeavor, they are as capable, as competent, as virtuous, as they have always been and as men are.

There is an element of magic in this reversal. How does a subject turn herself around, from a state of ideological abjection to a doubled affirmation? How does the subject counter the negative determinism of a hostile ideology, precisely in the field of subjective constitution? The question is important for theory of subjectivity and of revolution. Derrida dismisses it: "The subject is a fable," and a theory of the subject "is incapable of accounting for the slightest decision."[30] Similarly, for Slavoj Žižek, if an act has a subject, it is an uncannily acephalous and gutless subject, whose freedom coincides with "the utmost passivity, with a reduction to a lifeless automaton who blindly performs its gestures."[31] Neither can begin to address Christine's turnaround.

Two aspects of Christine's act are relevant. First, she makes common cause with a collectivity. Secondly, she lodges in the "empty" experiential a dimension of ideological meaning grafted onto her desire. Both aspects act as reinforcements, prostheses enabling the constitutive writing of performative fictions. By example, the female writing subject "Christine de Pizan" engages a far more ambitious trajectory, marked by two phrases. She uses a standard ploy, the "poor little woman,"[32] and presents her authorial self repeatedly as solitary and peripheral, *seulette a part*: the phrase becomes an authorial signature.[33] It dramatizes the notarial formula of the *Pseudo-Turpin*: her "*moi, Christine*," her "*je, Christine*," may be drawn from her husband's occupation as court notary or her own experience in chancellorial court:[34] it was derivative, serving the writer's self-authentication in the quest for authority. Above all, thirst for authority impels the text: authority to counter the ideology that negativizes her as subject, along with all other women.

Fortified by her work on ideology and the (re)construction of a feminine subjectivity, Christine de Pizan addresses the most fundamental issues facing the polity in the vernacular, as if she were the king's intimate adviser, repeatedly recycling the "mirror of princes" tradition. The *Livre du corps de policie* (1406–7) redeploys John of Salisbury's organic metaphor in discussing state governance, taking "police" as the pastoral duties of the prince, in spite of conventional or reactionary positions.[35] She addresses the political problem that haunts Western history and "*la chose publique*," war and peace, in *Le Livre de la paix* (1412–14). As always, the writing subject is a class subject.[36] From the perspective of an upper-middle-class woman, working-class rebellion is nothing but violent terror, "*cruaulte, pillage, et tyrannie soubz umbre de justice*." Criticism of the king or nobles is a sin; she inveighs against the "foul and miserable people, the inane government of small, bestial people," who dare to speak of "what it does not pertain for them to speak of": a political meeting is "a diabolical assembly," "execrations."[37] "The *menu peuple* should have neither authority, arms or function in war: the poor and indigent who live off their daily labor always seek war, especially civil war, so as to jump the rich."[38]

Reason, for Christine, is not oriented toward original social analysis: it is a merely administrative virtue (*l'administreresse*) that puts into operation the orders of a good understanding—like a *bailli* or a provost.[39] Its politics is not only undemocratic in the light of modern political ideals,[40] it is partial and patently conservative if not reactionary.[41] She distrusts electoral systems, fears popular uprisings, and exalts the monarchy of Charles V. Nowhere does she consider the armature of society: feudal institutions are reduced to their economic role; representative assemblies and the whole range of parish, village, communal, commercial and professional organizations vanish: guilds, the Hansa, Italian commercial companies might as well never have existed. The church is so corrupt it must remain under the prince's control. The mass of the third estate, its subjects, remain an undifferentiated collection of suspicious individuals. Her ideological values and norms are God's commandments, the law of Nature, and "rights and customs." What really counts is ancient, well tested, respectable: change is to be avoided, innovation distrusted. The transmission of norms and values is of greater interest than their promulgation. Even the prince, the only legitimate power, rarely legislates: existing laws, customs, and usages suffice. Are Christine's views traditionalist as regards men but innovative when it comes to women? Her traditionalism tends toward the utopian. A stratified pyramid of subjects functions without representation or associations: only respect for custom gives the state any cohesion, hence the necessity of endless hectoring, the interminable task of the people's indoctrination: the necessity of ideology.

Christine's texts contain enough political discourse to make a historian of political theory cite her repeatedly.[42] She repeatedly returned to the situation of women, often autobiographically, in the moral terms conventional for the interpretation of political issues. Sheila Delany compares her to Phyllis Schlafly, the vocal, aggressive, right-wing "feminist" of our own time.[43] I would add another comparison, to individuals of marginal identities who have achieved integration in the state: two Associate Justices of the United States Supreme Court, Sandra Day O'Connor and Clarence Thomas. Both perform as progressive ideologemes—representation of women and blacks on the Court—while their pronouncements and votes are usually reactionary.[44] Their fusion of contradictories ensured their acceptability to the right-wing administrations that appointed them and made the iconically progressive signals of their appointments acceptable to the antifeminism and racism that course through Congress and the electorate. Tokenism of vocal subaltern groups is a political fact. Such mixtures should no longer surprise. Christine's ideological foregrounding of "woman" comports certain retrograde "hypothecs." A balanced judgment, cognizant of the problem of anachronism, is that Christine's "feminist consciousness" lacks any concrete social program and is paired with retrograde attitudes in other political areas. She had "a plausible kind of feminism."[45] Her complex and contradictory figure enters the genealogy of feminism as much obstacle as early standard-bearer, as much reactionary patriarch as a progressive matriarch: to shoulder the responsibilities of widowhood, she had to imagine herself transformed into a man.[46] Her politics and her achievements in cultural history do not erase each other.

"Rewriting woman good" in 1405 was a complex, highly contradictory project. Paradoxically, it required a writing "beyond gender" which—unlike modern feminisms—did not challenge existing power structures and largely accepted the traditional patriarchal moral values.[47] It required construction of the ideologeme of woman out of a language and a tradition of writing defined by males.[48] The project required "civilized violence" against those males and their tradition, as well as obsequiousness to those in power—a distasteful combination, but not unpredictable. As against her function as a heroic icon for early modern feminism, Christine de Pizan today performs as a refracting surface of the reader's own ideology and subjectivity, allowing for multiple mirrorings. Her texts bear a vernacular political discourse aimed at the processes of power, forcefully injecting secular ideology into history, addressing overtly and directly immediacies of political action. The vernacular addresses power, in the voice of a notarial virago perhaps, but one who used the common language. Her right-wing sympathies and opinions, her thirst for escaping the danger of poverty and peripheral marginality in upward social mobility,[49] may be judged regrettable. The cultural and ideological triumph is undeniable, and its process is hardly incomprehensible. It is one process by which marginals make their way against oppressive ideologies. It allowed her to produce one voice of the female subject, at her time.

Alain Chartier's "Invasion of Words": National Ideology and the Subject

Shortly after the Second World War, a prestigious anthology of French medieval literature concluded with Alain Chartier's *Quadrilogue invectif.*[50] This inclusion made sense in an age which identified "literature" with rhetoric grasped as a textual technology and a necessity for civic discourse.

The name "Chartier" associates with "charters" and notaries, but the author presents it more humbly: *Alain Charretier* is closer to "carter," the man who drives a cart, than to a scribe's official paperwork. Alain Chartier enjoyed a long career as cleric, canon, and diplomat before serving as the king's *humble secretaire*. He was also the benchmark French poet of the fifteenth century. Like Pizan, he was a scribe and notary.

The *Quadrilogue* was written in 1422, at a disastrous moment in French history. The *haute noblesse* of France is decimated at Agincourt (1415); Charles VI, the mad king, is declared a bastard and dies; Henry VI of England, still a child, is proclaimed heir to France by English heralds at Saint-Denis. The Dauphin, whom Chartier served, is outlawed.[51] The country, wasted by the Black Plague, invasion, and civil war, is demoralized by anarchy and pillage. Charles VII retains a tiny demesne encircled by enemies: he is ironically labeled "The King of Bourges." Chartier's prologue gives the state of the union as "grievous" and "pitiful." Its weakness is internal, lacking "order, discipline, and rule."[52] Harsh necessity overdetermines the text. The war on the ground was extended by widespread political polemics in the vernacular. Polylogues were the order of the day. In the *Débats des hérauts d'armes de France et d'Angleterre*, representatives of the two warring nations hurl praises of their own nation at each other; it exists in both French and English. The country's territory is fragmented, so are its political organization and its texts. Unity asserts itself as the dialetical awakening of national self-consciousness.[53]

No work of the period foregrounds these contradictory forces more sharply—and problematically—than the *Quadrilogue invectif.* It textualizes a *parlement* in the original sense: discussion, conversation, including the king's council and the Estates General. The text's kernel is a trialogue of personifications, laying bare the *différends* that rend the body politic in the multiple grievances of a harshly segmented country: the nobility (*le chevalier*), the clergy (*le clergé*), and the people (*le peuple*).

Discourse

The prologue reinscribes the state's disarray in discourse. After Guillaume de Lorris, Jean de Meun, and Christine de Pizan, Alain Chartier casts his own political discourse in the conventional poetic form of the dream allegory. His text, though relatively short, grounds a totalized class analysis of French society in an ancient sociology already inadequate three centuries earlier: its personifications repeat the "three orders" ideology . . . with a difference. More even-handed than Christine's patrician superciliousness, Chartier's allegory is no longer driven by identity politics: it both affirms and eludes the problematics of political totalization. The analysis is inconclusive. Its subjective representation gives voice to the classes of French society and problematizes their status. A new "protorealism" differentiates their discourses stylistically: the knight is pompous and disdainful; the cleric's discourse is long, fulsome, and cannily structured; the people of labor are granted direct discourse. Beyond style, the text's performative goal requires it to remain an open text, even as it focuses on a concrete sociohistorical referent.

The debate begins with the most humble and numerous: the people are given far greater voice than with Christine, to whom commoners are an embarrassment. *Le Peuple* depicts itself as a beast of burden, spurred and beaten to do the impossible in providing other classes with necessities. The order of justice has been twisted by those in power:

> The labor of my hands nourish the cowardly and lazy, who persecute me with hunger and the sword. . . . They live off of me, I die for them.

The law of just exchange has been broken: the people cannot bear it. Their only hope is to imitate those enriched by spoliation, who prefer booty to the honor of war:

> It is not war that is fought in this country, but private robbery, unlimited theft, the public force overshadowed by arms and violent rapine, allowed by an absence of justice and good governance.[54]

An ideologeme of social justice underlays the people's pathemic discourse, an unformulated theory of social exchange asserted by implication. Peasant labor sustains the rest of society: justice requires proper treatment in exchange. *Le Peuple* (male) dies while living, watching wife and children die, desiring his own death. Exiled in his own house, prisoner of friends, assaulted by defenders, he is attacked by soldiers paid with his own savings. Land remains uncultivated, inhabited by widows and miserable orphans, begging and sorrowing as the strong steal goods from those who earned them. Law keeps silent, Justice has abandoned her seat to arbitrary rule. Then comes the ringing declaration of the people's right in the common-wealth:

> The people is an illustrious member of a kingdom, without which neither nobles nor clergy can suffice to govern nor to sustain their status nor their lives.[55]

The idea of interdependence itself is traditional: its placement as a declaration of the people, its self-laudatory evaluation, is new. The people's discourse closes with a dual invocation, of God (the Father) and France (the Mother). Yet its last word marks ultimate alienation: the speaker, abandoned by both father and mother, lives *en orphaneté*.

The knight responds, attacking the people to assert his own lordship. The people are easily deceived and seduced, enduring neither the ease of peace nor the harshness of war. You lean toward sedition (*toute sedicion*) and lose true obedience. You complain and ask God for vengeance, but you, your wife, and children eat your bread in safety each day, each in his place under governance, wishes fulfilled with all good things, without loss, without wrong.[56] The people, in their madness, desire only change, eager for what is most damaging. Its own lies and fickle belief have brought on this most bitter division.

> This war was begun and has worsened by you and the political parties [*les partiz*] you have madly created and adhered to with obstinate willfulness. . . . War . . . comes from lack of justice; if we were all just, we would not require force of arms.[57]

For the knight, defending class interest, a burgher has nothing to do but count his pennies, a wealthy canon spends his time eating and sleeping. Both live in comfort, complain that knights do not fight, and chase off enemies, but neither would lay out a single penny were it not for the power of princes. The greatest clamors and complaints come from those who are better off than we knights, but the affliction is on the working people (*le peuple de labour*), while we garner the pains and the effort. Those who grumble the most care nothing for governance except to be close to profits and far from losses; they prefer to disavow their natural lord (*leur naturel seigneur*), to increase their wealth, than suffer losses and remain loyal. Would it please God that all kept their eyes on the common good and the honor of the government (*le bien publique et l'onneur de la seigneurie*). Alas, such is not the case. Afflictions come from mutations, division, change of government (*mutacion de gouvernement*). Adversity is common to the entire kingdom.

> In war, where force reigns and steel governs, law cannot dominate; but whoever looks carefully will find that commoners and people of low estate . . . are guilty of these horrible excesses, and that evil is born among the people, and falls in turn on the people.[58]

Blaming the victim is not an invention of the twentieth century.

The people's rejoinder resonates with ancient and contemporary debates, insisting on the problematics of violence:

> Violence legitimates itself by force where it has no right. You claim I cause this damned war, but the folly of lesser people is based on the outrages of the great . . . depending on how the princes and high-placed men live the life of their state, the people takes from them its rule and its example . . . your immoderate life, your disordered government causes our impatience and the beginning of the evils we endure.[59]

And this personification of the lower classes coins a phrase that resonates and gave the title of Jules Vallès's newspaper during the Commune of 1870: *La Voix du Peuple*. In former times,

> *the people's voice* was like the cry of seagulls, signaling the ebb and flow of the sea, for our words, which you call discontented grumbling, signified even then the evil that for these reasons was to come.[60]

The people conclude by restating a theme that is remarkably contemporary as the twenty-first century begins, the socioideological determination of character. Society forms its population according to the ideologies and examples it produces and harvests what it sows. *La voix du peuple* defines subjectification by ideology.

Clergé speaks shrewdly, allying first with the dominant powers, briefly rehearsing the discourse of the mirror of princes. The prince requires knowledge, wealth, and obedience. Wars and internal divisions have placed the yoke of servitude on high powers, forcing them to become serfs and subjects in order to acquire or retain their seigneuries. Citing biblical history, he argues for the prince's knowledge and constancy. Exactions are defended as drawing not on revenue but on industry and diligence (it's a tax on production, not individuals!), before an abyss of necessity in which everything melts. Even though private gain subverts *le salut publique* and *la chose publique*, obedience to the prince is required, for no community can maintain itself without justice, not even a thieves' gang or a family: their will must be lodged in a chief, their powers limited to the obedience of one who can enforce justice by force of arms.

The knight's final rebuttal disclaims specialized knowledge. How should obedience to the rules of warfare be maintained, unless it is granted to those who make war? Failing its devolution from the great, should it come from below? How would the governed keep to the rules of obedience, if their sovereigns corrupt it? This argument is, in fact, similar to the people's: How should the armed forces be responsible for obedience, if they are not given models by those who rule?

Such is the trialogue of Ciceronian rhetoric, much abbreviated, often moving, earlier ideological elements sedimented into more recent discourses. Those who labor, those who fight, and those who pray have been given discursive space, voice, and differentiated instruments of signification that include the resources of grammar, rhetoric, dialectic, and a dosage of classical and biblical history. Personifications represent class subjectivities relayed by medieval ideology in systemic and reciprocal accusations, defenses, and counteraccusations. They are arraigned before a nonexistent, hoped-for entity, neither the Lord God nor a Lord King. Religious and monarchical apexes are displaced and replaced by a new political entity, that once-and-future "imagined community" of the nation "France."

The problem that remains after their triune debate is familiar: no positive results are reached. The discourses hang there, the reciprocal critiques of social alterities pungent but indeterminate. Social fragmentation is textualized and retained, at a strategic and rhetorical level. Confronted with each others' negative perspectives, the different classes are told to reform themselves accordingly. The noncloturnal ending opens on a future eventuality, posited but undefined, a concerted deontic indeterminacy conveyed in a complex verbal structure. A nonexistent "France" is addressed by being textualized in order to make it real: it is a performative proleptic apostrophe, in France's own vernacular.[61] What subject(s) will respond to its call?

Language

Its discourse incorporates a broad theoretical vocabulary, structured by the semantics of state and subject formations: the text is suffused with technical words from the art and political theory of governance, invested with the performative power of creating the very entities its desire names. The prologue recalls "the state of our infelicity" and describes the text itself by a metaphoric fusion of language and military action: it is "invective" insofar as it proceeds by "way of a verbal attack as the form of critique" [*par maniere d'envaïssement de paroles et par forme de reprendre*].

Seigneury, one of its heaviest words, makes multiple appearances in the text. For the earlier Middle Ages, it designated all the means by which a master appropriates the value produced by those he rules, in the cellular fragment dominated by a castle.[62] By the fifteenth century, it loses the connotation of localism, to become a synonym of *gouvernement*, even at a national scale. In the *Quadrilogue*, it means the nation itself, as in "the high seigneury and glorious house of France," which suffers "subjection of seigneury" under the English occupation. It retains a sense of "protective" domination, as when the knight asserts the advantages the peasant enjoys *soubz la seigneurie*. Throughout, it means the active governance of a population. For *clergé*, the prince requires the assistance of people with knowledge. A close synonym is the familiar *police*, in the sense Foucault resurrected. When the people complain that "our French *police*" resembles the household of an incompetent manager, or a madman biting himself and tearing his own limbs it has more to do with governance than cops.[63] *Gouvernement* itself makes an appearance; as with *police*, its absence leads to complaint: the present state of France is due to lack of proper government.[64] Governance, however, requires subjects, a population beyond the political fragmentation of local seigneuries: "France" requires the constitution of a new kind of subject. The state demands a universal class of subjects, subject to new ideologies.

What constitutes the subject for Alain Chartier? The *subgiet* appears more than once, with different implications. The knight's rhetoric threatens with the fear of a *mutacion* we might call "revolution": an equalization of subjects and masters.[65] Correct subjectivity, for the knight, lies entirely in subjection. Similarly, clergy cites "murmurs of subjects and complaints of the people" among the troubles that assail rulers. The peasant's life in his small hut is a happier one, of more security, freedom, contentment, along with the "*faculté de vivre à son gré*," than the prince's life in the palace, reduced to the harsh necessities of defending lordship (seigneury)![66] Again, the *subgiet* is defined by subjection, as clergy embraces the knight's theme of the political world turned upside down when the high and mighty are fallen to the status of serfs and subjects!

Later in clergy's discourse, however, the subject appears in its paradoxical nature. Having captured the knight's benevolence, clergy seeks superiority to both classes of laymen and allows complaints about the warriors. Some officers appropriate their soldiers' wages, forcing them to plunder, forage, and devastate the countryside. Clergy opines, "A loyal subject must not abandon honor for the profit of war."[67] Those targeted are not soldiers but their captains, middlemen who larcenously pocket monies destined to their soldiers' wages. They are lieutenants, representatives of power, subjects subject to contradictory ideologies: accumulation of profit as against loyal self-restraint. Whence comes to a subject the ability and power to limit his own acquisitiveness? Where, in fact, do subjects come from? The answers are recognizable: ideology as history; living models; discipline; plebeian reactions to oppression, sometimes violent; and a fourth source, not specified, but implicit in the very structure of the work. "Ideology" does not appear in the text, but its function of modeling behavior in narrative does. Great men model behavior for the lower classes: "The people take its rule and its example, whether of good or evil, whether of peace or riot," from the behavior of princes and great men.[68] If some of the lower classes behave badly, "such as they are, you made them"; therefore, say the people, the knight is to blame.[69] Such models come in living form; they also come—as Christine de Pizan had realized—as the narratives of history that move us emotionally: "Ancient histories can move us" to obey the "*ordre des armes et discipline de chevalerie*."[70]

More than ideology, Alain privileges discipline as a means of subjectivation. It is of major concern to the *Quadrilogue*: the term recurs in various contexts. Bearing witness to the grievous fortune and piteous state that has settled on the glorious house of France, *l'Acteur* ascribes disloyalty and *nostre persecucion* to the lack of *ordre, discipline et regle*, which characterize the state.[71] So do measure and reason: the knight ascribes war to a lack of justice which is contrary to *ordre, mesure, raison*: he, in turn, is reproached for the *lack* of discipline.[72] It is absurd to seek "order, measure, and reason" in the state of war, which makes all violence comprehensible. Against the arrogance of the professionals of war, clergy argues that obedience is due, not to personal lineage, but

> to whomever, by intelligence, courage and the authority of the prince, must be obeyed . . . obedience is due to the office and order of arms and the *discipline* of chivalry, which every noble must prefer to all other honor.[73]

This ideal linkage of chivalry with discipline has already been invoked by clergy: "*discipline de chevalerie*" resounds twice in consecutive sentences, in conjunction with a *justice d'armes* characterized as *droicturiere*.[74] "Discipline" is specific knowledge and know-how whose deontology constitutes individuals as military subjects. If it is to curb individual acquisitiveness, it must be a self-discipline, enabling choice between competing ideological values.

The third source of subjectivity is what both knight and clergy fear: the counterviolence of rebellion, fueled by the injustice argued by the people, the quality Foucault called the *plebs*: rebellion has its own medieval tradition. A fourth source of subjectivity is not so much exemplified or argued by the text as implicit in its very structure. The *Quadrilogue* displays ideological investments, reveals the problematics of discipline, cites plebeian revolt. . . . Yet, both the final injunction of France, and the very structure of the text, call for a different reaction than any of these. Rather than ideology, discipline, or violence, the text solicits consideration of the complaints of all participants, weighing their historical situation, and the sociopolitical invention of necessary accommodations. It is the thought, not of a unity reductive to a single ideological value, but the coordination of rival claims in the name of an entity that returns thought to the reciprocal interdependence of the entity's constitutive classes. Those who labor, those who fight, those who pray, each requires the other two. Their coexistence requires a process of negotiation whose first step is attending to alterities. It is the problematic of the nation-state, in monarchy as in republic. The constitutive conflict of ideologies, in the very structure of their textualization, indexes a supraideological discursive space . . . or a superideological one: the ideology of state disguises itself as an absence of ideology. Since each personification is to reform itself in reaction to the others' criticism, its supplementary space is identical with a psychic space of self-analysis, self-control, and self-fashioning.

Governance, properly exercised and received by the population of subjects concerned, could produce the order of discipline and rule. The disciplines of different estates could work coherently, in recognition of a shared element, that which is *commun*, a shared element recognized lexically as the *communité*. A *communité* can be any collective, any *compagnie*, so long as it is ruled by justice . . . even a community of thieves.[75] It is also a socius of shared values under a single governance, marked in its very absence:

> Never were the honor, virtue, and generalized civility of a community
> of government less inscribed in hearts than at present.[76]

Community is imagined coexisting with government, possibly even an effect of its governance.

The classical *res publica* disseminates a particularly rich vernacular progeny. The radical, egotistical individualism of late capitalism is directly critiqued by France herself: a man

> must little value his birth and even less desire continuation of his life
> who spends his days, as if a man born for himself alone, without
> fructifying the common utility.[77]

The discourses of the text are replete with expressions like *commune desertion, commune utilité, bien publique, service publique, salut publique, necessité publique*, as well, of course, as the direct translation of the *res publica*: *la chose publique*.

This verbal cortège of commonality accompanies the projection of a putative "France" on a future screen: it gives theoretical specificity to the grandest ideologeme of the text, that of "France," not as geographical entity, nor as the concrete bureaucracy of state, not even as the king whose dual corporeality betrays his mystic identity with the state, but as that postulated, imagined unity and principle of coherence that might undergird the fragmented, conflictual reality: the class divisions that sap the unity and self-defense of the nation-state. The multiplicity of these phrases insists on their crucial role: they index a principle of political identity, not to erase differences but to sublate them. A postulated communitarian unity, perhaps always invented after the fact, in reaction, as here, to the all-too-evident dismemberment of the body politic. That principle of unity is the universal of all separate, concrete identities.

The verbal exchange of the three speakers is foreseen in the very structure of the historical parliament. What is new here goes beyond these elements. To the trialogue, which understands class as a combination of economics and culture, the poet-turned-ideologue adds further figures, which together constitute the text's narrative frame. First is the figure of "France" as a universalizing identitarian ideologeme. Its supervening discourse leaves all opinions voiced intact. None is irrelevant or discarded: all remain on the table. Rather than respond to the arguments presented, France demands an *Aufhebung*, the subsumption of particularistic interests. Dissension, rather than discarded, returns to the speakers in deontic reflexivity. France's charge to each is: take to heart the critiques made by the representatives of the other classes. No decision-making structure is given: though it cites the king, this *parlement* addresses neither him nor the regent, who appear initially only to secure the speaker's identity. Christine de Pizan is a major source for Chartier:[78] unlike her political discourses, his text addresses the totality of the French population, in the guise of its ancient tripartite sociology. In complete circularity, the text addresses precisely those figures it textualizes by giving them voice: the fragmented totality of a future nation. The textual subject(s) are also the subject(s) to whom the text is addressed; the subjects of the future state of "France." It has a weak purchase on reality. It is "pure ideology": the principle of hope. As the unity of enmities, it is the ideologeme par excellence, arbitrarily linked to geographical territory. Not quite the invention of the fifteenth century, "France" is the product of an ideological evolution that began with the *Roland*'s invocation of *Franceis* alongside *Francs* and of *douce France*, to posit the necessity of a new polity.

"France" is the fourth interlocutor in the title's concert of voices, marked by a hopefulness that betrays the distance between wish and fact. It becomes all the more incumbent to insist on an unresolved coherence. "The state of our infelicity" infuses the four-part polyphony that allegorizes the necessary interdependence of the classes represented.[79] None is a synecdoche hegemonically representing the whole, hence the urgency of keeping the whole present to the reader's mind:

> I do not want anyone to read one part without the other, so that one
> might think that all the blame is placed on one estate. But if any part
> of it is worthy reading, then let it be worth the space of time to visit
> and read the surplus.[80]

This modernist insistence on textual integrity devolves specifically from the fragmentary nature of its elements, the unresolved discourses that compose it: precisely their fragmentary nature requires retotalization. The text's postmodern fragmentation is folded into the hope of its modernist totalization. "France" is the imagined community whose self-examination will acknowledge the opposing claims of the conflictual classes, whose self-reformation will produce the undefined changes that will allow its realization. It both pleads with the classes to reform and is given as the value for the sake of which they should reform. It is both the blank check offered one and all, and the reserve bank that guarantees payment on presentation.

The *Quadrilogue invectif* is the theoretico-ideological culmination of the medieval invention of the state. It witnesses the initiation of the state's shell game, disguising its multiple existences as war machine, bureaucratic policing, and pastoralism, under the guise of the fictive tribal birth-unity that is a "nation": an ethnic unity that never existed. Multiple ethnicities characterize the state from the beginning. "France" was never just the nation of Franks, any more than Germany was the abode of "racially pure" Teutons, or America the Land of Free WASPs only. Polyglottal multiethnic populations of diverse origins make up all the world's major populations. National identity is the fictional identity the state offers in the stead of resolutions of other, more haunting injustices. Whether that fiction is *necessarily* constitutive of collective life in the state remains a present question.

As a general rule, and against general assumption, the state precedes the nation.[81] The "nation" is the state's central ideologeme. It is proposed by a writer of "liberal," sensitive decency, whose text enjoys a subtle, self-de-

constructive structuration and a curiously empty acknowledgment of subjectivity. After an imposing prologue, a sudden linguistic shift occurs from
French to Latin for a subtitle: "Here starts the Four-Voiced Rap of Blame
for the Correction of Gallic Ways": here starts, in fact, the "frame" of a
noncarnavalesque debate, more dialogue than dialogical.[82] It leads into a
prose version of the Dreamer's sudden awakening in *Rose I* and the arrival,
on the scene of his *ymaginacion*, of the trialogue's personifications: the
scene of the sociohistorical conflict among the three constituents of France.
The author's psyche is the ground of history.

Concomitant with the *res publica* of France, a second figure also enters,
a textual creature with ancient roots and an imposing progeny: *l'Acteur*.
The ideologeme France, given voice and textual space, requires its opposite
number: the creature on the ground. "*L'acteur*" combines "author," "actor,"
and "agent." Earlier, the "actor" was distinguished from the kind of author
also considered an "authority": *actor* and *auctor* designated different kinds
of writers.[83] Medieval writers often struggled to shift themselves from *actor* to *auctor*.[84] Alan the Carter chooses the more modest term that coheres
better with its implied subordination to France. At the end of the text, *l'acteur* gives himself as being called on by "France": "*Adoncques m'appella*":
"she called on me." Well, yes, if we accept being framed by the frame of the
text. But it is, of course, the author who says so, as represented by the personification of the narrator, raising the question: Who called on whom?
France, to a subject? The author to himself, through the relay of France,
self-reflexively? The author as subject, to France? Earlier, *l'acteur* had initiated the sequence of discourses with a stage direction: "L'ACTEUR COM-
MENCE": "the author/actor starts." The writing subject initiates the sequence of discourses, which in turn calls on the self-same author to
conclude, closing a circle of reflexive self-referentiality whose allegorical artifice insists on its external reference to history. The constitutive aporia of
language, which calls on an "external" reality *and* constitutes that reality in
its systemic self-referentiality, could not be more incisively inscribed.

This *acteur/auctor* performs a number of different roles, all subordinate.
He observes and reports on the present state of the country, anticipating
the Balzacian novelist's secretarial role. He narrates his own awakening and
describes the person, vestments, and arrival of the Lady France. He acknowledges a complex, hierarchical intentionality in the phrase "*intention*

principale."[85] He recurs as the figure that allows the various personifications to speak in turn, a parliamentary chair. At the end, he has the final words, reporting the order he receives from "France" to write up the discussion he has just facilitated, as its secretary, hoping each reader will interpret his text favorably, recognizing it as moved by compassion for public weal rather than self-presumption, by the desire to profit from good exhortation rather than reproaching others.[86]

L'acteur represents the author in the text, but his performance as subject of verbal actions is political. He figures the structuring force of the textual process, out of which is to rise the unity and coherence of France. He is the subject of words as discourse, discourse as political, the subject that orchestrates the representation of the polity's ideological conflicts. Through and by him, contradictory perspectives find voice: through the loan of his voice and its discursive potentials. Alan the Carter as *acteur* emblematizes the role of the medieval writing subject, the *acteur*/author/subject who organizes the figures of historicity that may realize that goal in the space of textuality. *Acteur* is the subject of France, whose subjectivation is a necessary condition of the very creation of France, the sine qua non of the polity: that subject whose speech allows all other subjects to address its besetting issues. Subjectivity, the ideology of the state, finds voices for the actual classes of the state through the voice of its *auctores*, functioning as its *acteurs*: its authors, whose texts are acts. It is the self-reflexivity of writing, a technology of self-knowledge the *auctor* possesses, that allows *writing*, oral and written, to establish the political *parlemenz*. In lending his voice, does that writing subject also model subjectivity for others? The closing injunction constitutes him as a writing subject. It is extraordinarily broad and formulates a universal state ideology of service: "Serve the public thing as [best] you can."[87]

In his functions as secretary, descriptor, analyst of emotions and intentions, herald of speakers, parliamentary chair, *l'Acteur* represents a theoretical acknowledgment of a function that has been of prime importance since the twelfth century, long recognized as essential to medieval storytelling, that of the supple and serviceable narrator. But, of course, the narrator impersonates the author in a simulacrum without origin. He textualizes the instance of textual production, of history and ideology. If France orders him to "serve the public thing as best you can," that is hardly accidental. The injunction is addressed, not only to Alain's Narrator, but to any and all sub-jects in and of the nascent state. The subject, creature of the state, exists to serve the state, in both the specific rules and order or particular disciplines and in the breadth of his individual *ymaginacion*. The writer becomes the model of the subject of the state: an "organic intellectual."

CHAPTER 15

"Love for Sale": François Villon's
Textament of Solidarity

S ubjectivity is that reserved and necessary possibility of making choices among contradictory constitutive ideological codes, plus the psychic space to accommodate that function: a possibility of encompassing the terms of a contradiction, a stretch of dubiety and hesitation. But subjectivity is not only constructed as a *terra reservata*, perhaps surrounded by protective walls. It is also a self-extension, a psychic gesture the twelfth century noted as largesse, the seventeenth as *générosité*. Both overlap with *caritas*, subtracting the religious dimension.

François Villon was born about the time of Christine de Pizan's death. Her last work celebrated Joan of Arc, one of his "Ladies of the Past." The prissy, ambitious, upper-middle-class woman and the lowlife, criminal cleric and wastrel shared a language, a country, and possibly a profession as notaries. Otherwise, they had little in common. He was adopted out of poverty by a priest, given a clerical education, and grubbed out a living at the lower edges of officialdom. She is a snob, he is a prole. Christine looked above her in the social hierarchy for images of a desired self. Villon looked up only for help in legal manipulations: he looked to the street for community, including the Mafia of the Coquillards. He was constituted as a subject by the Other that claimed universality: the university, which graduated him as Master. He presumably knew Latin, but always wrote in French or in the thieves' argot that was its linguistic spin-off. As cleric, he was entitled to protection from the church and was taught charity and discipline. He used his poetic skill to vent rage: his text savages a bishop for having tortured and perhaps sodomized him. He also demonstrated some injudiciousness of conduct: he took part in a major theft and murdered a cleric in a tavern brawl.

At the end of life's trajectory, death too is ambiguous. Villon figures himself as hanging on the gibbet among other criminals, to produce the harrowing "Ballade of the Hung Men," also known as his "Epitaph," one of *humanité*'s crowning poetic achievements. Juxtaposed to that ballade, a quatrain turns the poet's death to a hanging joke:

> Frank's my name, weighted with regret,
> Born in Paris, not far from Pontoise,
> By a rope full six-foot long,
> My neck will learn my ass's weight.

Neither is included in the anthology of Villon's earlier work inserted in the "Testament." Why?

François Villon was a problematic subject. He is known by two sets of documents: his poems, and a criminal record. His two major poems rehearse death in the same poetic convention, a last will and testament.[1] Their form is identical, the perfect square, 8 x 8: octosyllabic stanzas of eight lines each, rhymed ababbcbc. The difference between the two, aside the question of "greatness," is specific. The second, longer version includes an anthology of the poet's earlier work, the series of intercalated ballades, many famous enough in their own time for the poet Clément Marot, who established Villon's first critical edition, to collect them orally as songs in the streets of Paris from those who had learned them from the poet himself. Their inclusion defines the question of the Epitaph's exclusion.

Beginning with Aposiopesis

The fundamental technique of both testaments is the same as the "Congés" from Arras: the address to contemporaries that staples the surface of the writer's body-text to survivors, real persons often well known enough to leave archival traces. A collectivity defines the poet to ensure his survival. The bequests are to friends and colleagues in the *basoche*, law clerks and notaries working around the halls of state power: the Parlement of Paris, the Court of Justice, the Treasury.[2] Villon's relations to officialdom are complex and contradictory. He may have been a member of the *basoche* himself: he knew its circles and treated some figures with familiarity. In times of need, he manipulates its legal potentials. Such institutional con-

nections seem a "natural" continuation of his studies at the university, leading to scribal and notarial functions. If so, he was a representative of power,
albeit a lowly one. His peers function, in his bequests, as *points de capiton*
that staple his being to theirs.

In spite of their differences, the opening of the "Testament" resembles
that of the *City of Ladies* in structure: four stanzas of radical interruption
and disjunction from the institutional world: the experience of desubjectification, in a radical secession of the individual from constitutive subjection. The opening tone of serene composure was conventionally appropriate to one undertaking his moral reckoning as he faced death:

> In the thirtieth year of life,
> Having drunk all my shames,
> Not all mad, not all wise,
> Notwithstanding many punishments endured.

The syntactical hypotaxis bespeaks control of self and language, willful
self-domination, as does the legal *nonobstant*: "notwithstanding." The
grammatical hypotaxis continues two more lines, as Villon's persecutor, the
bishop of Orléans, enters the scene:

> All of which I endured
> Under Thibault d'Aussigny's hand.

With line six, disjunction interrupts, in the aposiopesis that breaks linguistic control:

> Under Thibault d'Aussigny's hand . . .
> He signs the cross in the street, like a bishop:
> That he's mine, I deny, him and it!

Syntactic subordination in a well-established socioreligious hierarchy, broken by the irruption of a cold, calculating rage of long-suppressed verbal
revenge, the aposiopesis marks rejection of the institutional subjection that
constituted the enunciator a social subject and defined his social insertion.
The savage linguistic vengeance assures Thibault d'Aussigny's survival as
the false and possibly sodomite agent of Villon's harsh summer in the
bishop's prison, and possible torture.

Paul defines the bishop as "a man of unimpeachable character . . . hospitable, right-minded, temperate, just, devout, and self-controlled."[3] Denying he is "under" the bishop in religion or vassalage, denying he owes him faith or homage, denying he is his serf, buck (= *cerf*) or doe, Villon suggests he *was* forcibly "under" him in all these roles. Negation is a form of an affirmation:[4]

> He fed me the crumb of a tiny *bite*
> And cold water all one summer long;
> Big or small, he was cheap.[5]

Linguistic innuendo of small [sexual] size bypasses direct accusation of starvation, of torture or homosexual sadism, as intense rage takes symbolic vengeance, crowned by invoking God in the name of equitability: May God treat him as he did me! and goes on two stanzas more, with regular repetition of this last line: let God be as pitiful (that is, as cruel and harsh) to him as he was to me. The reading is confirmed by a mock confession which implies an earlier sinfulness: "I am wrong and ashamed, Whatever he did to me, I leave him to God."[6] Its meaning is the contrary of its statement: Villon asks God to wreak vengeance on Thibault d'Aussigny, bishop of Orléans.

God the avenger[7] becomes the poet's representative against the representative of his church: the subject reverses roles with the Subject. Nothing in the text attacks belief in God or religion directly, but does the church escape all contamination from the vengeance requested of God? Consider the role of the *basoche*. The association of clerics and law clerks was subject to criticism, censure, and legal attack. The king outlawed its satirical allusions, the parliament jailed its members, the Faculty of Theology pronounced interdiction in 1444.[8] Does the "Testament" further a preexisting rivalry between the *basoche* and the church as metonymy for other institutions of power, with *Taque d'Aussigny* its personalization? The initial aposiopesis marks not only a subject escaping from self-control, but a confrontation of contradictory constitutive codes. Such confrontations are the fodder of the "Testament." Is the alienation from an institutional hierarchy also a disjunction from the collective, from the Other? What subjectivity is left, when the subject rejects his Subject?

Bequests or Death-jokes?

The convention of stapling the body of a poem to contemporaries is enacted through the bequests to real-life beneficiaries. Too numerous for even a partial inventory, they are historical *realia* whose names turn into linguistic matrices of verbal games. Villon's *points de capiton* are destabilized by puns, repeatedly of an erotic register.[9] If the poet identifies "Jehan le Lou" as "a good man and an honest merchant" (*homme de bien et bon marchant*: l. 1110), it is in part because Johnny the Wolf was a merchant (= *marchand*, phonetically identical to *marchant*, striding, walking), who supplemented his income by cleaning Paris ditches and as a police informant. But *bon marchant* can also mean that his equipment worked well: by antiphrasis, that he was impotent.[10] Indeterminacy here is the poetic point, not a regrettable cost of communication. The joy of the text lies precisely in the repeated explosions of the linguistic basis of signification, the implosions of reference, in willfully liberating poetic abuse of analytico-referential discourse. Joy is linguistic anarchy pitted against the "serious" use of language.

Villon will pray for Jean Cotart's soul . . . as he will for Thibault d'Aussigny (l. 34)! In official city archives, Cotart appears as *procurator* and *promotor curie*; Villon names him as his own lawyer (l. 1231).[11] Cotart's bequest takes the form of a prayer, which traces his genealogy back to Noah, the father of all drunks, each stanza echoing with the refrain

the soul of good-God-rest-his-soul Master Johnny Cotart![12]

including the final *envoi*, which has Cotart so drunk he is incapable of even spitting on the ground:

Always yelling "Hey! my throat's burning up!"
He never could slake his thirst,[13]

which rather undermines any presumed reliability as a legal representative. Villon also mentions owing Cotart "a small amount"[14] (a substantial sum?), "which [he] has just remembered."

Guy Tabarie is mentioned in the bequest to Villon's "more-than-father," Guillaume de Villon:

> I leave him [Guillaume de Villon] my library
> And the Novel of the Devil's Fart,
> Fattened and deformed by Master
> Guy Tabarie, a truthful man.
> It's in notebooks under a table;
> Though roughly made,
> Its material is so noteworthy
> It compensates the crime.[15]

Tabarie copied and amplified the "Novel of the Devil's Fart"? Leaving no other trace, it has occasioned scholarly debates: Was it written in verse or in prose?[16] The mention seems innocent enough to fit between the heart-felt stanzas addressed to Villon's adoptive parents. But unity of tone or meaning are the last qualities to look for in Villon, or in medieval textuality: "tone" varies enormously even within a single work and is not a criterion of textual coherence.

Historical connotations pullulate. The "Roman du Pet au Deable" has left no trace: it may be an invention of Villon's. Its title has historical reference, however. The "Devil's Fart" was a stone marker at the residence of a wealthy, well-connected widow, Mademoiselle de Bruyères. Students stole the marker and carried it to their own neighborhood behind the Place Maubert in 1451. The king's officers reclaimed it, storing it for safe keeping within the precincts of the Palace of Justice. Mademoiselle de Bruyères replaced it with another stone. Students, with the support of *basochiens*, forced their way into the Palace, reclaimed the original stone, placed it behind the Place Maubert once more, reinforcing its implantation with iron bars and plaster, and topped it with its replacement, also stolen. They danced the night away around their trophy, demanding respect from passers-by: even the king's officers had to doff their hats. Inspired by success, the students next attacked commercial insignia in Paris and ripped off the butchers' iron hooks around Sainte-Geneviève. City burghers were scandalized, as was the king's justice. The provost of Paris took personal charge of the affair, reclaimed stone markers, insignia, iron hooks, and confiscated a small cannon and a collection of swords.

Was this caper the story of the "Novel of the Devil's Fart"? Did Villon actually write a mock epic on these fantasmagoric student pranks or political actions? It would have been his only narrative text. Was its evocation heavily connoted in the original audience? Or is a third historical fact more telling? Guy Tabarie participated in the 1457 theft at the Collège de Navarre, in which Villon and several other clerics broke in, picked the locks of its treasury and made off with 500 golden crowns—a large sum. Guy, as lookout, received 10 gold *écus* for his services and his silence. Picked up by the police, however, he confessed during interrogation. Does the content of the nonexistent "novel" then become, not the student prank of 1451, but the far more serious crime of 1457, which would haunt Villon all his life? Unlike his other misadventures, his poems never refer to it directly, which may indicate its gravity. The frequency of antiphrasis and double encodings establishes these as decoding rules, potentially valid, but not absolute. Does the characterization of Guy Tabarie as *homs veritable* mean that his confession to the police was false? Does the orthography *cayers* hide *cailler*, phonetically identical: A stool pigeon? Is that confession what lies in the *cayers soubz une table*, a nonexistent text (the "Rommant du Pet au Deable") masking a lying one (Tabarie's "confession")?

Historical information is essential for reading the text. Rarely does one find so convincing a demonstration, however, that history does not function to clear up misunderstandings, "disambiguate" or delimit indeterminacies in cloturing monovalence. On the contrary, what history brings to interpretation are potentialities of meaning, additional sources of polysemantics, hence more destabilizations of meaning and escapes from semantic determinacies, one of whose forms is historical determination. The insistence on textual analysis, formal and structural, narrative and verbal, is not purely aesthetic: its pragmatic effect is historical too.

The implication of the "Testament" is bonding with the survivors. An internal discrepancy, however, undermines this implication. The imposing moment of self-analysis at approaching death is continually undercut by the farcical in-jokes of a street-savvy, ironic, and cynical jailbird. A psychic severance has always already occurred in Villon, assumed as "fact" by the text as a whole. His legacies are absurd ironies. The poverty-stricken poet leaves as heirlooms objects he does not own or that do not exist, assigning them to heirs who have no use for them. The poem deconstructs the legal performative it mimics, as well as any fictive union of individual subject and historical community: the performative and its collectivity are always already denounced. The very notion of psychic survival is an absurdity: the body subtracted, no subject survives. The undoing of the "shapely, self-mastering humanist agent into . . . a fluid, multifarious polyvocality" has always already occurred for Villon and exceeds that flattering compass.[17] The helpless passivity of the corpses hanging from the gibbet in the "Ballade des pendus," bodies washed by rain and blackened by sun, eyes pecked out, beards and eyebrows torn out by crows and magpies, buffeted by the wind, is merely the endpoint, beyond the "Testament" itself, of a desubjectification always already in force: the basis of a life, the mining of a subject.

Extensions

Ironies account for much of the "Testament," but not all. The "Testament," riveted to multitudes, is a "Textament." It fuses body and text with effects both dispersive and cohesive. Linguistic indeterminacy, parlayed into fragmentation, grounds a medieval subject in indeterminacy: not as being "without determinations," but in unlimited instability. The dispersals of subjective indeterminacy are the topic of several poems outside the "Testament." They inscribe the fundamental split between "*je*" and its "heart"; assert the subject's total knowledge, except of himself; mimic the very notion of truth by a series of countertruths; ridicule totalizing traditional wisdom in the form of proverbs.[18] One ballade, in perfectly correct, comprehensible language, consists entirely of self-contradiction:

> I die of thirst at the fountain . . .
> I laugh in tears . . .
> Potent am I, lacking force and power,
> Well received, rejected by all.[19]

Language is loosed from the law of noncontradiction: paradox and oxymoron triumph.

In the narrative "Testament," aside the intercalated ballades, the constitutive contradiction is that of multiple voices in the perfection of squared quatrains: the victim, the penitent, the martyred lover, the poor student, the nostalgic senior, the self-negating authority on love, theology, music, and language; above all, the poet playing with semantic multiplicity and ideational heterogeneity. The unitary quality that legitimates voiced authority is continually dispelled as heterogeneity drives language and its representations of subjective voicings. Villon's poetic presence is the most unmistakable in the Middle Ages, affirming itself in the continuous deconstruction of unitary subjectivity. The subject's voicings are protean: a specific subjectivity, outside the play of language, is inexistent.

The constitution of the subject by discipline or ideology incites the *plebs'* flight. Inversely, indeterminate subjectivity occasions its own dialectical countergeneration of determinate enunciations, performed by concretized extrasubjective voices of alterity. Irony accounts for the paradoxical "body" of the poem: the bequests that give it the testamentary force it parodies. Something radically different also occurs in the "Textament," in intercalated ballades of slightly varying forms: octosyllabic octets, or the more imposing decasyllabic ten-line stanzas, also a perfect square 10 x 10, both with appropriate *envois*. These ballades, marked by formal alterity, frequently shift the subject voice from the testamentary "François Villon" to another "I," in remarkable extensions of enunciation accompanied by shifts of tone. In the three ballades for Past Ladies and Lords, the voice is extended to the famous dead of the past; the third substitutes place names for personal proper nouns: possibly a parody of the first two.[20] There is little overt religious content, except for the mention of "good Joan of Lorraine" and of the "sovereign Virgin": *souvraine* rhymes with *Lorraine*. The enunciatory subject in these three poems is an impersonal one, the one who always already knows the answer to the refrain, "where are last year's snows?"

There is more direct religious content in the "Ballade to Pray Our Lady," written for Villon's "poor mother, who God knows had bitter grief and much sadness on my account": the earthly mother now can pray directly to the heavenly.[21] The chasm between them does not destroy the parallelism, analogous to the relation between subject and Subject: this "subject," however sympathetically, even tenderly presented, undergoes no ideological contradiction. On the contrary, the poem affirms the unity of subject and faith. It begins imposingly with Latinate vocabulary (*regente terrienne, Emperiere des infernaux palus . . .*), but its most affective lines are later, where the old woman examines images of paradise and hell:

> One frightens, the other joys me;
> Send me to joy, high goddess,
> Whom all sinners call on,

> Fill me with faith, nothing false or lazy:
> In this faith, I live and die.[22]

The lettered discipline endows the old woman with words of new prayer, amazed, frightened, and desirous at images painted on the walls of her parish church, the illiterate ekphrasis of poverty. Disregarding the earlier invention of Purgatory, they proffer the radical ideological binarism of salvation/damnation.[23]

Age and sex are the same in another text, but the morality is not. The "Ballade of the Helmet-Maker's Wife" is introduced by ten stanzas of her "Regrets" among the most moving of the poem, in pendant to the ballade for his mother.[24] The Old Woman regrets her age, its losses, the power youthful beauty once gave her over merchants and clerics: none would have refused to abandon everything he owned for her. She rejected many, for the sake of a young lover who wanted only her money. All that's left is shame and sin. She goes nearly mad at the sight of naked herself: poor, dry, skinny, shriveled. What happened to the smooth brow, blonde hair, high-arched eyebrows, the coy glance that caught the subtlest men, that beautiful nose of perfect size, cute little ears, dimpled chin, bright well-drawn face, and beautiful red lips? What became of handsome shoulders, long arms and fine hands, small breasts and ample hips, high, separate, perfect for amorous combat; the large loins, that tight sex on firm, round thighs, in its little garden?

The evocation of youth, beauty, and erotic desire is paralleled by old age in devastating juxtaposition. Now she squats with other poor foolish old women, in poverty, on their knees, bunched like balls of wool. . . . Having retraced her own degradation, the logic of the Belle Heaulmiere's advice to the whores of Paris is clear, impeccable, and implacable. To her peers, the Beautiful Haberdasher, Blanche the Shoemaker, the Sausage-maker, the Tapestry Lady, Little Jane the Hatmaker, Katherine the Purse-maker (or the Treasurer, or the Madame?), to them all, she says: take right and left, spare none, refuse no man,

> For old women are worthless,
> Coins out of circulation.[25]

The women of the street are made to speak: the harsh, amoral wisdom of the street, condemned by propriety, excluded from poesy, is given voice.

The marginalization of discourse reaches its extreme with "Fat Margot's Song": a whore and her pimp the subject. The poem has been dismissed as nothing more than a conventional *sotte chanson*. It trespasses even this text's rather loose "standards." Complicity between pimp and whore legitimates their relationship: What's shameful, if I love and serve the beauty? She's got what it takes to satisfy the most demanding customers. They arrive, I fetch a pitcher of wine, serve water, cheese, bread, fruit. If they pay well, I'll invite them back

to this whorehouse where we hold our state.[26]

But if she comes to bed penniless, I can't stand her, I hate her, I hock her dress. She protests? I grab a broken potsherd and "write a note" right on her nose. Intimate violence is followed by repulsive reconciliation: we make up, she lays me a huge fart like some slimy beetle. Laughing she cracks my head with her fist, calls me Gogo, and whacks my ham. Both drunk, we sleep like logs. We wake, her stomach growls, she climbs on me so as not to spoil her fruit (Nature's call? A child?). I groan underneath, she flattens and kills me with sex:

In this whorehouse where we hold our state.

The *envoi*'s acrostic inscribes Villon. Wind, hail, frost, my bread's baked. I'm a bawd, she's a bawd, who's worth more? With the same model, we deserve each other: bad rat, bad cat. We love filth; filth follows us. We flee honor; it flees us:

In this whorehouse where *we hold our state.*

What is "the state": A whorehouse? A philosophical state of being? A rank within a stable hierarchy, a professional calling, a craft? The phrase "*tenir estat*" applies to royalty, as when, on entry into official residence, heralding an audience or court of justice, the king displays the panoply of rank.[27] No semantic closure is available to this indeterminacy, no safe limitation. The repugnance the poem arouses raises the question: Is the reader's life itself such a whorehouse? Just how much better is any auditor or reader, than the repulsive pimp and whore? Is such vulgarity mere self-indulgence? Is the interest of the ballades only a picturesque grotesquery, however joyful or sensual? Are the ballades really a senseless failure?[28]

The intercalation of ballades in the "Testament" is the textual body's incorporation of its formal alterity. It also incorporates the poem's structural alterities: their multiplicity of voices. The poet's voice, in the bequests, is subject to the dispersals of indeterminacy. In the ballades, constituted in heterogeneity, voice and message tend toward greater determinacy, though never absolute. The enunciator obtains purchase on textual identity by speaking through another: sincerity of expression arrives in the invention of fictions, in impersonation, in the simulacra of identity. Identifying with the supposed subjects of the ballades, the subject metamorphoses into their experiential location: by Rousseau's "pity," by "extension."[29]

The subjects of these ballades are a class of women ordinarily absent from a poetic world still dominated by courtly codes: those excluded also from the "City of Ladies." Villon's self-extension gives voice to those who had none in the world of official cultural textuality: thus the "Ballade of the Women of Paris." They are compared to Florentines, Venetians, good talkers all; to Lombards, Romans, and Genoese; to Neapolitans, Germans, Prussians, Greek, Egyptian, Hungarians, Spaniards, and Catalonians; to Bretons, Swiss, Gascons, Toulousans, those of Lorraine, England, and Calais—"is that a lot?"—even Picards from Valenciennes: sorry, give it up, "There's no good talk outside of Paris":

> "Il n'est bon bec que de Paris."

The Parisian patter of two herring women from the Petit Pont will liquidate all others. The same is true, not only of excluded voices, of excluded social categories, but of excluded languages—see Villon's poems in argot—and their messages. The immorality of the Helmet-Maker's Wife is the logic of the street: discrepancy signals the encounter of class ideologies.

Before representation of the subaltern was problematized,[30] the subject extends himself to other genders, other classes, than those well placed in the world of textuality. It is an extension of self that will have repercussions throughout European history, political as well as literary: revolutions result, when potential leaders cross class lines. The subject opens textuality to presences of the excluded, giving voice to the socially voiceless. The "Testament" makes room for its alterities, and those of the socius. If voice means subjectivity, François Villon's great gift, his greatest bequest, is the voiced being of subjectivity to those who lacked it. In the whorehouse of life, there is room for that gift, that self-extension of the subject. Are the voiceless to whom the poetic subject extends being our stand-ins, as readers, our lieu-tenants, in the poem's diegesis? After the enunciating subject's multiple, fictitious identifications, can the reader, the auditor of his poems follow?

We may now return to the initial question: Why is that text, which may be Villon's greatest poem, his "epitaph," the "Ballade of the Hung Men," excluded from the anthology of the "Textament"? The poet and his editor Marot were presumably aware of its value. It may not have been included because it was written after the "Testament" was already constituted. Perhaps its subject did not fit the poetic category intended by the collected ballades and the conception of the work as a whole. Perhaps its thematization of the message of solidarity—"Brother humans, who live after us, have pity and pray for us"—is best left unsaid among the ballades for the voiceless. It asks for the audience's self-extension toward the subject and his mates, reversing and reaffirming his own self-extension to others.

The Medieval Crucible

> The tradition of the oppressed teaches us that the "state of emer-
> gency" in which we live is not the exception but the rule.
> *Walter Benjamin,*
> *"Theses on the Philosophy of History"*

T he crucible of the Middle Ages manufactures a new amalgam
that transforms earlier practices into a new kind of political organization, strongly different from its past, oriented toward the captation
of increased surplus value, power, and political cohesion, which has never
settled into quiescent stability. Violence, subject, state, and representation
are major elements. They participate in each other's formation without entire amalgamation: their relations undergo perpetual friction, adjustment,
and slippages. The death of each element has been trumpeted repeatedl for
over a century: their death throes are extended.

The state, produced as the crystallization of recentralization in a major geographical expansion of the application of power for political and
economic aggrandizement, responds to violence by capturing, incorporating, and amplifying it. The state does not invent governance. Its governance realizes power in creating subjects as its representatives by processes
of identification with the state, its mechanisms, interests, and ideology:
bureaucracy and a population unified through identification are the end
result. These identifications are initially mediated by the figure of the
ruler, the monarch, as the personification of the state. A properly
"monotheistic" state, with only a single ideology, would be a totalitarian
one: the fascist state is one logical outgrowth of the state-form, one mode
of "the end of history."

A plurality of ideologies is characteristic of any evolving historical
state: social evolution results from contradiction. Ideology is both representation of values for the constitution of subjects and a "representation
for" other social segments. The enormous historical changes which consti-

tute the Middle Ages are obvious: compare the end of antiquity with what is now called "Early Modern Europe." The change is the travail of the Middle Ages: its enormity is the enormity of the period's constitutive contradictions.

The subject of subjection certainly exists in the Middle Ages, as exemplified in both monasticism and servitude. But the constitution of subjects, whether by ideology or discipline, works imperfectly. In part, that is due to the contrariousness of "human nature": the tendency for law to produce infraction and ideology transgression. But, too, the subject is inherently unstable. Its complexity and instability define its freedom. The political model of feudalism makes of all agents (except the king) simultaneously vassal and suzerain, simultaneously subject and Subject. A functionalist view of the state identifies its ideological constitution of subjects only as an element of society's self-reproduction. In fact, existence within a historical society means the coexistence of a plurality of contradictory ideologies. People are repeatedly forced into making concrete choices among conflicting ideologies.

There is no greater ethical, philosophical, or political problem than the "freedom" of such choices. Spinoza warns against confusing freedom with contingency: the standard American error, which absolutizes freedom as the given. From this perspective, Spinoza's assertion that "a thing is free, which exists and acts solely by the necessity of its own nature" can only seem paradoxical.[1] That is exactly what is dramatized in *Silence* as a supposedly "free" choice: Which form of determination, nature or nurture, will dominate? Which form of determination, nature or nurture, will the actant Silence "freely" choose as his or her "nature"? What surfaces repeatedly in medieval texts is the situation of contradiction which forces actants into acting as subjects making "free choices." Narrativized, freedom appears as the product of contradictory determinisms. That product is what, beyond subjugation, is called "the subject." Narrative is the privileged means of its textualization.

That subject is defined as early as the Oaths of Strasbourg, which constitute the subject as a structure of choice at a site of fissure. That fissure, constitutive of the state-and-subject invention, carries implications of autonomy, resistance, and eventually rebellion. Modernity's commitment to an ideologically fictitious representation of its medieval antecedence largely suppresses acknowledgment of the frequency of critique, of resistance, of rebellion, of open revolt, and all the pressure tactics to which a complex society gives rise.[2] Far more comfortable, for modernity's self-satisfaction, is the image of a Middle Ages quiescent in an acceptance of subjugation that grounds modernity's self-definition *a contrario*. Against this constitutive modernist delusion, the second model of the medieval subject is a split or a deviation from what is given in ideology or discipline. This "subject" names not a substance, a character type, nor a universal condition of humanity or citizenship, but rather a process one had hoped would model human history as a whole: from subjugation to freedom.

The subject is core to the paradoxical continuity of medieval and modern. Constituted as an integral part of historical state-formation, the subject becomes the defining thorn in the state's side. Rebellion, resistance, or critique does not come into existence without prior subjection to a scheme of values that forces questioning and dubiety. What Althusser called "state ideology" forms not only obedient subjects but subjects of questioning, critique, and revolution as well. Critical subjectivity grounds itself in the deconstruction of existing ideology, or of the discrepancies between praxis and ideology. The effort of the desubjectified, those constituted as victims or subjects of subjection, to reconstitute themselves as subjects in a fuller sense of the word is discontinuous but repeated across history. From Alexis as subject disconnected from the ideology of social codes and awaiting reconnection with the Christian God; Yvain in madness and "divorce"; Perceval denied being as knight; to Christine de Pizan, denied humanity as woman; these narrative subjects endure desubjectification and reconstruct themselves as subjects through narrative. That repeated effort may be the one basis left for an optimistic view of human freedom as a universal. Any such optimism is tempered by the recognition that, for most humans, freedom is less a permanent condition they are born to than an activity they are forced into: that forcing is intermittent only.[3]

Foucault critiqued a recent "invention of 'man.'" Writing in 1966, he dated the invention of the *figure of man* from a century and a half earlier. It was the *figure* of man that had changed, as part of the fundamental dispositions of knowledge—an epistemic change. Hence the ease with which that figure might now disappear, along with an approaching epistemic change. What is at stake, however, is not just the figure of man: that formulation accepts the traditional epistemic distribution of reality and representation. The human is a creature that feeds off its figurations, its representations, as ideologies. That is why they can have performative effect. So-called antihumanism was precisely the rejection of an immutable "human nature" beyond the reach of ideology. As the figures of man change, as man's self-representations change, so does what we call "human nature." Ideology in part determines what functions as "human nature." Our being is not in some beyond of representation, a putative real behind the Reals, posited as a mere but immutable hypothesis: our being changes along with its representations. Representation and the figure of man become an interface between the nature of the human and operative systems of power. That representational interface names the interdependence between the system of governance and the powers it instantiates on the one hand, and a human nature that evolves along with it as both its condition of possibility and its effect, on the other.

The medieval invention of the state, whose historicity Engels had remarked, was necessarily accompanied by its effect and condition of possibility: the subject. This dual invention incorporated a contingency of confluences: the Roman Empire as *trace* (the fact that controlling structure had existed, but existed no more); new populations arriving on the European continent by invasion and migrations, with energies and cultural codes of which little is known but which played a major creative role *ex hypothesis*; an evolving system of new inequalities and local exploitations, each of which reached for the controlled exercize of violence against other, competing local nuclei; and a new ideology, preaching and sometimes honestly seeking peace, whose claims to universalism readily fit with local exploitation and aggression directed at distant populations: the religion of Christianity. The heterogeneity of this confluence fueled an explosion of social fusions and cultural energy which state, and subject-formation tried to capture and channel . . . imperfectly.

Perspectivism, Violence, and Ideology

Violence is at once the occasion for the invention of the state, its ultimate instrument of power, and its permanent destabilization. Two extreme positions establish theoretical limits of possibility regarding the nature and career of human violence. One narrates an originary, Edenic matriarchal peaceability of sedentary calm, venerating a parthenogenetic Goddess as the single source of life manifest in all forms of nature.[4] The reign of the goddess was overthrown by eastern, horseback-riding nomads, warlike, patriarchal, hierarchical, with thrusting and cutting weapons, whose hilltop fortifications and burial mounds were ancestors of the "barbarian invasions." The other limit-position absolutizes violence. Prehistoric peace never existed. War and aggression are ahistorical, integral to human nature. Existence itself is a fact of aggression. Humans eat: digestion and assimilation are combat, a war of the individual organism on its food. "War is universal and total."[5]

Between these two limit-positions, one may hazard that the human *potential* for violence is universal. Its *manifestations* are modulated by historical and social circumstances. Simple equations of "*the* medieval" with "violence" and "*the* modern" with "peace" are no longer tenable, if they ever were.[6] Characterizations like Giambattista Vico's of the Middle Ages as uniquely rampant with "violence, rapine, and murder . . . because of the extreme ferocity and savagery of these most barbarous centuries"[7] are nothing more than an ideological strategy of self-definition by successive modernities which cast the Middle Ages as the violent, inverted mirror-image of an innately peaceable and rational modernity—a claim modern history renders preposterous.

Variations in the degree and modes of violence exist. The historical question: Was the feudal dispensation particularly violent? is unanswerable in the absolute. The social evenementiality in question, the real, is unavailable; it never existed in any case as a singular entity. The medieval experience was not unitary, but complex. Many of its texts indicate serious concerns, on various sides, with violences that resound emphatically among its multiple Reals. Some social groups profited from violence and considered it normal; their representations reveled in it. Others held physical violence in horror and attempted to exclude or reduce it to symbolic rituals. Some complex texts incorporated codes from these contradictory attitudes: the *Song of Roland* expresses admiration for the beauty of violence, just as does Bertrand de Born, but incorporates that admiration in a narrative structure oriented toward peace. The core population, the peasantry, was dedicated to the struggle with nature in the production of food and the construction of a social life at the village level, much of which escapes the modern historical gaze. It was neither dedicated to violence, nor claimed abhorrence as did the monks. Each group had a different perspective on the phenomenon of violence.

Multiple perspectives operated within the historical past: modern monomanias, whether nostalgic or politically invested, falsify our images of the past, its burgeoning variety, contradictions, and deferrals under continual transformation. Not only is the real behind the documented Reals forever beyond our grasp: no single, unitary, totalizing real ever existed. The real of the past—its reality—was the multiplicity of its own Reals. Written texts, interpreted by modern historians as evidentiary documents, were often not composed as historical documents, but as legal claims or polemical instruments. They constructed competing Reals, whose collocation allows for the perspectival complexity of a postulated real. A nonexclusive historiographical perspectivism takes these differences into account. A representation of the past is required which takes account of its perspectival complexity, within a horizon of a conflictual social totality.

Various historiographies privilege one perspective over others. The clerical perspective is that of the modern academic historian's predecessors; some find the perspective of the nobility more congenial. Both adapt a rhetoric of continuity in furtherance of the ideological claims of genealogy, always oriented toward legitimation of present possession.[8] Ideologies of order sustain society's self-representation with an image of continuous, stabilized self-identity. More adequate appears to be the view that insists on a relatively sharp and violent change. Some saw lordship as inherently illegitimate:

> rulers "derive their origin from men ignorant of God who raise themselves above their fellows by pride, plunder, treachery, murder . . . "[9]

The aggressive growth of new lordships, centered in the eleventh century, though with earlier roots and later after-effects, particularly in the ideological field of the twelfth, was perhaps too radical for the term "mutation": "revolution" is more appropriate.[10] In a sudden rapid, all-transforming change, an old world seemed to burst apart, a new one to thrust forward.[11] In spite of revisionism, that moment remains "what must be called the Feudal Revolution."[12]

Such views remain hypothetical. What is more certain is that the Peace documents—whatever the accuracy of their representation of social reality—demonstrate the existence of an *ideological crisis* of the first order. Ideology emerged from this revolution as a relatively autonomous field for the negotiation of social conflicts, subtracted from clerical institutionalization. While its cultural production, especially in written form, was associated initially with the princely courts' bureaucratizing mode of governance, its vernacularization made it more unpredictable than its clerical antecedents and signaled its continuity with present forms of ideology.

Absolutely speaking, the Middle Ages did not invent ideology, the subject, or governance. Nor did it create the scene of ideological representation *ab ovo*: subjects from Antigone to Augustine, governments from the Athenian Boule, the Roman Senate in the Republic, attest otherwise. What is true is that, as an integral part of the state, the Middle Ages (re)invented an ideological scene, in which different social groups addressed the issue of socially generated violence, an issue which perdures to the present. Its initial impulse mutated into permanent institutions of state, the increasingly representative assemblies initially termed "conversations" (*parlemens*), which turn into assemblies, parliaments, houses of representatives, senates . . .

Simultaneously, the Middle Ages constructed a narrative political subject as a representational emanation of the state. Functionally defined as the application of power and reproduction of society, the subject turned out to be contorted in complexity by contradiction, characterized less by graceful self-mastery, more by discord, fragmentation, and motion. Often, the texts oppose it to another precipitate of the human person, identity. Stable, fixed, devolving from social categories when not imposed by them, identity coheres ill with subjective motility. Subject and identity are not alternative substances: they are phases of the person, both apparently necessary. Rather than stability, subjectivity is a phase of existence, a moment of disquieted freedom, of hesitation and choice. Like identity, it depends on introjection of social value-systems as givens (Althusser's "ideology"). Unlike identity, it requires their interruption. Across the medieval centuries, fiction and discourse construct, test, and critique what will become the modern subject, in the compound determination and necessity of internalization and freedom. That imbrication of subjectivity, state, mediating

ideology of representation—a nexus of aporetic reactions to violence—
evolves continuously to the present.

This aporia is part and parcel of the radical transformations of a society
undergoing disciplinarization, with state-formation as its apex. Power recentralized at the dual levels of principality and what would become the
nation-states of modernity. Oddly enough, the triumph of state-formation
under Philippe Augustus had among its first effects, not consolidation of
the subject, but its problematization. Prose discourse is forged as a new medium, the instrument of ideological claims of truth as against poetic fiction, enabling the vernacular to participate in the momentous political discussions of policy, in the formation of minority identities, and in the
constitution of discursive public intellectuals. Lyric poetry itself becomes
the scene in which the gesture of self-extension toward others—folding in
clerical *caritas* and secular *générosité* or largesse—operates at a popular,
even vulgar level and signals the marginal intellectual's association with
marginalized illiterates.

Across the medieval centuries, fiction, poetry, and discourse model the
subject, subjected to the symbolic order of an absent ruler in the compounded necessity of internalization, contradiction, and freedom. There is
no absolute break, no radical *solution de continuité* between medieval textual practices of subjectivity and those of later periods.[13] The subject of
contradiction explored and constituted in medieval texts is continued by
the texts of a presumed modernity—continuity denied by a modernity
given to incantatory self-adulation. A recent—and very good—book on
political subjectivity insists that modernity is born of the "dissolution of
the Christian imaginary and the disintegration of medieval society," that
only "modern reason," only "modern political subjects" and the state are
"critically interdependent.[14] In fact, the "modern" subject and its implications of violence, the state, and representation, are inscribed in medieval
fictions and the practices of governance that stretch "the Middle Ages" into
"modernity." So is the gesture of a solidarity that transcends all identitarian binarisms.

Text

Texts are a privileged lens by which to view the process of constructing this
new civilization of the state. Text stages the problematics of representation,

as writing becomes a necessary means of surveillance, epistemic construction, and archiving: it stages the self-consciousness of writing as itself integral to representation. The *Life of Saint Alexis* reproduces itself in the text the saint composes just before dying, that he refuses to unclench from his hand even after death until the right destinatee presents himself. The *Song of Roland*'s social structure is emblematized through the perspective of the enemy ambassador who comes to the Frankish encampment. Marie de France's *lais* repeatedly stage the imbrication of sign and narrative within their narrative. Chrétien de Troyes suffuses his text with the self-consciousness of a writing subject whose identity as author or narrator is undecidable.

Representation, whether of agents or texts, is recursive: its *mise-en-abyme* acquires a deontological dimension as well as an ontological playfulness. It is the medium for the ideological constitution of subjects, individual or collective; their self-examination; and their eventual transformations. Text is exploratory, experimental, and playfully constructive; its self-reflexivity constructs the space in which the ideological sedimentation of the present by the past, of the individual by the collective, of the subject by its identities, can be modified. Representation, from governmental documentation to fiction writing to abstract theory, does not exist except within a collectivity. As thought, it is the medium in which the freedom available to humanity is achieved.

Text is not necessarily on the side of freedom: *vide* Virgil's servility to the cause of empire, even after acknowledgment of its deathly cost, in the seduction of writing by power. The problematic is inherent to a form of governance which alternates between force and representation, between the repressive state apparatuses and the ideological state apparatuses. Administrative textualities cleave most closely to fusion with the state: the prose of the analytic-referential lends itself most readily to totalitarian dominance. But both in its gaps and in the necessity of explanation to which it responds, AR-prose stands in dialectical relation to what it seeks to suppress. Text stages occasions for the choices of freedom by the very nature of its narrative backbone.[15] Philippe de Beaumanoir proposes a discursive theory of the *bailli* as subject, whose function is the enact the narrative performances of administration and judgment. The contemporary novel of cross-dressing of *Silence*, and the autobiographical fiction of Christine de Pizan a century and a half later, dramatize the dubitative and even anguished nature of choice. Alain Chartier's polyphonic discourse stages the necessity of submission to an overarching ideology of collectivity, at a moment in history when only the ideologeme of "nation" seems capable of promising peace. The subject struggles with an ideologically constituted identity at the service of hierarchical power, subject-positions, or cultural gendering. Insofar as human freedom exceeds the circular walls of Spinoza's paradoxical formulation in making ethical and political choices, narrative text is the medium of choice for its representation. Narrative, by its very nature, may also be the earliest figuration of human freedom.

Text here is not that of literary history, a late, disciplinary devolution from a Kantian transcendence, nor an instance of "art" in its modernist hypostasis as a substitute for religious transcendance. The modernist meditation on or play with the forms and materials of the art, cut off from their traditional function of representation, may attain an ultimate, Platonic reality (see the classic statements of Klee and Kandinsky). That trancendence subtracted, art may also present itself as a construct radically independent from all other realms of reality, resolutely antiplatonic, asserting itself as a radical. At this point, modernist experimentalism rejoins the notion of art which the Middle Ages inherits from classical antiquity: *ars* as the discipline of a craft. The technical discipline of text-making came from the past, but was oriented toward social or future effectivities. The traditional craft object is oriented by its maker's concrete social intent: the bootmaker wants to make and sell a shoe that fits and pleases. But so far as the modern reader is concerned, the medieval *ars* of writing produces a text subtracted from authorial as well as ontological intentionality. Wace presumably wanted to please his patron Henry II, but was led to formulate critiques that displeased: telling historical truth overrode the fear of the royal patron's displeasure.

A crafted work is a rationally organized collection of devices—narrative, rhetorical, and linguistic—superimposed and imbricated. This formalist model has been extended from fiction to all forms of representation. The repetition of permanent elements across large series of texts allows for recognition of their syntactical organizations. The model of language forces a shift from syntax to semantics, to focus on the production of meaning: "semantic" values are produced even by purely formal experiments. *Rose Novel I* may well have been generated as a formal experiment with the materials of its tradition and culture: the allegorization of courtly love. Its sensuous analycity leads to the shocking discovery of the persistence of violence.

Texts are collocations of values in multiplicities. These coexist either in agonistic coherence or the attenuated dispersals of their deconstruction. The distinction is not always clear: Eros and Thanatos do not settle into persuasive stability in the *Yvain*, nor is the identity of the courtly lady who endows the poetic world with meaning ineluctably stable, in spite of its repetitions through hundreds of poems. Both Marie de France and Chrétien de Troyes compose narratives of structural integrity, but that does not resolve the antinomy of the Celtic material drawn from vanquished populations and the political problematics of the conquerors and their continental neighbors. The political contradiction at the heart of their fabulations have only exceptionally been noted.[16]

Textual values cannot but draw on equivalences established in the social body. Yet some texts transform these equivalences into critiques or reversals. Texts are microlaboratories of society, in which experiments with form and structure can produce new formulations of meaning—as when the *Song of Roland* takes feudal themes of epic violence to limn a monarchical submission of the feudal nobility that, in the social text of the time, is purely theoretical. A century later, the monarchy performs that political subjugation with guile and violence. When a text undertakes to demonstrate the ultimate self-destruction of a polity which attempts to reconcile the feudalism that borders on anarchy with the monarchy that insufficiently distinguishes itself from the nobility, the logical coherence of *Raoul de Cambrai*'s demonstration deconstructs the very notion of narrative compositional unity.

Text and subject replay each other's problematics. As the state is more solidly established and looms more permanently on the sociopolitical landscape, the correlative subject undergoes more scrutiny. Initially, the personification allegory of Guillaume de Lorris separates out elements at work in the traditional love story of "romance." A recognizable narrative of quest, qualifying test, social encounter, affective cathexis, and pursuit is visible under the independence granted to the constitutive elements of the story. But in its "continuation" half a century later by Jean de Meun, the "romance" dwindles to a skeleton, and each of Guillaume's personifications, along with new ones, are given voice and discursive space to argue for their own subjective dominance. At the same time, the field of reference is no longer that of an interpersonal "love story." It touches on the connections that bond humans in any polity.

Simultaneous to the transformation of narrative personifications into subjects of relative autonomy, the exemplary political subject—the field agent representative of recentralizing power—speaks in his own voice, addressing both the situations of subjects in general and his own subjectivity in particular. Philippe de Beaumanoir is brought to speak of the subject as a natural extension of his administration of the polity in the count's name: his role as *bailli*, both bureaucrat and judge, is crucial to the *baillage*. The *bailli* as subject is the site of traversals of codes, power, strategies, and representations which define the life of the principality as polis.

Just about simultaneous to his *Customs of the Beauvaisis* is the fictional narrativization of the split Philippe acknowledges as a limit-case of the bailli's identity: the encounter as subject with the unacceptable risk of damnation. That split of identity and subject is the fissure constitutive of Silence. As subject, she carries out her father's ideology of protecting material wealth; she does so against the claims of her identity as a woman. As far as tone is concerned, *Silence* is a tale lightly told in rapidly moving octosyllables. But the split between subject and identity announces a major theoretical disjunction, replayed today in the opposition between a philosophy of universalism and a theory of identity as alternative grounds of democratic politics.

The alternative is also played out in the juxtaposition of Christine de Pizan, whose production is based in gender identity, and François Villon's self-extension to those outside his own identitarian sites. His identities as student, cleric, law clerk, criminal, and poet are necessary to understanding his text, but also to grasping the leap his text performs beyond those identitarian limits. That leap is a gesture of generosity, largesse, of charity. It was not entirely without preparation: the openness of Marie de France toward the culture of the conquered "Bretuns" was an earlier sign of the same subjectivity. In both the twelfth-century courtly woman poet and in the fifteenth-century university-trained criminal poet of the margins, identitarian limitations reach toward their transcendence.

Before the devastations of utter fragmentation which civil war joined to foreign invasion, Alain Chartier presents heartfelt voicings of identitarian ideologies: while the contradictions among them are noted, neither the historical author nor his intratextual representative criticizes any party. Instead, an image is proposed, an image which bears unquestioned resonance but less specifiable content, a representation whose very indefiniteness could allow it to function as a factor of unity. Before the nation gave rise to the depradations of nationalism, it figured as a potential of peace, the ideologeme which might unite the disparate populations of the state. The image of France is introduced as what might be called a "relative universal": "France" is universal for all parties present, and all recognize its relevance to them. "France" is that universal, relevant to those present, which might give them occasion to transcend their identitarian sitedness, without necessarily denying their identity.

Early Moderns and the Space of Philosophy

Five "postmedieval" figures develop the paradoxes of the medieval construction. There is no question of a discussion adequate to Montaigne, Shakespeare, La Boétie, Descartes, or Max Weber. At best, their continuity with the problematics examined earlier can be suggested. Montaigne's well-known proclivity to self-contradiction extends to subjectivity. The universalism of "each man bears the entire form of man's estate" implies the democratic principle that all moral philosophy can be attached to "a common and private life."[17] But difference and variability unsettle that universal reach. He rejects "the common error" of judging others by oneself, conceiving of "a thousand contrary ways of life," more easily admitting difference than resemblance.[18] An ordered subjective unity and the total self-knowledge it allows,[19] are countered by assertions of variation and evanescence: "The world is a perennial movement. . . . Stability itself is nothing but a more languid motion":[20] "Life is an uneven, irregular and multiform movement."[21] As one twelfth-century historian said, "This ensemble of land and sea . . . all the time it is in motion, for what can be found in the world that is not moving?"[22]

Straightforward acceptance of Montaigne's contradictoriness is preferable to an imposed, factitious unity. This includes a dedoubled subject: a private writing subject who seizes thought in the process of formulation, and a public individual subjected to his prince: "the social and political subject."[23] These two subjects redistribute Beaumanoir's duality: loyal submission to the superior is identical, but the possible negative judgment of the master turns into a space of privacy. Split, private and public subjects take odd forms. Subjects are freer than the king, the Subject who "cannot shed his political role," whereas the private individual's merely peripheral contact with public life allows withdrawal. Only those who seek out public service undergo the "real and essential subjection" to the sovereign, that collectivity of thinkers, statesmen, functionaries, and lawyers known as the *Politiques*:[24] a higher bureaucracy of representational analogues to sheriffs, provosts, bailiffs . . . As against Beaumanoir Montaigne demands a "natural and simple obedience," a "subjection" that excludes individual "discretion."[25] Public institutions and practices should not be submitted to the instability of *une privée fantaisie*: "Private reason has only a private jurisdiction."[26] Montaigne crystallizes Alain Chartier's association of the state with order and discipline in the phrase, the "ordinary discipline of a state," presupposing

> a body [politic] that holds together in its principal parts and
> functions, and a common consent to its observance and obedience.
> The law-abiding pace is a cold, deliberate, and constrained one, and
> is not the kind that can hold up against a lawless and unbridled
> pace.[27]

Rebellious lawlessness—violence—must be fought by subjugating it to "the ordinary discipline of a state." Exception is made for the diplomat, to whose representational function leeway is granted for on-the-spot judgment:

> Constrained obedience belongs only to precise and stated commands.
> Ambassadors have a freer commission, which in many areas depends
> in the last resort on their own judgment; they do not simply carry
> out, but also by their counsel form and direct their master's will.[28]

Up to this point, Montaigne legislates the division of the public domain of law from the private. But a domain "heterogeneous to political laws" exists,[29] that of the "sovereign friendship" based on the correspondence [*convenance*] of "one soul in bodies twain," as he phrased his relation to Etienne de la Boétie. *Contra* Derrida, Montaigne did not entertain "a fundamental apoliticism": his distrust and fear "of those who seek to disturb and change the state of our government without worrying whether they will improve it"[30] is fundamentally conservative. Nevertheless, the fraternity of sovereign friendship based on correspondence has as its transcendent consequence a communal and even communist holding of everything together: "their wills, goods, wives, children, honor and lives," all held together so close that ultimately the friends can neither lend nor give each other anything.[31] Unlike Villon's self-extension, Montaigne's requires a narrower field: correspondence is limited by gender and class to men of position.

Beaumanoir's discrepancy within subjectivity allows for a potential exceptionalism, which interrupts ordinary encodings to remove a parcel of subjectivity from subjection to a superior power, allowing the individual to function as momentary judge of his superior. Montaigne limits any exceptionalism to diplomacy. Other subjects are also split, but without license to overturn hierarchy: the other half of subjectivity is remaindered to the private sphere. In the evolution from the thirteenth century to the sixteenth, a measure of critical autonomy has beaten a retreat to privacy.

Montaigne and his friend Etienne de la Boétie were both members of that select group of *politiques* Montaigne discusses—men who chose a political and administrative career. It is not generally recognized that La Boétie addresses this class of men in his classic text, *On Voluntary Servitude*.[32] The focus of the text—strange, difficult, as paradoxical as its topic—is on the phenomenon of its title: the fact that men, born free, voluntarily submit to the domination of another, the "One" of an alternative title: "*Le contr'Un.*" "Servitude" is the status of any person subjected to the state. The "One" who dominates is indifferently termed "king" or "tyrant": the distinction is obliterated. There is no legitimate rule, nor is there a legitimate king.

La Boétie's text is a radical political tract. Its sinuous composition—"tortuous" might be more exact—ends with a section that examines the question: How is that a single person imposes illegitimate rule on an entire country? The question is to some degree a practical one . . . but is a mystery, stresses the author. Force of arms—Althusser's "Repressive State apparatus"—is not the answer. Not really. It is not, he says, hauberks, protective armor, castle watches that defend tyrants. At first, a small handful, four or five men only maintain the tyrant: just four or five keep the entire country in servitude; five or six have the tyrant's ear, approaching on their own initiative or summoned by him, to become accomplices of his cruelties, companions of his pleasures, pimps of his sensualities, shareholders in his pillages. Under these six men, six hundred more draw profits; the six in turn manipulate their six hundred just as they do the tyrant. These six hundred rule over six thousand, assigned to govern the provinces or manipulate the finances: in this manner, their avarice and cruelty remain under control. A great column follows after, a hundred thousand, nay millions more are attached to the tyrant by this rope. As many find tyranny profitable as prefer freedom. It is not only evil, the dregs of a kingdom, a pile of twisted thievelets who gather around when a king declares himself tyrant; but those who are touched by burning ambition and particular greed to take part in the booty become tyrannicules under the great tyrant himself.[33]

What La Boétie describes as a creeping suffusion of the kingdom by ambition, greed, and cruelty is a dialectic whose historical beginning was noted in Chapter 9 (on representative agency): what begins as a princely or a royal court expands into a functioning bureaucracy, which ultimately suffuses the entire state. This, says La Boétie, and not force of arms, is the secret spring of domination, the support and foundation of tyranny. The agents representing the prince or the king, the initial subjects of the state, are those who enforce its demands for taxes, services, and eventually ideological submission, upon the general population. More radical than his friend Montaigne, La Boétie does not discuss that parcel of reserved psychic space which is freedom's mortgage.

The parcel of reserved psychic space that can be tracked from Beaumanoir to Montaigne became a major philosophical problem for the seventeenth century's experience of "crisis and uncertainty."[34] That crisis did not result from a sharp discontinuity between medieval and modern times. Pascal returns to the medieval anguish of a space empty of certain signification. His reaction to free thought, appealing to God for protection from the extremes of the very great and the very small, demonstrates the continuity of the Christian's hope as bettor, cast into "a tortured equanimity." Descartes also "manages" doubt and uncertainty, but in a radically different manner, hoping to counter "the corrosive effects of skeptical doubt" by enactments of doubt and finitude. Beaumanoir's limited critical subjective space, transformed into a private indeterminate space by Montaigne, is subtracted by Descartes from history as the ground of philosophical thought, to achieve "the self-certainty of an autonomous subject," a self-reflexivity spatialized as interiority.[35]

The spatial dimension which constituted the medieval subject as representation of the absent Subject has been internalized. A fixed, self-certain, self-possessed subjectivity, surveying the world around it, reduces it to mere extension, on whose surface may be imposed a discipline of geometrical analysis oriented toward possession. The subject's radical autonomy vis-à-vis a world of pure extension, despiritualized and objectified, resembles an abstraction of the feudal chatelain, viewing the agricultural extension around his fortress as space to be conquered, dominated, and exploited. Cartesian abstraction announces the violent reduction of the other for surveillance and control,[36] as in the panoptic schema of the disciplinary society.

Descartes's rigorous foundational binarism has dubious foundations. The autonomy of philosophy, geared to truth, depends on the baroque allegory of a writing subject "obsessed with fiction,"[37] who deploys heterogeneous modes—autobiographical, moral, metaphysical, scientific, and elegiac—as successively receding frames to an authorial self-portrait of the author, itself nothing more than a frame. The ambiguous author as subject, insisting that with him, philosophy enters a radically new epoch, establishes crisis as the normal mode of modernism. Descartes's effort to ground philosophy anew guaranteed its instability.

Philosophical ideas are not disjoined from political history. The spatial isotopy, essential to the constitutive binarism of Cartesian subjectivity, is a defining reality of the nation-state. The state is that form of human community that exercises "the monopoly of the legitimate use of physical force *within a given territory*."[38] The cookie cutter of modern statehood rests on precise territorial delineations. Within them, each state applies its quotient of self-legitimated violence. Beyond its borders, any particular state practices violence without that self-legitimation: for any specific state, the geographical expanse beyond its borders is the space of delegitimized violence, that is, barbarism.[39] That binary topology—"our" civilized space, the Other's "barbaric" space—licenses all barbarous activities beyond "our" borders, in overt colonialism and conquest, in the fire-bombing of Dresden, in the rape of My Lai, in the economic colonialism of (post)modern capitalism that goes under the name of "globalization." That "barbarian" space is now formally governed by another sovereignty is a face-saving supplement.

The "rational civility" of philosophy depends on its inclusion within the organized space of a disciplined, legitimated violence, which reciprocally legitimates philosophy's claim to nonviolence. Descartes, whose method stresses order, rule, and discipline, claims that his thinking substance requires no place or other material thing to exist. He makes that claim, however, a page after specifying that the solitary and withdrawn life within which the discourse on method was developed, depended on the well-ordered discipline of the Dutch armies that guaranteed peace and security while he wrote.[40] Philosophy depends on the political border "between internal civility and external barbarity": it is ontologically a dependent protopod of the state, whose borders both exclude and extrude legitimized violence against barbarism. Philosophy attempts to recast itself in a self-possession abstracted from violence. Descartes attempted to reconstitute philosophy by its/his own bootstraps, abstracted from a passable world in which the *res cogitans* was the condition of personal thought, in a rejection of history and memory, as the very ground of knowledge and action on a world of "external" extension.[41]

Not without an "hypothec," however. Possession, in itself an illegitimate claim on extension, is secured by barbaric violences which may be profitable and afford an improved standard of living for some; it does not leave unscathed the self-assurance of philosophy. Methodological doubt figures self-doubt: philosophy pays its debt to the state in installing dubiety as a fundamental condition of the thought which inhabits the extension protected by the "border." The border becomes an object of anxiety, protecting an "interior" sustained by a lawless violence beyond the border, reflected back into civil society as internalized doubt and insecurity. The geographical border divides philosophical discourse from the practices of violence, as well as the autonomy of disciplines and faculties, to be defended with appropriate violences. Hence the disquiet of disciplines before the violences of interdisciplinary thought.

The "border" makes possible institutionalized thought within territorial confines that guarantee the relative autonomy of the bounded nation-state and the equally bounded individual subject. Max Weber problematized both as aspects of modernity. In "a resolutely historicist vein," he argued for "a new conception of freedom, a new personality, a new subjectivity."[42] But he warned that the pursuit of subjectivity is inherently dangerous, particularly in relation to political life. Whoever wants to engage in politics "lets himself in for the diabolical forces lurking in all violence." In the face of political forces, the subject will be driven to say: "'Here I stand; I can do no other.'"[43] Writing these words as a quotation, the theoretician of bureaucracy re-marked the decisionary aporia of subjectivity sketched out by the *bailli* of Clermont.

The hypothec resulting from the philosophical subject's claimed autonomy within state borders holding at bay the violences that maintain political borders, implies the reproduction of political violence. If Descartes installs systematic doubt and hesitation, his procedure reproduces the aporia of political history at the very heart and goal of philosophy. The absolute certainty aimed at as the foundation of a new philosophy parallels the absoluteness of Louis XIV's monarchy, encapsulated in the assertion that seemingly liberates the king from all traditional institutional restraints: "L'état, c'est moi." Louis's absolutism replayed Descartes's philosophical transcendence of history. It endows the modernity of subjectivity with an ideology of absolute self-determination—the modern understanding of "freedom"—which not only flies in the face of common sense and experience: it also leads to modernity's permanent crisis.

Historicism: Sacred/Profane

The continuity of the subject raises the question of the sacred, the profane, and the model of "secularization" of culture and society implicit in "the disenchantment of the world."[44] The two models cited at the threshold of this study, from Benedict of Nursia and the Oaths of Strasbourg, seem to identify the subject with the secular, while the subject of obedient subjection is religious. This is not entirely false, but it is not entirely correct either. Within the church itself, subjects found ground for contradiction, dissent, and differentiation. The rights of the subject are discussed by William of Ockham in the context of the contradictory claims of monarchy and papacy, around 1335–40. He argues that subjects have a right to know the nature of the power that is set over them, a matter understood only through arguments, assertions, questions, objections, answers, studies, and other modes of inquiry. Only through such free inquiry can the subjects learn the extent of the pope's powers, and to what point they must obey the sovereign pontiff. The pope must not be indignant that scholars inquire into his powers:

> Subjects have the right to know the nature and extent of the pope's power over them . . . so that they are not subjected more than is necessary.[45]

Subjection is a condition of life in this world. The degree, the nature, and the comprehensibility of subjection—its theory—are not given, but grounds of inquiry and struggle, defying the pope to name his limitations as pope.

Lay people for the most part continued to think themselves Christians, even when their practices bear values distant from modern ideals of Christianity. Our retrospective view imposes all too readily a binary categorization, assuming that such and such an activity must have been *either* profane *or* sacred. It is not at all clear, however, that medievals experienced that binarism as patent.[46] The opposition between the laity and the clericality (including all religious orders) was fundamental and reinforced by the Gregorian reforms. But it did not have the same status of meaning as in modernity. Rather than refer to doctrinal belief or its absence, it had more to do with a mode of life. Had the individual submitted to a ritual ordination? Was he or she living "in the world," or in a religious community? The distinctions might be mobile: they were not erased for all that. It can reasonably be assumed that, within Europe, outside the Jewish communities, most individuals would have been likely to self-identify as "Christians" . . . allowing that the specific content of that label could be enormously varied.[47]

Paradoxically, the church itself can be thought to have initiated desacralization, insofar as its critical vocation led it to recognize that the sacred occupies a *limited* sphere, to be examined in a rigorous and disciplined manner by a specific "science" named "theology." The term itself dates from the twelfth century, apparently invented by a thinker whose major contributions were not theological at all: Peter Abelard, an outsider in more ways than one. The identification of a field of thought, a problem, or an individual person as separate and autonomous from a cotext implicitly recognizes its epistemic separability and susceptibility to critique. That said, the question of religion is rarely raised by the texts here, and then only occasionally and ritually. After the *Saint Alexis*, the major exception is Philippe de Beaumanoir. Whether religion, in these cases, functions as anything more than the name of a superior lord, is not the question. Religion, here, creates the contradiction which forces subjective choice on the person. It does not produce automatic submission, nor does secularity automatically produce subjectivity or freedom. Far from it . . .

Overall, religion does not intrude. It functions largely as an assumption, held somewhere "off-stage." Christianity, the Divine, occur only as formalities in *De Scaccario* or in Grosseteste's "*reules*" on governing a noble manor. The marriage of Yvain and Laudine is performed without religious interference, except that clerics waste candles: it is not thereby antireligious. Absence is not denial or rejection. The suspension of the category of religion does not make of these texts anti-Christian writings. For all practical purposes, most of the narratives discussed in these pages suspend religion.

In the dialectic of history, this suspension does not install the texts as doctrinally "lay," dedicated to an antireligious secularism. The possibility of such a suspension, however, does establish nameless islands of the profane, before that category's separateness from the religious is overtly, consciously acknowledged: before its "ontologization." That bracketing may not permanently remove the text or practice in question from its philosophical immanence, but it opens the possibility of a retrospective vision of historical presentism which sees, in that suspension or bracketing, the initiating gesture of a new profanity, a new secularism, more active and more self-conscious later than in its initiation. On that basis, even in a period ideologically designated as "Christian," textual archipelagos and practices become visible which ultimately gave rise to a recognition of the secular as distinct from the religious . . . in spite of underground survivals.

Bracketing religion and the divine allowed epistemic spaces in which developed technical analyses of grammar, rhetoric, dialectic, and poetics; the financial processes required both by commerce and the construction and expansion of the state; fictional representations of lay concerns with power, violence, and erotic affective bonds; the understanding of the manor as a social cell with its own internal structure and processes. They imply a growing epistemic distinction that ends by constructing a de facto domain of secularity in thought and imagination. At first, the secular inheres in the religious, the profane in the sacred. The religious construction of the divine initially harbors and nourishes the secular and the profane. By dint of repetition and critique, they grow into a separateness of culture and ideology, proleptically traced by the ecclesiastical distinction between lay and clerical.

Any simple binarism of a modern profane against a medieval religiosity is also undermined from the other end. Contemporary thinkers, turning to students of the past,[48] are beginning to realize what some of the latter have long understood, that a complex, sinuous continuity obtains between the two. It is recognizable only to a retrospective view willing to assume, in its examination of the past, the responsibility of identifying the initiation of processes that eventually produce the present. As against a historicism which refuses to recognize what the past did not understand about itself, a certain presentism is required. Contemporary thinkers view with increasing skepticism notions of radical secularism, of desacralization, of the world's "disenchantment." Such views, which supposedly mark the break with a Christian religiosity, can themselves be seen as too Christian.[49] The discussion, unfortunately, tends to continue a constitutive essentialism. What is not discussed is the *degree* to which the process of "secularization" actually gets away from its theological origins. Does bearing a trace of the past reconvert the subject to that past completely? Does that trace corrupt the bearer entirely, by a kind of historical metonymy? Is "purity" a criterion to be imposed on history? Is an epistemological break ultimately conceivable? Can gradations or complex involutions be tracked? These questions, and others like them, cannot be addressed without a thoughtfully proportionate mixture of historicism and presentism.

The related binarisms of medieval/modern, of sacred/profane, do not state mutually exclusive contraries. The medieval inheres in and continues to vivify and entrap the modern; structures of sacrality worm their way into the practices of the profane. So did they earlier. When medieval vintners hawked the price of their wine in the nave of Chartres Cathedral,[50] it had less to do with wine as symbol of sacrality than the financial loss of its impending turn into vinegar at the end of the season. The question is not an "either-or," but rather the degree to which the inherence of the other vitiates either term, the degree to which "spectrality" dispels identity.[51] What needs to be addressed is not a terminological purity to ground their essential absoluteness, but the necessary bifocalism required by the fact that our cognitive categories distinguish aspects of practices that were less perfectly separate for their practitioners. Both categories must be brought to bear as practices are examined that did not recognize the distinction. Analytic categories are not existentially exclusive. Pure unity belongs to models: applied to social history, it is always a figment of the imaginary.

This recognition of purity as imaginary is also what makes of epistemological returns to originary purity under the guise of historicism so many fictions. The recapture of a past in itself, without corruption of the present, is a self-delusional daydream in scholarship, as it is in politics. Something happens in history, which can no longer be denominated simply as "progress," but which changes the board we play on. That change is necessarily arguable, but its *différance* has always already occurred, and ineluctably places obstacles between us and that strange object of desire, an originary past of transcendent, Edenic purity. A constitutive obstacle is our own situatedness outside that object of desire and study. Epistemologically, our origins are *inter feces and urinam*, never pure, always torsious.

It is that *différance* between the medieval and the modern which grounds their resemblances as uncannily discomfiting to modern identity. Descartes's foundation of modernity reenacts Christianity's claim at a radical newness, in the very fact of differentiation. The absoluteness of both legitimates a crusading expansionism in philosophical revolution as in the recapture of Jerusalem or the colonialism of early capitalism. *What* is asked of the subject is historically specific; the *structure* of the modern subject is not radically different in nature from subjectivities adumbrated, constructed, and formulated in the Middle Ages.

The hiker realizes his trails, signed and mapped, reworks the trail of deer, which re-marked the trail of smaller animals. The modern subject—a posttextual construct—retraverses paths of violence, rationality, and governance for the extraction of power and profit laid down in the Middle Ages' practices and ideologies. Its vaunted freedom is a structural feature of un-reliable representation within the constitutive framework of the state. Our discomfiture, our guilt and anxiety, our helplessness at the machinations of systems and officials of power, devolve from structures of subjective con-sciousness rooted in the continuing medieval construction of modernity. Within this paradoxicality, which readily turns into a sense of impending tragedy, the attentive reader repeatedly stumbles across the thirst, among multiple and oppressive determinations of subjectivity, the parched, un-ending thirst, in the records of the past, for human peace and freedom.

Notes

INTRODUCTION

1. Paul Viollet, *Histoire des institutions politiques et administratives de la France, 1890–1903*; cited in *Mediaeval Contributions to Modern Civilization*, ed. F. J. C. Hearnshaw (London: George Harrap, 1921; rpt. New York: Barnes and Noble, 1967), p. 212.

2. Jacques Derrida, *Politics of Friendship*, tr. George Collins (London: Verso, 1997), p. 162; referring to Carl Schmitt, *Political Theology*, tr. George Schwab (Cambridge, Mass.: MIT Press, 1985).

3. Joseph R. Strayer, *On the Medieval Origins of the Modern State* (Princeton, N.J.: Princeton University Press, 1970).

4. Harold J. Berman, *Law and Revolution: The Formation of the Western Legal Tradition* (Cambridge, Mass.: Harvard University Press, 1983), passim, esp. 113–15.

5. Giles Constable, *The Reformation of the Twelfth Century* (Cambridge: Cambridge University Press, 1996–98), p. 301.

6. Peter Brown, "Society and the Supernatural: A Medieval Change," *Daedalus* 104, no. 2 (1975): 133–51.

7. Fredric L. Cheyette, "The Invention of the State," in *Essays on Medieval Civilization*, ed. Bede Karl Lackner and Kenneth Roy Philp (Austin: University of Texas Press, 1978), pp. 143–78.

8. Emile Benveniste, *Problèmes de linguistique générale*, 2 vols. (Paris: Gallimard, 1966), 1:260.

9. Medbh McGuckian, "Harem Trousers," in *On Ballycastle Beach* (Oxford: Oxford University Press, 1988).

10. Jacques Lacan, "Le stade du miroir comme formateur de la fonction du Je," *Ecrits*, 2 vols. (Paris: Seuil, 1966), 1:89–97.

11. In contrast, see Žižek account of the Lacanian "authentic act": "From 'Passionate Attachments' to Dis-Identification," *UMBR(a)* 1 (1998): 3–18.

12. Louis Althusser, "Ideology and Ideological State Apparatuses," *Lenin and Philosophy* (New York: Monthly Review/NLB, 1970), pp. 127–86.

13. Michel Foucault, esp. "The Subject and Power," in *Michel Foucault, Beyond Structuralism and Hermeneutics*, ed. Hubert L. Dreyfus and Paul Rabinow (Chicago: University of Chicago Press, 1982), pp. 208–26; and the four volumes of the *History of Sexuality*.

14. Gayatri Chakravorty Spivak, "Subaltern Studies: Deconstructing Historiography," in *In Other Worlds: Essays in Cultural Politics* (London: Routledge, 1987–88), pp. 197–221, 204.

15. Ernesto Laclau and Chantal Mouffe, *Hegemony and Socialist Strategy* (London: Verso, 1985).

16. Haidu, "Althusser Anonymous . . . ," *Exemplaria* 7 (1995): 55–74.

17. Alain Badiou, *Théorie du sujet* (Paris: Seuil, 1982), p. 275.

18. Judith Butler, *The Psychic Life of Power* (Stanford, Calif.: Stanford University Press, 1997), p. 197.

19. Slavoj Žižek, *The Ticklish Subject* (London: Verso, 1999), p. 257.

20. See particularly Alexandre Leupin, *Barbarolexis* (Cambridge, Mass.: Harvard University Press, 1989).

21. Fredric M. Jameson, "Third World Literature in the Era of Multinational Capital," *Social Text* (fall 1986): 65–88.

22. Aijaz Ahmad, "Jameson's Rhetoric of Otherness and the 'National Allegory' (1987)," *Social Text* 17 (1987); rpt. in Terry Eagleton and Drew Milne, eds., *Marxist Literary Theory* (Oxford: Blackwell, 1988), pp. 375–98.

23. Haidu, "Realism, Convention, Fictionality and the Theory of Genres in *Le Bel Inconnu*," *L'Esprit Créateur* 12 (1972): 37–60. 24. Haidu, "Narrative Structure in *Floire et Blancheflor*: A Comparison with Two Romances of Chrétien de Troyes," *Romance Notes* 14 (1972): 1–4.

25. Compare Jacques le Goff, *Pour un autre Moyen Age: Temps travail et culture en Occident: 18 essais* (Paris: Gallimard, 1977); English edition: *Time, Work, and Culture in the Middle Ages*, tr. Arthur Goldhammer (Chicago: University of Chicago Press, 1980), to Jacques le Goff, *Un autre Moyen Age* (Paris: Gallimard [Quarto], 1999).

26. In the long view of French history, the "nation" and "civil society" alike are products of the state.

27. Walter Benjamin, "Critique of Violence," in *Reflections*, tr. Edmund Jephcott (New York: Harcourt Brace Jovanovich, 1978), pp. 277–300; Jacques

Derrida, *Force de loi* (Paris: Galilée, 1994); Giorgio Agamben, *Homo Sacer*, tr. Daniel Heller-Roazen (Stanford, Calif.: Stanford University Press, 1998).

CHAPTER 1

1. "*Nullus in monasterio proprii sequatur cordis uoluntatem, neque praesumat quisquam cum abbate suo proterue aut foris monasterium contendere*" (Adalbert de Vogüé and Jean Neufville, *La règle de saint Benoît*, 7 vols. [*Source chrétiennes: Série des textes monastiques d'Occident, no. 34*] [Paris: Cerf, 1972]), vol. 1, ch. 3, pp. 8–9, 454.

2. Theodor Adorno, *Negative Dialectics*, tr. E. B. Ashton (New York: Continuum, 1973–85), p. 277.

3. Giles Constable, "Liberty and Free Choice in Monastic Thought and Life, especially in the Eleventh and Twelfth Centuries," *La notion de liberté au Moyen Age Islam, Byzance, Occident*, ed. George Makdisi, Dominique Sourdel, and Janine Sourdel-Thomine (Paris: Les Belles Lettres, 1985), pp. 99–118, p. 106.

4. Yves Delègue, *Les machine du sens: Fragments d'une sémiologie médiévale* (Paris: Editions des Cendres, 1987), p. 28.

5. *Nithardi historiarum libri IV*, 3d ed., E. Müller, *Monumenta Germaniae historica, Scriptores regnum Germanicarum in usum scholarum ex monumentis Germaniae historicis recusi* (Hanover/Leipzig, 1907), 3:5; tr. Bernhard Walter Scholz and Barbara Rogers, *Carolingian Chronicles* (Ann Arbor: University of Michigan Press, 1972–95), p. 161. On the Oaths, see Renée Balibar, *L'institution du français: Essai sur le colinguisme des Carolingiens à la République* (Paris: PUF, 1985), pp. 78–81; Bernard Cerquiglini, *La naissance du français* (Paris: PUF, 1991), pp. 68–84; and Susume Kudo, "La naissance d'une langue nationale: Réflexions politico-linguistiques sur les Serments de Strasbourg," *Il miglior fabbro . . . Mélanges Pierre Bec* (Poitiers: University of Poitiers, 1991), pp. 273–84, 275.

6. Compare with Jacques Derrida, *The Ear of the Other*, ed. Christie McDonald, tr. Peggy Kamuf (Lincoln: University of Nebraska Press, 1988), p. 125.

7. Dismissal of the Oaths as mere literary conceit disregards their political implications in order to resacralize Latin, the historian's primary-source language: Rosamond McKitterick, "Latin and Romance: An Historian's Perspective," in *Latin and the Romance Languages in the Early Middle Ages*, ed. Roger Wright (University Park: Pennsylvania State University Press, 1991–96), pp. 130–45.

8. Jeanette M. A. Beer, *Early Prose in France: Contexts of Bilingualism and*

Authority (Kalamazoo: Western Michigan University, Medieval Institute Publications, 1992), pp. 15–36.

9. Philippe Contamine, "La segmentation féodale," in *Histoire militaire de la France*, vol. 1: *Des origines à 1715* (Paris: PUF, 1992), pp. 43–76.

10. Jan Dhondt, *Etude sur la naissance des principautés territoriales en France (IXe–Xe siècles)* (Bruges: Rijksuniversiteit te Gent, Werken uitgegeven door de Faculteit van de Wijsbegeerte en Letteren, 102: 1948).

11. Contamine, p. 45.

12. Marc Bloch's epochal work: *La société féodale* (Paris: Albin Michel, 1939).

13. Roger Berger, *Le nécrologe de la confrérie des jongleurs et des bourgeois d'Arras*, 2 vols. (Arras: Commission Départmentale des Monuments historiques du Pas-de-Calais, 1970), 2:241, n. 11.

14. "*L'encellulement*": see Robert Fossier, "La naissance du village," in *Le roi de France et son royaume autour de l'an mil*, ed. Michel Parisse et Xavier Barral i Altet (Paris: Picard, 1992) ("Actes du Colloque Hugues Capet 987–1987, La France de l'an Mil," Paris-Senlis, June 22–25, 1987), pp. 219–21; and Robert Fossier, *La société médiévale* (Paris: Armand Colin, 1991), pp. 196–99; and *L'enfance de l'Europe*, 2 vols. (Paris: PUF, 1982), 2:288–601.

15. See Jean-Claude Schmitt, *Les revenants. Les vivants et les morts dans la société médiévale* (Paris: Gallimard, 1994); Patrick J. Geary, *Living with the Dead in the Middle Ages* (Ithaca, N.Y.: Cornell University Press, 1994); and Patrick J. Geary, *Phantoms of Remembrance: Memory and Oblivion at the End of the First Millennium* (Princeton, N.J.: Princeton University Press, 1994).

16. Jacques Derrida, *Spectres de Marx* (Paris: Galilée, 1993), p. 177, emphasis added.

17. "*Nudi pontifices sine fine sequantur aratrum/Carmina cum stimulo primi cantando parentis*" (Adalbéron de Laon, *Poème au roi Robert*, ed. Claude Carozzi [Paris: Les Belles Lettres, 1979], l. 41f.).

18. Michel Mollat and Philippe Wolff, *Ongles bleus, Jacques et Ciompi* (Paris: Calman-Léuy, 1970), pp. 192–94.

19. Rodney Hilton, *Bond Men Made Free: Medieval Peasant Movements and the English Rising of 1381* (New York: Viking, 1973), p. 211.

20. Johan Huizinga, *The Waning of the Middle Ages* (Garden City, N.Y.: Doubleday Anchor, 1954), p. 53.

21. See Paul Freedman, *Images of the Medieval Peasant* (Stanford, Calif.: Stanford University Press, 1999).

22. Georges Duby, *Guerriers et paysans* (Paris: Gallimard, 1973).

23. Robert Bartlett, *The Making of Europe, Conquest, Colonization and*

Cultural Change 950–1350 (Princeton, N.J.: Princeton University Press, 1993), pp. 86ff.

24. "Tesaurus, uestis cunctis sunt pascua serui./ Nam ualet ungenuus sine seruis uiuere nullus./ Cum labor occurit sumptus et habere peroptant,/ Rex et pontifices seruus seruire uidentur./ Pascitur a seruo dominus quem pascere sperat" (Adalbéron de Laon, *Poème du roi Robert,* ll. 289–93).

25. Carolyn Webber and Aaron Wildavsky, *A History of Taxation and Expenditure in the Western World* (New York: Simon and Schuster, 1986), p. 174.

26. A classic description is that of F. L. Ganshof, *Qu'est-ce-que la féodalité?* (Brussels: Office de Publicité, 1957); major critiques are those of Alain Gerreau, *Le feudalisme: Un horizon théorique* (Paris: Le Sycomore, 1980); and Susan Reynolds, *Fiefs and Vassals: The Medieval Evidence Re-interpreted* (Oxford: Oxford University Press, 1994); further references in Haidu, *The Subject of Violence* (Bloomington: Indiana University Press, 1993), p. 220f., n. 26.

27. Robert Fossier, *L'enfance de l'Europe,* 2 vols. (Paris: PUF, 1982), 2:956.

28. Joseph R. Strayer, "The Two Levels of Feudalism," in *Life and Thought in the Early Middle Ages,* ed. R. S. Hoyt (Minneapolis: University of Minnesota Press, 1967); Dominique Barthélémy, *La société dans le comté de Vendôme de l'an mil au XIVe siècle* (Paris: Fayard, 1993), p. 362.

29. Fossier, *La société médiévale,* p. 199.

30. Dominique Barthélémy, "La crise châtelaine des principautés," in *L'ordre seigneurial XI-XIIe siècle,* vol. 3: "Nouvelle Histoire de la France Médiévale" (Paris: Seuil, 1990), pp. 13–51.

31. Eric Bournazel and Jean-Pierre Poly, *La mutation féodale* (Paris: PUF, 1980).

32. Georges Duby, *La société aux XIe et XIIe siècles dans la région mâconnaise* (Paris: SEVPEN, 1971).

33. Webber and Wildavsky, p. 214.

34. *Bede, coustuma, questa; exactio, tonsio, tolta, tallia.*

35. *The New Science of Gianbattista Vico . . . ,* tr. Thomas G. Bergin and Max H. Fisch (Ithaca, N.Y.: Cornell University Press, 1948), p. 105.

36. Bloch, *La société féodale,* pp. 566–69.

37. Philippe Contamine, *Histoire militaire de la France,* vol. I: *Des origines à 1715,* ed. Philippe Contamine (Paris: PUF, 1992), p. 75f.

38. In addition to Georges Duby's bibliography, major works most immediately pertinent are: Pierre Bonnassie, *La Catalogne du milieu du Xe à la fin du XIe siècle* (Toulouse: Publications de l'Université de Toulouse-Le Mirail, 1975); Eric Bournazel and Jean-Pierre Poly, *La mutation féodale* (Paris: PUF, 1980); and

Thomas N. Bisson, *Tormented Voices: Power, Crisis, and Humanity in Rural Catalonia 1140–1200* (Cambridge, Mass.: Harvard University Press, 1998).

39. They include a rejoinder by Poly and Bournazel ("Que faut-il préférer au 'mutationnisme'? ou le problème du changement social," *Revue historique de droit français et étranger* 4th ser., no. 72 [1994]); a substantive article by Thomas Bisson ("The 'Feudal Revolution,'" *Past and Present* 142 [Feb. 1994]: 6–42); a rejoinder by Barthélémy in the same journal (ibid., p. 152 [1996]: 197–205); a contribution by Stephen D. White (ibid., 205–23), who also contributes a thoughtful review article of Barthélémy's *La société dans le comté de Vendôme* (*Speculum* 71 [1996]: 116–20), only to differ finally in accepting the necessary category of "violence," even if "very reluctantly." Most recently, see Barthélémy, *La mutation de l'an mil a-t-elle eu lieu? Servage et chevalerie dans la France du Xe et du XIe siècles* (Paris: Fayard, 1997).

40. Barthélémy, *La société dans le comté de Vendôme*, pp. 351, 423, 1006f.

41. Patrick J. Geary, "Vivre en conflit dans une France sans état: Typologie des mécanismes de règlement des conflits, 1050–1200," *Annales ESC* 41 (1986): 1107–33; now in Geary, *Living with the Dead*, pp. 125–60.

42. Barthélémy, *La société dans le comté de Vendôme*, p. 1006f; emphasis added.

43. Geary, *Living with the Dead*, p. 160; emphasis added.

44. Barthélémy's alternative to "violence": *La mutation*. Duby prefers "violence" to "brutality": *An 1000 an 2000 sur les traces de nos peurs* (Paris: Textuel, 1995).

45. Ratherius Veronensis, *Praeloquia*, 4, 15, ed. Peter L. D. Reid, *CCCM* 46A (1984): 119; cited in John Van Engen, "Sacred Sanctions for Lordship," in *Cultures of Power: Lordship, Status and Process in Twelfth-Century Europe*, ed. Thomas N. Bishop (Philadelphia: University of Pennsylvania Press, 1995), pp. 203–30, p. 204.

46. Barthélémy, *La mutation*, p. 83.

47. Olivier Guillot, "La liberté des nobles et des roturiers dans la France du XIe siècle: L'exemple de leur soumission à la justice," *La notion de liberté au Moyen Age: Islam, Byzane, Occident*, ed. Georges Makdisi, Dominique Sourdel, and Janine Sourdel-Thomine (Paris: Société d'Édition les Belles Lettres, 1985), pp. 155–67.

48. Max Gluckman, *Custom and Conflict in Africa* (Oxford: Oxford University Press, 1956), pp. 1–26; cited by Thomas Head and Richard Landes, "Introduction," *The Peace of God: Social Violence and Religious Response in France Around the Year 1000* (Ithaca, N.Y.: Cornell University Press, 1992), p. 16.

49. Renato Rosaldo, *Ilongot Headhunting, 1883–1974: A Study in Society*

and History (Stanford, Calif.: Stanford University Press, 1980), p. 273; and Renato Rosaldo, *Culture and Truth: The Remaking of Social Analysis* (Boston: Beacon, 1989–93), on how grief and rage feed social relations of violence.

50. Pierre Clastres, "Archéologie de la violence: la guerre dans les sociétés primitives," *Libre* 1 (1977): 137–73; rpt. in *Recherches d'anthropologie politique* (Paris: Seuil, 1980), pp. 171–206.

51. "*Surprélèvement*": Barthélémy, *L'ordre seigneurial*, p. 97f.

52. Fossier, *La société médiévale*, p. 218.

53. See below, Chapter 2.

54. "*Foyers de violence*": Pierre Bonnassie, "Les paysans du royaume franc au temps d'Hugues Capet et de Robert li Pieux (987–1031), in *Le roi de France et son royaume autour de l'an mil*, ed. Michel Parisse and Xavier Barral i Altet (Paris: Picard, 1992) ("Actes du Colloque Hugues Capet 987–1987, La France de l'an Mil," Paris-Senlis, June 22–25, 1987), pp. 117–30.

55. W. W. Warren, *The Governance of Norman and Angevin England, 1086–1272* (London: Edward Arnold; Stanford, Calif.: Stanford University Press, 1987), p. 7f.

56. Fossier, *La société médiévale*, pp. 242–45.

57. *Cartulaire de Saint-Aubin d'Angers*, ed. B. de Broussillon, vol. 2, Sept. 17, p. 1138; cited by Bloch, *La société féodale*, p. 567, emphasis added.

58. Robert Jacob, "Le meurtre du seigneur dans la société féodale. La mémoire, le rite, la fonction," *Annales ESC 45* (1990): 247–63; Freedman, pp. 177–203.

59. Elisabeth Magnou-Nortier, "The Enemies of the Peace: Reflections on a Vocabulary, 500–1100," in *The Peace of God: Social Violence and Religious Response in France around the Year 1000*, ed. Thomas Head and Richard Landes (Ithaca, N.Y.: Cornell University Press, 1992), pp. 58–79. Barthélémy repeats his argument variously, esp. *La société dans le comté de Vendôme*.

60. Geary, "Vivre en conflit."

61. Dominique Barthélémy, "Qu'est-ce que la chevalerie en France aux Xe et XIe siècles?" *Revue historique 587* (July–Sept. 1993): 15–74.

62. Head and Landes.

63. Henri Dubois, "La paix au moyen âge," in *Les fondements de la paix. Des origines au début du XVIIIe siècle*, ed. Pierre Chaunu (Paris: PUF, 1993), pp. 95–108.

64. R. I. Moore, "Postscript: The Peace of God and the Social Revolution," in *The Peace of God: Social Violence and Religious Response in France around the Year 1000*, ed. Thomas Head and Richard Landes (Ithaca, N.Y.: Cornell University Press, 1992), pp. 308–26, referring to Barbara Rosenwein,

To Be Neighbor of St. Peter: The Social Meaning of Cluny's Property, 909–1049 (Ithaca, N.Y.: Cornell University Press, 1989), pp. 312, 315f.

65. Althusser characterized the opposition as that between repressive state apparatuses and ideological state apparatuses.

66. Timothy J. Reiss, *The Discourse of Modernism* (Ithaca, N.Y.: Cornell University Press, 1982), pp. 55–107.

67. Magnou-Nortier, pp. 58–79.

68. Barthélémy, *La société dans le comté de Vendôme*. Concerns with violence are repeatedly smeared as colonialist prejudice against non-Western populations, even when occurring in a thirteenth-century text such as the *La mort le roi Artu*! In other words, *La mort Artu*, ca. 1230, reflecting on the violence of its own society, is guilty of orientalism!

69. Stephen White, "The Feudal Revolution," *Past and Present* no. 142 (1994): 205–23, p. 210.

70. Ibid., p. 217, emphasis added.

71. Barthélémy, *La société dans le comté de Vendôme*, p. 351.

72. Dominique Barthélémy, "L'état contre le lignage: un thème à développer dans l'histoire des pouvoirs en France au XIe, XIIe, et XIIIe siècles," *Médiévales* 10 (1986): 37–50, p. 50, emphasis added.

73. Charles Tilly, *Coercion, Capital, and European States, AD 990–1992* (Oxford: Blackwell, 1990–92), p. 67.

74. Eric Hobsbawm, "Barbarism: A User's Guide," *New Left Review* 206 (1994): 44–54; see also Hobsbawm's *The Age of Extremes: The Short Twentieth Century, 1914–1991* (London: Michael Joseph, 1994).

75. Hobsbawm, "Barbarism."

76. For the last phrase: Barthélémy, *Past and Present*, p. 201.

77. Dominique Barthélémy, "La Paix de Dieu dans son contexte (989–1041)," *Cahiers de civilisation médiévale* 40 (1997): 3–35, p. 14.

78. Fossier, *L'enfance de l'Europe*, 2:952.

79. Bloch, *La société féodale*, p. 568.

80. Ibid.; Fossier, *La société médiévale*, p. 141f.

81. Georges Duby, *Le Dimanche de Bouvines* (Paris: Gallimard, 1973), p. 137.

82. Magnou-Nortier, pp. 58–79.

83. Latin *consuetudo* > Old French *cou[s]tume* > modern English *custom*.

84. Eric Hobsbawm and Terence Ranger, eds., *The Invention of Tradition* (Cambridge: Cambridge University Press, 1983).

85. Hans-Werner Goetz, "La paix de Dieu en France autour de l'an mil: Fondements et objectifs, diffusion et participants," in *Le roi de France et son royaume autour de l'an mil*, ed. Michel Parisse and Xavier Barral i Altet (Paris: Picard, 1992), pp. 131–45.

86. The technical term *inermes* designated, not the total absence of weapons, but restriction to nonknightly weapons. In fact, peasants did possess certain weapons: Bonnassie, "Les paysans du royaume franc," p. 121f.

87. Contamine, p. 51.

88. Guy Lobrichon, "The Chiaroscuro of Heresy: Early Eleventh-Century Aquitaine as seen from Auxerre," in *The Peace of God: Social Violence and Religious Response in France around the Year 1000*, ed. Thomas Head and Richard Landes (Ithaca, N.Y.: Cornell University Press, 1992), pp. 80–103.

89. White, 205–23.

90. Charroux: original texts in Giovanni Mansi, *Sacrorum conciliorum nova, et amplissima collectio*, 31 vols. (Florence and Venice, 1759–98); rev. and continued by J. Martin and L. Petit, 60 vols. (Paris, 1899–1927); reprinted Graz, 1961–present; translations in the Appendix to Head and Landes, pp. 327–42.

91. This is from a fairly late marginal council, called by the count of Barcelona in 1064: *The Usatges of Barcelona: The Fundamental Law of Catalonia*, tr. Donald J. Kagay (Philadelphia: University of Pennsylvania Press, 1994), p. 104.

92. Thomas Head and Richard Landes, "Document 6," tr. Richard Landes, in *The Peace of God: Social Violence and Religious Response in France around the Year 1000*, ed. Thomas Head and Richard Landes (Ithaca, N.Y.: Cornell University Press, 1992), pp. 332–34.

93. Bloch, *La société féodale*, p. 150f.

94. Head and Landes, p. 332f.

95. André Debord, "The Castellan Revolution and the Peace of God in Aquitaine," in *The Peace of God: Social Violence and Religious Response in France around the Year 1000*, ed. Thomas Head and Richard Landes (Ithaca, N.Y.: Cornell University Press, 1992), pp. 135–64, 157.

96. Contamine, p. 52.

97. *Die Entstehung des Kreuzzungsgedankens* (Stuttgart: W. Kohlhammer, 1935); cited by Head and Landes, p. 18.

98. Georges Duby, "Les laïcs et la paix de Dieu," *Hommes et structures du moyen âge* (The Hague: Mouton, 1973), pp. 227–40, 237.

99. Georges Duby, *Les trois ordres ou l'imaginaire du féodalisme* (Paris: Gallimard, 1978), p. 193. Barthélémy confuses "model" with "description."

100. Georges Duby, *Le Moyen Age, 987–1460: De Hugues Capet à Jeanne d'Arc (987–1460)* (Paris: Hachette, 1987), p. 218.

101. Edward Peters, ed. *The First Crusade* (Philadelphia: University of Pennsylvania Press, 1971), pp. 2–5.

102. Clerical attempts at direct, violent military countermeasures proved self-delegitimizing, as Aimon, archbishop of Bourges, learned. His social role as archbishop precluded the direct use of force: Andrew of Fleury, *Mirac. s. Benedicti*, in *The Peace of God: Social Violence and Religious Response in France around the Year 1000*, ed. Thomas Head and Richard Landes (Ithaca, N.Y.: Cornell University Press, 1992), pp. 339–42.

103. Robert Fossier, "Remarques sur l'étude des 'commotions' sociales aux XIe et XIIe siècles," *Cahiers de civilisation médiévale* 16 (1973): 45–50, 49f.

104. Frederick S. Paxton, "History, Historians, and the Peace of God," in *The Peace of God: Social Violence and Religious Response in France around the Year 1000*, ed. Thomas Head and Richard Landes (Ithaca, N.Y.: Cornell University Press, 1992), p. 38.

105. Barthélémy, "La paix de Dieu dans son contexte."

106. My debt to Louis Althusser's famous essay on ideology is obvious. The work is now available in its original context: *Sur la reproduction* (Paris: PUF, 1995).

107. Duby, *Guerriers et paysans*, p. 60.

108. Patrick J. Geary, ed., *Readings in Medieval History* (Peterboro, Ontario: Broadview Press, 1991), p. 404.

109. Reynolds, p. 20.

110. Geary, *Readings*, p. 405.

111. George Beech, Yves Chauvin, and Georges Pon, *Le conventum (vers 1030): Un précurseur aquitain des premières épopées* (Geneva: Droz, 1995); and Stephen D. White, "Stratégie rhétorique dans la *Conventio* d'Hugues de Lusignan," in *Mélanges offerts à Georges Duby*, 4 vols. (Aix-en-Provence: Publications de l'Université de Provence, 1992), 2:147–58.

112. Karl Marx, *The German Ideology* (Moscow: Progress, 1976), p. 190.

113. Karl Marx, *Capital*, 4 vols. (Moscow: Progress, 1954–77), 1:81f.

114. Jean-François Lyotard, *Le différend* (Paris: Minuit, 1983).

115. Jacques Derrida, "Archive Fever," *Diacritics* 25 (1995): 9–63, 13.

116. Which a contemporary theoretician now calls for as necessary but not yet existent in the first decade of the twenty-first century: Etienne Balibar, *Politics and the Other Scene*, tr. Christine Jones, James Swenson, and Chris Turner (London: Verso, 2002), p. xif.

117. Duby, *Les trois ordres . . .* , p. 188; *Guerriers et paysans . . .* , p. 60 and passim.

118. Contamine, *Histoire militaire de la France*, pp. 45–53.

CHAPTER 2

1. The word *romanz* initially means "in the vernacular," as opposed to Latin.

2. Auerbach imposed the nineteenth-century aesthetic of his subtitle on texts of all periods in *Mimesis: The Representation of Reality in Western Literature* (New York: Doubleday Anchor, 1957): it is especially damaging in "The Knight Sets Forth," pp. 107–24. Northrop Frye's typology in the *Anatomy of Literature* made "romance" nonpertinent for any serious consideration of history. That typology inspires Fredric Jameson's neo-Marxist criticism in *The Political Unconscious*.

3. John Dunbabin, *France in the Making 843–1180* (Oxford: Oxford University Press, 1985–91).

4. The convention here is that capitalized "Real" denotes representations referring to a putative, lowercase "real" which is not directly available.

5. "Bien les vit a esploit venir / et aprés lui du bois issir; / trestout le cuer l'em rit de joie" (*Le Roman de Thebes*, 2 vols., ed. Guy Raynaud de Lage [Paris: Champion, 1966], 1: ll. 3581–83).

6. "Qan vei per campaignas rengatz / cavalliers e cavals armatz. / E platz mi qan vei apres lor / granren d'armatz corren venir, / E platz m'e mon coratge / qan vei forz chastels assegatz / e.ls barris rotz et esfondratz, / e vei l'ost el ribatge / q'es tot entorn claus de fossatz, / ab lissas de fortz pals serratz" (Bertran de Born, "Be'm platz lo gais temps de pascor," text from *The Poems of the Troubadour Bertran de Born*, ed. William D. Paden Jr., Tilde Sankovitch, and Patricia H. Stäblein [Berkeley and Los Angeles: University of California Press, 1986], pp. 338–45; tr. Paul Blackburn, *Proensa: An Anthology of Troubadour Poetry*, ed. George Economou [Berkeley and Los Angeles: University of California Press, 1986], pp. 168ff. Blackburn used a different edition).

7. "Toute la terre vi plaine d'aversiers, / Viles ardoir et violer moustiers, / Chapeles fondre et rebuchier clochiers, / Mameles tortre a cortoises moilliers, / Que en mon cuer m'en prist si grant pitié, / Molt tendrement plorai des eulz del chief" (*Le Charroi de Nimes*, ed. J.-L. Perrier [Paris: Champion 1967], ll. 570–75).

8. "Ce jor chevalchent a force et a estri. / La veïsiez tant vent elme bruni; / Cuevrent les plaignes, la terre et li larri. / Li ardeor se sunt par devant mis; / Les coraors garde Isorez li gris; / Et li forrier corent par le païs. / Lieve la noise et enforce li cris. / Par[mi] ces chanz veïsiez genz fuïr, / Ces pastoriax lor vaches acoillir; / Es bors se tiennent, ilec quident garir; / Ce ne vaut rien, que trop furent sospris. / Li coraor ont partot le feu mis / Dedenz ces viles et la fumee en ist. / Les proies chacent et mainnent vilain pris. / La gent s'escrie, si esforce

li cris. / Jusqu'a Canbrai ne sunt mie alentis; / A .i. liue ont li bordiax espris. / Li apiax sone, li citez s'estormist. . . . / Li s[en]eschax a la fenestre en vint, / Parmmi la plainne vit chevaliers venir / Et les vers elmes flanboier et luisir; / Vit toz les chanz des chevaliers covrir; / Par ces champaignes vit les proies saisir, / Asnes et bués et prendre et retenir; / Vit le feu metre et la flame saillir, / Ces pastoriax et [ces] vilains fuïr" (Josephine Elvira Vallerie, ed., *Garin le Loheren* [Ann Arbor, Mich.: Edwards Brothers, 1947], ll. 2945–79).

9. Matthew Bennett, "Wace and Warfare," in *Anglo-Norman Warfare, Studies in Late Anglo-Saxon and Anglo-Norman Military Organization and Warfare*, ed. Matthew Strickland (Woodbridge, Eng.: Boydell, 1992), pp. 230–50.

10. "Tenez al rei d'Escoce la fiance afiee! / Qu'il vus aït de guerre, hastif, / senz demuree, / Destruice voz enemis e guaste lur cuntree: / Par fu e par enbrasement tute seit alumee! / Ne lur laist defors chastels, n'en forest ne en pree, / Dunt il puissent al matin aveir une disnee; . . . / Issi deit l'em cumencier guerre—ço m'est vis— / Primes guaster la terre e puis ses enemis" (*Jordan Fantosme's Chronicle*, ed. R. C. Johnston [Oxford: Oxford University Press, 1981], ll. 441–50).

11. "Alez par cest païs ardant, / maisons e viles destruiant, / pernez la robe e la vitaille, / porz e oeilles e aumaille, / que Normant vitaille ne troissent / ne nule rien donc vivre poissent" (*Le Roman de Rou de Wace*, ed. A. J. Holden, 3 vols. [Paris: Picard, 1971], 3:6927–32).

12. John Gillingham, "Richard I and the Science of War in the Middle Ages," in *War and Government in the Middle Ages*, ed. John Gillingham and J. C. Holt (Cambridge, Eng.: Boydell, 1984), pp. 78–91, 84.

13. Michael Prestwich, *Armies and Warfare in the Middle Ages: The English Experience* (New Haven, Conn.: Yale University Press, 1996), p. 198.

14. *De re militari*, 69; quoted by Gillingham, pp. 78–91.

15. Prestwich, pp. 1–10.

16. Bennett, p. 232.

17. "Dunc pristrent la terre a destruire; . . . / Maisuns ardent, viles destruient; / Les chevaliers e les vilains, / Les clers, les muines, les nuneins, / Batent e chacent e ocient; / La lei Damnedeu cuntralient. / Mult veïssiez terre eissillier, / Femmes hunir, humes percier, / Enfanz en berz esbüeler, / Aveirs saisir, preies mener, / Turs abatre, viles ardeir" (*Brut*, ll. 13,473–87; p. 233).

18. John Gillingham, "War and Chivalry in the *History of William the Marshal*," in *Anglo-Norman Warfare: Studies in Late Anglo-Saxon and Anglo-Norman Military Organization and Warfare*, ed. Matthew Strickland (Woodbridge, Eng.: Boydell, 1992), pp. 251–63, 256.

19. Ibid.

20. "Kar riches sunt d'almaille, de bofs e de chevals, / E dels bels vaches, de brebiz, e d'aigneaus, / De dras, et de muneie, de nusches, e d'eneaus" (Fantosme, ll. 1182–84).

21. Maurice Keen, "Chivalry, Nobility and the Man-at-Arms," in *War, Literature and Politics in the Late Middle Ages*, ed. C. T. Allmand (Liverpool: Liverpool University Press, 1976), p. 45.

22. John R. E. Bliese, "The Just War as Concept and Motive in the Central Middle Ages," *Medievalia et Humanistica* 17 (1991): 1–26. See also Frederick Russel, *The Just War in the Middle Ages* (Cambridge: Cambridge University Press, 1975).

23. Augustine, *Contra Faustum*, 22.74; Bliese, p. 9.

24. Chichester's burning (*Brut*, ll. 13,533–624); regarding the civil war, see *Brut*, ll. 2,712–839.

25. Benoît de Sainte-Maure, *Le Roman de Troie*, 6 vols., ed. Léopold Constans (Paris: Firmin-Didiot "Société des Anciens Textes Français," 1904–12), 2:ll. 12,803–13,064.

26. *Sämtliche Lieder des Trobadors Giraut de Bornelh*, ed. A. Kolsen (Halle: M. Niemeyer, 1910), n. 65, pp. 414–15; Gillingham, "War and Chivalry," p. 262.

27. Honoré Bonet, *The Tree of Battles*, ed. G. W. Coopland (Cambridge: Cambridge University Press, 1949), p. 189; cited by Gillingham, "War and Chivalry," p. 263.

28. Bertrand is William's sidekick.

29. "Prennent les chars et les bués et les tones. / Li bon vilain qui les font et conjoignent / Ferment les tonnes et les charrues doublent. / Bertran ne chaut se li vilain en grocent: / Tieus en parla qui puis en ot grant honte, / Perdi les eulz et pendi par la goule" (ibid., ll. 959–63).

30. Thomas N. Bisson, *Tormented Voices: Power, Crisis and Humanity in Rural Catalonia, 1140–1200* (Cambridge, Mass.: Harvard University Press, 1998).

31. Ibid., p. 29.

32. Jacques le Goff, *La civilisation de l'Occident médiéval* (Paris: Arthaud, 1964), p. 373.

33. Rodney Hilton, *Bond Men Made Free: Medieval Peasant Movements and the English Rising of 1381* (New York: Viking, 1973); and Rodney Hilton, *Class Conflict and the Crisis of Feudalism* (London: Verso, 1985–90).

34. Eric J. Goldberg, "Popular Revolt, Dynastic Politics, and Aristocratic Factionalism in the Early Middle Ages: The Saxon *Stellinga* Reconsidered," *Speculum* 70 (1995): 467–501.

35. See also Paul Freedman, *Images of the Medieval Peasant* (Stanford, Calif.: Stanford University Press, 1999).

36. Hilton, *Bond Men Made Free*, p. 71.

37. Guillaume de Jumiéges, *Gesta Normannorum*, ed. Jean Merx (Rouen/Paris: Lestringant, 1914), col. 823–4; Pierre Bonnassie, "Les paysans du royaume franc au temps d'Hugues Capet et de Robert li Pieux (987–1031), in *Le roi de France et son royaume autour de l'an mil*, ed. Michel Parisse and Xavier Barral i Altet (Paris: Picard, 1992) ("Actes du Colloque Hugues Capet 987–1987, La France de l'an Mil," Paris-Senlis, June 22–25, 1987), pp. 117–30.

38. *Chronique des ducs de Normandie par Benoît*, ed. Carin Fahlin, 4 vols. (Uppsala: Almqvist and Wiksells; Wiesbaden: Otto Harrassowitz; The Hague: Martin Nijhoff; and Geneva: Droz, 1951–79), 2: ll. 28,869–900.

39. "De ce sordent noz achaisons: / Tuit querent noz destructions. / Qui porreit tanz prevoz sofrir, / Ne tanz baillis en gré servir / N'a tanz forestiers n'a bedeiaus / Faire n'acomplir lor aveiaus? / . . . Mieuz nos en vendreit toz foïr / Que c'endurer ne ce sofrir. / Mauvais avun esté e fous / Dum tant avun plaissiez les cous, / Quer hommes sommes forz e durs, / Plus adurez e plus seürs / Et moct plus menbru e plus grant / Que il ne sunt ou autretant. / Por un qu'il sunt, sommes nos cent. / Me force ne desfendement / N'ont il vers nos ne ja n'avront / Ne ja, por tant cum il vivront, / Des qu'eissi iert la chose emprise. / Ne feront mais sor nos justise. / S'or ne nos faut cuers e hommece, / Moct porron aveir grant largece / De ce dum si nos garde l'on, / Dum ja es denz ne nos ferron: / Des cers, des sengleers e des dains, / Dum ja ne mangera vilains. / Toz les buens peisons porron prendre / Qu'il nos funt veer e desfendre" (ibid., 2: ll. 28907–938).

40. J. G. Gouttebroze, "Le duc, le comte et le peuple. Remarques sur une sédition des paysans en Normandie, autour de l'an mil," *Le Moyen Age* 101 (1995): 407–23.

41. "Le *cumune* remest atant, / n'en firent puis vilain semblant" (l. 847f.), *Le roman de Rou de Wace*, ed. A. J. Holden, 3 vols. (Paris: Picard, "Société des Anciens Textes Français," 1970–73).

42. Gouttebroze, p. 411. My comments on the peasantry in "Althusser Anonymous," *Exemplaria* 7 (1995): 55–74, were erroneous.

43. *Rou*, ll. 867–71.

44. Hilton, *Bond Men*, p. 72; and *Class Conflict*. General comments on peasant rebellions by Robert Fossier, *L'enfance de l'Europe*, 2 vols. (Paris: PUF, 1982). Dolores Buttry comments that the passage "could almost be called Jeffersonian, if not Marxist" ("Contempt or Empathy? Master Wace's Depiction of a Peasant Revolt," *Romance Notes* 37, no. 1 [1996]: 31–38, 37). I regret that I

came across this article only when this book was in production. And Paul Freedman, *Images of the Medieval Peasant* (Stanford, Calif.: Stanford University Press, 1999).

45. Baruch Spinoza, *The Political Treatise*, tr. Samuel Shirley (Indianapolis: Hackett, 2000). Since Althusser's brief remarks, Spinoza studies have undergone an extraordinary rejuvenation. I have benefited greatly from Warren Montag, *Bodies, Masses, Power* (London: Verso, 1999), ch. 3, entitled "The Body of the Multitude," which is especially pertinent to this discussion.

46. Partha Chatterjee, "More on Modes of Power and the Peasantry," in *Selected Subaltern Studies*, ed. Ranajit Guha and Gayatri Chakravorty Spivak (Oxford: Oxford University Press, 1988), p. 374 and preceding; for Marx, see the *Grundrisse*, tr. Martin Nicolaus (Hamondsworth, Eng.: Vintage, 1973), pp. 471ff.

47. Alexandre Leupin, "Naming God: *La vie de saint Alexis*," in *Barbarolexis: Medieval Writing and Sexuality*, tr. Kate M. Cooper (Cambridge, Mass.: Harvard University Press, 1989), pp. 39–58.

48. Brigitte Cazelles, *Le corps de sainteté* (Geneva: Droz, 1982), p. 48f.

49. *La Vie de saint Alexis*, ed. C. Storey (Geneva: Droz, 1968), ll. 170, 11. 171.

50. "D'icest honur nem revoil ancumbrer" (l. 188).

51. A twelfth-century rewriting demonstrates unease with the avoidance of names, personal feelings, and the fact that no one asks Alexis's name during the seventeen years spent in his father's house: Alison Goddard Elliott, *The Vie de saint Alexis in the Twelfth and Thirteenth Centuries* (Chapel Hill: University of North Carolina Press, 1983), p. 30.

52. "Seignors, que faites?" ço dist li apostoilie. / "Que valt cist crit, cist dols ne cesta noise? / Chi chi se doilet, a nostr'os est il goie, / Quar par cestui avrum boen adjutorie; / Si li preiuns que de tuz mals nos tolget" (Christopher Storey, ed., *La vie de saint Alexis* [Geneva and Paris: Droz and Minard, 1968], ll. 501–4). Old French and Latin texts and an English translation are also available in Carl J. Odenkirchen, *The Life of Saint Alexius* (Brookline, Mass.: Classical Folia Editions, 1978).

53. Donald L. Maddox, "Pilgrimage Narrative and Meaning in Manuscripts L and A of the *Vie de saint Alexis*," *Romance Philology* 27 (1973): 143–57, 146.

54. Giovanni Miccoli, "Théologie de la vie monastique chez Saint Pierre Damien (1007–1072)," in *Théologie de la vie monastique* (Paris: Aubier, 1962), p. 473.

55. "*Penat sun cors el Damnedeu servise*" (l. 162).

56. A. Latreille, E. Delaruelle, and J. R. Palanque, *Histoire du catholicisme en France*, vol. 1: *Des origines à la chrétienté médiévale* (Paris: Spes, 1957), p. 262f.

57. Jean Hubert, "La place faite aux laïcs dans les églises monastiques et dans les cathédrales aux XIe et XIIe siècles," *I laici nella 'societas christiana' dei secoli XI e XII* (Milan: Vita e Pensiero, 1968), pp. 470–87, 473.

58. Jean Leclerq, "Le monachisme clunisien," in *Théologie de la vie monastique* (Paris: Aubier, 1961), p. 457.

59. Ibid., p. 438.

60. Miccoli, p. 459.

61. "O bele buce, bel vis, bele faiture, / Cum est mudede vostra bele figure! / Plus vos amai que mule creature. / Si grant dolur or m'est apar[e]üde! / Melz me venist, amis, que morte fusse" (ibid., ll. 481–85).

62. On Peter, see Herbert Grundmann, *Religious Movements in the Middle Ages*, tr. Steven Rowan (Notre Dame, Ind.: University of Notre Dame Press, 1995), pp. 25–27, 190, 211.

CHAPTER 3

1. "Donna Aaliz la reïne, / Par qui valdrat lei divine, / Par qui cresitrat lei de terre / E remandrat tante guerre / Por les armes Henri lu rei, / E par le cunseil qui ert en tei" (Benedeit, *Le voyage de Saint Brandan*, ed. Ian Short [Paris: UGE (10/18), 1984], ll. 1–6). The queen named in l. 1 varies according to the king's marriages.

2. See below, Chapter 7.

3. This is the epic world according to Bertrand de Bar-sur-Aube's *Girart de Vienne* and *Doon de Mayence*, in Ulrich Mölk, *Französisches Literarästhetik des 12. und 13. Jahrhunderts* (Tübingen: Niemeyer, 1969), pp. 9f., 13f.

4. Foremost among these: Tony Hunt, "The Dialectic of *Yvain*," *Modern Language Review* 72 (1977): 285–99; Tony Hunt, "Aristotle, Dialectic and Courtly Literature," *Viator* 10 (1979): 95–129; and Eugene Vance, *From Topic to Tale, Logic and Narrativity in the Middle Ages* (Minneapolis: University of Minnesota Press, 1987).

5. "Pur sun seignur deit hom susfrir granz mals / E endurer e forz freiz e granz chalz, / Sin deit hom perdre del sanc e de la char" (*La Chanson de Roland*, ed. Joseph Bédier [Paris: UGE: 10/18], ll. 1117–19). Bédier's edition remains authoritative.

6. Hans-Erich Keller, "*The Song of Roland*: A Mid-Twelfth Century Song of Propaganda for the Capetian Kingdom," *Olifant* 3 (1976): 242–58; Stephen G. Nichols, "Fission and Fusion: Meditations of Power in Medieval History

and Literature," *Yale French Studies* 70 (1986): 21–42; and Stephen G. Nichols, *Romanesque Signs: Early Medieval Narrative and Iconography* (New Haven, Conn.: Yale University Press, 1983).

7. Haidu, *The Subject of Violence . . . : The Song of Roland and the Birth of the State* (Bloomington: Indiana University Press, 1993).

8. Elaine Scarry, *The Body in Pain: The Making and Unmaking of the World* (Oxford: Oxford University Press, 1985); Michel Foucault, *Surveiller et punir: Naissance de la prison* (Paris: Gallimard, 1975).

9. "Que que Rollant a Guenelun forsfesist, / Vostre servise l'en doüst bien garir. / Guenes est fels d'iço qu'il le traït; / Vers vos s'est parjurez e malmis" (ll. 3827–30).

10. The progress of education in the twelfth century affected secular knowledge of Latin only marginally. The beneficiaries of the cathedral schools and the later university were clergy, many headed toward secular careers.

11. The exchequer inscribed their presumption of "illiteracy": see below, Chapter 8.

12. Haidu, "The Episode as Semiotic Module in Twelfth Century Romance," *Poetics Today* 4, no. 4 (1983): 655–81.

13. Haidu, "Toward a Socio-Historical Semiotics: Power and Legitimacy in the *Couronnement de Louis*," *Kodikas/Code* 2 (1980): 155–69.

14. See Jean Dunbabin, *France in the Making 843–1180* (Oxford: Oxford University Press, 1985–91).

15. "En talent ot qi'il li colpast le chief, / Quant li remembre del glorios del ciel, / Que d'ome ocire est trop mortel pechiez. / Il prent s'espee, el fuere l'embatié, / Et passe avant; quant se fu rebraciez, / Le poing senestre li a meslé el chief, / Halce le destre, enz el col li assiet: / L'or de la gole li a par mi brisié; / Mort le trebuche a la terre a ses piez" (*Le couronnement de Louis*, ed. Ernest Langlois, 2d ed. [Paris: Champion, 1966] ["Classiques Français du Moyen Age," no. 22], ll. 125–33).

16. This split grounded Erich Köhler's analyses of feudal literature: *L'aventure chevaleresque: Idéal et réalité dans le roman courtois* (Paris: Gallimard, 1956); "Observations historiques et sociologiques sur la poésie lyrique des troubadours," *Cahiers de civilisation médiévale* 7 (1964): 27–51.

17. Other classes were internally differentiated as well, including the clergy (not a class in the Marxist sense) and the peasantry. Imposing impossible standards of theoretical purity on an analytic concept such as "class" is a polemical weapon in the effort to discard it as an instrument of reflexion.

18. Jacques le Goff, "Le rituel symbolique de la vassalité," *Pour un autre*

Moyen Age: Temps, travail et culture en Occident (Paris: Gallimard, 1977), pp. 349–420.

19. Robert Bresson's *Lancelot du Lac* explores the centrality of the horse's point of view to the culture of this class. The self-destruction of a polity by its highest ideal (passionate "chivalric" love) is shot in moral and cinematic darkness from the perspective of the horse's eye: the symbol of the class becomes the means of its perspectival deconstruction.

20. Joseph Strayer's classic essay, originally in *Life and Thought in the Early Middle Ages*, ed. R. S. Hoyt (Minneapolis: University of Minnesota Press, 1967).

21. See the remarks on Etienne de Fougères and Hugh of St Victor, below.

22. Jean-François Lemarignier, *Le gouvernement royal aux premiers temps capétiens (987–1108)* (Paris: 1965); Jean-François Lemarignier, "Aux origines de l'état français. Royauté et entourage royal aux premiers temps capétiens," in *L'Europe aux IXe–XIe siècles: Aux origines des Etats nationaux* (Warsaw: Panstwowe Wydawnictwo Naukowe, "Institut d'Histoire de l'Académie Polonaise des Sciences," 1968), pp. 43–55; and Eric Bournazel, *Le gouvernement capétien au XIIe siècle, 1108–1180: Structures sociales et mutations institutionnelles* (Paris: PUF, 1975).

23. Max Weber, *The Theory of Social and Economic Organization*, ed. Talcott Parsons (Oxford: Oxford University Press, 1947–64), p. 156f.

24. Joseph R. Strayer, *On the Medieval Origins of the Modern State* (Princeton, N.J.: Princeton University Press, 1970), p. 5.

25. Etienne de la Boétie, *Le discours de la servitude volontaire* (Paris: Payot, 1976–93).

26. Jacques Krynen, *L'empire du roi. Idées et croyances politiques en France. XIIIe-XVe siècle* (Paris: Gallimard, 1993), p. 68.

27. Pierre Riché, "Les Clercs carolingiens au service du pouvoir," in *Idéologie et propagande en France*, ed. Myriam Yardeni (Paris: Picard, 1987), pp. 11–18.

28. Ibid., p. 17f.; Daniel Bell, *The End of Ideology—On the Exhaustion of Political Ideas in the Fifties* (Glencoe, N.Y.: Free Press, 1960).

29. Georges Duby, "Remarques sur la littérature généalogique en France aux XIe et XIIe siècles," *Hommes et structures du moyen âge* (The Hague: Mouton, 1973), pp. 287–98.

30. Krynen, p. 36.

31. Jean Batany, "Du *bellator* au chevalier dans le schéma des 'trois ordres' (étude sémantique)," in *La guerre et la paix au moyen âge* (Lille: Actes du 101e congrés National des Sociétés Savantes, 1976), pp. 232–34.

32. Aryeh Graboïs, "La royauté sacrée au XIIe siècle: manifestation de la propagande royale," in *Idéologie et propagande en France*, ed. Myriam Yardeni (Paris: Picard, 1987), pp. 31–41; Jacques le Goff, "Aspect[s] religieux et sacré[s] de la monarchie française du Xe au XIIIe siècle," *Pouvoirs et libertés au temps des premiers capétiens*, ed. Elisabeth Magnou-Nortier (Editions Hérault, 1992), pp. 309–22.

33. Suger, *Vie de Louis VI le Gros*, ed. Henri Waquet (Paris: Les Belles Lettres, 1964), ch. xiv, pp. 84–89.

34. Krynen, p. 38.

35. Le Goff, p. 311f.

36. Ibid., p. 313.

37. Graboïs.

38. Riché, p. 13. On the limitations imposed on ritual's ability to form consensus by political, rhetorical, and strategic manipulations, see Philippe Buc, *Dangereux rituel. De l'histoire médiévale auxx sciences sociales*, Paris: PUF, 2003.

39. A. Luchaire, *Histoire des institutions monarchiques sous les premiers Capétiens (987–1180)*, 2 vols. (Paris: Picard, 1883), 1:69.

40. Graboïs, p. 39.

41. Krynen, p. 39.

42. Details on Louis's reign from Yves Sassier, *Louis VII* (Paris: Fayard, 1991).

43. Ibid., pp. 205–7.

44. Ibid., p. 258.

45. Ibid., p. 263f.

46. Ibid., p. 265.

47. Krynen, p. 42.

48. Jacques le Goff, "Genèse de la France (milieu IXe-fin XIIIe siècle): Vers un état monarchique français," in *Histoire de la France*, ed. André Burguière and Jacques Revel (Paris: Seuil, 1989), p. 34.

CHAPTER 4

1. Norbert Elias, *Über den Prozess der Zivilisation: Soziogenetische und psychogenetische untersuchunger . . .* (Basel: Haus Zum Falken, 1939); Joachim Bumke, *Höfische Kultur: Literatur und Gesellschaft im hohen Mittelalter*, 2 vols. (Munich: Deutscher Taschenbuch Verlag, 1986); Stephen Jaeger, *The Origins of Courtliness—Civilizing Trends and the Formation of Courtly Ideals—939-1210* (Philadelphia: University of Pennsylvania Press, 1985).

2. Stephen Jaeger, "Courtliness and Social Change," in *Cultures of Power: Lordship, Status and Process in Twelfth Century Europe*, ed. Thomas N. Bisson (Philadelphia: University of Pennsylvania Press, 1995), p. 299.

3. Major studies are those of Jack Goody, *The Domestication of the Savage*

Mind (Cambridge: Cambridge University Press, 1977–78); Jack Goody, *La logique de l'écriture: Aux origines des sociétés humaines* (Paris: Colin, 1986); and M. T. Clanchy, *From Memory to Written Record: England 1066–1307* (Oxford: Blackwell, 1979; 2d ed. 1993). See also Brian Stock, *The Implications of Literacy* (Princeton, N.J.: Princeton University Press, 1983); Henri-Jean Martin, *The History and Power of Writing*, tr. Lydia G. Cochrane (Chicago: University of Chicago Press, 1994); Jacques le Goff, *Les intellectuels au moyen âge* (Paris: Seuil, 1957).

4. Haidu, "La sémiose dissociative: la signification historique du phénomène stylistique 'Chrétien de Troyes' en France du nord au XIIe siècle," *Europe* 642 (Oct. 1982): 36–47.

5. Sarah Kay, *Subjectivity in Troubadour Poetry* (Cambridge: Cambridge University Press, 1990), p. 2.

6. Roman Jakobson, *Shifters, Verbal Categories, and the Russian Verb*, Russian Language Project (Cambridge, Mass.: Harvard University Press, 1957); Nicolas Ruwet, tr., "Les embrayeurs, les catégories verbales et le verbe russe," *Essais de linguistique générale* (Paris: Minuit, 1963), pp. 176–205. Its medieval problematic boasts an impressive bibliography, from Leo Spitzer, "A Note on the Poetic and the Empirical 'I' in Medieval Authors," *Traditio* 4 (1946): 414–22, to Paul Zumthor, "Le grand chant courtois," *Essai de poétique médiévale* (Paris: Seuil, 1972), pp. 189–243, and the three essays grouped under the subtitle, "Le 'je' du poète," in *Langue, texte, énigme* (Paris: Seuil, 1975), pp. 163–213.

7. "Farai un vers de dreit nïen; / Non er de mi ni d'autra gen, / Non er d'amor ni de joven / Ni de ren au / Qu'enans fo trobatz en durmen / Sus un chivau" (*Farai un vers de dreyt nien*," ed. and tr. Paul Blackburn, in *Proensa: An Anthology of Troubadour Poetry*, ed. George Economou [Berkeley and Los Angeles: University of California Press, 1978], p. 7), modified. Texts are from a different edition than that used by Blackburn: *The Poetry of William VII, Count of Poitiers, IX Duke of Aquitaine*, ed. with a translation by Gerald A. Bond (New York: Garland, 1982), p. 14. A member of the Collège de France with a book on subjectivity considers reflexivity a *"tarte à la crème"* of the 1970s: Michel Zink, *Actes du XXe Congrès International de Linguistique et Philologie Romanes*, ed. Gerold Hilty, 6 vols. (Tübingen and Basel: Francke Verlag, 1993), 5:162.

8. "Farai un vers, pos mi sonelh / E.m vauc e m'estauc al solelh" (Bond, p. 18). The theme of composing while asleep will be retained and parodied in a fourteenth-century *fatras*: Uns ours emplumés / Fist semer uns blés / De Douvre a Wissent; / Uns oingnons pelez / Estoit aprestés / De chanter devant, /

Quant sor un rouge olifant / vint uns limaçons armés / qui alors allait en s'écriant / 'Fils a putain, ça venez / je versifie en dormant" [A feathered bear / Had wheat sown / from Dover to Wissant; / A peeled onion / Was ready and waiting / To sing on ahead / When on a red elephant / Came an armed snail / Who then went yelling / "Son of a whore, come here / I'm versifying in my sleep"] (Lambert C. Porter, *La Fatrasie et le fatras* [Geneva: Droz, 1960], p. 135).

9. "Tant las fotei com auziretz: / Cen e qatre vint et ueit vetz! / Qe a pauc no.i rompet mos conretz / E mos arnes, / E no.us pues dir lo malaveig / Tan gran m'en pres" (Blackburn, *Proensa*, pp. 9—11, modified; Bond, p. 22).

10. "Farai chansoneta nueva / Ans que vent ni gel ni plueva: / Ma dona m'assaya e.m prueva, / Quossi de qual guiza l'am; / E ja per plag que m'en mueva / No.m solverai de son liam. / / Qu'ans mi rent a lieys e.m liure / Qu'en sa carta.m pot escriure; / E no m'en tengatz per yure / S'ieu ma bona domna am; / Quar senes lieys non puesc viure / Tant ai pres de s'amor gran fam" (Blackburn, *Proensa*, p. 17, modified; Bond, p. 44).

11. Giorgio Agamben, *Stanze*, tr. Yves Hersant (Paris: Rivages, 1981–98), pp. 184–206.

12. Paul Zumthor, *Langue et techniques poétiques à l'époque romane (XIe–XIIe siècles)* (Paris: Klincksieck, 1963); Paul Zumthor, *Essai de poétique médiévale*, pp. 231f., 239–42, 251f.; "Registres linguistiques et poésie aux XIIe–XIIIe siècles," *Cultura neolatina* 34 (1974): 151–61.

13. The literature on women's medieval history is voluminous. Georges Duby's classic works on marriage are: *Medieval Marriage: Two Models from Twelfth-Century France*, tr. Elborg Forster (Baltimore, Md.: Johns Hopkins University Press, 1978); and *The Knight, the Lady and the Priest: The Making of Modern Marriage in Medieval France*, tr. Barbara Bray (New York: Pantheon, 1983). Beyond marriage, see also Penny Schine Gold, *The Lady and the Virgin: Image, Attitude and Experience in Twelfth-Century France* (Chicago: University of Chicago Press, 1985); and Christiane Klapisch-Zuber, ed., *Silences of the Middle Ages*, vol. 2 of *A History of Women*, ed. Georges Duby and Michelle Perrot (Cambridge, Mass.: Harvard University Press, 1992–94).

14. Georges Duby, "Pour une histoire des femmes en France et en Espagne: Conclusion d'un colloque," *Mâle moyen age* (Paris: Flammarion, 1988), pp. 118–26, 121f.

15. R. Howard Bloch, "Medieval Misogyny," *Representations* 20 (fall 1987): 1–24; and R. Howard Bloch, *Medieval Misogyny and the Invention of Western Romantic Love* (Chicago: University of Chicago Press, 1991); and the debate in *Medieval Feminist Newsletter* 6 (1988) and 7 (1989).

16. Jane Burns, "The Man Behind the Troubadour Lyric," *Romance Notes*

25 (1985): 254–70; Jean-Charles Huchet, *L'amour discourtois: La "fin'amors" chez les premiers troubadours* (Toulouse: Privat, 1987).

17. The subtitle of Auerbach's *Mimesis*.

18. See below, Chapter 10.

19. E. Jane Burns, Sarah Kay, Roberta L. Krueger, and Helen Solterer, "Feminism and the Discipline of Old French Studies: *Une bele disjointure*," in *Medievalism and the Modernist Temper*, ed. R. Howard Bloch and Stephen G. Nichols (Baltimore, Md.: Johns Hopkins University Press, 1996), pp. 225–66, 240.

20. Ibid., p. 242.

21. Jacques Lacan, *L'éthique de la psychanalyse* (Paris: Seuil, 1968), p. 151.

22. Jacques Lacan, *Le Séminaire, Livre XX, Encore, 1972–1973* (Paris: Seuil, 1975), p. 65.

23. Ibid., pp. 68–72, 153.

24. Ibid., p. 78.

25. Lacan, *L'éthique de la psychanalyse*, p. 128f.

26. "*Une époque où tout de même, on baisait ferme et dru*" (ibid., p. 163).

27. Ibid., pp. 212–17.

28. Sigmund Freud, *Civilization and its Discontents* (Chicago: University of Chicago; rpt. textbook for Humanities II, ca. 1950), p. 85f.

29. Friedrich Nietzsche, *The Genealogy of Morals*, tr. Horace B. Samuel, in *The Philosophy of Nietzsche* (New York: Modern Library), bk. 2, sections 16–18, pp. 75–81.

30. Sigmund Freud, concluding words, "Anxiety and Instinctual Life," Lecture xxxii, *New Introductory Lectures on Psychoanalysis*, in *Complete Introductory Lectures on Psychoanalysis* (New York: W. W. Norton, 1966), p. 574f., emphasis added.

31. Sigmund Freud, "Reflections upon War and Death," in *Character and Culture*, ed. Philip Rieff (New York: Collier, 1963), p. 130.

32. R. Howard Bloch, *Medieval Misogyny and the Invention of Western Romantic Love* (Chicago: University of Chicago Press, 1991).

33. Karl Marx and Friedrich Engels, *The German Ideology* (Moscow: Progress, 1976), p. 42.

34. *Ab la dolchor del temps novel*, l. 24; *Farai chansoneta nueva*, l. 7f. Interestingly, it is Blackburn the poet who picks up on the economic image, which scholars like Jeanroy and Nelli and Lavaud elide in their translations; *Pos de chantar m'es pres talentz*.

35. Zumthor, *Essai de poétique médiévale*, pp. 189ff.; Haidu, "Text and History: The Semiosis of XIIth Century Lyric as Socio-Historical Phenomenon,"

Semiotica 33 (1980–81): 1–62; and Haidu, "Semiotics and History," *Semiotica* 40 (1982): 187–228.

36. On the transformation of lyric into narrative, see Paul Zumthor, "De la chanson au récit: 'La châtelaine de Vergi," in *Langue, texte, énigme*, pp. 219–36; and Eugene Vance, "The Châtelain de Coucy: Enunciation and Story in Trouvère Lyric," in *Mervelous Signals: Poetics and Sign Theory in the Middle Ages* (Lincoln: University of Nebraska Press, 1986), pp. 86–110.

37. On feudal vocabulary in courtly lyric, see Roger Dragonetti, *La technique poétique des trouvères dans la chanson courtoise, contribution à l'étude de la rhétorique courtoise* (Bruges: Rijksuniversiteit Gent, 1960), pp. 61–113.

38. "Tous jours soies en son dangier, / Puis qu'empris et comencié l'as. / Ja, mon los, plenté n'ameras, / Ne pour chier tans ne t'esmaier; / Biens adoucist par delaier, / Et quant plus desiré l'auras, / Plus t'en ert douls à l'essaier" (Chrétien de Troyes, "D'Amors qui m'a tolu," in *Les chansons courtoises de Chrétien de Troyes*, ed. Marie-Claire Zai [Berne and Frankfurt: Lang and Lang, 1974], ll. 39–45).

39. William Paden, "The Troubadour's Lady: Her Marital Status and Social Rank," *Studies in Philology* 72 (1975): 28–49.

40. Ernst Kantorowicz, *The King's Two Bodies* (Princeton, N.J.: Princeton University Press, 1957).

41. Robert Guiette, *Questions de littérature* (Gand: 1960); Dragonetti; and Zumthor, *Langue et techniques poétiques*.

42. Matilda Tomaryn Bruckner, "The Women Troubadours," *Speculum* 67 (1992): 865–91; see also Sarah Kay, "The Poetry of the *Trobairitz*," *Subjectivity in Troubadour Poetry* (Cambridge: Cambridge University Press, 1990), pp. 101–11.

43. As W. T. H. Jackson, of revered memory, once suggested.

44. Judith Butler, *Gender Trouble* (London: Routledge, 1990), pp. 142–49.

CHAPTER 5

1. For example, Christine Brooke-Rose, "Woman as a Semiotic Object," in *The Female Body in Western Culture*, ed. Susan Rubin Suleiman (Cambridge, Mass.: Harvard University Press, 1985–86), pp. 305–16.

2. Colin Morris, *The Discovery of the Individual, 1050–1200* (London: SPCK, 1972); Robert Hanning, *The Individual in Twelfth Century Romance* (New Haven, Conn.: Yale University Press, 1977); Janet Coleman, "The Individual and the Medieval State," in *The Individual in Political Theory and Practice*, ed. Janet Coleman (Oxford: Clarendon: 1996), pp. 1–34.

3. See Chapter 2, above.

4. Erich Auerbach, *Mimesis: The Representation of Reality in Western Literature* (Princeton, N.J.: Princeton University Press, 1953); Northrop Frye, *The Anatomy of Criticism* (Princeton, N.J.: Princeton University Press, 1957); Fredric Jameson, *The Political Unconscious* (Ithaca, N.Y.: Cornell University Press, 1981).

5. Haidu, *Aesthetic Distance in Chrétien de Troyes: Irony and Comedy in* Cligés *and* Perceval, and *Lion-queue-coupée: L'écart symbolique chez Chrétien de Troyes,* both published in Geneva by Droz, 1968 and 1972, respectively.

6. Caroline A. Jewers, *Chivalric Fiction and the History of the Novel* (Gainesville: University of Florida Press, 2000), pp. 34–45.

7. Thus, Linda Hutcheon, *A Theory of Parody: The Teachings of Twentieth-Century Art Forms* (London and New York: Methuen, 1985), transforms a universal characteristic of textuality to a marker of modernism . . . as in *Irony's Edge* (London: Routledge, 1994).

8. Jacques le Goff, "Naissance du roman historique au XIIe siècle?" *NRF* no. 238 (1972): 163–73, p. 170.

9. *Le Roman de Brut de Wace,* 2 vols., ed. Ivor Arnold (Paris: Société des Anciens Textes Français, 1940), 2: ll. 14865f.

10. Matilda Tomaryn Bruckner, *Shaping Romance: Interpretation, Truth, and Closure in Twelfth-Century French Fictions* (Philadelphia: University of Pennsylvania Press, 1993).

11. Matilda Tomaryn Bruckner, *Narrative Invention in Twelfth-Century French Romance: The Convention of Hospitality (1160–1200)* (Lexington, Ky.: French Forum, 1980).

12. Haidu, "Text and History: The Semiosis of XIIth Century Lyric as Socio-Historical Phenomenon," *Semiotica* 33 (1980–81): 1–62.

13. Jacques Lacan, *L'éthique de la psychanalyse* (Paris: Seuil, 1986), p. 151.

14. Compare with Jean-Claude Schmitt, for whom the knight was merely an individual, not a subject—a status he reserves for the monk (*Le corps, les rites, les rêves, le temps: Essais d'anthropologie médiévale* [Paris: Gallimard, 2001], p. 20).

15. Donald Maddox, *Structure and Sacring: The Systematic Kingdom in Chrétien's Erec et Enide* (Lexington, Ky.: French Forum, 1978).

16. Haidu, *Lion-queue-coupée.*

17. "Les anges don les janz se plaingnent, / Qui ocient quanqu'il ataingnent" (Christian von Troyes, *Der Percevalroman (Li contes del graal),* ed. Alfons Hilka [Halle: Niemeyer, 1932], ll. 399f.).

18. On Perceval's mother, see Matilda Tomaryn Bruckner, "Rewriting

Chrétien's *Conte du graal*—Mothers and Sons: Questions, Contradictions, and Connections," in *The Medieval Opus: Imitation, Rewriting, and Transmission in the French Tradition*, ed. Douglas Kelly (Amsterdam: Rodopi, 1996), pp. 213–44; Matilda Tomaryn Bruckner, "Election Politics and Coronation Trials: Manessier Ends Chrétien's Grail Campaign," forthcoming; and Rupert T. Pickens, *The Welsh Knight: Paradoxicality in Chrétien's Conte del graal* (Lexington, Ky.: French Forum, 1977), ch. 2, "Point of View."

19. Chrétien de Troyes, *Le Chevalier au lion (Yvain)*, ed. Mario Roques (Paris: Champion, 1980) ("Classiques Français du Moyen Age," l. 89), ll. 3479ff.

20. Béatrice Fraenkel, *La signature, genèse d'un signe* (Paris: Gallimard, 1992).

21. Michel Pastoureau: "La diffusion des armoiries et les débuts de l'héraldique," in *La France de Philippe Auguste: Le temps des mutations*, ed. Robert-Henri Bautier (Paris: CNRS, 1982), pp. 737–60; "Le regard héraldique," *Les Cahiers du Musée National d'Art Moderne* 37 (fall 1991): 22–31 ("Visions"); "La naissance des armoiries," in *Le XIIe siècle, mutations et renouveau en France pendant la première moitié du XIIe siècle*, ed. Françoise Gasparri (Paris: Le Léopard d'Or, 1994), pp. 103–22; *Traité d'héraldique*, 2d ed. (Paris: Picard, 1993).

22. Brigitte Bedos Rezak, "Les sceaux au temps de Philippe Auguste," in *La France de Philippe Auguste: Le temps des mutations*, ed. Robert-Henri Bautier (Paris: CNRS, 1982), pp. 721–36.

23. Jean-Luc Chassel, "L'usage du sceau au XIIe siècle," in *Le XIIe siècle*, ed. Françoise Gasparri (Paris: Le léopard d'or, 1994), pp. 61–102, 64.

24. Le roi demaund par amour: / "Ou qy este vus, sire Joglour?" / "Le baron ma dame, par ma foy. / —Quy est ta dame par amour? / —Sire la femme mon seignour. / —Comment estes vus appellee? / —Sire, come cely qe m'ad levee. / —Cesti qu te leva quel noun aveit? / —Itel come je, sire, tot dreit. / —Où vas tu?—Je vois de là. / —Dont vien tu?—Je vienk de sà" and so on (Anatole de Montaiglon and Gaston Raynaud, eds., *Recueil général et complet des fabliaux* [Paris: 1872–90; rpt. Geneva: Slatkine, 1973]; 2:243).

25. Hildegard Emmel, *Formprobleme des Artusromans und der Graldichtung* (Berne: Francke, 1951).

26. Haidu, "La valeur: Sémiotique et marxisme," *Sémiotique en jeu: A partir et autour de l'oeuvre d'A. J. Greimas*, ed. Michel Arrivé and Jean-Claude Coquet (Paris-Amsterdam-Philadelphia: John Benjamins, 1987), pp. 247–63.

27. Paul Zumthor, *Essai de poétique médiévale* (Paris: Seuil, 1972), p. 108.

28. Joan Tasker Grimbert, *"Yvain" dans le miroir: Une poétique de la réflex-*

ion dans le Chevalier au lion de Chrétien de Troyes (Amsterdam: Benjamins, 1988), p. 106.

29. Georges Duby, "Les 'jeunes' dans la société aristocratique dans la France du Nord-Ouest au XIIe siècle," in *Hommes et structures du moyen âge* (The Hague: Mouton, 1973), pp. 213–26.

30. "Se *essoines* me detenra / de malage ne de prison" (ll. 2592f.).

31. "Nus *essoines* ne vos atant / tant con vos sovanra de moi" (ll. 2600f.).

32. Ibid., ll. 2572–616.

33. On the feudal contract, see F. L. Ganshof, *Qu'est-ce-que la féodalité?* (Brussels: Office de Tourisme, 1947); on the marriage contract, Duby, *The Knight, the Lady and the Priest*; on commercial contracts, Jacques le Goff, *Marchands et banquiers du moyen âge* (Paris: PUF, 1972), pp. 20–24; and Robert S. Lopez, *The Commercial Revolution of the Middle Ages, 950–1350* (Cambridge: Cambridge University Press, 1976), pp. 73–79; Raymond de Roover, *Business, Banking, and Economic Thought in Late Medieval and Early Modern Europe* (Chicago: University of Chicago Press, 1974); and Richard David Face, "The Caravan Merchants and the Fairs of Champagne: A Study in the Techniques of Medieval Commerce," Ph.D. dissertation, University of Wisconsin, University Microfilms, 1975.

34. Donald Maddox, *The Arthurian Romances of Chrétien de Troyes* (Cambridge: Cambridge University Press, 1991), p. 139.

35. Roberta L. Krueger, *Women Readers and the Ideology of Gender in Old French Verse Romance* (Cambridge: Cambridge University Press, 1995), p. 42f.

36. On the image of the forest, see Jacques le Goff, *The Medieval Imagination*, tr. Arthur Goldhammer (Chicago: University of Chicago Press, 1988), pp. 47–59 and pp. 107–31.

37. Haidu, "The Hermit's Pottage: Deconstruction and History in Yvain," *Romanic Review* 74 (1983): 1–15; appears also in *The Sower and the Seed: Essays on Chrétien de Troyes*, ed. Rupert T. Pickens (Lexington, Ky.: French Forum, 1983), pp. 127–45.

38. Compare with Jacques Derrida, *Donner le temps: 1. La fausse monnaie* (Paris: Galilée, 1991); *Critique* 596–97 (Jan.–Feb. 1997): *L'échange de la civilité à la violence*.

39. "Mestiers li est qu'aïde truisse / qui li aïst et qui l'en maint" (*Les romans de Chrétien de Troyes, IV, Le chevalier au lion (Yvain)*, ed. Mario Roques [Paris: Champion, 1960] ["Classiques Français du Moyen Age," no. 89], ll. 3034f.).

40. "Et cil, qui grant mestier eüst / d'aïde" (ibid., ll. 3043f.).

41. "Dameisele, or me dites donc / se vos avez besoing de moi?" (ibid., ll. 3074f.).

42. Haidu, "The Episode as Semiotic Module in Twelfth Century Romance," *Poetics Today* 4, no. 4 (1983): 655–81.

43. Robert S. Corrington, *An Introduction to C. S. Peirce* (Lanham, Md.: Rowman and Littlefield, 1993), pp. 118–41.

44. Fraenkel, esp. pp. 98–121.

45. Earlier studies of subjectivity based themselves on Emile Benveniste's view of subjectivity as defined by the use of the pronoun "I": Michel Zink, *La subjectivité littéraire au siècle de saint Louis* (Paris: PUF, 1985); and Sarah Kay, *Subjectivity in Troubadour Poetry* (Cambridge: Cambridge University Press, 1990).

46. Ll. 1432–1510 and 6500–16.

47. See also Haidu, "Temps, histoire, subjectivité: aux XIIe et XIIIe siècles," *Le nombre du temps (Mélanges Zumthor)* (Paris: Champion-Slatkine, 1988), pp. 105–22.

48. In addition to the works by Morris, *Discovery*; Hanning, *Individual in Twelfth Century*; and Coleman, "Individual and the Medieval State," see Carolyn Walker Bynum, "Did the Twelfth Century Discover the Individual?" in *Jesus as Mother* (Berkeley and Los Angeles: University of California Press, 1982), pp. 82–109; Jean Wirth, "Le sujet médiéval," *Penser le sujet aujourd'hui*, ed. Elisabeth Guibert-Sledzieski and Jean-Louis Vieillard-Baron (Paris: Klincksieck, 1988); Jean-Claude Schmitt, "La 'Découverte de l'individu': Une fiction historiographique?" *La fabrique, la figure, et la feinte: Fictions et statut des fictions en psychologie*, ed. Paul Mengal and Françoise Parot (Paris: Vrin, 1989), pp. 213–36; and Haidu, "Althusser Anonymous in the Middle Ages," *Exemplaria* 7, no. 1 (1995): 55–74.

49. Barbara Nelson Sargent-Baur, "*Dux bellorum / rex militum /* roi fainéant: la transformation d'Arthur au XIIe siècle," *Le Moyen Age* 90 (1984): 357–74; Kristin Lee Over, "Kingship, Conquest, and *Patria*: Literary and Cultural Identities in the Medieval French and Welsh Arthurian Romances," Ph.D. dissertation, University of California, Los Angeles, 2002.

50. Edward Peters, *The Shadow King: Rex inutilis in Medieval Law and Literature, 751–1325* (New Haven, Conn.: Yale University Press, 1970).

51. Michel Bur, *La formation du comté de Champagne, v. 950–v. 1150* (Nancy: Université de Nancy, 1977); and Theodore Evergates, *Feudal Society in the Bailliage of Troyes under the Counts of Champagne, 1152–1284* (Baltimore, Md.: Johns Hopkins University Press, 1975).

52. Kathryn Gravdal, *Ravishing Maidens: Writing Rape in French Literature and Law* (Philadelphia: University of Pennsylvania Press, 1991).

53. Krueger, p. 19.

54. Jacqueline Murray, "Thinking About Gender: The Diversity of Medieval Perspectives," in *Power of the Weak: Studies on Medieval Women*, ed. Jennifer Carpenter and Sally-Beth MacLean (Urbana: University of Illinois Press, 1995), pp. 1–26, p. 9.

55. Ibid., p. 16.

56. Gravdal, p. 22.

57. Sue-Ellen Case, "Re-Viewing Hrotsvit," *Theater Journal* 35 (1983): 533–42.

58. Gravdal, p. 67.

59. Ibid., p. 50f.

60. Krueger, p. 51.

61. Georges Duby, "Pour une histoire des femmes en France et en Espagne," *Male moyen âge* (Paris: Flammarion, 1988), pp. 118–26, p. 120.

62. Haidu, "Hermit's Pottage."

63. James R. McGuire, "L'onguent et l'initiative féminine dans Yvain," *Romania* (1991): 65–82, p. 82.

CHAPTER 6

1. Richard Baum, *Recherches sur les oeuvres attribuées à Marie de France* (Heidelberg: Carl Winter, 1968).

2. *"Marie ai num, si sui de France"* (Marie de France, *Fables*, ed. and tr. Harriet Spiegel [Toronto: Medieval Academy of America, 1987–94], p. 256); and "Epilogue," ll. 1–8.

3. Jean-Charles Huchet, "Nom de femme et écriture féminine au moyen âge: Les Lais de Marie de France," *Poétique* 48 (1981): 407–30.

4. Simon Gaunt, *Gender and Genre in Medieval French Literature* (Cambridge: Cambridge University Press, 1995), p. 335.

5. "E dame Marie autresi, / Ki en rime fist e basti / E compassa les vers de lais, / Ki ne sunt pas del tut verais; / E si en est ele mult loee / E la rime par tut amee, / Kar mult l'aiment, si l'unt mult cher / Cunte, barun e chivaler; / E si enaiment mult l'escrit / E lire le funt, si unt delit, / E si les funt sovent retreire. / Les lais solent as dames pleire, / De joie les oient e de gré, / Qu'il sunt sulum lur volenté" (Denis Piramus, *La Vie de Seint Edmund le rei*, ed. H. Kjellman [Göteborg: Elanders Boktryckeri Aktieholag, 1935]).

6. Matilda Tomaryn Bruckner, "Textual Identity, and the Name of a Col-

lection: Marie de France's *lais*," in *Shaping Romance: Interpretation, Truth, and Closure in Twelfth-Century French Fictions* (Philadelphia: University of Pennsylvania Press, 1993), pp. 157–205.

7. Yves Sassier, *Louis VII* (Paris: Fayard, 1991), pp. 354–68, 367f., emphasis added.

8. Michael J. Curley, ed., *Saint Patrick's Purgatory: A Poem by Marie de France* (Binghamton, N.Y.: MRTS, 1993), p. 5f.

9. "Il ne l'osot nïent requere; / Pur ceo qu'il ert d'estrange tere / Aveit poür, s'il li mustrast, / Qu'ele l'enhaïst e esloinast" (Marie de France, *Lais*, ed. Jean Rychner [Paris: Champion, 1983] ["CFMA" 93], ll. 477–80).

10. "Hum estrange descunseillez, / Mut est dolenz en autre tere, / Quant il ne seit u sucurs quere!" ("Lanval," ll. 36–38; ibid., p. 73).

11. Doris Desclais Berkvam, "La chose et le signe dans *Le Fresne*," in *L'imaginaire courtois et son double*, ed. Giovanna Angeli and Luciano Formisano (Salerno and Naples: Edizioni Scientifiche Italiana, 1991), pp. 235–44.

12. Robert Sturges, *Medieval Interpretation: Models of Readings in Literary Narrative, 1000–1500* (Carbondale and Edwardsville: Southern Illinois University Press, 1991), pp. 75–124.

13. Elizabeth Wilson Poe, "The Problem of the Tournament in *Chaitivel*," in *In Quest of Marie de France: A Twelfth Century Poet*, ed. Chantal A. Maréchal (Lewiston, N.Y.: Mellen, 1992), pp. 175–92.

14. Alexandre Leupin, "The Impossible Task of Manifesting 'Literature': On Marie de France's Obscurity," *Exemplaria* 3 (1991): 221–42, 225.

15. Marie de France, *Lais*, ed. Jean Rychner (Paris: Champion, 1983), p. 273.

16. Katharine Gingrass-Conley, "La 'Venue' à l'écriture de la dame dans *Le Chaitivel*," *Romanic Review* 83 (1992): 149–60.

17. Michelle Freeman, "The Power of Sisterhood: Marie de France's 'Le Fresne,'" in *Women and Power in the Middle Ages*, ed. Mary Erler and Maryanne Kowaleski (Athens: University of Georgia Press, 1988).

18. "Tu m'as abatu al juster: / A merveille te puis amer!" (l. 443f.).

19. "Le laustic li trametrai, / L'aventure li manderai / En une piece de samit / A or brusdé e tut escrit / Ad l'oiselet envolupé" (ll. 133–37).

20. "Ne vus sans moi, ne jeo sanz vus" ("Chievrefoil," l. 78).

21. Ibid., ll. 107–11.

22. Ann Banfield, *Unspeakable Sentences: Narrative and Representation in the Language of Fiction* (London: Routledge, 1982); against see Bernard Cerquiglini, "Le style indirect libre et la modernité," *Languages* 73 (1984):

7–16; and Matilda Tomaryn Bruckner, "Marie's Fusion of Voices," in *Shaping Romance: Interpretation, Truth, and Closure in Twelfth-Century French Fictions* (Philadelphia: University of Pennsylvania Press, 1993), pp. 184–89.

23. "Ne poeit vivre sanz li. / D'euls deus fu il tut autresi / Cume del chievrefoil esteit / Ki a la cordre se perneit: Quant il s'i est laciez e pris / E tut entur le fust s'est mis, / Ensemble poënt bien durer, / Mes ki puis les voelt desevrer, / Li cordres muert hastivement / E li chievrefoilz ensement / 'Bele amie, si est de nus: Ne vus sanz mei, ne jeo sans vus'" (ll. 67–78). I discard the editor's quotation marks, which partially resolve the question of (in)direct discourse.

24. Marie de France, *Lais*, ed. Jean Rychner (Paris: Champion, 1983), pp. 276–79.

25. Compare with R. Howard Bloch, "The Medieval Text—*Guigemar*—as a Provocation to the Discipline of Medieval Studies," *Romanic Review* 79 (1988): 63–73.

26. "Le chastel a destruit e pris / e le seignur dedenz ocis. / A grant joie s'amie en meine. / Ore a trepassee sa peine" (ll. 879–82).

27. Kathryn I. Holten, "Metamorphosis and Language in the Lay of *Bisclavret*," in *In Quest of Marie de France: A Twelfth Century Poet*, ed. Chantal A. Maréchal (Lewiston, N.Y.: Mellen, 1992), pp. 193–211, 193.

28. Kirby F. Smith, "An Historical Study of the Werewolf in Literature," *PMLA* 9 (1984): 2–3.

29. Matilda Tomaryn Bruckner, "Of Men and Beasts in *Bisclavret*," *Romanic Review* 81 (1991): 251–69.

30. Rupert Pickens, "Marie de France and the Body Poetic," in *Gender and the Text in the Later Middle Ages*, ed. Jane Chance (Gainesville: University of Florida Press, 1996), pp. 135–71, 138f.

31. Judith Butler, *The Psychic Life of Power* (Stanford, Calif.: Stanford University Press, 1997), p. 64.

32. Joan Ferrante, *To the Glory of Her Sex: Women's Roles in the Composition of Medieval Texts* (Bloomington: University of Indiana Press, 1997), p. 197.

33. On thresholds, see Gérard Genette, *Seuils* (Paris: Seuil, 1987).

34. See editor's footnote to ll. 13–16, p. 265.

35. John le Patourel, *The Norman Empire* (Oxford: Oxford University Press, 1976); François Neveux, *La Normandie des ducs aux rois, Xe-XIIe siècle* (Rennes: Ouest-France, 1998).

36. "La geste des Bretons / Et la lignee des baruns / Ki del lignage Bruti vindrent" (Epilogue to *Le Roman de Brut de Wace*, 2 vols., ed. Ivor Arnold [Paris: Société des Anciens Textes Français, 1940], ll. 14859–61).

37. Gilles Deleuze and Félix Guattari, *Kafka: Toward a Minor Literature*, tr. Dana Polan (Minneapolis: University of Minnesota Press, 1986), p. 16f.

38. "Pur les paroles remembrer" ("Chievrefoil"); and "pur remembrer / Qu'hum nel deüst pas oblier" ("Eliduc").

39. Patrick J. Geary, *Phantoms of Remembrance: Memory and Oblivion at the end of the First Millenium* (Princeton, N.J.: Princeton University Press, 1994), p. 29.

40. Homi K. Bhabha, *The Location of Culture* (London: Routledge, 1994), p. 206f.

41. Eva Rosenn, "The Sexual and Textual Politics of Marie's Poetics," in *In Quest of Marie de France: A Twelfth Century Poet*, ed. Chantal A. Maréchal (Lewiston, N.Y.: Mellen, 1992), pp. 225–42.

42. Bruckner, "Of Men and Beasts in *Bisclavret*," pp. 265ff.

43. Compare with Jacques Derrida, "L'invention de l'autre," *Psyché, Inventions de l'autre* (Paris: Galilée, 1987), p. 60.

CHAPTER 7

1. Sarah Kay, ed. and tr., *Raoul de Cambrai* (Oxford: Oxford University Press, 1992); same edition, with modern French translation: ed. William Kibler (Paris: Livre de poche, 1996).

2. Alexandre Leupin, "*Raoul de Cambrai*: The Illegitimacy of Writing," in *The New Medievalism*, ed. Marina S. Brownlee, Kevin Brownlee, and Stephen G. Nichols (Baltimore, Md.: Johns Hopkins University Press, 1991), pp. 131–54, p. 131.

3. On the narrative structure of the text, see Sarah Kay, "La composition de *Raoul de Cambrai*," *Revue belge de philologie et d'histoire* 62 (1984): 474–92.

4. Martin Gosman, "'*Rex Franciae, Rex Francorum*': La chanson de geste et la propagande de la royauté," in *Aspects de l'épopée romane*, ed. Hans van Dijk and Willem Noomen (Groningen: Egbert Forsten, 1995), pp. 451–60. Gosman's work is based on seven contemporary epics from the early thirteenth century.

5. The identification of the narrator's voice with that of the son as hero in turn falsifies the representations of the text's women: Thelma S. Fenster, "The Son's Mother: Aalais and Marsent in *Raoul de Cambrai*," *Olifant* 12, no. 2 (1987): 77–93.

6. Stephen D. White, "The Discourse of Inheritance in Twelfth-Century France: Alternative Models of the Fief in '*Raoul de Cambrai*,'" *Law and Government in Medieval England and Normandy*, ed. George Garnett and John Hudson (Cambridge: Cambridge University Press, 1994), pp. 173–97.

7. Leupin, p. 135.

8. See Sarah Kay, "L'éthique dans Raoul de Cambrai," *Op. cit.* 13 (1999): 5–10.

9. Simon Gaunt focuses exclusively on the *compagnonnage* of Raoul and Bernier and sees the text exhibiting "a nostalgia for a formerly heroic world . . . a yearning for a lost perfect world is manifest in virtually all *chansons de geste*" (Simon Gaunt, *Gender and Genre in Medieval French Literature* [Cambridge: Cambridge University Press, 1995], p. 62).

10. On the question of genre, compare Kay, *The chanson de geste in the Age of Romance: Political Fictions* (Oxford: Clarendon, 1995) and Gaunt with Haidu, "Romance: Idealistic Genre or Historical Text?" in *The Craft of Fiction: Essays in Medieval Poetics*, ed. L. A. Arrathoon (Rochester, Mich.: Solaris Press, 1984), pp. 1–46.

11. Ll. 1300ff.

12. Ll. 1468, 1518, 1560, 1569, 1677ff., 1708ff., 1721, 1839–44.

13. Emanuelle Baumgartner and Laurence Harf-Lancner, *Raoul de Cambrai: L'impossible révolte* (Paris: Champion, 1999), p. 88.

14. "Lie la dame qe isil aroit prise, / car molt a los de grant chevalerie; / qi le tenroit tot nu soz sa crotine, / miex li valroit qe nule rien qi vive / . . . Q[u]i le loroit acoler et baisier / miex li v[a]lroit qe boivre ne mengier.' / Puis dist en bas, c'ele puet esploitier, / qe le tenra encor ains l'anuitier" (ll. 5409–12; Kay's translation, slightly modified).

15. "Mari vos qier por mon cors deporter" (l. 5607).

16. Laisses 2, 3, 4, 5, 6, 8, 9, 10, 11, and so on.

17. Ll. 855–99.

18. Matilda Tomaryn Bruckner, "Rewriting Chrétien's *Conte du graal*—Mothers and Sons: Questions, Contradictions, and Connections," in *The Medieval Opus*, ed. Douglas Kelly (Amsterdam: Rodopi, 1996).

19. Carolyn Walker Bynum, *Jesus as Mother* (Berkeley and Los Angeles: University of California Press, 1982), p. 143.

20. Juliet Mitchell, *The Selected Melanie Klein* (New York: Free Press, 1986–87), pp. 74ff.

21. Bernier would want to deny it, but cannot (l. 1679).

22. Ll. 6817–27.

23. See, most recently, Sophie Marnette, *Narrateur et points de vue dans la littérature française médiévale: Une approche linguistique* (Bern: Peter Lang, 1998).

24. Gabrielle Spiegel, *Romancing the Past: The Rise of Vernacular Prose His-*

toriography in Thirteenth Century France (Berkeley and Los Angeles: University of California Press, 1993).

25. Spiegel, pp. 31–44; see also John Baldwin, *The Government of Philip Augustus* (Berkeley and Los Angeles: University of California Press, 1986), p. 99f.

26. Spiegel, p. 95.

27. *La Chronique de Waulsort,* cited Baumgartner and Harf-Lancner, p. 159.

28. Gilles Deleuze and Félix Guattari, *Kafka, Toward a Minor Literature,* tr. Dana Polan (Minneapolis: University of Minnesota Press, 1986).

CHAPTER 8

1. Frederick Engels, *The Origin of the Family, Private Property and the State,* ed. Eleanor Burke Leacock (New York: International, 1972–93), p. 232; the passage is cited by Lenin, *The State and Revolution* (Peking: Foreign Languages Press, 1976), p. 18f.

2. Max Weber, "Politics as a Vocation," in *From Max Weber,* ed. and tr. H. H. Gerth and C. Wright Mills (Oxford: Oxford University Press, 1946), pp. 77–28, 78, emphasis original.

3. Louis Althusser, "Ideology and Ideological State Apparatuses," in *Lenin and Philosophy,* tr. Ben Brewster (New York: Monthly Review / NLB, 1971), pp. 127–86; now in its original form and context: *Sur la reproduction* (Paris: PUF, 1995), pp. 269–314. Michel Foucault, *Discipline and Punish,* tr. Alan Sheridan (New York: Random House, 1977); *The Foucault Effect: Studies in Governmentality,* ed. Graham Burchell, Colin Gordon, and Peter Miller (Chicago: University of Chicago Press, 1991); and John S. Ransom, *Foucault's Discipline: The Politics of Subjectivity* (Durham, N.C.: Duke University Press, 1997).

4. On tyrannicide, see Richard and Mary Rouse, "John of Salisbury and the Doctrine of Tyrannicide," *Speculum* 42 (1967): 693–709; Cary J. Nederman, "A Duty to Kill: John of Salisbury's Theory of Tyrannicide," *Review of Politics* 50 (1988): 365–89; and Kate L. Forhan, "Salisburian Stakes: The Uses of 'Tyranny' in the *Policraticus,*" *History of Political Thought* 11 (1990): 397–407. On bureaucracy, see Jean Dunbabin, "Government," in *The Cambridge History of Medieval Political Thought, c. 350–c. 1450,* ed. J. H. Burns (Cambridge: Cambridge University Press, 1988–91), p. 479.

5. Michel Senellart, *Machiavélisme et raison d'Etat* (Paris: PUF, 1989); and *Les arts de gouverner: Du regimen médiéval au concept de gouvernement* (Paris: Seuil, 1995).

6. But see John W. Baldwin, *Masters, Princes and Merchants: The Social*

Views of Peter the Chanter and his Circle, 2 vols. (Princeton, N.J.: Princeton University Press, 1970).

7. R. W. Southern, *Medieval Humanism and Other Studies* (New York: Harper, 1970), p. 176.

8. Compare with Cary J. Nederman and Kate Langdon Forhan, *Medieval Political Theory—A Reader: The Quest for the Body Politic, 1100–1400* (London: Routledge, 1993), pp. 10, 16. See also D. E. Lunscombe and G. R. Evans, "The Twelfth Century Renaissance," in *The Cambridge History of Medieval Political Thought c. 350–c. 1450,* ed. J. H. Burns (Cambridge: Cambridge University Press, 1988–91), pp. 306–38. The origins in medieval theology of modern thought on the state are "the real unthought of our culture": Senellart, *Machiavélisme*, p. 12; and Pierre Legendre, *L'amour du censeur* (Paris: Seuil, 1974). But more recently, see Derrida, *Politics of Friendship*, tr. George Collins (London: Verso, 1997).

9. The classic work is Jan Dhondt, *Etudes sur la naissance des principautés territoriales en France (IXe–Xe siècles)* (Bruges: 1948); see also the more recent synthesis of Jean Dunbabin, *France in the Making, 843–1180* (Oxford: Oxford University Press, 1985–91).

10. Karl Ferdinand Werner, "La genèse des duchés en France et en Allemagne," in *Vom Frankenreich zur Entfaltung Deutschlands und Frankreichs* (Sigmaringen: Jan Thorbecke, 1984), pp. 278–310; and "Histoire de France," *Les origines*, ed. Jean Favier, vol. 1 (Paris: Fayard, 1984).

11. René Germain, "Les sires de Bourbon et le pouvoir: de la seigneurie à la principauté," in *Les princes et le pouvoir au moyen âge*, XXIIIe Congrès de la Société des historiens médiévaux de l'enseignement supérieur public (Paris: Publications de la Sorbonne, 1993), pp. 195–210.

12. Michel Bur, "La Champagne féodale," in *Histoire de la Champagne*, ed. Maurice Crubellier (Toulouse: Privat, 1975), pp. 115–73, 121.

13. James W. Fesler, "French Field Administration: The Beginnings," *Comparative Studies in Society and History* 5 (1962): 76–111, p. 81.

14. Jean Favier, *Le temps des principautés de l'an mil à 1515* (Paris: Fayard, 1984).

15. Dunbabin, *France in the Making*, p. 44.

16. Bernado Davanzati, *Lezione della monete*, in *Ecrits notables sur la monnaie: xvie siècle, Copernic à Davanzati*, ed. Jean-Yves le Branchu, 2 vols. (Paris: Félix Alcan, 1934), 2:228; cited Timothy J. Reiss, *The Meaning of Literature* (Ithaca, N.Y.: Cornell University Press, 1992), p. 93f.

17. Marcel Pacaut, "Recherche sur les termes *Princeps, principatus, prince, principauté* au Moyen Age," (Bordeaux: Société des historiens médiévistes de

l'enseignement supérieur public, 1979), pp. 19–27. In some cases, royal authority remained in effect: Robert Fossier calls them "royal principalities" ("Sur les principautés médiévales, particulièrement en France," *Les principautés au moyen-âge*, pp. 9–17).

18. Olivier Guillot, *Le comte d'Anjou et son entourage au XIe siecle* (Paris: Picard, 1972), p. 365f.

19. "Ché non fa scienza, sanza lo ritenere, avere inteso" (*Paradiso*, V.41–42): the letter to Francesco Vettori, cited in Machiavelli, *The Prince*, ed. Quentin Skinner and Russell Price (Cambridge: Cambridge University Press, 1988–91), pp. 93–95.

20. Althusser, "Machiavel et nous," in *Ecrits philosophiques et politiques*, 2 vols. (Paris: Stock, 1995), 2:59.

21. Ibid., 2:8.

22. Machiavelli, p. 14. His admiration of France did not prevent him from noting the blunders of Louis XII in annexing Milan, and criticizing the French for allowing the church to accumulate so much power!

23. Allan H. Gilbert, *Machiavelli's Prince and Its Forerunners: "The Prince" as a Typical Book "de Regimine Principum"* (Durham, N.C.: Duke University Press, 1938).

24. Martin Coyle, "Introduction," in *Niccolò Machiavelli's The Prince: New Interdisciplinary Essays*, ed. Martin Coyle (Manchester: Manchester University Press, 1995), p. 2.

25. Skinner and Price, p. 93; Machiavelli, *The Discourses*, ed. Bernard Crick, tr. Leslie J. Walker (London: Penguin, 1970), 2:1, p. 273.

26. Compare with Senellart, *Les arts de gouverner*, p. 20f. Outside some incidental remarks, this excellent book addresses medieval theory only, not medieval practices.

27. Coyle, p. 8; and Janet L. Nelson, "Machiavelli's *via moderna*: Medieval and Renaissance Attitudes to History," pp. 40–64.

28. The *regimen* precedes the *regnum*: "the government preceded the State": Senellart, *Les arts de gouverner*, p. 23.

29. Machiavelli, *The Discourses*, 2:2, p. 275.

30. S. E. Finer, *The History of Government*, 3 vols. (Oxford: Oxford University Press, 1997–99), 2:921f.

31. Jacques Derrida, *Donner le temps, 1. La fausse monnaie* (Paris: Galilée, 1991). This development is drawn from Haidu, "1194–1941–1994: Five Bucks and the Suitcases of State," *Suitcase* 1 (1995): 28–35.

32. Fossier, p. 11.

33. "Le maintient dans la présence par la médiation de l'envoi," in Bruno Latour, *Nous n'avons jamais été modernes* (Paris: La Découverte, 1991), p. 175.

34. Michael Clanchy, "Literacy, Law, and the Power of the State," in *Culture et idéologie dans la genèse de l'état moderne* (Rome: L'Ecole Française de Rome, 1985), pp. 25–34; and Michael Clanchy, *From Memory to Written Record: England 1066–1307* (London: E. Arnold, 1979; 2d ed. Oxford: Blackwell, 1993).

35. Foucault, "Governmentality," *Foucault Effect*, pp. 87–104, 104.

36. Beccaria, *Elementi di economia pubblica* (Milan: 1804), p. 22f.; these are notes of lectures given in 1769: Pasquale Pasquino, "*Theatrum politicum*: The Genealogy of Capital," in Foucault, *Foucault Effect*, pp. 105–18, 109.

37. Foucault, *Foucault Effect*, p. 102.

38. Erwin Panofsky, *Gothic Architecture and Scholasticism* (New York: World, 1951–68); Walter Horn and Ernest Born, *The Plan of St. Gall*, 3 vols. (Berkeley and Los Angeles: University of California Press, 1979); Lorna Price, *The Plan of St. Gall in Brief* (Berkeley and Los Angeles: University of California Press, 1982); and Charles M. Radding and William W. Clark, *Medieval Architecture, Medieval Learning: Builders and Masters in the Age of Romanesque and Gothic* (New Haven, Conn.: Yale University Press, 1992).

39. Haidu, "The Episode as Semiotic Module in Twelfth Century Romance," *Poetics Today* 4, no. 4 (1983): 655–81.

40. Robert Henri Bautier, "Les Foires de Champagne: Recherches sur une évolution historique," in *La Foire* (Recueils de la Société Jean Bodin), vol. 5 (Brussels: Editions de la Librairie Encyclopédique, 1953), p. 97.

41. N. J. G. Pounds, *An Economic History of Medieval Europe* (New York: Longmans, 1974), p. 356. On the Champagne fairs, see Félix Bourquelot, *Etudes sur les foires de Champagne, sur la nature, l'étendue et les règles du commerce qui s'y faisait aux XIIe, XIIIe et XIVe siècles*, 2 vols. (Paris: L'Imprimerie Royale, 1865); Bautier, pp. 97–145; Richard David Face, "The Caravan Merchants and the Fairs of Champagne: A Study in the Techniques of Medieval Commerce," Ph.D. dissertation, University of Wisconsin, 1975, University Microfilms; and Michel Bur, *La formation du comté de Champagne, v. 950–v. 1150* ("Publications de l'Université de Nancy") (Nancy: Mémoires des Annales de l'Est, 1977), 2:54.

42. Bautier, p. 114f.

43. Bur, *La formation*, p. 299f.

44. Pounds, p. 355; Bautier, p. 133.

45. Bur, "L'essor économique," in *La formation*, pp. 292–307, 296f.

46. Ibid., p. 305.

47. Foucault, *Discipline and Punish*; and *The Birth of the Prison*.

48. Robert Fossier, *Polyptyques et censiers* (Turnhout: Brepols, 1978) ("Typologie des Sources du Moyen Age Occidental," fasc. 28).

49. Alexander Murray, *Reason and Society in the Middle Ages* (Oxford: Oxford University Press, 1978–91), pp. 188, 195.

50. *The American College Dictionary* (New York: Random House, 1964).

51. Like many such, it was revised later, in 1167 and 1168: R. H. C. Davis, "Domesday Book: Continental Parallels," in *Domesday Studies*, ed. J. C. Holt (Woodbridge, Eng.: Boydell and Brewer, 1987), pp. 15–39, 24.

52. W. W. Warren, *The Governance of Norman and Angevin England, 1086–1272* (London: Edward Arnold; Stanford, Calif.: Stanford University Press, 1987), p. 72.

53. C. Warren Hollister, "1066: The Feudal Revolution," in *Monarchy, Magnates and Institutions in the Anglo-Norman World* (London: Hambledon, 1986), pp. 1–16.

54. Ibid., p. 24.

55. Thomas K. Keefe, *Feudal Assessments and the Political Community under Henry II and His Sons* (Berkeley and Los Angeles: University of California Press, 1983), pp. 154–88.

56. Frank Stenton, *The First Century of English Feudalism 1066–1166*, 2d ed. (Westport, Conn.: Greenwood Press, 1961), p. 136.

57. Isaac Johsua, *La Face cachée du moyen âge: Les premiers pas du capital* (Paris: La Brèche, 1988).

58. Ibid., p. 137f., n., and p. 11.

59. Jean-Pierre Genêt, "Féodalisme et naissance de l'Etat moderne: A propos des thèse de Charles Tilly," in *Villes, bonnes villes, cités et capitales. Etudes d'histoire urbaine (XIIe–XVIIIe siècle) offertes à Bernard Chevalier*, ed. Monique Bourin (Caen: Paradigme, 1993), pp. 239–46.

60. Keefe, p. 73.

61. Keefe, "Appendix I The Norman *Infeudationes militum*: 1172," in *Feudal Assessments*, pp. 141–53.

62. Thomas N. Bisson, *Fiscal Accounts of Catalonia under the early count-kings (1151–1213)*, 2 vols. (Berkeley and Los Angeles: University of California Press, 1984), 1:27f. On Catalonia, see also the important research of Pierre Bonnassie.

63. John W. Baldwin, *The Government of Philip Augustus. Foundations of French Royal Power in the Middle Ages* (Berkeley and Los Angeles: University of California Press, 1986–91), p. 287.

64. Theodore Evergates, *Feudal Society in the Bailliage of Troyes under the*

Counts of Champagne, 1152–1284 (Baltimore, Md.: Johns Hopkins University Press, 1975).

65. Goody, "What's in a List?" in *The Domestication of the Savage Mind* (Cambridge: Cambridge University Press, 1977–78), pp. 74–111.

66. Ecclesiastics were far more advanced in record keeping than the lay nobility. The *Foeda campanie* underline the accession of a specific class.

67. Evergates, p. 61.

68. Pierre Feuchère, *De l'épée à la plume. Les châtelains d'Arras* (Arras: 1948) ("Commission départementale des Monuments historiques du Pas-de-Calais," vol. 6, fasc. 1), p. 13.

69. Its registers include a census of all the communes of the kingdom: Michel Nortier, "Les actes de Philippe Auguste: notes critiques sur les sources diplomatiques du règne," in *La France de Philippe Auguste: Le temps des mutations*, ed. Robert-Henri Bautier (Paris: CNRS, 1982), pp. 429–53.

70. Fossier, *Polyptiques et censiers*, p. 37.

71. Georges Duby, *Les trois ordres ou l'imaginaire du féodalisme* (Paris: Gallimard, 1978); text of Adalberon de Laon's *Poème au roi Robert*, ed. and tr. Claude Carozzi (Paris: Les Belles Lettres, 1979), with an important introduction.

72. Jacques Krynen, *L'empire du roi: Idées et croyances politiques en France, XIIIe–XVe siècle* (Paris: Gallimard, 1993), p. 18.

73. Etienne de Fougères, *Le livre des manières*, ed. R. Anthony Lodge ("Textes Littéraires Français," no. 275) (Geneva: Droz, 1979), editor's introduction.

74. Jean Batany, "Du bellator au chevalier dans le schéma des 'trois ordres' (étude sémantique)," *La guerre et la paix au moyen âge*. Actes du 101e Congrés National des Sociétés Savantes (Paris: Bibliothéque Nationale, 1976), pp. 232–34.

75. "Molt devon cher aveir nos homes, / quar li vilen portent le[s] sonmes / don nos vivon quanque nos sunmes, / et chevaliers et clers et domes" (ibid., pp. 577–80).

76. "Li clerc deivent por toz orer, / li chevalier sanz demorer / deivent defendre et ennorer, / et li païsant laborer" (ibid., ll. 673–76, p. 84).

77. On burghers, see ll. 801–972; on women, ll. 973–1252. Half a century earlier, Hugh of Saint Victor had already exploded the seven liberal arts to twenty-one, including the "mechanical" arts: *The Didascalion of Hugh of St. Victor*, ed. Jerome Taylor (New York: Columbia University Press, 1961–68), pp. 31, 74–79.

78. Brian Stock, *The Implications of Literacy* (Princeton, N.J.: Princeton University Press, 1983).

79. Elizabeth M. Hallam, *Domesday Book Through Nine Centuries* (London: Thames and Hudson, 1986), p. 17.

80. Ibid., p. 18f.

81. In addition to Fossier's *Typologie*, see John Percival, "The Precursors of Domesday: Roman and Carolingian Land Registers," in *Domesday Book: A Reassessment*, ed. Peter Sawyer (London: Edward Arnold, 1985), pp. 5–27.

82. V. H. Galbraith, *The Making of Domesday Book* (Oxford: Oxford University Press, 1961), p. 1f.

83. The prologue of the *Inquisitio Eliensis*, a collection of returns from the abbey of Ely, an early stage of *Domesday Book*: Hallam, p. 22, emphasis added.

84. *The Anglo-Saxon Chronicle*, tr. and ed. Michael Swanton (New York: Routledge, 1998), p. 215f.

85. Davis, pp. 15–29, 28.

86. H. R. Lyon, "The Beyond of Domesday Book," in *Domesday Studies*, ed. J. C. Holt (Woodbridge, Eng.: Boydell, 1987), pp. 1–13.

87. F. M. Stanton, *Preparatory to Anglo-Saxon England*, ed. D. M. Stanton (Oxford: Oxford University Press, 1970), p. 325.

88. Robin Fleming, *Kings and Lords in Conquest England* (Cambridge: Cambridge University Press, 1991), pp. 107–44, 184f.

89. Peter Sawyer, "1066–1086: A Tenurial Revolution?" in *Domesday Book: A Reassessment*, ed. Peter Sawyer (London: Edward Arnold, 1985), pp. 71–85.

90. Fleming, p. 145.

91. *The Ecclesiastical History*, 2 vols., ed. and tr. Marjorie Chibnall (Oxford: Oxford University Press, 1969–90), 2:266; in Fleming, p. 107. Orderic describes the redistribution of lands and the humiliation of the indigenous population: pp. 260ff.

92. Davis, p. 27.

93. Baldwin, *Masters, Princes and Merchants*, p. 421.

94. Baldwin, *Government of Philip Augustus*, pp. 412–18.

95. Gérard Sivéry, "La description du royaume de France par les conseillers de Philippe-Auguste et par leurs successeurs," *Le Moyen Age* 90 (1984): 65–85; documents in De Wailly, Delisle, and Jourdan, *Scripta de foedis at regem spectantibus et de militibus ad exercitum vocandis*, in "Recueil des Historiens des Gaules et de France," vol. 23 (Paris: 1894).

96. Sivéry, p. 73.

CHAPTER 9

1. Anthony Giddens, *The Nation-State and Violence*. Vol. 2: *A Contemporary Critique of Historical Materialism* (Berkeley and Los Angeles: University of California Press, 1987), p. 75f.

2. Janet L. Nelson, "Literacy in Carolingian Government," in *The Uses of Literacy in Early Medieval Europe*, ed. Rosamond McKitterick (Cambridge: Cambridge University Press, 1990–92), pp. 258–96, 272ff.

3. Karl Ferdinand Werner, "Les Robertiens," in *Le roi de France et son royaume autour de l'an mil*, ed. Michel Parisse et Xavier Barral i Altet (Paris: Picard, 1992), pp. 15–26, 22.

4. Ibid., p. 45.

5. John W. Baldwin, *The Government of Philip Augustus* (Berkeley and Los Angeles: University of California Press, 1986), p. 35f.

6. Ibid., p. 125f.

7. "*Plain pouvoir de faire toute chose autretant con li seignor*" (Geoffroy de Villehardouin, *Conquête de Constantinople*, ed. Edmond Faral [Paris: Les Belles Lettres 1938–39], 1:14ff.).

8. Gaines Post, "*Plena potestas* and Consent in Medieval Assemblies," *Studies in Medieval Legal Thought: Public Law and the State, 1100–1322* (Princeton, N.J.: Princeton University Press, 1964), pp. 91–108, 107.

9. W. L. Warren, *Henry II* (Berkeley and Los Angeles: University of California Press, 1973–91), pp. 281–83.

10. Ibid., pp. 287–90.

11. M. Moheau, *Recherches et considérations sur la population de France* (Paris: 1778), p. 20; in Pasquale Pasquino, "*Theatrum Politicum*: The Genealogy of Capital—Police and the State of Prosperity," in *The Foucault Effect: Studies in Governmentality*, ed. Graham Burchell, Colin Gordon, and Peter Miller (Chicago: Chicago University Press, 1991), pp. 105–18, 115.

12. Jacques Beauroy, "Centralisation et histoire sociale: Remarques sur l'*Inquisitio Vicecomitum* de 1170," *Cahiers de Civilisation Médiévale* 37 (1994): 3–24.

13. Olivier Guillot, *Le comte d'Anjou et son entourage au XIe siecle* (Paris: Picard, 1972), pp. 421–25.

14. Baldwin, p. 130f.

15. On the Capetian *baillis*, see ibid., pp. 125–36.

16. Wayne M. Senner, "Theories and Myths on the Origin of Writing: A Historical Overview," in *The Origins of Writing*, ed. Wayne M. Senner (Lincoln: University of Nebraska Press, 1989), pp. 1–26; and Denise Schmandt-Besserat, "Two Precursors of Writing: Plain and Complex Tokens," in *The Origins of Writing*, ed. Wayne M. Senner (Lincoln: University of Nebraska Press, 1989), pp. 27–42; Ernest Gellner, *Plough, Sword, and Book: The Structure of Human History* (Chicago: University of Chicago Press, 1988), pp. 70–75; and Alexander Murray, *Reason and Society in the Middle Ages* (Oxford: Oxford University Press, 1978–91), pp. 194–203.

17. Charles Johnson, ed. and tr., *Dialogus de Scaccario The Course of the Exchequer, by Richard Fitz Nigel and Constitution Domus Regis The Establishment of the Royal Household* (Oxford: Oxford University Press, 1983).

18. Warren, p. 315.

19. Ibid., p. 13.

20. "Dedication," ibid., p. 1–2.

21. In fact, the accounting technology was already known in classical Athens: Carolyn Webber and Aaron Wildavsky, *A History of Taxation and Expenditure in the Western World* (New York: Simon and Schuster, 1986), pp. 209–21.

22. C. Warren Hollister, "The Origins of the English Treasury," *Monarchy, Magnates and Institutions in the Anglo-Norman World* (London: Hambledon, 1986), pp. 209–22.

23. *De scaccario*, p. xlii.

24. Hollister, p. xliv.

25. Such "tallies" were still used in the nineteenth century in parts of Europe.

26. Johnson, *De scaccario*, p. 25f.

27. *A.S.C.*, s.a. 1086 [E] [*recte* 1087]; Fleming, p. 107.

28. Johnson, *De scaccario*, p. 39f.

29. Ibid., p. 61f.

30. Thomas R. Keefe, *Feudal Assessments and the Political Community under Henry II and His Sons* (Berkeley and Los Angeles: University of California Press, 1983).

31. Eric Bournazel and Jean-Pierre Poly, *La mutation féodale* (Paris: PUF, 1980), p. 284.

32. Baldwin, p. 218.

33. Sidney Painter, *Studies in the History of the English Feudal Barony*, p. 20; cited by J. O. Prestwich, "War and Finance in the Anglo-Norman State," in *Anglo-Norman Warfare, Studies in Late Anglo-Saxon and Anglo-Norman Military Organization and Warfare*, ed. Matthew Strickland (Woodbridge, Eng.: Boydell, 1992), pp. 59–83, 61.

34. Frank Stenton, *The First Century of English Feudalism, 1066–1166* (Oxford: Clarendon, 1932), pp. 50, n. 1, 214, 191; more recently, Michael Prestwich, *Armies and Warfare in the Middle Ages: The English Experience* (New Haven, Conn.: Yale University Press, 1996), pp. 57–75.

35. A. L. Poole, *Obligations of Society in the XII and XIII centuries*, pp. 3–4; cited in J. O. Prestwich, *Armies and Warfare in the Middle Ages: The English Experience* (New Haven, Conn.: Yale University Press, 1996), pp. 59–61.

36. John Baldwin, "The Royal Income, 1202/3," in *The Government of*

Philip Augustus (Berkeley and Los Angeles: University of California Press, 1986), pp. 152–73. On the details of royal taxation, see Elisabeth Magnou-Nortier, "Pouvoir, finances et politiques des premiers capétiens," in Elisabeth Magnou-Nortier, ed., *Pouvoirs et libertés au temps des premiers capétiens* (Editions Hérault, 1992), pp. 125–68.

37. Georges Duby, *Le Moyen Age 987–1460: De Hugues Capet à Jeanne d'Arc (987–1460)* (Paris: Hachette, 1987), p. 337.

38. Such as that in the depths of the Louvre, and another of equal size at Dun.

39. Baldwin, "War and Finances," in *The Government of Philip Augustus* (Berkeley and Los Angeles: University of California Press, 1986), pp. 166–75.

40. Prestwich, pp. 69–73.

41. Georges Duby, *Le Dimanche de Bouvines* (Paris: Gallimard, 1973), p. 145f.

42. John Gillingham, "Richard I and the Science of War in the Middle Ages," in *War and Government in the Middle Ages*, ed. John Gillingham and J. C. Holt (Cambridge, Eng.: Boydell, 1984), p. 83.

43. Ibid., pp. 78–91.

44. John Gillingham, "War and Chivalry in the *History of William the Marshal*," in *Anglo-Norman Warfare, Studies in Late Anglo-Saxon and Anglo-Norman Military Organization and Warfare*, ed. Matthew Strickland (Woodbridge, Eng.: Boydell, 1992), pp. 251–63.

45. *De re militari*, p. 69.

46. Matthew Bennett, "Wace and Warfare," in *Anglo-Norman Warfare, Studies in Late Anglo-Saxon and Anglo-Norman Military Organization and Warfare*, ed. Matthew Strickland (Woodbridge, Eng.: Boydell, 1992), p. 234.

47. R. Allen Brown, *English Castles*, 3d ed. (London: B. T. Batsford, 1976), p. 209; cited by Matthew Strickland, "Securing the North: Invasion and the Strategy of Defense in Twelfth-Century Anglo-Scottish Warfare," in *Anglo-Norman Warfare, Studies in Late Anglo-Saxon and Anglo-Norman Military Organization and Warfare*, ed. Matthew Strickland (Woodbridge, Eng.: Boydell, 1992), pp. 208–29.

48. The small keeps at La Turbie, north of Monaco, are examples.

49. Strickland, p. 211f.

50. Gillingham, "Richard I and the Science of War," p. 90.

51. By contrast, in the whole of his reign, he only spent £7,000 on all English castles. The closest thing to Château Gaillard was the nearly £7,000 spent on Dover during the decade between 1180 and 1190 (Gillingham, "Richard I and the Science of War," p. 90).

52. Alain Erlande-Brandenburg, "L'architecture militaire au temps de Philippe Auguste: Une nouvelle conception de la défense," in *La France de Philippe Auguste*, ed. Robert-Henri Bautier (Paris: CNRS, 1982), pp. 595–603.

53. Philip Augustus's register A in the Vatican Library.

54. *Cartulaire de la Trinité de Vendome*, 1: no. 2. The charter is from the 1180s but dates its arrangements before 1030; Keefe, p. 76.

55. Duby, *Dimanche de Bouvines*, pp. 100–10.

56. Andrew Ayton and J. L. Price, "Introduction: The Military Revolution from a Medieval Perspective," in *The Medieval Military Revolution: State, Society and Military Change in Medieval and Early Modern Europe*, ed. Andrew Ayton and J. L. Price (London: Tauris, 1995), pp. 1–22, 3; with reference to Michael Mann, *The Source of Social Power*, 2 vols. (Cambridge: Cambridge University Press, 1986–92), 2:453–58, 2:475–83.

57. Johnson, *De Scaccario*, p. 2.

58. For England, see Prestwich, p. 76; for France, see Baldwin, *Government of Philip Augustus*.

59. A contrast later repeated by Gerald of Wales: Linda E. Marshall, "The Identity of the 'New Man' in the *Anticlaudianus* of Alan of Lille," *Viator* 10 (1979): 77–94.

60. Baldwin, *Government of Philip Augustus*, pp. 193–95.

61. Except as noted, I follow Duby's classic account, *Le Dimanche de Bouvines*.

62. Baldwin, *Government of Philip Augustus*, pp. 207–19.

63. Duby, *Dimanche de Bouvines*, p. 43; see the map facing p. 50.

64. Ibid., p. 287.

65. Gabrielle M. Spiegel, *Romancing the Past: The Rise of Vernacular Prose Historiography in Thirteenth Century France* (Berkeley and Los Angeles: University of California Press, 1993), pp. 269–313.

66. Baldwin, *Government of Philip Augustus*, p. 365f.; Duby, *Le Moyen Age*, p. 353f.

67. Ibid., pp. 380–88.

68. Robert-Henri Bautier, "Le règne de Philippe-Auguste dans l'histoire de France," in *La France de Philippe-Auguste: Le temps des mutations*, ed. Robert-Henri Bautier (Paris: CNRS, 1982), p. 27.

69. Spiegel, pp. 305–9.

70. Jacques Krynen, *L'empire du roi: Idées et croyances politiques en France, XIIIe-XVe siècle* (Paris: Gallimard, 1993), pp. 51–67.

71. Ibid., p. 392f.

72. Baldwin, *Government of Philip Augustus*, pp. 359–62.

73. Recent historiography is rich in the study of Capetian ideology: see Baldwin, *Government of Philip Augustus*, pp. 362–93; Jacques le Goff, "L'imaginaire politique: Mémoire et idéologie," in *Histoire de la France*, vol. 2, ed. Jacques le Goff, *L'Etat et les pouvoirs* (Paris: Seuil, 1989), pp. 53–91.

74. Spiegel, pp. 269, 312.

75. Haidu, "Toward a Socio-Historical Semiotics: Power and Legitimacy in the *Couronnement de Louis*," *Kodikas / Code* 2 (1980): 155–69; Sarah Kay, *The Chansons de geste in the Age of Romance*, p. 124.

76. Kay, pp. 137–44.

77. Max Weber, *The Theory of Social and Economic Organization*, ed. Talcott Parsons (New York: Free Press, 1964), p. 156; and *On Charisma and Institution Building*, ed. S. N. Eisenstadt (Chicago: University of Chicago Press, 1968), p. 75.

78. Hagen Schulze, *States, Nations and Nationalism*, tr. William E. Yuill (Oxford: Blackwell, 1994–98), p. 16.

79. Weber, p. 337.

80. Jean Dunbabin, "Government," in *The Cambridge History of Medieval Political Thoughts, c. 350–c. 1450*, ed. J. H. Burns (Cambridge: Cambridge University Press, 1988–91), pp. 479–82.

81. John of Salisbury, *Policraticus*, 2 vols., ed. C. C. J. Webb (Oxford: Clarendon, 1909); partial translations by John Dickinson, *The Statesman's Book* (New York: Alfred A. Knopf, 1927); J. B. Pike, *The Frivolities of Courtiers and the Footprints of Philosophers* (Minneapolis: University of Minnesota Press, 1938); Cary J. Nederman, *Policraticus* (Cambridge: Cambridge University Press, 1990); Walter Map, *De nugis curialium: Courtiers' Trifles*, ed. and tr. M. R. James, rev. C. N. L. Brooke and R. A. B. Mynors (Oxford: Oxford University Press, 1983). On Walter, see Siân Echard, "Map's Metafiction: Author, Narrator and Reader in *De nugis curialium*," *Exemplaria* 8, no. 2 (1996): 287–314.

82. Krynen, p. 53; on the later distinction of vassal and subject, see André Bossuat, "The Maxim 'The King Is Emperor in his own Kingdom': Its Use in the Fifteenth Century before the Parlement of Paris," in *The Recovery of France in the Fifteenth Century*, ed. P. S. Lewis (New York: Harper and Row, 1971–72), pp. 185–95, 195.

83. Johnson, *De scaccario*, p. l. The next royal document of this kind was Edward's Household Ordinance in 1279: T. F. Tout, *Chapters in the Administrative History of Mediaeval England*, 6 vols. (Manchester: Manchester University Press, 1920; rpt. 1967), pp. 10–62; text in 2:158–63.

84. "Homme qe veut bien aprendre / des terres garder e acountes prendre / cest livre bien ly aprendra / coment par tut bien sey contendra" (Dorothea

Oschinsky, ed., *Walter of Henley and Other Treatises on Estate Management and Accounting* [Oxford: Clarendon, 1971], p. 296).

85. Ibid., p. 8.

86. In English: steward, bailiff, and reeve.

87. Oschinsky, p. 151f., and the text, pp. 308–43.

88. Ibid., p. 340f.

89. The text is given in Oschinsky, pp. 388–407.

90. "Par un u deus des plus *privez* e *leals* ke vus eyez *priveement* fetes comparisun des roulles des acuntes rendues."

91. "Trestuz les hostes seculaers e religius."

92. Oschinsky, p. 7.

93. Gérard Sivery, "La description du Royaume de France par les conseillers de Philippe Auguste et par leurs successeurs," *Moyen Age* 90 (1984): 65–85.

94. Krynen, pp. 53ff.

95. C. Warren Hollister, "The Rise of Administrative Kingship: Henry I," *Monarchy, Magnates and Institutions in the Anglo-Norman World* (London: Hambledon, 1986), pp. 223–45, 232, with reference to R. L. Poole, *The Exchequer in the Twelfth Century* (London: 1912).

96. "Par le fer et par le feu, the roi assainissait" (Duby, *Le Moyen Age*, p. 335f.).

97. "Foi et savoir," in *La religion*, ed. Jacques Derrida and Gianni Vattimo (Paris: Seuil, 1996), pp. 9–86, 75f.

98. Michael T. Clanchy, *From Memory to Written Record, England 1066–1307*, 2d ed. (Oxford: Blackwell, 1979–93), p. 32.

99. "*Decreuit subiectum sibi populum iuri scripto legibusque subicere*," Johnson, *De scaccario*, p. 62.

100. Ibid., p. 63.

101. Max Weber, "Meaning of Discipline," in *On Charisma and Institution Building*, ed. S. N. Eisenstadt (Chicago: University of Chicago Press, 1968), pp. 28–42, 36.

102. W. W. Warren, *The Governance of Norman and Angevin England, 1086–1272* (London: Edward Arnold; Stanford, Calif.: Stanford University Press, 1987), p. 169.

103. This notion of "civilization" differs substantially from Norbert Elias's celebratory concept in *Über den Prozess der Zivilisation*.

104. Jacques le Goff, *Les intellectuels au moyen âge* (Paris: Seuil, 1965); Antonio Gramsci, "The Intellectuals," in *Selections from the Prison Notebooks*, ed.

and tr. Quentin Hoare and Geoffrey Nowell-Smith (Moscow: International Publishers, 1971), pp. 3–23.

105. Bossuat, pp. 185–95; and Barthélemy-Amédée Pocquet du Haut-Jussé, "A Political Concept of Louis XI: Subjection instead of Vasselage," in *The Recovery of France in the Fifteenth Century*, ed. P. S. Lewis (New York: Harper and Row, 1971–72), pp. 185–215.

106. Philippe Buc, *L'ambiguïté du livre* (Paris: Beauchesne, 1994).

107. Trinh T. Minh-ha, *Woman, Nature, Other: Writing, Postcoloniality, and Feminism* (Bloomington: Indiana University Press, 1989), p. 16f.

CHAPTER 10

1. Roger Dragonetti, "Pygmalion ou les pièges de la fiction dans le *Roman de la rose*," in *Orbis mediaevalis, mélanges . . . Reto R. Bezzola* (Berne: Francke, 1978), pp. 89–111.

2. David Hult, *Self-fulfilling Prophecies: Readership and Authority in the First Roman de la rose* (Cambridge: Cambridge University Press, 1986), pp. 6, 24.

3. Alan M. Gunn, *The Mirror of Love: A Reinterpretation of the Romance of the Rose* (Lubbock: Texas Tech Press, 1952).

4. Erich Köhler, "Narcisse, la fontaine d'amour, et Guillaume de Lorris," in *L'humanisme médiéval dans les littératures romanes du XIIe au XIVe siècle*, ed. Anthime Fourrier (Paris: Klincksieck, 1964), pp. 147–64, 163.

5. Marc-René Jung, *Etudes sur le poème allégorique en France au moyen âge* (Berne: Francke, 1971), p. 290.

6. Guillaume de Lorris and Jean de Meun, *Le Roman de la rose*, 3 vols., ed. Félix Lecoy ("Classiques Français du Moyen Age," 92 vols.) (Paris: Champion, 1965), 1:16.

7. "Li plusor songent de nuiz / maintes choses covertement / que l'en voit puis apertement" (ll. 18–20).

8. Sigmund Freud, *The Interpretation of Dreams*, in *The Basic Writings of Sigmund Freud*, ed. A. A. Brill (New York: Random House, 1938), particularly ch. 6, "The Dreamwork," pp. 319–467.

9. "En ce songe onques rien n'ot / qui tretot avenue ne soit / si con li songes recensoit. / Or veil cel songe rimeer" (ll. 28–31).

10. Jean Batany, "Paradigmes lexicaux et structures littéraires au moyen âge," *Revue d'histoire littéraire en France* 70 (1970): 819–35, p. 824.

11. Armand Strubel, *Le Roman de la rose* (Paris: PUF, 1984), p. 50.

12. Emmanuèle Baumgartner, "The Play of Temporalities; or, the Reported Dream of Guillaume de Lorris," in *Rethinking the Romance of the Rose*,

ed. Kevin Brownlee and Sylvie Huot (Philadelphia: University of Pennsylvania Press, 1992), pp. 21–38, 25.

13. "Grant servise et doz et plesant / aloient li oisel fesant; / lais d'amors et sonoiz cortois / chantoient en lor serventois. / li un haut, li autre en bas. / De lor chant, n'estoit mie gas, / la douçor et la melodie / me mist el cuer grant reverdie" (ll. 699–706).

14. "L'odor de li entor espent; / la soautume qui en ist / tote la place replenist; / et quant jou senti si fleirier, / je n'oi talant de repairier, / ainz m'en apressai por le prendre" (ll. 1666–71).

15. Ll. 1729f., ll. 3459–72.

16. "Et quant du bessier me recors, / qui me mist une odor ou cors / assez plus douce que de basme, / par un poi que je ne me pasme, / qu'ancor ai ge ou cuer enclose / la douce savor de la rose" (ll. 3755–60).

17. Compare with Strubel, pp. 36–41.

18. Jean Rychner, "Le mythe de la Fontaine de Narcisse dans le *Roman de la rose* de Guillaume de Lorris," in *Du Saint-Alexis à François Villon* (Geneva: Droz, 1985), p. 319.

19. 1: ll. 1423–1520; 2: ll. 1521–68; 3: ll. 1569–2762.

20. Combining elements from Ovid and a twelfth-century rewriting: Ovid, *Metamorphoses* III, 344–503; M. M. Pelan and N. C. W. Spence, ed., *Narcissus* (Paris: Les Belles Lettres, 1964).

21. Frederick Goldin, *The Mirror of Narcissus in the Courtly Love Lyric* (Ithaca, N.Y.: Cornell University Press, 1967), p. 53.

22. Giorgio Agamben, *Stanze*, tr. Yves Hersant (Paris: Rivages, 1981–88), p. 139.

23. "Dedenz n'ousai esgarder, / ainz començai a coarder, / que de Narcisus me sovint / cui malement en mesavint. / Mes me pensai que a seür, / sanz peor de mauvés eür, / a la fontaine aler pooie; / par folie m'en esloignoie" (ll. 1513–20).

24. Jung, p. 300.

25. Goldin, p. 54.

26. E. B. Vitz, "The *I* of the *Roman de la rose*," *Genre* 6 (1973): 49–75.

27. Alain Badiou, *Théorie du sujet* (Paris: Seuil, 1982), p. 275.

28. *Aesthetic Distance, ad finem.*

29. Félix Lecoy ("Classiques Français du Moyen Age," 92 vols.) (Paris: Champion, 1965), p. 275, n. to ll. 1541–68.

30. *Ii. pierres de crystal* (l. 1536); *li cristaus sanz decevoir / tot l'estre dou vergier encuse* (ll. 1558f.).

31. "Anc non agui de me poder / Ni no fui meus de l'or'en sai / Que-m

laisset en sos olhs vezer / En un miralh que mout me plai. / Miralhs, pus me mirei en te, / M'an mort li sospir de preon, / C'aissi-m perdei com perdet se / Lo bels Narcisus en la fon." "Can vei la lauzeta mover" (René Nelli and René Lavaud, *Les troubadours*, 2 vols. [Paris: Desclée de Brouwer, 1960], 2:74).

32. "Qui en ce miroër se mire / ne puet avoir garant ne mire / que il tel chose as ieuz ne voie / qui d'amors l'a mis tost en voie" (ll. 1753–56).

33. The totalizing claim that Luce Irigaray attacks in her *Speculum de l'autre femme* (Paris: Minuit, 1974); English edition: Gillian C. Gill, tr., *Speculum of the Other Woman* (Ithaca, N.Y.: Cornell University Press, 1985).

34. Ll. 1569, 1573, 1578, 1607, 1613.

35. I follow Lecoy, whose reading of B. N. fr. 1573 represents the *difficilior lectio:* "Mes ja mes n'oroiz miels descrivre / la vérité de la matere, / quant j'avré *apost* le mistere" (ll. 1598–1600); an *apost* is a word *in apposition* to another in order to explain it. It belongs to the same semantic family as *gloser.*

36. Is it the same kind of space as that of a clerical consciousness, treading on the ground of religious belief? Or is it closer to a consciousness of emptiness? Georges Didi-Hubermann, "Ce que nous voyons, ce qui nous regarde," *Les cahiers du musée national d'art moderne* 37 (fall 1991): 33–59.

37. Jean-Charles Huchet, *L'amour discourtois: la "fin'amors" chez les premiers troubadours* (Toulouse: Privat, 1987), p. 175f.

38. Charles Muscatine, "The Emergence of Psychological Allegory in Old French Romance," *PMLA* 68 (1953): 1160–82.

39. Batany, p. 825.

40. Strubel, pp. 42–44.

41. The entry in Tobler-Lommatzsch runs about six columns and includes "La signorie et le *dangier*"; "Hé, douche amie . . . Se jou creïsse ton talent, Couronne, terre ne avoirs Ne signorie ne pöoirs Ne *dangiers* de nul hyretage N'amendroit ton pucelaige, Por qu'a tel honte fust perdus"; and *Merchant of Venice,* IV.i.179.

42. Giles of Rome (ca. 1246–1316), in *De potestate ecclesiastica:* John B. Morrall, *Political Thought in Medieval Times* (New York: Harper, 1958–62), p. 86f.

43. "Amors et ma mestresse, je sui en son dangier," and "Soufrir lor estuet le dangier, Quant amors les veut justicier" (Tobler-Lommatzsch).

44. "Vasaus, pris estes, rien n'i a / de destorner ne de desfendre, / ne fai pas dangier de toi rendre . . . / Il est fox qui moine dangier / vers celui que doit losengier / et qu'il covient a souploier" (ll. 1882–89).

CHAPTER II

1. Lewis Thorpe, ed., *Le Roman de Silence* (Cambridge, Eng.: Heffer, 1972). Regina Psaki reedited the text: *Le Roman de Silence* (New York: Garland, 1991). I have used *Silence*, ed. and tr. Sarah Roche-Mahdi (East Lansing, Mich.: Colleagues Press, 1992).

2. Félix Lecoy, "Le *Roman de Silence* d'Heldris de Cornualle," *Romania* 99 (1978): 109–25. In fact, Roche-Mahdi lists two earlier notices: R. W. H. Stevenson, *Report on the Manuscripts of Lord Middleton at Wollaton Hall, Nottinghamshire* (Historical Manuscripts Commission, 1911); F. A. G. Cowper, "Origins and Peregrinations of the Laval-Middleton Manuscript," *Nottingham Medieval Studies* 3 (1959): 3–18; and one study, Heinrich Gelzer, "Der Silenceroman von Heldris de Cornualle," *Zeitschrift für romanische Philologie* 27 (1927): 88–99.

3. Kate Mason Cooper, "Elle and *L*: Sexualized Textuality in *Le Roman de Silence*," *Romance Notes* 25, no. 3 (1985): 341–60; and Michèle Perret, "Travesties et transsexuelles: Ydes, Silence, Grisandole, Blanchandine," *Romance Notes* 25, no. 3 (1985): 328–40.

4. Thorpe, p. 15.

5. Suzanne Conklin Akbari, "Nature's Forge recast in the *Roman de Silence*," *Literary Aspects of Courtly Culture*, ed. Donald Maddox and Sara-Sturm-Maddox (Cambridge, Eng.: Brewer, 1994), pp. 39–46, 45f.; Akbari cites Kathleen J. Brahney, "When Silence was Golden: Female Personae in the *Roman de Silence*," in *The Spirit of the Court*, ed. Glyn S. Burgess and Robert A. Taylor (Cambridge, Eng.: Boydell and Brewer, 1985), p. 60.

6. Elizabeth A. Waters, "The Third Path: Alternative Sex, Alternative Gender in *Le Roman de Silence*," *Arthuriana* 7, no. 2 (summer 1997): 35–45.

7. R. Howard Bloch, *Etymologies and Genealogies: A Literary Anthropology of the French Middle Ages* (Chicago: University of Chicago Press, 1983), pp. 195–97; R. Howard Bloch, "Silence and Holes: The *Roman de Silence* and the Art of the Trouvère," *Yale French Studies* 70 (1986): 81–99.

8. R. Regina Psaki, "The Modern Editor and Medieval 'Misogyny': Text Editing and *Le Roman de Silence*," *Arthuriana* 7, no. 2 (summer 1997): 78–86, p. 79.

9. Peter Allen, "The Ambiguity of Silence: Gender, Writing, and Le Roman de Silence," in *Sign, Sentence, Discourse: Language in Medieval Thought and Literature*, ed. Julian N. Wasserman and Lois Roney (Syracuse, N.Y.: Syracuse University Press, 1989), pp. 98–112; Simon Gaunt, "The Significance of Silence," *Paragraph* 13, no. 2 (1990): 202–16.

10. Deuteronomy 22:5.

11. James A. Brundage, *Law, Sex, and Christian Society in Medieval Europe* (Chicago: University of Chicago Press, 1987), p. 108; for the rest of this paragraph, see pp. 250, 314, 473.

12. Valerie R. Hotchkiss, *Clothes Make the Man: Female Cross-Dressing in Medieval Europe* (New York: Garland, 1996), p. 39.

13. *Eneas, Roman du XIIe siècle*, 2 vols., ed. J.-J. Salverda de Grave ("Clasiques Français du Moyen Age," nos. 44 and 62) (Paris: Champion, 1964 and 1929), 1: ll. 7399–411.

14. John Boswell, "Revolutions, Universals and Sexual Categories," in *Hidden from History: Retaining the Gay and Lesbian Past*, ed. Martin Bauml Duberman, Martha Vicinus, and George Chauncey Jr. (New York: Penguin, 1991), pp. 17–36. See also Brundage; Joan Cadden, *Meanings of Sex Difference in the Middle Ages* (Cambridge: Cambridge University Press, 1993); and John Benton, *The Language of Sex: Five Voices from Northern France Around 1200* (Chicago: University of Chicago Press, 1994).

15. *Eneas*, ll. 7388–93.

16. In practice, even the exemplum is not that simple: Claude Bremond, Jacques le Goff, Jean-Claude Schmitt, *L'Exemplum* (Turnhut: Brepols, 1982); and Jean-Claude Schmitt, ed., *Prêcher d'exemples* (Paris: Stock, 1985).

17. Jorge Luis Borges, "From Allegory to Novel," in *Selected Fictions*, ed. Eliot Wienberger, tr. Esther Allen, Suzanne Jill Levine, and Eliot Weinberger (New York: Viking, 1999), pp. 337–39.

18. Angus Fletcher, *Allegory: Theory of a Symbolic Mode* (Ithaca, N.Y.: Cornell University Press, 1964).

19. Haidu, "Introduction," in *Aesthetic Distance . . .* (Geneva: Droz, 1966).

20. Alexandre Leupin, *Fiction et incarnation: Littérature et théologie au moyen âge* (Paris: Flammarion, 1993).

21. "Mais el roiame n'en a trois / Dont la mellor presisse mie / S'une m'en faut, bele Eufemia" (ll. 982–84, punctuation modified).

22. Biele Eufemie, cho est l'une / A cui li cuers Cador s'aüne! / De l'une est Eufemie gloze, / Mais que sor li prendre ne l'oze, / Qu'en li n'a pas tat d'ozer / Qu'ele sor li l'oze glozer (ibid., ll. 985–90, emphases added).

23. "Or voel a l'enfant repairier / Et demostrer et esclairier / Liquels cho fu, masle u femiele. / Segnor, cho fu une puchiele / Nature i mostre tolte s'uevre . . . Nature qui moult grant force a / Vint a l'enfant, si sesforça / Dist: "Or voel faire ouvre forcible" (ll. 1795–1807).

24. "Quante faire violt un vallant home / Que voelle ovrer par majestyre"

(ll. 1826f.). The last word is a punning neologism, combining majesty, mastery, and mystery.

25. "Se vos, bials sire, nel savés, / Je vos di c'une fille avés. S'est la plus biele creäture / C'ainc en cest monde fesist Nature" (ll. 2017–20).

26. "Miols val li graindres del menor" (l. 2312).

27. "En un poi de vil noreture / Empire plus bone nature / Que longhe aprisons de bienfaire / Puist amender cuer de pute aire" (ll. 2339–42).

28. "Tel n'oï onques! / Silencius! qui sui jo donques? / Silencius ai non, je cui, / U jo sui altres que ne fui. / Mais cho sai jo bien, par ma destre, / Que jo ne puis pas altres estre! / Donques sui jo Scilentius, / Cho m'est avis, u jo sui nus" (ll. 2531–38).

29. "Dont se propense en lui-meïsme / Que Nature li fait sofime: / Por cho que l'-us est encontre us / N'a pas a non Silentius. / Aler en violt a la costure / Si con li a rové Nature, / Car por fief, ne por iretage, / Ne doit mener us si salvage" (ll. 2539–46).

30. "Lassciés ester ma noreçon, / Nature, a la maleÿçon. / Jo l'ai tolte desnaturee / N'avra ja voir o vus duree. / Se ne lassciés icest anter / Bien vos porés al loig vanter / Se jo ne fac par noreture / .m. gens ovrer contre nature. / Jo noris tres bien, c'est la some, / D'un noble enfant un malvais home. / Jo te desferai tolt ton conte. / Nature, envoies o ta honte" (ll. 2593–2604).

31. Jacques Derrida, "'Il faut bien manger' ou le calcul du sujet," *Confrontation* 20 (winter 1989): 91–114; Jacques Derrida, *Who Comes After the Subject?* [Après le sujet qui vient], tr. and ed., Eduardo Cadava, Peter Connor, and Jean-Luc Nancy (New York: Routledge, 1991). The translation disambiguates the title (the French could also mean "After the subject that comes").

32. Translation modified.

33. Philippe Buc, *L'ambiguïté du livre* (Paris: Beauchesne, 1940).

34. "Qu'ensi fuscent d'une voellance / Com il sunt fait d'une sustance, / Andoi eüscent un voloir, / A l'esjoïr, et al doloir. / Entr'ome et feme a grant commune, / Car d'als .ii. est la sustance une" (ll. 1707–12).

35. Matilda Tomaryn Bruckner, *Shaping Romance: Interpretation, Truth, and Closure in Twelfth-Century French Fictions* (Philadelphia: University of Pennsylvania Press, 1993), pp. 60–156; on (non)exclusive disjunctions, see Julia Kristeva, *Semiotiké* (Paris: Seuil, 1969).

36. "Et se ses vils cuers li fait faire / Qu'il ne s'en puiscce pas retraire, / Dont est il sers et ses cuers sire, / Espi! quant tels cuers le maistyre" (ll. 2429–32).

37. "Desuser and refuser son bon viel us . . . por us de feme" (ll. 2629–31).

38. "Miols vialt vialt li us d'ome / Que l'us de feme, c'est la some. 'Voire,'

fait il, 'a la male eure / Irai desos, quant sui deseure. Deseure sui, s'irai desos? . . . Car vallés sui et nient mescine. / Ne voel perdre ma grant honor, / Ne la voel cangier a menor. Ne voel mon pere desmentir . . . Por quanque puete faire Nature / Ja n'en ferai descoverture" (ll. 2637–56).

39. "Savés que dist mes corages? / Que bien ait tols jors bons usages. / Bons us tolt moult vilonie / Et fait mener cortoise vie. / Car bons us a qui bone vie uze / Et villonie le refuse. / Mains hom fait tols jors desonor / Que s'il eüst flairié honor / Et maintenue dé l'enfance / Ki n'avroit cure de viltance. / S'il fait le honte n'en puet nient / Qu'a cho qu'il a apris se tient. / Silence ne se repent rien / De son usage, ains l'ainme bien. / Chevaliers est vallans et buens. / Mellor n'engendra rois ne cuens" (ll. 5165–80).

40. "Car la verté ne doi taisir" (l. 1669).

41. Allen, p. 110.

42. Perret.

43. Timothy J. Reiss, *Mirages of the Selfe: Patterns of Personhood in Ancient and Early Modern Europe* (Stanford, Calif.: Stanford University Press, 2003).

44. Jacques le Goff, "Culture ecclésiastique et culture folklorique au Moyen Age: saint Marcel de Paris et le dragon," in *Pour un autre moyan âge* (Paris: Gallimard, 1977), pp. 236–79.

45. Loren Ringer, "Exchange, Identity and Transvestitism in *Le roman de Silence*," *Dalhousie French Studies* 28 (1994): 3–13, pp. 4ff.

46. Alexandre Leupin, "Naming God: *La vie de saint Alexis*," in *Barbarolexis* (Cambridge, Mass.: Harvard University Press, 1989), pp. 39–58.

47. Perret, p. 332. Bloch, "Silence and Holes," p. 85.

48. Henrietta Moore, "The Problem of Explaining Violence in the Social Sciences," in *Sex and Violence: Issues in Representation and Experience*, ed. Penelope Harvey and Peter Gow (London: Routledge, 1994), pp. 138–55, 150.

49. "Et tols jors eert pres a contraire / A cho que ses cuers voloit faire. / Et qui ouevre contre voloit / Soventes fois l'estuet doloir" (ll. 2677–80).

50. Ll. 6300, 6304, 6309, 6311,6312, 6314; 6321, 6330; 6385, 6395, 6399; 6423, 6425, 6425; 6443, 6446, 6453, 6457; 6472, 6480; 6552; 6593, 6596, 6601, 6611, 6614, 6626, 6627, 6641, 6693; I omit less emphatic forms like *j'en*.

51. Ll. 1–106, particularly ll. 23, 30, 38, 39, and 88.

52. "Par covoitise / Tolt a main home sa francise, / Et plus avoec—quant s'i amort / Troter le fait jusque a la mort" (ll. 329–32).

53. "Se jo sui manans ele iert riche" (l. 2060).

54. "Fu ainc mais feme si tanee / De vil barat, ne enganee / Que cho fesist par covoitise?" (l. 2583–85).

55. See the essays in the special issue of *Arthuriana* 7, no. 2 (summer 1997).

56. Georges Duby, "Les 'jeunes' dans la société aristocratique dans la France du Nord-Ouest au XIIe siècle," *Hommes et structures du moyen âge* (The Hague: Mouton, 1973), pp. 213–26; tr. Cynthia Postan in *The Chivalrous Society* (Berkeley and Los Angeles: University of California Press, 1977), pp. 112–22.

57. "Il n'i a celui de nos / Ki n'en ai l'un l'altre escarni" (l. 6478f.).

58. Compare ll. 2656 and 6519.

59. *For They Know Not What They Do—Enjoyment as a Political Factor*, 2d ed. (London: Verso, 2002), p. 56.

CHAPTER 12

1. Perhaps during the second half of 1202: Pierre Ruelle, ed., *Les Congés d'Arras (Jean Bodel, Baude Fastoul, Adam de la Halle)* (Paris: PUF and Presses Universitaires de Bruxelles, 1965). I have also consulted Pierre-Yves Badel, ed., *Adam de la Halle, Oeuvres complètes* (Paris: Livre de Poche, 1995), pp. 404–11.

2. Compare with Jacques Derrida's recreation of a differentiated semantic field in "La pharmacie de Platon," *La dissémination* (Paris: Seuil, 1972), pp. 69–197.

3. Saul Nathaniel Brody, *The Disease of the Soul: Leprosy in Medieval Literature* (Ithaca, N.Y.: Cornell University Press, 1974).

4. Paul Zumthor, "Entre deux esthétiques: Adam de la Halle," *Mélanges Frappier*, 2 vols. (Geneva: Droz, 1970), 2:1155–71.

5. J. Lestoquoy, *Les villes de Flandre et d'Italie sous le gouvernement des patriciens (XIe–XVe siècles)* (Paris: PUF, 1952).

6. Jakemon Pouchinois: l. 103.

7. "Encor soit Arras fourmenés, / S'i a il des bons reniés / A cui je voeil prendre congiet, / Qui mains grans reviaus ont menés / Et souvent biaus mengiers donnés, / Dont li usages bien dechiet, / Car on i a si pres faukiet / C'on leur a tout caupé le piet / Seur coi leur deduis ert fondés. / Chil on fait grant mortel pechiet / Qui tant onot a rive sakiet / Que tés viviers est esseués" (strophe III, ll. 26–36).

8. The split subjectivity of men whose careers shift them between the clerical and secular cultures becomes a social type in the twelfth century: Haidu, "Temps, histoire, subjectivité: Aux XIIe et XIIIe siècles," in *Le nombre du temps (Mélanges Zumthor)* (Paris: Champion-Slatkine, 1988), pp. 105–22.

9. "Arras, Arras, vile de plait / Et de haïne et de detrait, / Qui soliés estre si nobile, / On va disant qu'on vous refait, / Mais sediex le bien n'i ratrait, / Je ne voi qui vous reconcile. / On i aime trop crois et pile / . . . Ailleurs vois oïr l'E-

vangile, / Car chi fors mentir on ne fait" (ll. 13–24). *Haïne* often names not the emotion of hate but behaviors that could most readily be explained in its terms.

10. Carolyn Walker Bynum, "Did the Twelfth Century Discover the Individual?" *Journal of Ecclesiastical History* 31 (1980): 1–17.

11. "Du jour est li vespre tesmoins" (l. 144).

12. "Pour estre de valeur au loins" (l. 140).

13. Haidu, "La valeur: Sémiotique et marxisme," *Sémiotique en jeu: A partir et autour de l'oeuvre d'A. J. Greimas*, ed. Michel Arrivé and Jean-Claude Coquet (Paris-Amsterdam-Philadelphia: John Benjamins, 1987), pp. 247–63.

14. "Aler doit hors de men lieu" (l. 121).

15. *Prendre congé*: ll. 27, 37, 99, 146.

16. "Arras, Arras, Vile de plait / Et de haïne et de detrait" (ll. 13f.).

17. Roger Berger, *Littérature et société arrageoises au XIIIe siècle: Les chanson et dits artésiens* (Arras: Commission Départementale des Monuments Historiques du Pas-de-Calais, 1981), pp. 25–54, see also the map inside the back cover.

18. "La Vile est bien alee a nient / De coi Cités bonne devient" (l. 115f.).

19. Ruelle, pp. 185–213; Berger, pp. 88–116, esp. pp. 297–425; and Roger Berger, *Le Nécrologue de la Confrérie des Jongleurs et des Bourgeois d'Arras (1194–1361)* (Arras: Commission Départementale des Monuments Historiques du Pas-de-Calais, 1970).

CHAPTER 13

1. Timothy J. Reiss, *The Discourse of Modernism* (Ithaca, N.Y.: Cornell University Press, 1982); *The Uncertainty of Analysis* (Ithaca, N.Y.: Cornell University Press, 1988); and *The Meaning of Literature* (Ithaca, N.Y.: Cornell University Press, 1992).

2. On medieval prose, see Brian Woledge and H. P. Clive, *Répertoire des plus anciens textes en prose française depuis 842 jusqu'aux premières années du XIIe siècle* (Geneva: Droz, 1964); Hermann Tiemann, "Zur Geschichte des altfranzösischen Prosaromans," *Romanische Forschungen* 63 (1951); Omer Jodogne, "La naissance de la prose française," *Bulletin de la Classe des Lettres et des Sciences Morales et Politiques* (Brussels) 5 (1963): 296–308; Jeffrey Kittay and Wlad Godzich, *The Emergence of Prose: An Essay in Prosaics* (Minneapolis: University of Minnesota Press, 1987); and Jeanette Beer, *Early Prose in France: Contexts of Bilingualism and Authority* (Kalamazoo, Mich.: Medieval Institute, 1992).

3. Henri de Curzon, ed., *La Règle du Temple*, Paris: Reynouard, 1886.

4. Beer, pp. 66–69.

5. John E. Matzke, ed., *Lois de Guillaume le Conquérant en français et en latin* (Paris: Picard, 1899).

6. Ernest-Joseph Tardif, ed., *Coutumiers de Normandie*, 2 vols. (Rouen: Cagniard, 1881–93; rpt. Geneva: Slatkine Reprints, 1977).

7. Peter Dembowski, *La chronique de Robert de Clari: Etude de la langue et du style* (Toronto: University of Toronto Press, 1963).

8. Jacques Monfrin, "L'emploi de la langue vulgaire dans les actes diplomatiques du temps de Philippe Auguste," in *La France de Philippe Auguste: Le temps des mutations*, ed. Robert-Henri Bautier (Paris: CNRS, 1982), pp. 785–92, 786ff.

9. M. Aug. de Loisne, "Anciennes chartes inédites en langue vulgaire reposant en original aux archives du Pas-de-Calais, 1221–1258," in Comité des Travaux historiques et Scientifiques, *Bulletin historique et philologique* 1899, no. 1, pp. 65–78; Pierre Feuchère, *De l'épée à la plume: Les châtelains d'Arras* (Arras: 1948), pp. 123ff.

10. *Les Etablissements de Saint Louis*, ed. Paul Viollet, 4 vols. (Paris: Renouard, 1881–86).

11. Jacques le Goff, *Saint Louis* (Paris: Gallimard, 1996), p. 688.

12. Haidu, "Repetition: Modern Reflections on Medieval Aesthetics," *MLN* 92 (1977): 875–87.

13. Marcia Colish, *The Mirror of Language: A Study in Medieval Theory of Knowledge* (New Haven, Conn.: Yale University Press, 1968); Margaret W. Ferguson, "Saint Augustine's Region of Unlikeness: The Crossing of Exile and Language," *Georgia Review* 29 (1975): 842–64.

14. Gabrielle Spiegel, *Romancing the Past: The Rise of Vernacular Prose Historiography in Thirteenth Century France* (Berkeley and Los Angeles: University of California Press, 1993); and Gabrielle Spiegel's earlier *The Chronicle Tradition of Saint-Denis: A Survey* (Brookline, Mass.: Medieval Classics, Texts and Studies, 1978).

15. "Issi vos an feré le conte / Non pas rimé, qui an droit conte, / Si com li livres Lancelot / Ou il n'a de rime un seul mot, / Por mielx dire la verité / Et por tretier sans faussté; / Quar anviz puet estre rimée / Estoire ou n'ait ajosté / Mançonge por fere la rime" (ll. 99–107). Paul Meyer, "Prologue en vers français d'une histoire perdue de Philippe-Auguste," *Romania* 6 (1877): 494–98, p. 498; cited by Pierre Botineau, "L'histoire de France en français de Charlemagne à Philippe-Auguste," *Romania* [post-1964]: 79–99, p. 92, n. 2.

16. Spiegel, *Romancing the Past*, p. 70.

17. In one of the earliest and most independent adaptations: Ronald N. Walpole, ed. *The Old French Johannes Translation of the Pseudo-Turpin Chron-*

icle (Berkeley and Los Angeles: University of California Press, 1976), see pp. 97–122.

18. "Et por ce que rime se velt afeitier de moz conqueilliz hors de l'estoire, voust li cuens que cist livres fust sanz rime selonc le latin de l'estoire que Torpins l'arcevesque de Reins traita et escrist si com il le vit et oï" (p. 130).

19. Like modern French *histoire*, Old French *estoire* means both tale and history. An earlier version asserts that ordinary singers and jongleurs speak nothing but lies and don't know what they're talking about. No rhymed tale is true: everything they say is lie; for they know nothing except at second hand (see Kittay and Godzich, p. xiiif.).

20. Spiegel, *Romancing the Past*, pp. 55–98.

21. "Les escrivit par nuit et par jor quant il an veit lisir, si cum il li avenoient le jor" (p. xiv).

22. "Aprés ce venimes ensemble a Viane, et je, Torpins, remés ilec molt agravez de plaies et de cous que je avoie sofferz en Espaigne. Adonc priai je Charle et requis sor l'amor qu'il avoit a moi, qu'il me feist savoir le jor de son trespassement s'il trespassoit ainçois de moi, et je li creantai que je li feroie le mien savoir se je trespassoie ançois de lui. Je, Torpins, l'arcevesque, remés ensint a Viane" (Walpole, p. 175).

23. Robert-Henri Bautier, *Chartes, sceaux et chancelleries* (Paris: Ecole des Chartes, 1990), vol. 1. Béatrice Fraenkel, *La Signature, genèse d'un signe* (Paris: Gallimard, 1992), pp. 26–29.

24. Citations from LII, p. 163 and LXXVI, p. 179, respectively.

25. In an appendix to Alan M. Gunn, *The Mirror of Love: A Reinterpretation of the* Roman de la rose (Lubbock, Texas: Rice University Press, 1952).

26. Janet M. Ferrier, *French Prose Writers of the Fourteenth and Fifteenth Centuries* (Oxford: Pergamon, 1966), p. 102.

27. R. Howard Bloch, *Medieval Misogyny and the Invention of Western Romantic Love* (Chicago: University of Chicago Press, 1991), pp. 13, 48, final emphasis added.

28. Daniel Poirion, ed., *Le roman de la rose* (Paris: Garnier-Flammarion, 1974), ll. 8467–9360.

29. Helen Solterer, *The Master and Minerva: Disputing Women in French Medieval Culture* (Berkeley and Los Angeles: University of California Press, 1995), ch. 6, pp. 151–75.

30. Ibid., p. 49, emphasis added. On this first *"querelle des femmes,"* see Eric Hicks, *Le débat sur le "Roman de la rose"* (Paris: Champion, 1977).

31. Solterer, p. 162.

32. Sarah Kay, "Women's Body of Knowledge: Epistemology and Misogyny

in the Romance of the Rose," in *Framing Medieval Bodies*, ed. Sarah Kay and Mimi Rubin (Manchester: University of Manchester, 1994), pp. 211–35, 225.

33. "Compains, cist fos vilains jalous . . . [qui] se fait seignor de sa fame, / qui ne redoit pas estre dame, / mes sa pareille et sa compaigne, / si con la loi les acompaigne, / et il redoit ses compainz estre, / sans soi fere seigneur ne mestre" (ll. 9391–400, emphasis added).

34. "N'encor n'avoit fet roi ne prince / meffez, qui l'autrui tost et pince. / Trestuit pareill estre soloient / ne riens propre avoir ne voloient" (ll. 8415–17).

35. "Riche estoient tuit egaument / et s'entramoient loiaument . . . Lors iert amor sanz symonie" (ll. 9491–96; other mss. have *sanz seignorie*).

36. "Avarice et Covoitise / ont es queurs des homes assise / La grant ardeur d'avoir aquerre" (ll. 9545–47).

37. "La prumiere vie lessierent, / de maufere puis ne cessierent, / car faus et tricheür devindrent. / Aus proprietez lors se tindrent, / la terre meïsmes partirent . . . li plus forz les plus granz parz orent . . . Un grant vilain entr'eus eslurent, / Le plus torsu de quanqu'il furent, / Le plus corsu et le grignor, / Si le firent prince et seignor" (ll. 9559–612). Same condemnation of Avarice and Greed in Jean de Meun as in Heldris de Cornualle.

38. P. B. Milan, "The Golden Age and the Political Theory of Jean de Meun," *Symposium* 23 (1969): 137–49.

39. H. G. Walther, "Utopische Gesellschaftskritik oder satirischer Ironie? Jean de Meun und die Lehre des Aquinaten über die Entstehung menschlicher Herrschaft," *Soziale Ordnungen im Selbstverständnis des Mittelalters Miscellanea Medievalia* [Berlin] 12, no. 1 (1980): 84–105, n. 101; and Philippe Buc, *L'ambiguité du livre* (Paris: Beauchesne, 1940), p. 108f., nn. 98–100.

40. Wolfgang Stürner, *Peccatum und Potestas* (Sigmaringen: J. Horbecke, 1987), p. 187, n. 2; Buc, p. 109, n. 100.

41. Buc, p. 108.

42. For Marx's scattered comments on primitive communism, see William H. Shaw, *Marx' Theory of History* (Stanford, Calif.: Stanford University Press, 1978), esp. pp. 115–19.

43. Karl Marx and Friedrich Engels, *The German Ideology* (Moscow: Progress, 1976), p. 38.

44. Karl Marx, *Grundrisse*, tr. and ed. Martin Nicolaus (New York: Random House / Vintage, 1973), p. 472.

45. "Li siecles [ert] mout precieus. / N'ierent pas si delicieus / ne de robes ne de viandes; / Il cuilloient es bois les glandes / por pains, por chars et por poissons, / Et cerchoient par ces boissons, / par vaus, par plains et par mon-

taignes / pommes, poires, noiz et chastaignes / boutons et meures et pruneles, / framboises, freses et ceneles" (ll. 8331–40).

46. Brunetto Latini, *Li livres dou tresor*, ed. Francis J. Carmody (Berkeley and Los Angeles: University of California Press, 1948), p. xxii.

47. Alexander Murray, *Reason and Society in the Middle Ages* (Oxford: Oxford University Press, 1978–91), p. 222; and Fraenkel, "Les officiers de plume," in Fraenkel, *La signature*, pp. 26–29.

48. Einar Mar Jonsson, "Le sens du titre *Speculum* aux XIIe et XIIIe siècles et son utilisation par Vincent de Beauvais," in *Vincent de Beauvais. Intentions et réceptions d'une oeuvre encyclopédique au Moyen-Age*, ed. Monique Paulmier-Foucart, Serge Lusignan, and Alain Nadeau (Paris: Bellarmin-Vrin, 1990), pp. 11–32. Paul Barrette and Spurgeon Baldwin, *Brunetto Latini, The Book of the Treasure (Li Livres dou Tresor)* (New York: Garland, 1993), p. xii.

49. Adapted: Latini, p. 317; Barrette and Baldwin, p. 279.

50. Jesse Gellrich, *The Idea of the Book in the Middle Ages: Language Theory, Mythology, and Fiction* (Ithaca, N.Y.: Cornell University Press, 1985), p. 136.

51. F. R. P. Akehurst, tr., *The Coutumes de Beauvaisis of Philippe de Beaumanoir* (Philadelphia: University of Pennsylvania Press, 1992), p. xiii.

52. "Ci Commence li Livres des coustumes et des usages de Beauvoisins selonc ce qu'il couroit ou tans que cest livres fu fes, c'est assavoir en l'an de l'incarnacion Nostre Seigneur .M.cc.IIIxx et trois" (Philippe de Beaumanoir, *Coutumes de Beauvaisis*, ed. Am. Salmon, 2 vols. [Paris: Picard, 1899 and 1900], "Collection de Textes Pour Servir à l'Etude et à l'Enseignement de l'Histoire," ll. 24 and 30).

53. Ibid., §2–6, pp. 2–4.

54. Ibid., §9, p. 6. Richard H. Rouse and Mary A. Rouse, "*Statim invenire*: Schools, Preachers, and New Attitudes to the Page," in *Renaissance and Renewal in the Twelfth Century*, ed. Robert L. Benson, Giles Constable, and Carol D. Lanham (Cambridge, Mass.: Harvard University Press, 1982), pp. 201–25.

55. Beaumanoir, *Coutumes de Beauvaisis*, §689f.

56. Ibid., §1243, pp. 141–43.

57. "Ne les aiment fors que pour ce qu'ils les cr*ie*ment et doutent" (ibid., §13, p. 17; to be considered whenever the semantics of *amor* are discussed).

58. "Couroucier le riche homme qui avroit a fere contre le povre" (ibid., §16, p. 19).

59. "Ne se prent garde a quel fin il puet venir de ce qu'il entreprent" (ibid., §16, p. 20).

60. Ibid., §15.

61. Ibid., §20, p. 25.

62. "Par la soutilleté de l'examinacion, leur cuers et leur opinions soit conneue et la verités esclarcie de leur tesmoignage" (ibid., §1224, p. 131).

63. Ibid., §18.

64. "Car li sires n'est pas bons a servir qui prent plus garde a fere sa volenté que a droit et a justice maintenir" (ibid., §18, p. 21f.). Philip also recommends that the *bailli* leave his lord's service in case of a division between the lord and his counsel (ibid., §19, p. 24).

65. Alain Badiou, *Théorie de la subjectivité* (Paris: Seuil, 1982), p. 275.

66. Lee Patterson, *Chaucer and the Subject of History* (Madison: University of Wisconsin Press, 1991), p. 46; for the following remarks, compare with p. 32.

67. Max Weber, "Politics as a Vocation," in *From Max Weber*, ed. Hans H. Gerth and C. Wright Mills (New York: Oxford University Press, 1946), p. 95.

68. Beaumanoir, *Coutumes de Beauvaisis*, §19, pp. 22ff.

69. For example, see §26, p. 29f.

70. "Our passion is as subject / As are our wretches fetter'd in our prisons" (*Henry V*, I:ii).

71. Beaumanoir, *Coutumes de Beauvaisis*, §1042, p. 368.

72. "Car de teus quereles doit li cuens user entre ses sougiès selonc la coustume que si homme usent entre les leur sougiès."

73. Beaumanoir, *Coutumes de Beauvaisis*, §37; p. 34.

74. Ibid., §40, p. 35.

75. Ibid., §30, pp. 31ff.; §42, p. 36.

76. Ibid., §34; §35, p. 33.

77. "Aliances fetes contre seigneur ou contre le commun pourfit" (ibid., §883, p. 446).

78. Ibid., §884, p. 446f.

79. Ibid., §844, p. 447.

80. Ibid., §885, p. 447f.

81. "Par toutes ces choses sont servitudes venues avant, car selonc le droit naturel chascuns est frans; mes cele naturele franchise est corrompue par les acquisicions dessus dites" (ibid., §1438, p. 227).

82. Michel Foucault, *L'ordre du discours* (Paris: Gallimard, 1971), p. 12.

83. Reiss, *Discourse of Modernism*; *Uncertainty of Analysis*; and *Meaning of Literature*.

84. Michel Foucault, *Les mots et les choses* (Paris: Gallimard, 1966).

85. Reiss, *Discourse of Modernism*, ch. 1.

86. Carlo Ginzburg's work is exemplary here.

87. Antonio Gramsci, "The Formation of Intellectuals," in *The Modern Prince*, tr. Louis Marks (New York: International, 1957/92, pp. 118–25; p. 118.

88. Ibid., p. 121 f.

CHAPTER 14

1. Colette Beaune, "Les lois de la guerre à la fin du moyen âge," in *Les fondements de la paix. Des origines au début du XVIIIe siècle*, ed. Pierre Chaunu (Paris: PUF, 1993), pp. 109–12.

2. Jean-Philippe Genêt, "Le médiéviste, la naissance du discours politique et la statistique lexicale: Quelques problèmes," in *L'écrit dans la société médiévale*, ed. Caroline Bourlet and Annie Dujour (Paris: CNRS, 1991), pp. 289–98, 295.

3. On Christine as "professional author," see Marcella Munson, "Constructing the Subject: Author and Nation in Christine de Pizan's Prose Epistles," Ph.D. dissertation, University of California, Los Angeles, 2000.

4. Daniel Poirion, *Littérature française: Le moyen âge. 1300–1480* (Paris: Arthaud, 1971), p. 206.

5. Charity Cannon Willard, ed., *The "Livre de la Paix" of Christine de Pizan* (The Hague: Mouton, 1958); English edition: *Christine de Pizan, Her Life and Works* (New York: Persea, 1984), p. 223; Peter Dembowski, "Recent Studies in Old French Literature," *Medievalia et Humanistica* 15 (1987): 202. An essential research tool is Edith Yenal, *Christine de Pizan: A Bibliography*, 2d ed. (Metuchen, N.J.: Scarecrow Press, 1989).

6. *Lavision-Christine*: Introduction and Text, ed. Mary Louise Towner (Washington, D.C.: Catholic University of America, 1932; rpt. New York: AMS, 1969).

7. Joan Kelly, "Early Feminist Theory and the *Querelle des femmes*: 1400–1789," *Women, History and Theory* (Chicago: University of Chicago Press, 1984), pp. 65–109.

8. Charity Cannon Willard, "A Fifteenth Century View of Women's Role in Medieval Society: Christine de Pizan's *Livre des trois vertus*," in *The Role of Women in the Middle Ages* (Albany: State University of New York, 1975), pp. 90–120, 108, 116.

9. Christine Reno, "Christine de Pizan: 'At Best A Contradictory Figure'?" in *Politics, Gender, and Genre: The Political Thought of Christine de Pizan*, ed. Margaret Brabant (Boulder, Colo.: Westview Press, 1992).

10. Eric Hicks, "The Political Significance of Christine de Pizan," in *Politics, Gender, and Genre: The Political Thought of Christine de Pizan*, ed. Margaret Brabant (Boulder, Colo.: Westview Press, 1992), p. 11.

11. Lenin, quoting Chernychevsky's celebrated title *What Is to Be Done?* (1902).

12. Philippe Buc, *L'ambiguité du livre* (Paris: Beauchesne, 1940, p. 40.

13. Genêt, pp. 289–98.

14. *Le champion des dames* (1440–42): Renate Blumenfeld-Kosinski, in the Introduction of her *Selected Writings of Christine de Pizan* (New York: W. W. Norton, 1997).

15. Christine de Pizan, *Le Livre de la cité des dames*, 2 vols., ed. Maureen Cheney Curnow (Ann Arbor: University of Michigan Press, 1975).

16. Maureen Quilligan, *The Allegory of Female Authority: Christine de Pizan's Cité de Dames* (Ithaca, N.Y.: Cornell University Press, 1991), p. 49f.

17. Kevin Brownlee, "Discourses of the Self: Christine de Pizan and the Rose," *Romanic Review* 79 (1988): 199–221.

18. *The Book of the City of Ladies*, tr. Earl Jeffrey Richards (New York: Persea / Quality, 1982–92), p. 259; *La Cité des dames*, tr. Eric Hicks and Thérèse Moreau (Paris: Stock, 1986–96).

19. Quilligan, p. 47; Carolyn Walker Bynum, *Holy Feast and Holy Fast: The Religious Significance of Food to Medieval Women* (Berkeley and Los Angeles: University of California Press, 1987).

20. Pizan, 2:617.

21. "Et nom mie seulement un ou deux ou cestuy Matheolus, qui entre les livres n'a aucune reputacion et qui traitte en maniere de trufferie, mais generaument aucques en tous traittiez philosophes, pouettes, tous orateurs desquelz les noms seroit longue chose, semble que tous parle par une meismes bouche et tous accordent une semblable conclusion, determinant *les meurs feminins enclins et plains de tous les vices*" (Pizan, 2:618, emphasis added).

22. R. Howard Bloch, "Medieval Misogyny," *Representations* 20 (fall 1987): 13–36. R. Howard Bloch, *Medieval Misogyny and the Invention of Western Romantic Love* (Chicago: University of Chicago Press, 1991).

23. Claire Nouvet, "Writing (in) Fear," in *Gender and the Text in the Later Middle Ages*, ed. Jane Chance (Gainesville: Florida University Press, 1996), pp. 279–307, 301.

24. "Et ainsi m'en rapportoye plus au jugement d'autruy que ad ce que moy meismes en sentoye et savoye" (Pizan, 2:619).

25. "Ville chose fist Dieux quant il fourma femme" (Pizan, 2:620).

26. "Adonc moy estant en ceste penssee, me sourdi une grant desplaisance et tristesce de couraige en desprisant moly meismes et tout le sexe feminin, si come ce ce fust monstre en nature" (Pizan, 2:620).

27. "'Helas! Dieux, pourquoy ne me faiz tu naistre au monde en mascu-

line sexe . . . ?' . . . me tenoye tres malcontente de ce qu'en corps feminin m'ot fait Dieux estre au monde."

28. Liliane Dulac, "Authority in the Prose Treatises of Christine de Pizan: The Writer's Discourse and the Prince's Word," in *Politics, Gender, and Genre: The Political Thought of Christine de Pizan*, ed. Margaret Brabant (Boulder, Colo.: Westview Press, 1992), pp. 129–40.

29. There is "en ce monde [nulle] chose qui plus face a fouyr, a droite ver-ité dire, que fait la mauvaise femme dissolue et perverse si come monstre en nature . . . gittes hors ses ordes pierres broçonneuses et noires de ton ouvrage, car ja ne seront mises ou bel ediffice de ta cité" (Pizan, 2:642f.).

30. "'Il faut bien manger,' ou le calcul du sujet—Entretien (avec J-L. Nancy)," *Cahiers Confrontation* 20 (winter 1989): 91–114, p. 97; and *Politics of Friendship*, tr. George Collins (London: Verso, 1997), p. 68.

31. Slavoj Žižek, *The Ticklish Subject* (London: Verso, 1999), p. 375.

32. Joan Ferrante, "Public Posture and Private Maneuvers: Roles Me-dieval Women Play," in *Women and Power in the Middle Ages*, ed. Mary Erler and Maryanne Kowaleski (Athens: University of Georgia Press, 1988), pp. 213–29.

33. Jacqueline Cerquiglini, "L'étrangère," *Revue des langues romanes* 92 (1988): 239–51; Mary McKinley, "The Subversive 'seulette,'" in *Politics, Gender, and Genre: The Political Thought of Christine de Pizan*, ed. Margaret Brabant (Boulder, Colo.: Westview Press, 1992), pp. 157–69, 158.

34. Charity Cannon Willard, ed., *The "Livre de la Paix" of Christine de Pizan* (The Hague: Mouton, 1958), p. 50; and Willard, *Christine de Pizan, Her Life and Works*, p. 46f.

35. Christine de Pizan, *Livre du corps de policie*, ed. Robert H. Lucas ("Textes Littéraires Français") (Geneva-Paris: Droz-Minard, 1967), p. xxxiii; Kate Langdon Forhan's, "Polycracy, Obligation, and Revolt: The Body Politic in John of Salisbury and Christine de Pizan," in *Politics, Gender, and Genre: The Political Thought of Christine de Pizan*, ed. Margaret Brabant (Boulder, Colo.: Westview Press, 1992), pp. 33–52.

36. Willard, *The "Livre de la paix,"* p. 37.

37. "Le vile et chetive gente, le fol gouvernement de menu et bestial peu-ple" (ibid., p. 1); "de ce de quoy il ne leur apertient a parler" (Pizan, *Livre du corps*, 1:3); "celle diabolique assemblee" (Willard, *The "Livre de la paix,"* p. 11). See Delany, "'Mothers to Think Back Through,' . . . " p. 187f. Christine M. Reno's response, "Christine de Pizan: 'At Best a Contradictory Figure'?" (in Bra-bant, *Political Thought of Christine de Pizan*) occasioned a reply from Delany, "History, Politics, and Christine Studies: A Polemical Reply," in Brabant, *Po-*

litical Thought of Christine de Pizan, pp. 193–206. Delaney's key point—overlooked in the continuing debate—is that far less reactionary positions than Christine's existed *among contemporaries*. Quilligan denies such alternatives were available, dismisses "the king's eccentric friendliness to the people's cause," and denies such appointments were indices of "nascent democratic thought" (p. 265): they did not exist . . . and besides, they were ridiculous! In fact, she cites evidence they existed: Caboche, the leader of the revolt, was a very wealthy commoner of the same class as Christine, but with more progressive opinions, appointed to government posts by the king himself (p. 266f., n. 13), which led Christine to advise against appointment of commoners in the *Livre de la paix*. Quilligan offers evidence that Christine is "more royalist than the king," and more retrograde as well (Delany, "'Mothers,'" p. 187).

38. ". . . pour ce que tel gent sont povres et indigens et ne peuent avoir riens se de jour en jour à leurs labours ne le gaingnent, vouldroient tousjours guerre, par especial civill, afin de courir sus aux riches . . . n'est plus grant folie à prince . . . que de donner licence au menu commun de soy armer" (*Livre de la paix*, 3:12).

39. "Raison . . . est l'administreresse de faire mettre a excecucion par oeuvre si come baillif ou prevost des mandemens du bon et sain entendement" (Christine de Pizan, *The Epistle of the Prison of Human Life*, ed. Josette A. Wiseman [New York: Garland, 1984], p. 34).

40. Ibid. "Ahistoricism" is an ideologeme sometimes floated to justify Christine's conservatism against historically grounded criticism. *Every* historical situation comports elements that are forward-looking, conservative, and reactionary.

41. Marie-Thérèse Lorcin, "Christine de Pizan analyste de la société," in *The City of Scholars: New Approaches to Christine de Pizan*, ed. Margarete Zimmermann and Dina De Rentiis (Berlin: Walter de Gruyter, 1994), pp. 197–205. The third book of the *Livre de policie* exemplifies Christine's views of "the people."

42. Jacques Krynen, *L'empire du roi. Idées et croyances politiques en France, XIIIe-XVe siècle* (Paris: Gallimard, 1993).

43. Delany, "A City, a Room: The Scene of Writing in Christine de Pizan and Virginia Woolf," in Delany, *Writing Woman: Women Writers and Women in Literature, Medieval to Modern* (New York: Schocken, 1983), pp. 181–97; "Rewriting Woman Good: Gender and the Anxiety of Influence in Two Medieval Texts," in *Chaucer in the Eighties*, ed. Julian N Wasserman and Robert J. Blanch (Syracuse, N.Y.: Syracuse University Press, 1986), pp. 75–92; as well as critical reviews published in *Signs* and *Women's Studies*. The comparison to

Phyllis Schlafly occurs in "'Mothers to Think Back Through': Who Are They? The Ambiguous Example of Christine de Pizan," in *Medieval Texts and Contemporary Readers*, ed. Laurie Finke and Martin B. Schichtman (Ithaca, N.Y.: Cornell University Press, 1987), pp. 177–97.

44. Written before the Supreme Court decision in *Grutter v. Bollinger*, June 23, 2003, for which Justice O'Connor wrote the majority opinion.

45. Beatrice Gottlieb, "The Problem of Feminism in the Fifteenth Century," in *Women in the Medieval World: Essays in Honor of John H. Mundy*, ed. Julius Kirschner and Suzanne Wemple (Oxford: Blackwell, 1985), pp. 337–64.

46. *Le Livre de la Mutacion de Fortune*, 4 vols., ed. Suzanne Solente ("Société des Anciens Textes Français") (Paris: Picard, 1959–66).

47. Rosalind Brown-Grant, *Christine de Pizan and the Moral Defense of Women: Reading Beyond Gender* (Cambridge: Cambridge University Press, 1999), pp. 214–19.

48. See, for example, Donna J. Oestreich, "Christine de Pizan's *Book of the City of Ladies*: Paradigmatic Participation and Eschewal," in *Representations of the Feminine in the Middle Ages*, ed. Bonnie Wheeler (Dallas, Texas: Academia ["Feminae Medievalia 1"], 1993), pp. 253–75.

49. See Otto Gerhard Oexle, "Christine et les pauvres," pp. 206–20.

50. Albert Pauphilet, *Jeux et sapiences du moyen âge* (Paris: Gallimard ["Pléiade"], 1951); the standard edition, used here, is Alain Chartier, *Le Quadrilogue invectif*, ed. E. Droz (Paris: Champion, 1950) (CFMA #32).

51. Georges Duby, *Le Moyen Age, 987–1460* (Paris: Hachette, 1987), p. 448.

52. "Faulte de donner et recevoir *ordre, dicipline et regle* a mettre en oeuvre le povoir que Dieu nous a laissié" (Chartier, p. 6, emphasis added).

53. Michel Mollat du Jourdin, *Genèse médiévale de la France moderne, XIVe-XVe siècle* (Paris: Seuil, 1977), pp. 113–31.

54. "Que appelle je guerre? Ce n'est pas guerre qui en ce royaume se mayne, c'est *une privée roberie*, ung *larrecin habandonné*, force publique soubz umbre d'*armes et violente rapine*, que *faulte de justice et de bonne ordonnance* fait estre loisibles" (Chartier, p. 21).

55. "Le peuple si est membre notable d'un royaume, sans lequel les nobles ne le clergé ne pevent suffire a faire corps de police ne a soustenir leurs estas ne leur vie" (ibid., p. 23f.).

56. "Recognois au moins que tu, ta femme et tes enfans, mengiez vostre pain en sceurté chascun jour, chascun sur son lieu et soubz la seigneurie, comblé de tous biens, sans perte et sans dangier" (ibid., p. 26).

57. "Par toy et par les partiz que tu as choisiz folement et soustenuz de obstinee voulenté est ceste guerre sourse et aggravée. . . . Guerre, de sa propre

naissance, vient par defaulte de justice; car, se tous estions justes, force d'armes ne nous auroit besoing" (ibid., p. 27).

58. "En guerre, ou la force est et regne et le fer seigneurit, ne peut droit dominer; mais a bien enquerir, il sera trouvé que les gens de peuple et de bas estat, qui se mettent sus soubz le nom d'armes, sont coupable de ces horribles excez, et naist d'entre ceulz du peuple le mal qui sur le peuple redonde" (ibid., p. 33).

59. "Violence se donne droit par la force ou elle n'a riens. . . . Tu diz que je suis cause de ceste tresmaudite guerre. . . . Si te respons que la folie des mendres hommes est fondee sur l'outraige des plus grans . . . selon ce que les princes et les haulx hommes se maintiennent en estat et en vie, le peuple y prent sa rigle et son exemple soit de bien ou de mal, de paix ou d'esclandre. . . . Si est vostre desmesuree vie et vostre desordonné gouvernement cause de nostre impacience et commencement de nos maulx" (ibid., p. 37).

60. "Si estoit *la voix du peuple* comme les mouettes qui par leur cry denoncent les floz de la mer, car nos parolles, que tu apelles murmure, signifioient des lors le meschief qui pour ces causes estoit a advenir" (ibid., p. 38, emphasis added). This quotation appeared on the first page of each edition of the newspaper.

61. On the opposition of Latin and French for praising France, see Colette Beaune, *Naissance de la nation France* (Paris: Gallimard [Folio], 1985), pp. 414–16.

62. Pierre Bonnassie, *Les 50 mots clefs de l'histoire médiévale* (Toulouse: Privat, 1981), pp. 180ff.

63. See Chartier, p. 22f.

64. *Par faulte de gouvernement convenable* (ibid., p. 12).

65. Ibid., p. 36. The Knight's *anti-mutationnisme* marks a political class interest: Is that implicit also in the current historians' debate on the same theme?

66. Ibid., p. 47f. The paradox will recur in Montaigne: see below, Conclusion.

67. "Loial subgiet ne doit pour le prouffit de la guerre en delaissier l'onneur" (Chartier, p. 52).

68. "La folie des mendres hommes est fondee sur l'outraige des plus grans . . . selon ce que les princes et les haulx hommmes se maintiennent en estat et en vie, le peuple y prent sa rigle et son exemple soit de bien ou de mal, de paix ou d'esclandre" (ibid., p. 37).

69. "Telz qu'ilz sont tu les as faiz" (ibid., p. 39).

70. "Mouvoir nous pevent a ce faire moult d'anciennes histoires" (ibid., p. 58).

71. "Me vint en ymaginacion la douloureuse fortune et le piteux estat de la haulte seigneurie et glorieuse maison de France" (ibid., p. 6).

72. See ibid., p. 22f.

73. "Les lignaiges ne font pas les chiefs des guerres, mais ceulz a qui Dieu, leurs sens ou leurs vaillances et l'auctorité du prince, en donnent la grace, doivent estre pour telz obeiz. Laquelle obeissance n'est mie rendue a la personne, mais a l'office et ordre des armes et discipline de chevallerie, que chascun noble doit preferer a tout autre honneur" (ibid., p. 58).

74. See ibid., p. 54f.

75. See ibid., pp. 24, 55.

76. "Je puis sceurement dire que oncques honneur, vertu, et salut universel de la communité de seigneurie ne fut moins empraint es couraiges qu'il est de present" (ibid., p. 32). "Salut" may also mean salvation, of course.

77. "Peu doy priser sa naissance et moins desirer la continuation de sa vie qui passe ses jours, ainsi que fait homme nez pour soy seulement, sans fructifier a la commune utilité" (ibid., p. 11).

78. See especially her *Epistre de la prison de vie humaine*, ed. Josette A. Wiseman (New York: Garland, 1984); and *Le chemin de longue estude*, ed. Andrea Tarnowski (Paris: Livre de poche, 2000).

79. "L'estat de nostre infellicité" (Chartier, p. 5).

80. "Si ne veuille aucun lire l'une partie sans l'autre, afin que l'en ne cuide que tout le blasme soit mis sur ung estat. Mais s'aucune chose y a digne de lecture, si vaille pour attrait a donner aucun espace de temps a visiter et lire le sourplus" (ibid., p. 5).

81. Immanuel Wallerstein, "La construction des peuples: Racisme, nationalisme, ethnicité," in *Race, nation, classe: Les identités ambiguës*, by Etienne Balibar and Immanuel Wallerstein (Paris: La Découverte, 1988–97), pp. 95–116, 110; as well as Otto Hintze. "The Formation of States and Constitutional Develpment: A Study in History and Politics." *The Historical Essays of Otto Hintze*, ed. Felix Gilbert and Robert M. Berdahl (Oxford, 1975); pp. 159–77 (as essay published in 1902); Bernard Guenée, *Politique et histoire au Moyen Age* (Paris: Publications de la Sorbonne, 1981); Jacques le Goff, "Genèse de la France (milieu IXe-fin XIIIe siècle): vers un Etat monarchique français," in *Histoire de la France*, ed. André Burguière and Jacques Revel, *L'Etat et les pouvoirs*, vol. ed. Jacques le Goff, Paris: Seuil, 1989; E.J. Hobsbawm, *Nations and Nationalism since 1780. Programme, Myth, Reality* (Cambridge, 1990/5).

82. "Incipit Quadrilogium invectivum et comicum ad morum Gallicorum correctionem" (ibid., p. 5).

83. A. J. Minnis, *Medieval Theory of Authorship* (London: Scholar, 1984), p. 26.

84. See Brownlee, *Political Identity in Guillaume de Machaut* (Madison: University of Wisconsin Press, 1984); the article on Christine de Pizan in *Brabant, Politics, Gender, and Genre*; and Quilligan.

85. See Chartier, p. 9.

86. See ibid., p. 65f.

87. "Sers a la chose publique de ce que tu pués" (ibid., p. 65).

CHAPTER 15

1. On the testamentary convention, see W. H. Rice, *The European Ancestry of Villon's Satirical Testaments* (Syracuse University Monographs, 1941).

2. Pierre Guiraud, *Le Testament de Villon ou le gai savoir de la basoche* (Paris: Gallimard, 1970), pp. 11–52.

3. *Titus*, 1: 7–9.

4. William Empson, *Seven Types of Ambiguity* (New York: Meridian, 1955), p. 232.

5. "Mon seigneur n'est ne mon evesque, / Soubz luy ne tiens, s'il n'est en friche; / Foy ne luy doy n'hommage avecque, / Je ne suis son serf ne sa biche. / Peu m'a d'une petite miche / Et de froide eau tout ung esté; / Large ou estroit, moult me fut chiche: / Tel luy soit Dieu qu'il m'a esté!" (François Villon, *Oeuvres*, 4th ed., ed. Auguste Longnon and Lucien Foulet [Paris: Champion, 1967]; *Testament*, II, ll. 9–16). I have also consulted the admirable edition of Louis Thuasne: François Villon, *Oeuvres*, 3 vols. (Paris: Picard, 1923). *Bite* is translingual, both English, as in "to bite the hand that feeds you," and French, like *miche*, vulgar slang for "cock" or "prick."

6. "'J'ay tort et honte, / Quoi qu'il m'ait fait, a Dieu remis!'" (l. 31f.).

7. Evelyn Birge Vitz, *The Crossroads of Intention: A Study of Symbolic Expression in the Poetry of François Villon* (The Hague: Mouton, 1974), p. 68.

8. Guiraud, p. 96.

9. Ibid., pp. 55–76.

10. Longnon and Foulet, p. 149; Guiraud, p. 64; Jean Dufournet, *Recherches sur le Testament de Villon* (Paris: SEDES, 1966), 1:6.

11. Longnon and Foulet, p. 145.

12. "L'âme du bon feu maistre Jehan Cotart!" (ll. 1245, 1253, 1261, 1265).

13. "Prince, il n'eust sceu jusqu'a terre crachier; / Tousjours crioit: 'Haro! la gorge m'art.' / Et si ne sceust oncq sa seuf estanchier" (ll. 1262–64).

14. "Ung patart," a small Flemish coin (l. 1232).

15. "Je luy donne ma librairie, / Et le Rommant du Pet au Deable, / Lequel maistre Guy Tabarie / Grossa, qui est homs veritable. / Par cayers est soubz une table; / Combien qu'il soit rudement fait, / La matiere est si tres notable / Qu'elle amende tout le mesfait" (ll. 857–64).

16. See the introduction and notes to Thuasne's edition, 1:57f., 3:696; as well as Jean Dauvillier, "Les Procès de François Villon," *Bulletin de l'Université et de l'Académie de Toulouse* 7 (1943): 261–310.

17. H. Marshall Leicester Jr., *The Disenchanted Self: Representing the Subject in the Canterbury Tales* (Berkeley and Los Angeles: University of California Press, 1990), p. 415.

18. "Le Débat du cuer et du corps de Villon" (Longnon and Foulet, pp. 92–94). "Ballade des menus propos" (Longnon and Foulet, p. 80f.). "Ballade des contre-vérités" (Longnon and Foulet, p. 81f.). "*Tant crie l'on Noel qu'il vient*" ("Ballades des proverbes," Longnon and Foulet, p. 79f.).

19. "Je meurs de seuf auprès de la fontaine . . . Je ris en pleurs . . . Puissant je suis sans force et sans povoir, / Bien recueully, debouté de chascun" ("*Ballade du concours de Blois*," Longnon and Foulet, p. 84).

20. Villon's control of Old French was shaky; one editor counts twenty-six mistakes (François Villon, *Oeuvres*, ed. André Mary [Paris: Garnier, 1951], p. xxii).

21. "Item, donne a ma povre mere / Pour saluer nostre Maitresse, / (Qui pour moy ot douleur amere, / Dieu le scet, et mainte tristesse)" (ll. 865–88). The relative pronoun *qui* could equally well refer to *nostre Maitresse*: the content of the lines suggests it refers to Villon's mother.

22. "Femme je suis povrette et ancïenne, / Qui riens ne sçay; oncques lettre ne lus. / Au moustier voy dont suis paroissienne / Paradis paint, ou sont harpes et lus, / Et ung enfer ou dampnez sont boullus: / L'ung me fait paour, l'autre joye et liesse. / La joie avoir me fay, haulte Deesse, / A qui pecheurs doivent tous recourir, / Comblez de foy, sans fainte ne paresse: / En ceste joy je vueil vivre et mourir" (ll. 893–902).

23. Jacques le Goff, *La naissance du purgatoire* (Paris: Gallimard, 1981).

24. Villon's "belle qui fut hëaulmiere" could be a beauty who sold helmets, an employee of the helmet maker, the helmet maker's wife, or the historical personage, mistress of Nicholas d'Orgemont who was treasurer and canon at Notre-Dame, a famous lady more than eighty years old when Villon wrote the "Testament"; Villon's figure also recalls in Jean de Meun's la Vieille.

25. "Car vieilles n'ont ne cours ne estre, / Ne que monnoye qu'on descrie" (ll. 539f.).

26. "En ce bordeau ou tenons nostre estat." The poem occupies ll. 1591–1627; the line quoted is the refrain.

27. David Kuhn, *La poetique de François Villon* (Paris: Armand Colin, 1967), p. 29.

28. Ibid., p. 350.

29. I am grateful to Nadia Margolis for calling my attention to Jane Taylor's fascinating discussions of Villon (Jane H. M. Taylor, *The Poetry of François Villon: Text and Context* [Cambridge: Cambridge University Press, 2001]), who rediscovers the aesthetic pleasures of linguistic polyvalence and the fragmented subject. While I do not believe that Villon addressed the political or theoretical issues of "the woman's cause" at all (Taylor, p. 112), there was no sham whatsoever in his concrete sympathies and even identifications with the women for whom and in whose name he wrote. The subject "Villon" managed to make aggressivity and tenderness, cynical irony and empathetic projection, dominance and submission, and a host of other binary opposites, coexist, if not in harmony, then in the same existential neighborhood.

30. Gayatri Chakravorty Spivak, "Can the Subaltern Speak?" *Wedge* 7/8 (winter–spring 1985): 120–30; and in the extensive discussion this essay has aroused, see most recently, Stephen Morton, *Gayatri Chakravorty Spivak* (London: Routledge, 2003).

CONCLUSION

1. *The Chief Works of Spinoza*, tr. R. H. M. Elwes, 2 vols. (New York: Dover, 1951), 2:390; see also the *Political Treatise*, tr. Samuel Shirley (Indianapolis, Ind.: Hackett, 2000), p. 40f.

2. Chief among the exceptions noted in these pages have been Pierre Bonnassie, Robert Fossier, Rodney Hilton, and most recently, Paul Freedman.

3. The self-evidence "that all Men are created equal, that they are endowed by their Creator with certain unalienable Rights, that among these are Life, Liberty and the Pursuit of Happiness" is at stake. Rather than a "Creator," one might see equality, freedom, and rights, insofar as they actually come into existence, as effects of history.

4. Marija Gimbutas, *The Civilization of the Goddess: The World of Old Europe* (San Francisco: Harper Collins, 1991).

5. Roland Mousnier, "Préface," in Philippe Contamine, ed., *Histoire militaire de la France* (Paris: PUF, 1992), p. v.

6. Jacques Derrida has argued for a universal violence that includes social organization and language (*De la grammatologie* [Paris: Minuit, 1966]).

7. *The New Science of Gianbattista Vico,* tr. Thomas G. Bergin, and Max H. Fisch, Ithaca: Cornell, 1948. p. 105.

8. R. Howard Bloch's far-reaching *Etymologies and Genealogies: A Literary Anthropology of the French Middle Ages* (Chicago: University of Chicago, 1983), disregards the ideological dimension of appeals to the past; compare Georges Duby, who saw the nobility as a homogeneous "*société d'héritiers*" and their genealogies as legitimating their power: *Hommes et structure du moyen âge,* Paris: Mouton, 1973, pp. 405 and 290 f.

9. Letter to Bishop Hermann of Metz, March 15, 1081; quoted by Thomas N. Bisson, "The 'Feudal Revolution,'" *Past and Present* no. 142 (Feb. 1994): 6–42, p. 42.

10. Robert Fossier, *La société féodale,* p. 195 f.

11. R. I. Moore, "Postscript: The Peace of God and the Social Revolution," in *The Peace of God: Social Violence and Religious Response in France around the Year 1000,* ed. Thomas Head and Richard Landes (Ithaca, N.Y.: Cornell University Press, 1992), pp. 308–26.

12. Guy Bois, "Mutation de l'An mil et changement social," *Cahiers d'histoire* 64 (1996): 11–20; see also Guy Bois, *La mutation de l'An Mil: Lournand, village mâconnais de l'Antiquité au féodalisme* (Paris: Fayard, 1989).

13. Outside the misleading, self-serving claims of programmatic tracts like Du Bellay's *Deffence et Illustration de la Langue Françoyse.* The Pléiade poetic production is imposing; the disregard of its continuity with prior poetic and critical practice at the basis of claims to revolutionary "modernizing" originality are pompous balderdash and bowdlerization of literary history.

14. David Campbell and Michael Dillon, "Introduction," in *The Political Subject of Violence* (Manchester: Manchester University Press, 1993), p. 3, emphasis added.

15. Hayden White's *Metahistory* made the point in 1973.

16. Erich Köhler's name comes to mind.

17. Michel de Montaigne, *Essais,* ed. Albert Thibaudet (Paris: Gallimard ["Pléiade"], 1950), 3:2, p. 900; Donald Frame, tr., *The Complete Essays of Montaigne* (Stanford, Calif.: Stanford University Press, 1958), p. 611.

18. As in the essay "Of Cato the Younger": Thibaudet, p. 266; Frame, p. 169.

19. Montaigne, 3:2, p. 908/616.

20. Ibid., 3:2, p. 899/610.

21. Ibid., 3:3, p. 915/621.

22. "Mais qui le munt [vect] dreit nonmer, / C'est cel ensemble e terre e mer. / Por c'est nonmez monz dreitement / Que toz jorz est en movement, / Quer que est ce que l'on i trove / Qui eu mont est qui ne se move?"

(*Chronique des ducs de Normandie par Benoît,* ed. Carin Fahlin, 4 vols. [Uppsala: Almqvist and Wiksells; Wiesbaden: Otto Harrassowitz; The Hague: Martin Nijhoff; and Geneva: Droz, 1951–1979], 1:13–18).

23. Timothy J. Reiss, "Montaigne and the Subject of Polity," *Literary Theory / Renaissance Texts,* ed. Patricia Parker and David Quint (Baltimore, Md.: Johns Hopkins University Press, 1986), pp. 115–49, 117. See also François Rigolot, "Perspective modernes sur la subjectivité montaignienne," in *La problématique du sujet chez Montaigne,* ed. Eva Kushner (Paris: Champion, 1995), pp. 149–70, esp. p. 168f.

24. Reiss, p. 127.

25. Ibid., p. 123.

26. Montaigne, 1:23, pp. 151, 88.

27. "La discipline ordinaire d'un Estat . . . presuppose . . . un commun consentement à son observation et obeissance. L'aller légitime est un aller froid, poisant et contraint, et n'est pas pour tenir bon à un aller licencieux et effrené" (Montaigne, 1:23, pp. 152, 89).

28. Montaigne, 1:17, pp. 97, 51.

29. Jacques Derrida, *Politics of Friendship,* tr. George Collins (London: Verso, 1997), p. 182; I draw on the entire chapter, "He Who Accompanies Me," pp. 171–93. Montaigne's text, of course, is "De l'amitié" (1:28), "Of Friendship."

30. "Ceux qui cherchent à troubler et changer l'estat de nostre police, sans se soucier s'ils l'amendront" (Montaigne, 1:23, p. 231f.)

31. Ibid., p. 184f.

32. Etienne de la Boétie, *Le discours de la servitude volontaire,* ed. Miguel Abensour and Marcel Gauchet, text ed. Pierre Léonard (Paris: Payot, 1976–93).

33. Ibid., pp. 153–55.

34. Howard Caygill, "Violence, Civility and the Predicaments of Philosophy," in *The Political Subject of Violence,* ed. David Campbell and Michael Dillon (Manchester: Manchester University Press, 1993), pp. 48–72.

35. Mitchell Greenberg, *Subjectivity and Subjugation in Seventeenth-Century Drama and Prose: The Family Romance of French Classicism* (Cambridge: Cambridge University Press, 1992), p. 28.

36. Caygill, p. 49f.

37. Dalia Judovitz, *Subjectivity and Representation in Descartes: The Origins of Modernity* (Cambridge: Cambridge University Press, 1988), p. 5.

38. Max Weber, "Politics as a Vocation," in *From Max Weber: Essays in Sociology,* tr. and ed. H. H. Gerth and C. Wright Mills (Oxford: Oxford Uni-

versity Press, 1946–58), pp. 77–128, 78, my emphasis; see also R. B. J. Walker, "Violence, Modernity, Silence: from Max Weber to International Relations," in *The Political Subject of Violence*, ed. David Campbell and Michael Dillon (Manchester: Manchester University Press, 1993), pp. 137–60.

39. See repeated modern elisions of the congressional declarations of war required by the American Constitution.

40. René Descartes, *Discourse and Method and Meditations on First Philosophy*, 4th ed., tr. Donald A. Cress (Indianapolis, Ind.: Hackett, 1998), pp. 17ff.

41. Compare with Timothy J. Reiss, "Denying the Body? Memory and the Dilemmas of History in Descartes," *Journal of the History of Ideas* 57, no. 4 (1996): 587–607; "Revising Descartes: On Subject and Community," *Life Studies: Biography and Autobiography in Early Modern Europe*, ed. Patrick Coleman, Jill Kowalik, and Jayne Lewis (Cambridge: Cambridge University Press, 2000); and *Mirages of the Selfe: Patterns of Personhood in Ancient and Early Modern Europe* (Stanford, Calif.: Stanford University Press, 2003). I am grateful for the opportunity to have read the last two in manuscript form.

42. Walker, p. 148f.

43. Weber, p. 126.

44. Marcel Gauchet, *Le désenchantement du monde* (Paris: Gallimard, 1985).

45. Guillaume d'Ockham, Court traité du pouvoir tyrannique, tr. Jean-Fabien Spitz (Paris: PUF, 1999), pp. 102–4.

46. Jean-Claude Schmitt, the first two essays of *Le corps, les rites, les rêves, le temps* (Paris: Gallimard, 2001).

47. The surprise of the Christian asked whether he was a Christian in Meredith Monk's film *Book of Days* seems entirely right.

48. Carl Schmitt, Ernst Kantorowicz, Pierre Legendre, Michel Sennelart, and so on.

49. Jacques Derrida and Gianni Vattimo, *La religion* (Paris: Seuil, 1996), p. 85.

50. Jane Welch Williams, *Bread, Wine, and Money: The Windows of the Trades at Chartres Cathedral* (Chicago: University of Chicago Press, 1993), p. 80.

51. Jacques Derrida, *Spectres de Marx* (Paris: Galilée, 1993); Jacques Derrida, "Marx and Sons," in *Ghostly Demarcations*, ed. Michael Sprinker (London: Verso, 1999), pp. 213–69.

Index

Note: In this index "f" after a number indicates a separate reference on the next page, and "ff" indicates separate references on the next two pages. A continuous discussion over two or more pages is indicated by a span of numbers. "Passim" is used for a cluster of references in close but not consecutive sequence.

Not all mentions of "subject," "identity," "state," and "ideology" are indexed here.

FIGURAE: READING MEDIEVAL CULTURE

M. B. Pranger, *The Artificiality of Christianity: Essays on the Poetics of Monasticism*

Sarah Kay, *Courtly Contradictions: The Emergence of the Literary Object in the Twelfth Century*

Bruce Holsinger, *Music, Body, and Desire in Medieval Culture*

Rainer Warning, *The Ambivalences of Medieval Religious Drama*

Virginia Burrus, *'Begotten, Not Made': Conceiving Manhood in Late Antiquity*

Peter S. Hawkins, *Dante's Testaments: Essays in Scriptural Imagination*

Daniel Boyarin, *Dying for God: Martyrdom and the Making of Christianity and Judaism*

Catherine Brown, *Contrary Things: Exegesis, Dialectic, and the Poetics of Didacticism*

Paul Freedman, *The Image of the Medieval Peasant as Alien and Exemplary*

James F. Burke, *Desire Against the Law: The Juxtaposition of Contraries in Early Medieval Spanish Literature*

Armando Petrucci, translated by Michael Sullivan, *Writing the Dead: Death and Writing Strategies in the Western Tradition*

Renate Blumenfeld-Kosinski, *Reading Myth: Classical Mythology and Its Interpretations in Medieval French Literature*

Paul Saenger, *Space Between Words: The Origins of Silent Reading*

David Wallace, *Chaucerian Polity: Absolutist Lineages and Associational Forms in England and Italy*

Sylvia Huot, *Allegorical Play in the Old French Motet: The Sacred and the Profane in Thirteenth-Century Polyphony*

Ralph Hanna III, *Pursuing History: Middle English Manuscripts and Their Texts*

Theresa Tinkle, *Medieval Venuses and Cupids: Sexuality, Hermeneutics, and English Poetry*

Seth Lerer, ed., *Literary History and the Challenge of Philology: The Legacy of Erich Auerbach*

Martha G. Newman, *The Boundaries of Charity: Cistercian Culture and Ecclesiastical Reform, 1098–1180*

Brigitte Cazelles, *The Unholy Grail: A Social Reading of Chrétien de Troyes's 'Conte du Graal'*

John Kleiner, *Mismapping the Underworld: Daring and Error in Dante's 'Comedy'*

M. Victoria Guerin, *The Fall of Kings and Princes: Structure and Destruction in Arthurian Tragedy*